Society
&
Nature

For Anna

Society
&
Nature

Changing our Environment,
Changing Ourselves

PETER DICKENS

polity

The right of Peter Dickens to be identified as Author of this Work has been asserted in accordance with the UK Copyright, Designs and Patents Act 1988.

First published in 2004 by Polity Press Ltd.

Polity Press
65 Bridge Street
Cambridge CB2 1UR, UK

Polity Press
350 Main Street
Malden, MA 02148, USA

A catalogue record for this book is available from the British Library.

Library of Congress Cataloging-in-Publication Data
Dickens, Peter, 1940–
Society and nature : changing our environment, changing ourselves / Peter Dickens.
  p. cm.
  Includes bibliographical references and index. ISBN 0-7456-2795-1 (hb : alk. paper) – ISBN 0-7456-2796-X (pb : alk. paper)
  1. Social change – Environmental aspects. 2. Human ecology. 3. Nature – Effect of human beings on. 4. Social evolution. 5. Human evolution. I. Title.

HM856.D53 2004
303.4–dc21
                                      2003010716

Typeset in 10.5 on 12pt Sabon
by Graphicraft Limited, Hong Kong
Printed and bound in Great Britain by TJ International, Padstow, Cornwall

For further information on Polity, visit our website: www.polity.co.uk

Contents

Preface

This book is about the relationship between society and nature. It is different from other books on the subject because it considers people as part of nature. The book's central question is: how, as society transforms its environment, are people's own natures being transformed?

The Introduction locates this question in an historical context. In this way we can begin to understand why the relationships between society and nature are so important in the present day. Chapter 1 is also introductory. It presents a framework for understanding the links between society and nature and introduces some of the book's main themes. Chapters 2 and 3 are about our relationships with the environment or 'external' nature. Chapter 4 is a linking chapter. It is concerned with the impacts of society both on external nature and on internal nature, especially our own identities. Chapters 5 and 6 focus exclusively on the relationships between society and humans' own nature. Why and how are people being changed by the society in which they live and work? Furthermore, how do these changes relate to the transformation of external nature? Chapters 7 and 8 are about forms of politics. What kinds of politics might lead to better relations with the environment while allowing people to better fulfil their potential?

One of the central objectives of this book is to integrate understandings of natural scientists with those of social scientists. Natural as well as social scientists should find the book helpful. The Introduction and chapter 1 are intended as starting points for all readers. These are where the theoretical issues and underlying ideas are established. After that, students may turn to whichever set of chapters is particularly relevant to them. One possible start might be with the linking chapter, chapter 4. Here, some of the conventional understandings of humanity's relationships with nature are critically assessed. I hope, however, that students will finish up reading the whole text.

Understanding the relationships between society and nature entails not only crossing disciplinary divides, but also examining how the insights of disciplines can be combined. Transformations to internal and external nature are some of the most important issues of our times. Disciplinary boundaries must not be allowed to stop us talking to each other.

Finally, some readers will note that the main title of this book is the same as that of a book I published in 1992. Some explanation is in order. The first book was subtitled 'Towards a Green Social Theory'. Now, some twelve years later, the shape of a more comprehensive green social theory seems clearer. On the one hand, the ideas and debates associated with mainstream social theory remain highly relevant. On the other, modern social theory now incorporates a more sophisticated understanding of how society interacts with external nature and our own, internal, nature. This new book therefore combines older perspectives from social science while introducing concepts drawn from neighbouring disciplines such as biology and psychology. Such a fusion results in a much more developed understanding of modern society. Needless to say, however, the debates and arguments within such a framework continue.

Acknowledgements

This book has greatly benefited from the assistance of a number of people. Helpers at Sussex University included Andrew Chitty, Jenneth Parker, Pete Saunders and Graham Sharp. Cambridge assistance has come from Nick Bullock, Andrew Houston, Emile Perreau-Saussine, Martin Richards and Bryan Turner. And at a key stage the Master and Fellows of Fitzwilliam College provided the ideal physical and social setting necessary for writing a book. Ted Benton, James Ormrod and members of the Sociology Seminar at the University of Essex have been consistently helpful. Other major assistance was given by Julian Agyeman, David Barker, Kathryn Dean, Mervyn Hartwig, Lee Freese, Andrew Sayer, Andrew Whiten and the Red-Green Study Group.

This book started with a chance encounter with John Thompson of Polity in the Cambridge University Library. John, Sarah Dancy, Rachel Kerr and the staff at Polity have consistently been both creative and patient. I must also thank two anonymous readers whose ideas greatly improved the book. Finally, I must thank my daughter Emma. She is in the publishing business and her age is somewhere between mine and that of the intended student reader. She twice edited the whole text and did much to make my inaccessible prose accessible.

The author and publishers would like to thank the following for permission to reproduce copyright text:

British Broadcasting Corporation for material from their website pages, news.bbc.co.uk.

British Market Research Bureau for data included in figures 4.1–4.4 and Taylor & Francis Group Ltd for figures including this data from Mike Savage, James Barlow, Tony Fielding and Peter Dickens, *Property, Bureaucracy and Culture* (London: Routledge, 1992).

Cambridgeshire Action in Rural Communities for material by Chris Lea for the *Fenland Community Enterprise Bulletin*, Winter 1999/2000.

Campus Verlag GmbH, Frankfurt/New York for figure from Ulrich Beck, *The Brave New World of Work* (Cambridge: Polity, 2000), p. 105, fig. 1.

Curtis Brown Group Ltd on behalf of the Trustees of the Mass-Observation Archive, for material from Mass-Observation Archive, University of Sussex Library, Brighton, 23/2 (Autumn/Winter 1987). Copyright © Trustees of the Mass-Observation Archive.

Edinburgh University Press for figure from C. H. Waddington, *The Evolution of an Evolutionist* (1975), ch. 23, fig. 4.

The Egg Donor Program for material from the website <eggdonation.com/angel/ example.asp>

Environmental News Network for 'Oil Interests Eye Crude in Arctic Refuge', 26.5.00: <enn.com/news/enn-stories>

Guardian Newspapers Ltd for material from Duncan Campbell, 'Anarchism in the UK', *Guardian*, 18.4.01: copyright © 2001 The Guardian; Libby Brooks, 'May Day Demonstration', *Guardian*, 2.5.01: copyright © 2001 The Guardian; 'Cracking the Code of Human Life', *Guardian*, 2.12.99: copyright © 1999 The Guardian; and John Aldridge and Vanessa Thorpe, 'They Used to Want a Revolution', *Observer*, 19.11.00: copyright © 2000 The Observer.

Independent Newspapers for material from 'Production and Consumption: Making the Links', *Independent*, 13.6.02; 'Water companies and farms singled out as Britain's worst polluters', *Independent*, 25.7.02; and for 'New inquiry to check health of IVF babies', *Independent*, 22.10.02.

ISER for material from Heinz Schandl and Niels Schulz, 'Using Material Flow Accounting to Operationalise the Concept of Society's Metabolism: A Preliminary MFA for the UK for the Period of 1937–1997', ISER Working Paper 2000–3, University of Essex, UK.

Kogan Page Publishers for data from M. Redclift, *Wasted: Counting the Costs of Global Consumption* (London: Earthscan, 1996); and C. Flavin, 'Rich Planet, Poor Planet', tables 1–2, from L. Brown, *State of the World Yearbook 2001* (London: Earthscan); and figure from G. Tansey and T. Worsley, *The Food System: A Guide* (London: Earthscan, 1995), p. 163.

The McDonald Institute for Archaeological Research for figure from D. Erdal and A. Whiten, 'Egalitarianism and Machiavellian Intelligence in Human Evolution' (1996) in Paul Mellars and Kathleen Gibson (eds), *Modelling the Human Mind* (Cambridge: McDonald Institute Monographs, 1996); version included here repr. in Peter Dickens, *Social Darwinism* (Buckingham: Open University Press, 2000), with their permission.

Monthly Review Foundation for figure from J. Foster, *Marx's Ecology: Materialism and Nature* (New York, 2000), p. 162. Copyright © 2000 Monthly Review Press.

New Society Publishers for material from C. Plant and J. Plant, *Green Business: Hope or Hoax?* (Bideford: Green Books, 1991).

People Management for material from J. Atkinson and N. Meager, 'Is Flexibility Just a Flash in the Pan?', *Personnel Management*, September 1986.

Telegraph Group Ltd for material from Roger Highfield, 'Scientists discover gene that creates human intelligence', *Daily Telegraph*, 31.10.97.

Thomson Publishing Services for figures from P. Dickens, *Reconstructing Nature* (London: Routledge, 1996), p. 43; R. Wilkinson, *Unhealthy Societies* (London: Routledge, 1996), p. 76; and C. H. Waddington, 'The Complex System of Interactions Underlying the Epigenetic Landscape', in idem, *The Strategy of Genes* (London: Allen and Unwin, 1957).

Viva for poster, 'End Factory Farming'.

The Wilderness Society for material from 'Stand By Your Lands'.

Patricia J. Wynne for 'Homeobox genes', in E. De Robertis, G. Olliver and C. Wright, 'Homeobox Genes and Vertebrate Body Plan', *Scientific American*, 263/1 (1990): 26–32, p. 27.

Crown copyright material is reproduced under class Licence No. CO1W0000283 with the permission of the Controller of HMSO and the Queen's Printer for Scotland.

Labour is first of all a process between man and nature, a process by which man, through his own actions, mediates, regulates and controls the metabolism between himself and nature. He sets in motion the natural forces which belong to his own body, his arms, legs, head and hands, in order to appropriate the materials of nature in a form adapted to his own needs. Through this movement he acts upon external nature and changes it, and in this way he simultaneously changes his own nature.

Marx 1970: 177

Introduction: Society, Nature and Enlightenment

Changing Nature, Changing Ourselves

This book is about the environment and how it is being transformed by society. But it is not only about the environment or 'external' nature. It is also about the refashioning of humanity, of people's own internal nature. How, as society transforms external nature, does it transform internal nature?

External and internal nature are now being changed in extraordinarily far-reaching ways, and many people find these disturbing. The environment, at least since the eighteenth century, has been largely seen as a mere object, something there to serve human ends. Meanwhile, people have, for more than two centuries, been celebrated as independent individuals, capable of indefinitely improving themselves without reference to other people or their environment. Now, many of these assumptions are coming under question. Rampant individualism combined with environmental degradation and the destruction of species are leading many people to question humanity's original priorities. Let us explore how these priorities became established and the kinds of question that are now being asked.

The Age of Enlightenment

We still live in the Age of Enlightenment. Sometimes referred to as the Age of Reason, the Enlightenment is a philosophical and social movement which started developing in the eighteenth century. It is composed of a number of ideas which are considered 'progressive'. These include a commitment to reason and science and the freedom of the individual. Mysticism and appeals to ancient forms of philosophy were to be dismissed. In all these ways modern society was to make progress.

Many of these commitments dominate our thinking today. Yet they have come under a cloud. The Enlightenment is casting a shadow. Reason and science have not delivered all that they promised. If they are responsible for widescale environmental degradation, perhaps they should be rejected. And what of the freedom of the individual? Has it taken place? Is it even desirable? All these themes are relevant to an understanding of humanity's relations to nature.

Nature as a resource

Nature, both external and internal, was a key concept in the making of the new Age of Reason. Its understanding and its exploitation were central.

Isaac Newton was one icon. In 1687 he published *Mathematical Principles of Natural Philosophy*. There he produced mathematical descriptions of the laws of the universe, revealing the universal law of gravity, the motions of planets and the notion that planetary space is infinite. Francis Bacon was another icon. He was seen as the prophet of modern science. In the 1620s he rejected all forms of knowledge based on 'the enchantments of antiquity and authority' and proposed an alternative, rational, scientific approach to understanding humanity's place in nature. For both men, the priority was to reveal, to figure out, nature's fixed laws. This was to be done by the 'inductive method', whereby the truth was drawn from the world rather than via reasoning alone. It is a method frequently used in scientific and sociological research today.

Bacon's attempted uncovering of nature's secrets was just one step away from an attitude to nature with which we are also very familiar today. Joseph Glanvill, a philosopher contemporary of Bacon, paraphrased him as saying: 'nature being known . . . may be mastered, managed and used in the services of humane life' (cited in Porter 2001: 305; see also Porter 2000). Yet it is important not to let our concerns with environmental destruction colour the Enlightenment's attitudes. It is true that nature was seen as mainly designed for human purposes. On the other hand, as set down in the Bible, God had given the earth to humanity to manage. Its fruits were to be appropriated by Man, but in the context of a cooperative relation between humanity and nature. The earth was seen as analogous to a huge farm. It was self-balancing, but it could be managed even better by Man, cultivated in a rational way using the new sciences (including the science of chemistry) to fulfil God's duty.

Land-enclosure was seen as a key means to this end. The private ownership of land was the first step to rational conservation and husbandry. In much the same way as good husbandry kept a farm fertile and productive, science combined with human ingenuity and was seen as a way of ensuring that the God-given earth remained in balance. What better than private property as a way of ensuring that a balanced earth could be passed on to future generations?

A new kind of self

Clearing forests, making ditches, planting crops and mining were not only means for making wealth out of wasteland. They were also seen as making a new kind of person. This was an 'enlightened' person. Arthur Young, an early nineteenth-century commentator on the ongoing process of enclosure, put it as follows:

> The Oxford farmers . . . are now in the period of great change in their ideas, knowledge, practice, and other circumstances. Enclosing to a greater proportional amount than in almost any other county in the kingdom has changed the men as much as it has improved the country; they are now in the ebullition of this change; a vast amelioration has been wrought, and is working; and a great deal of ignorance remains. The Goths and Vandals of open fields touch the civilization of enclosures. Men have been taught to think, and till that moment arrives nothing can be done effectively. (Cited in Porter 2000: 566)

So a new kind of 'improved', 'rational' self was also in the making. The Enlightenment, in addition to developing a science of nature, was also developing a science of 'Man', a science of *internal* nature. There were differences between different philosophers as to what human nature consists of, but central to this new science was the rejection of ideas handed down from antiquity and the medieval era. There was no reason to suggest, for example, that man is innately sinful. Such suppositions, and superstitions, could not be scientifically proven. Human beings are certainly possessed of passions such as love, pride and ambition. But this does not make them inherently evil or destructive. If such desires and propensities could be channelled, they too could be recruited to the common cause of advancement and 'progress'. Like external nature, internal nature could only be understood by a process of scientific observation and further induction. A fixed human nature could not simply be assumed.

It began to be believed that human nature is revealed according to the environment in which people are operating. Human beings were seen as immensely plastic creatures, capable of enormous adaptation as they became acclimatized to new environments. They could therefore be envisaged as starting off in life as 'blank sheets'. They absorb new information, shape it, turn it into ideas and values about what ought to be the case. Education had an enormous role to play, this being one way in which the blank sheet could be written on and an 'improved man' created.

This, then, was seen as an evolutionary process. As humans modify the external world, went the thinking, they upgrade their own nature. It is another enormously influential picture, one we will encounter later.

A scientific politics

The new science could even be applied to politics. Enlightenment philosophers were concerned with the new nation-states and with the attempts by those in charge to claim sole authority over people living in their boundaries. Such claims could only be made, they argued, if governments were able to demonstrate to their people that they actually were securing their liberty. What the good life consists of should not concern governments; that is a matter for individuals. The priority of governments was to secure the freedom of individuals to make their own choices.

The new, scientific form of politics goes back to humanity's relations with nature. While Newton discovered the laws underlying the earth, political philosophers were attempting to discover a scientific and rational form of politics for humanity's relations with the earth. God had given mankind dominion over nature with Man having the right to use it, work on it and consume its produce. Politics was ensuring that these processes took place.

John Locke, whose arguments were especially influential when the United States Constitution was being drawn up, is the central figure here. He argued that private property was a natural outcome and necessity, which stemmed from humanity's relations with nature. A legal property system is necessary to protect individuals working on the land, ensuring that they gain adequate reward for their work. A system of legal property ownership is also necessary to protect the consumer. Consumption is a process only enjoyed at the level of the individual person. It is rational to ensure that people should not consume an item which does not belong to them. In all, therefore, Locke argued that a God-given system linking people and nature necessitates a legal system supporting private property rights. Such a legal system would protect property and individuals from being harmed by others. It was seen as a 'rational' form of governance. Newton and others had established the laws underlying the earth's structure. Locke and others were establishing the scientific laws necessary to ensure that the best, most progressive appropriation was made of it. Locke and Newton, we might note, were good friends. Newton, although he had some disagreements with his friend, broadly supported his proposals for a rational type of government.

Enlightenment and Romanticism

The philosophy of the Enlightenment emphasized the control and containment of nature in God's and Man's best interest. One result was an increasing premium on 'wildness'. As nature became tamed, mountains, precipices, craggy knolls, unploughed land and fast-flowing rivers became prized precisely because they had *not* been tamed. They were unharnessed and intimidating. As a result, they were described as 'dreadful' or 'awe-ful'. Many well-organized eighteenth-century country-house gardens, particularly in continental Europe, contained a small special area (sometimes known as an English Garden) which was a well-managed wilderness. The unknown and unpredictable could be appreciated here, albeit in a carefully controlled environment. Any 'surprises' had been carefully orchestrated.

This response to Enlightenment thought prefigured Romanticism. It was, and still is, a movement that turns away from rationality, rejecting the Enlightenment view of nature as a mere physical 'resource' to be used in a dispassionate, scientific way by humanity. Nature, both human and non-human, was seen by the Romantics as also a source of wonder, humility and awe. Human beings need an aesthetic and spiritual relationship with themselves and with their environment. Internal and external nature should therefore be appreciated for its own qualities and not for its value as a material resource or a commodity for humanity. Respect for non-human entities is therefore required. Indeed, it was believed that people become better human beings precisely as a result of recognizing nature's sublime qualities and turning away from industrialism, cash and 'progress'. Organisms, according to this view, are much more than machines and collections of atoms; they are independent and whole entities. And they help humans to see themselves in the wider order of things.

These two apparently opposing modes of thought often find themselves combined. In the sphere of politics and philosophy, for example, Marx insisted on the possibilities for human beings to realize their full potential while conquering and using the powers of nature. At the same time, his theory of alienation from nature (including human nature) relied on a Romantic idea of human salvation lying in appreciating the aesthetic and spiritual qualities of nature as an independent entity.

Some of the same ambivalences and contradictions continue today. They are to be found in, for example, the field of architecture and town planning. The Swiss architect, Le Corbusier (1887–1965), was highly influential during the twentieth century. The schemes he drew up in the 1920s for an ideal city seem, at first sight, to be the archetypal example of rationalist, Enlightenment thinking (see box I.1). Straight lines of communication are drawn across the landscape, the crooked route being what this master of the so-called 'Modern Movement' called 'the way of the donkey'. Similarly, vast machine-like edifices hovering above the landscape seem to epitomize the eighteenth-century ideal of nature being finally conquered and controlled in 'man's' best interests. Large swathes of medieval Paris were to be swept away in this fashion. Le Corbusier's *Plan Voisin*, published in 1925, envisaged considerable stretches of France's capital city being rationalized away; ancient buildings, along with ancient myths, were holding back the progress of humanity.

The buildings, in Le Corbusier's plans, were to be replaced by the rationalizers themselves: the bureaucrats working in the eighteen skyscrapers looking down on Notre Dame Cathedral. But note that Le Corbusier argued that such rationalization was precisely the way to realize human beings' aesthetic and spiritual needs. New technologies allowed buildings and roads to be fully segregated from the natural world. In this way human beings were able to enjoy nature (*'soleil, espace, verdure'*) as an independent, aesthetic resource.

The American Frank Lloyd Wright (1869–1959) was another of the most significant of the twentieth-century architects. His proposals for Broadacre City look at first sight like a return to an older primitive way of life in which people commune with nature (see box I.2). Here, surely, is Romanticism run wild. The whole of the USA was to be turned into a giant, decentralized city, with the family as its basic unit. American democracy was to be restored in this way, with families and individuals spending much of their time working on the land as part-time farmers. But, again, appearances are deceptive. Frank Lloyd Wright invested considerable faith in modern technology as a means of enabling this vision. America in the 1930s was beginning to see the mass ownership of cars and the massive spread of the telephone. Helicopters, as well as very advanced forms of automobile, flit in and

Box 1.1 Rationalization, Romanticism and city-planning: Le Corbusier's 'contemporary city'

Illustration 1.1A (this page) and **1.1B** (opposite) Urban utopias in the twentieth century

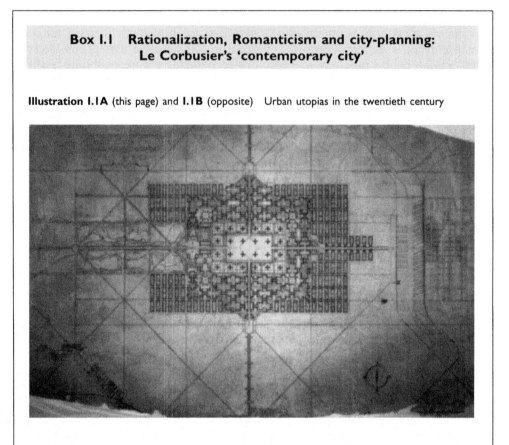

Le Corbusier's 1922 plan of the contemporary city placed a grid over nature and lifted buildings well above the trees and the land. The grid was organized around an exact north–south/east–west axis (see illus. 1.1A). At the centre of the city a massive transportation centre was proposed, with an aircraft runway on the roof. An elite of bureaucratic managers would have worked in high-rise towers and lived in luxury high blocks just outside the central business district. Workers would have lived and worked in satellite cities and industries outside the centre.

Le Corbusier's plan can be seen as Enlightenment ideas brought into the twentieth century. Nature is finally controlled and contained in 'man's best interests'. (Note, however, the space set aside for a 'wild' English garden to the west of the central business district (see illus. 1.1B).) But it diverged from classical Enlightenment thinking in two important ways.

First, the purpose of detaching human beings from nature, Le Corbusier argued, was precisely that of enabling them to appreciate a nature which is untouched by human beings. In this way their aesthetic, non-rational sensibilities will be enhanced.

Second, Le Corbusier's idea of individual freedom was based on a form of communism or anarchism known as 'syndicalism'. Property, including industry, would be publicly owned, the bureaucracy being freely elected by the industrial workers governing their factories and deciding what work they will do. Le Corbusier had hoped to nationalize all land, but he realized that this was unrealistic and proposed a close collaboration between the public and private sectors in a collective 'community'

Illustration 1.1B

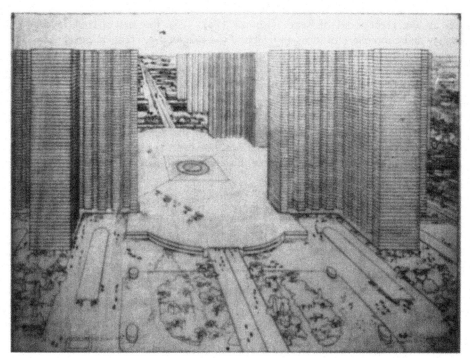

Photos La Fondation Le Corbusier, Paris, France. © ADAGP, Paris and DACS, London 2003

interest. Here were strong, collaborative links between state and industry, a long step away from the Enlightenment philosophers' insistence on minimal government and free trade.

out of Wright's vision of Broadacre. In short, modern technology was seen as the means of recovering humanity's engagement with the land, not just as a resource but also as a landscape which could spark the imagination and improve the soul. Nature and humanity were fully integrated. New technology was allowing the United States to become, as the Enlightenment thinkers of the Age of Reason had intended, something resembling a gigantic farm.

Box 1.2   Rationalization, Romanticism and city-planning: Frank Lloyd Wright's Broadacre City

Frank Lloyd Wright's vision of a decentralized 'non-city' looks like an unapologetic and Romantic mass return to rustic nature (see illus. 1.2A). But it does have close links with Enlightenment thinking. Here are families owning small pieces of land and spending substantial amounts of time working on them. The individual, the family and the family home are the basic building-block of this vision of a recovered American democracy. It was an anti-urban vision in the sense that Wright saw the city as 'the great locus of Rent' (Fishman 1982: 125). Renters of land, lenders of money and controllers of ideas all inhibited the productive, creative, potentially self-sufficient individual. The old nineteenth-century city was the renters' place of work and it would be overthrown by Broadacre City and the return to the land (see illus. 1.2B).

But note that Wright's return to a society in which people are integrated with land was facilitated by maximum use of new technologies. Mr Edison and Mr Ford would be the modern technical means by which the American social and political dream would be re-made. Wright could not, however, resist designing his own cars and, in the later versions of Broadacre, his own version of the personal helicopter (see illus. 1.2C).

Illustration 1.2B (this page) and **1.2A** and **1.2C** (opposite) Frank Lloyd Wright's Broadacre City

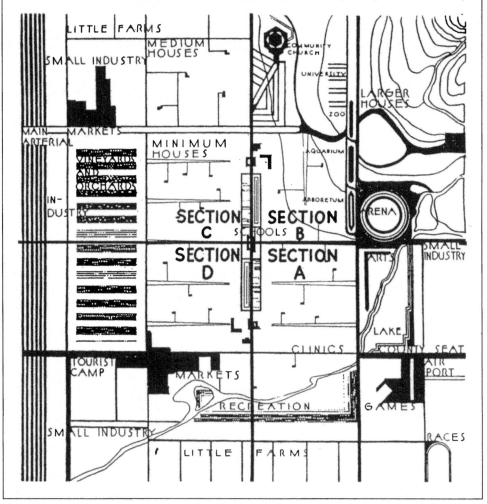

Illustration 1.2A

Illustration 1.2C

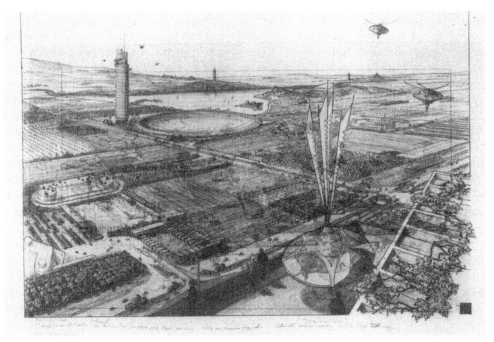

Enlightenment's Shadow

As the Romantic reaction suggests, the Enlightenment has brought deep moral criticism. The rationalization of nature, of industry, of human beings and even of politics led one of the most influential sociologists, Max Weber, to use the term 'disenchantment' to sum up the modern condition. According to him, rational thinking, what he calls 'intellectualism', means that the modern individual is trapped in an 'iron cage', stripped of moral value and religious meaning. In the early 1920s he wrote:

> As intellectualism suppresses belief in magic, the world's processes become disenchanted, lose the magical significance, and henceforth simply 'are' and 'happen' but no longer signify anything. As a consequence, there is growing demand that the world and the total pattern of life be subject to an order that is significant and meaningful. (Cited in Murphy 1994: 32)

Pessimism about the Enlightenment

Anti-Enlightenment thought was a feature of elements of the highly influential Frankfurt School of Sociology, which was established in the 1920s. Two members of this group, Theodor Adorno and Max Horkheimer, mounted a fearsome anti-Enlightenment critique in 1944. They argued that Enlightenment science had actually finished up dominating nature and further dominating human beings by stultifying their powers of imagination and morality. The Enlightenment had promoted 'rationality' but had never addressed what rationality actually was or to what ends it was to be used. Religion, mysticism, tradition and mythology had been dispensed with, but these did at least give humans a sense of identity and morality.

The Enlightenment had left a moral vacuum, into which, for example, modern anti-Semitism had stepped. Baumann (1989) took the thought still further. The Nazi extermination camps were organized along a rationalized, 'scientific' basis. Along similar lines, 'rationalism' actually resulted in vast numbers of individual tragedies, as those who were supposedly irrational had their behaviours adjusted (Foucault 1977). The 'rational' way of dealing with crime is to lock people into prisons with maximum surveillance, make them reflect on their sins, thereby ensuring that they make themselves into self-improving, eventually self-reformed characters (see box I.3). In practice, however, such rationalism produced increasing numbers of broken people, broken families and human misery.

Rationalism and the Enlightenment, according to the pessimists, is characterized by any number of disastrous, very often unintended, consequences. This is a position argued by a contemporary commentator on the Enlightenment, Ulrich Beck. In his influential book, *Risk Society* (1982), he argues strongly that the Enlightenment project is now coming to grief. Science now, far from offering 'truth' and 'progress', is itself generating any number of disastrous effects and mistakes. Furthermore, science is necessary for human society to disentangle itself from the very problems that science has created.

Box 1.3   The Panopticon and the improvement of the self

According to the modern French philosopher Michel Foucault, the Panopticon represents the way in which power has been organized from the period of the Enlightenment onwards. Designed in the late eighteenth century by Jeremy Bentham, this device contained in its open central hall ('E' on the cross-sectional drawing shown in illus. 1.3A) a controller housed in an 'inspection lantern' suspended in the central open space (see illus. 1.3B). The lantern has paper-thin walls pierced by small lenses through which the controller could observe the inmates.

The occupants on the outside of the building therefore do not know when they are being observed. Even more importantly, the controlling manager does not even need to be in the lantern for the prisoners to be pacified, self-reforming individuals. He or she may be there, or not. This is the kind of invisible power exercised in modern-day societies.

The Panopticon most obviously applies to the prison, but Foucault argues that it is a metaphor for the modern, 'rational' way of coercing whole populations. This is no longer achieved through physical violence (as occurred in the Middle Ages) but through the concentration of power and people improving or *self*-educating them-selves. (For further discussion and illustration with reference to human and external nature, see box 1.5).

Illustration 1.3A   Cross-section of Bentham's Panopticon (1791)

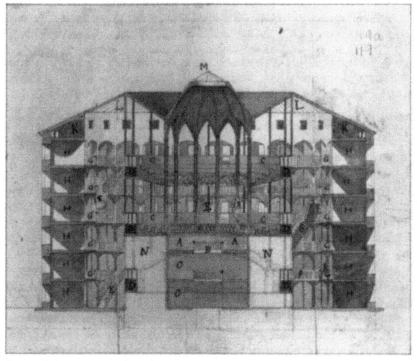

Courtesy of the Library, University College, London, ms. 119a, f. 24

Illustration I.3B The Panopticon's inspection lantern

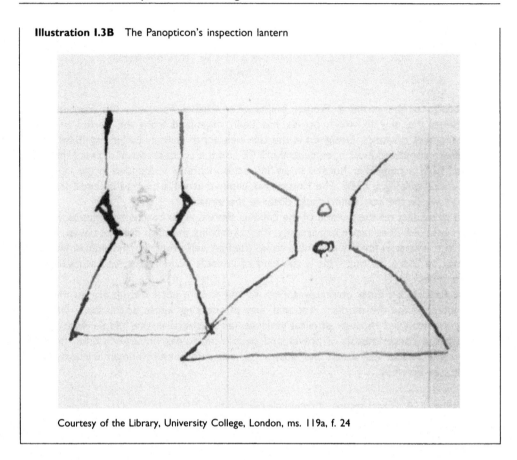

Courtesy of the Library, University College, London, ms. I19a, f. 24

Science is being taken off its pedestal. In contemporary society it is constantly being quizzed and interrogated. This applies, Beck argues, to many other forms of authority and tradition. 'Another modernity' is coming into being in which science, authority, religion, parents, schools, the law and all the institutions representing established ways of proceeding are coming under severe question. The Enlightenment project was reassuring and assumed inevitable progress. But these assumptions can no longer be relied on. Knowledge of all kinds needs constantly to justify itself. This is in many ways a good development, since it means that any vested interests behind supposed objectivity are flushed out into the open and made to justify themselves. Similarly, it recognizes the importance of people's own 'lay' understandings. But at the same time it is profoundly unsettling. There is little left as an anchor on which people can depend. Tradition, as well as science, can no longer be relied on. The Risk Society, according to Beck, is therefore not only to do with insecurities deriving from rational science, but follows also from the personal insecurities resulting from all previously relied-on sources of understanding and guidance being systematically undermined.

As regards the science of 'Man', many of the Enlightenment's assumptions are being questioned. The autonomous being exercising her or his state-protected rights is, for many, a pipe-dream. She or he actually cannot ever exist. Nor can people be simply considered as clean slates, created or reconstructed by education. Throughout their lives, individuals are inevitably caught up in social relations. People may like to think of themselves as independent beings, but this is not a logical possibility. It was not even a possibility at the time when the Enlightenment philosophers were working. New kinds of 'self' are certainly being made, but these selves are in large part a product of the social and environmental relations in which people are caught up.

Politics is also under scrutiny. The kind of politics handed down from the eighteenth century is, for many, increasingly inadequate as a means of offering people the kinds of 'freedom' which the Enlightenment celebrated. It offers, rather, little control over the institutions affecting people's lives. The particular idea of a 'scientific politics' promoted by Locke and others received wide support in its own day, especially from those fortunate enough to own property and who found themselves made into participating citizens. A property-owning democracy of autonomous individuals no longer has much purchase over present-day concentrations of economic power.

Finally, the Enlightenment idea of a general kind of science is very much open to question. The hope was that the kinds of science developed by Newton and Bacon could be readily applied to the understanding of human beings and their society. Auguste Comte, working in the 1830s and '40s and often said to be the very first sociologist, is a good example of the problem. The understanding of human society, he believed, would greatly gain by adopting the kinds of scientific principle used in the physical and natural sciences. To the extent that it rejected theological and mystical explanations, it too would develop as a proper science. Human society could only benefit (see box I.4).

Box I.4 Science as progress: Auguste Comte on science as the final stage of human evolution

In the theological state, the human mind, seeking the essential nature of beings, the first and final causes (the origins and purpose) of all effects – in short, Absolute Knowledge – supposes all phenomena to be produced by the immediate action of supernatural beings. In the metaphysical state, which is only a modification of the first, the mind supposes, instead of supernatural beings, abstract forces, veritable entities (that is, personified abstractions) inherent in all beings, and capable of producing all phenomena. What is called the explanation of phenomena is, in this stage, a mere reference of each to its proper entity.

In the final, the positive state, the mind has given over the vain search after Absolute notions, the origin and destination of the universe, and the causes of phenomena, and applies itself to the study of their laws – that is, their invariable relations of succession and resemblance. Reasoning and observation, duly combined, are the means of this knowledge. (Auguste Comte, *Cours de Philosophie Positive* (1842); cited in Gordon 1991: 290. For further information on Comte, science and progress, see Appendix.)

But it is very doubtful whether the kind of science done by Newton could ever be applied to human beings and their societies. Newton stated, for example, that all bodies in the universe attract each other with a force that is proportional to their mass, with the force getting weaker the further they are apart. These laws could be readily expressed in mathematical form and proved with reference to the evidence of the heavens. All this may be excellent as a means of understanding the universe, but it does not say much about people and human society here on earth. People, unlike planets or atoms, tend to be proactive, take stock of their situations and often behave unpredictably. They also know when experiments are being conducted on them and act accordingly. Enlightenment ideas as developed in physics and chemistry were always going to come to grief if applied too literally and mechanically. Furthermore, what status should be really attached to 'evidence' when we turn to human beings? Understanding how people behave and how societies change cannot fully rely on 'the facts'. The facts do not necessarily tell us much about the power relations and processes lying behind what we experience on a day-to-day basis. Furthermore, why are some 'facts' collected and given special status while others are not?

The problem of universalism

Many of these difficulties can be summed up by pointing to the high level of generality and abstraction associated with Enlightenment ideas. It is a tendency that some social philosophers refer to as 'universalism'. 'Science' is conceived by Enlightenment thinking at a very general level. There is not necessarily any real problem about this. Science is, after all, about developing general understandings of the world around us. The problem is that the Enlightenment's scientific *solutions* were, and to a large degree still are, also conceived at a very general level. Diversity is not part of the Enlightenment programme. Indeed, reason, as sought by the Enlightenment, actively celebrated the obliteration of diversity and particularity.

The solution to nature's improvement, for example, is seen as its subdivision and private ownership. But this general and apparently rational idea has often proved disastrous for communities in developing countries which have their own well-established ways of farming. There is no room for social or ecological variety within the single Enlightenment project, one trying to converge on a very specific kind of civilization. In our own time, for example, this kind of thinking is associated with the apparently 'scientific' solution of a mass-produced single type of crop or animal as a way of 'improving' developing countries. In many instances, however, this universal solution and denial of difference has proved ecologically and socially disastrous. Undermining existing traditions and cultures, such improvement has also rendered crops and animals prone to disease because of a lack of genetic diversity.

The problem of universality also applies to the making of 'Enlightened Man'. He or she is envisaged as an individual made to espouse modernity and advancement via modern science. In this way people find fulfilment. But what if some people have alternative ideas about fulfilment? Are, for example, more collective, less individualistic kinds of self to be seen as merely transitory types of identity, waiting to be rationalized into a single form? And why should other forms of knowledge held by people, particularly those of a more practical, everyday and qualitative kind, be neglected and even despised?

There is a paradox here. Humans are encouraged to act as individuals, 'rationally' making their choices. But the range of choices they are supposed to make is at the same time limited by Enlightenment ideals. Similarly, what about other kinds of politics? Why should the parliamentary model of democracy and freedom be seen as the optimal solution for all? Why are other kinds of politics not considered equally rational or liberating for a modern society?

In short, the kinds of universalism promoted by the Enlightenment, including that of representative democracy, could be and still are easily made into a means for exercising power over 'The Unenlightened'. Universalism has in practice been made into a way of exercising social and political influence (see box I.5).

Box I.5   Improving nature: Foucault revisited

THE CASE OF THE AMERICAN INDIANS

Robert Cushman, in a seventeenth-century book called *The Lawfulness of Removing out of England into the Parts of America*, argued that the Indians were basically non-industrious, 'neither having art, science, skill or faculty to use either the land or the commodities of it; but all spoils, rots and is marred for want of manuring, gathering, ordering. Etc. . . . [Indians] do but run over the grass, as do also the foxes and wild beasts' (cited in Drayton 2000: 56). This diagnosis meant that the English had not only the right but also the duty to take over and improve the Indians' land. But note that such improvement was seen as also bringing improvement to the Indians themselves. They would be transformed from being vagrants to being fully fed, modern, eventually rational people; a part of cultured human society rather than 'nature'.

THE CASE OF THE BRITISH LOWER CLASSES

John Lindley, a Professor at the University of London in the 1830s, was one of the chief supporters of the project for a giant glass house to be built in Kew, in London. This was to contain, and still contains, species of plants collected throughout the British Empire and elsewhere (see illus. I.5). In 1838 Lindley urged politicians of all sides to provide the money for this magnificent building, arguing that it would serve to educate and generally improve the rapidly growing numbers of working-class people. As his argument shows, his thinking was firmly in line with Enlightenment thinking:

> [Kew] would undoubtedly become an efficient instrument in refining the taste, increasing the knowledge, and augmenting the amount of rational pleasures of that important class of society, to provide for the instruction of which has become so great and wise an object with the present enlightened administration. (Cited in Drayton 2000: 156)

Illustration 1.5 Great Palm House at Kew Gardens

© CORBIS

Foucault's arguments would interpret these attempted 'improvements' of the American Indians and the British working classes as the means by which subordinated races and classes were pacified or made 'docile'. But Foucault also argued that the contemporary exercise of power is more subtle and diffuse than this. These forms of Enlightenment and Improvement are not simply repressive. Power induces knowledge, discourse and pleasure. The lower classes may well have enjoyed Kew even while they were being improved by their 'superiors'.

Optimism about the Enlightenment

But against all these negative assessments, some philosophers and social scientists hold out for the positive virtues of the Enlightenment. One of the most influential has been Jürgen Habermas. He argues forcibly that the Enlightenment saw the opening up of a 'public sphere' in which people – admittedly the middle classes – were able to engage in open dialogue and the search for truth. Politics and public policy could benefit from such rational and open debate. The Enlightenment, therefore, can still be seen in an emancipatory way, opening up the possibility for genuine debate and the active exchange of opinions and ideas. In this way a new kind of 'public person' can, in theory at least, be created. According to this view, then, Enlightenment thinking should be pursued and not abandoned in favour of Romanticism.

Society, Nature and Knowledge: Contemporary Debates

Such are some of the key themes of the Enlightenment and its critics. They have been necessarily simplified here. Major debates took place between proponents of Enlightenment thinking. For example, who exactly was going to define what human autonomy actually consisted of? Was it to be defined by the state acting on behalf of all individuals? Or was it literally to be left to each individual? Or should the Church still have a pivotal role? Despite these variations and arguments, the above is a reasonable preliminary account; one that helps us to situate the key debates covered here.

Social theory versus the Enlightenment: the cultural turn

One response to the problems of Enlightenment thinking has been for the social sciences to adopt a wholly cultural view of nature. That is, they argue that the increasing regulation of nature by society leaves the distinction between what is 'natural' and what is 'social' increasingly difficult to make. Both internal and external nature now seem fully infused with, and influenced by, social and political processes. Contemporary social theory also recognizes that Enlightenment thought has long been used as a form of domination, a means by which powerful people posing as objective are actually using general and scientific knowledge as a way of promoting themselves and marginalizing others.

A logical next step is to argue that there is in fact no difference between scientific and any other kind of knowledge. They are both a product of language and of society and science cannot make any particular claims. Its dethronement must be made complete, not least because it is used in a domineering manner by vested interests. Such are the influential views of contemporary cultural sociologists.

Latour argues, for example, that 'all of culture and all of nature get churned up every day' (1993: 2). He shows how the language of science and the language of society get constantly 'churned up' or 'mangled' in the media and, indeed, in everyday language (see box I.6). Again, there is no such thing as a pure nature. And, as Latour argues, this parallels the 'churning up' of nature and culture in the scientific world. What gets researched is a product of influential people, not least those who give research funds. This 'churning' or 'mangling' of society is a characteristic feature of society's actual relation with nature in modern society.

**Box 1.6   The churning up of culture and nature:
Latour on society and nature**

An important theme in contemporary sociology is the fusion between society and nature in language and power relations. Especially well known is the work of Latour (1987, 1988, 1993; see also Latour and Woolgar 1979) and his colleagues. Latour writes that 'all of culture and all of nature get churned up again every day' (1992: 2). By this he means that concepts of society and nature have become completely intertwined in contemporary society. He discusses, for example, a newspaper article concerning the thinning of the ozone layer over the Antarctic. Conventional categories of thought and language (nature, culture, science, politics and so on) are 'mangled' and deeply interlocked. As Latour puts it:

> The same article mixes together chemical reactions and political reactions. A single thread links the most esoteric sciences and the most sordid politics, the most distant sky and some factory in the Lyon suburbs, dangers on a global scale and the impending local elections of the next board meeting. The horizons, the stakes, the time frames, the actors – none of these is commensurable, yet there they are, caught up in the same story. (1993: 1)

The result of such 'mangling' is a series of 'hybrids' or 'quasi objects', neither being quite natural or social. Conventional science or social theory are incapable of capturing the richness and diversity of such objects. Research should focus on relations *between* such entities.

The feminist sociologist, Donna Haraway (1991), also points to the fusion between society and nature in modern society. The new reproductive technologies can be seen as heralding the development of a new kind of 'cyborg' creature, someone half machine, half human. Such interventions again serve to confuse the conventional categories of society and nature. Some feminists see these technologies as controlling female reproduction and hence as oppressive for women. But Haraway actively celebrates this fusion between 'the social' and 'the natural' since it threatens to undermine the oppressive distinctions between 'male' and 'female'. But her main point is still to challenge Enlightenment science and its 'truth claims' (see box I.7). All such claims, she argues, should be placed in their social and political contexts. The outcome is similar to that of Latour. There is no distinction to be made between science and culture. They are equally challengeable. Such a focus on the contemporary fusion between the social and natural worlds is important, not least because how people construe 'nature' and 'society' powerfully influences how society treats both internal and external nature. And most scientists would agree that their truth claims do need constantly questioning. But this approach still leaves the big issue untouched.

The counter-argument is that scientific understandings are surely about much more than discourse or the influence of fundgivers on science. It is still, as indeed the Enlightenment insisted, about understanding the reality of the world in which

---

Box I.7 The churning up of society and nature: Haraway on science as domination

Donna Haraway, like many feminist social scientists, challenges Enlightenment science and its notion of an objective or 'scientific' knowledge based on the evaluation of 'facts' independent of values and politics. Enlightenment 'objectivity' stems, it is argued, from a masculine demand to dominate nature and women. Haraway seeks a diversity of knowledges, rather than the 'Master' knowledge promoted by the Enlightenment. She writes:

> I, and others, started out wanting a strong tool for deconstructing the truth claims of hostile science by showing the radical historical specificity, and so contestability of every layer of the onion of scientific and technological constructions, and we end up with a kind of epistemological electro-shock, which far from ushering us into the high stakes table of the game of contesting public truths, lays us out on the table with self-induced multiple personality disorder. (1991: 186; original emphasis)

---

we live. The equalizing of all kinds of knowledge in the way proposed by these sociologists runs the real risk of leading to the suggestion that all forms of science are merely 'social constructions'. Newton's and Darwin's theories of the world are put on a par with conversation at the bar or dinner-party chatter. According to this view, there is no reality at all independent of power and language. It is all social construction. Such arguments are a kind of sociological imperialism, analogous to the scientific imperialism they attack. Both such views rapidly depart from common sense and an alternative approach to understanding society–nature relations must be found.

Enlightenment science revived: critical realism

Allowance must be made for a reality which exists beyond language and politics. But allowance must also be made for an understanding which not only recognizes the 'churning up' of society and nature but which also reassembles these different types of knowledge in a coherent way. Such a view is offered by contemporary critical realism. Some of the key features of this philosophy are outlined in box I.8.

Broadly, humans and other species develop and behave within the laws and mechanisms studied and outlined by the physical and natural sciences. Global warming and other forms of environmental change indicate, however, that human society is now having an impact on the precise ways in which these mechanisms are operating. As a result, humans and other species are being affected in new, sometimes disastrous, ways. But this does not affect the real underlying mechanisms themselves. Similarly, Darwin's theory of evolution posited a series of mechanisms underlying the evolution and development of species. All species and their relationships are influenced by these underlying mechanisms and processes, but precisely

---

Box 1.8 Critical realism: key elements

1 Knowledge is a product of society, but knowledge is not *only* a product of society. It can refer to real processes and mechanisms in the world.
2 Science is about establishing the causes underlying phenomena of interest. Real, relatively enduring structures and causal mechanisms in the physical, biological and social worlds underlie what we observe and experience. They do so in combination with one another and often in combination with contingent circumstances. 'Closed systems' are created artificially to develop understandings of causal mechanisms, but these are rare in society and nature.
3 The world is envisaged as hierarchically stratified. At the most general level are physical mechanisms (e.g. gravity). At a 'higher' level are chemical structures and mechanisms. Higher still are biological mechanisms (e.g. those generating an organism's growth). Finally, there are psychological and social mechanisms. Mechanisms at each level of reality are rooted in – but not reducible to – those operating at lower levels.
4 The nature of these structures and mechanisms is subject to constant critique and scientific development. This critique and development can also stem from practical, everyday experience.

For further discussion and an application, see box 6.5 (p. 184). Also see 'Further reading' section at the end of this chapter.

---

how they work out will depend on their context. Human beings, for example, have evolved with a strong sense of personal 'self' or identity. But, as chapters 4 and 5 suggest, this sense of identity can take very different forms in different kinds of society. Humans have also evolved with mechanisms designed to protect the developing infant. But chapter 6 will show that these mechanisms can be made to work in different ways for different classes of people. In some instances, like the mechanisms of the physical world, they are being made to operate in ways that are dangerous. In such ways, 'the risk society' is being actively created. The key point here about a critical realist position is its recognition of reality, independent of discourse and language.

This perspective therefore recognizes the 'churning up' of society and nature, but it also attempts to unpack and understand this churning up in a coherent, organized fashion. It also avoids the problem of empiricism; trying to deduce how the world is organized simply by interrogating 'the facts'. Similarly, it avoids the problem of positivism and the argument that the social world is inevitably best developed through the application of scientific methods developed in the physical and natural sciences. Critical realism certainly draws on Enlightenment-style attempts to develop general, scientific understandings of the world. But Enlightenment-style knowledge is made less dogmatic, more open to criticism from non-scientists, more self-critical, more open to alternative research methods and, where necessary, critical of the processes it is examining.

Structure of the Book

Chapter 1

This chapter introduces the four main lenses through which the relations between society and nature are to be viewed. These are evolution, industry, community and risk.

Why these particular lenses?

Evolution Darwin argued that there are minute differences between individuals. In a situation where populations grow much more quickly than resources, some individuals will have characteristics that enable them to survive. They will be the ones who survive and who reproduce into future generations. The result is endless improvement. Evolution has, for the past century and a half, been an extraordinarily influential idea, deeply affecting the thinking of the social as well as the natural sciences. As a concept, it also links well with Enlightenment ideas. A number of social scientists (and some biologists) strongly suggest that both biological and social evolution comprise an ongoing success story. At one time the British Labour Party adopted a pop song, 'Things Can Only Get Better'. Their belief was that only their party could achieve this end. Enlightenment philosophy took a longer view. Biological and social evolution are, over the long term, steadily evolving towards something better. But what is this 'better'? According to those critical of Enlightenment thinking, there is a tacit assumption here which needs critical assessment. The perfect model towards which biological and social evolution has all along been heading is apparently modern capitalist society and modern 'man'. Is such an assumption satisfactory?

Industry Industry is another core concept in the social sciences. The relationships formed in modern industry, the things produced and how people are treated at the workplace have long been central to modern social science. But there is a major gap here, one that urgently needs filling. Industry, or work, is the means by which nature is transformed into goods. 'Industry' needs recasting to take this basic fact into account. An industry lens allows us to focus on the transformation both of external nature and of the people in the industry: the workers.

Community 'Community' is perhaps *the* core unit idea in the contemporary social sciences, particularly sociology. An often-heard cry over the last two centuries is that 'community' is collapsing, that the old kinds of close relationship between people, and between people and nature, are collapsing as feudalism has given way to modern, capitalist ways of life. There are many debates in this area; many social scientists and others argue, for example, that old forms of community were not necessarily all that wonderful and that new kinds of community are continually in the making. Young people, it is sometimes argued, are the least likely to participate in the public realm. Their lives are more individualistic. They are 'non-joiners' (Putnam 2000). This is not the place to enter into these debates, but suffice it to say that 'community' is indeed one of the big ideas in modern social science.

Risk Using the concept of 'risk' as a lens to examine society's relations with nature might seem more questionable. It has, at least until recently, received little attention in social science. On the other hand, its inclusion reflects a growing concern in modern social science. To a growing extent humanity is making social life more risky. The unintended consequences of global warming, or the thinning of the ozone layer, are now becoming apparent. The results of transforming food for human purposes are also clear, the BSE disaster in the UK in the 1990s being just one example. Beck's notion of 'the risk society' expresses the idea that we now live in a society which is actively generating new kinds of danger. As we will see, there are arguments for and against this assertion. But including 'risk' as a lens is justified not only by what social scientists are saying, but also by the sometimes disastrous ways in which the causal powers of the natural world are being activated.

Chapter 2

This chapter focuses on industry and the way it transforms the powers of the environment or 'external nature'. It adopts a perspective first developed by Marx and Engels. These philosophers gave particular attention to the relationships made between people and between humanity and nature in the process of producing the things that individuals need. Marx and Engels were highly critical of modern capitalist society. They saw it as ruining not only the environment in increasingly disastrous ways, but also internal nature, people's health and well-being. Humanity needs an active engagement with the environment if its full human powers are to be adequately recognized and if further risks to human health are to be avoided. But such engagement had, Marx and Engels argued, been severed by modern capitalist societies. However, although critical of the kind of capitalist society which the Enlightenment celebrated, Marx and Engels also welcomed the modern world. This was because they envisaged it as an important and necessary stage towards the next stage of social evolution: the arrival of communism. In such a society, work life and community life would be combined. Furthermore, the rift between society and nature would be restored and human potential would be fully realized.

Chapter 3

The Enlightenment philosophers, as we have seen, welcomed the ownership, buying and selling of the earth. They saw all this as an essential further stage in social and human evolution. Realizing the fruits of the earth and realizing human potential as modern and rational remains a familiar cry today. The commercialization of the earth's surface and its integration into a world market are seen in economically and politically powerful circles as the answer to the world's food problems. And, contrary to the views of many of today's ecological activists and protesters, such commercialization is seen as the answer to environmental degradation. This is because rising prices resulting from the use of a commodified environment give an early indication that new resources should be found. The market operates according to what Adam Smith, the Scottish Enlightenment economist and philosopher (1723–90), called 'an invisible hand', and thus ensures that society moves in a progressive way – the beliefs of the Enlightenment are alive and well. But there are problems here. Private ownership and management is no longer seen as the basis of control. The powers of nature cannot be manipulated and controlled in the complete way envisaged by Enlightenment thinking. A key result is that nature has its 'revenge'. Humanity experiences risks that stem from its overarching ambition to dominate nature.

Chapter 4

At this stage the emphasis is on both external and internal nature. It is often said that the earth's resources are now in danger because, as a global society, humanity consumes too much. This chapter takes issue with such a view, arguing that it is too simple. Instead, certain groups of people (especially those with large amounts of disposable income) constitute the problem. Consumption has become an important, even dominant influence on development of human identity and community. For this reason it certainly cannot be wished away and it is central to any focus on society–nature relations. Environmental risk starts when the power of the dominant classes leads to considerable social and economic change. This power, which stems from the high levels of education and strategic position in the labour market of the elite, influences the attitudes and priorities of others. Consumerism and its values extend down to those without the material resources to fully engage in high levels of consumption.

Chapter 5

Here, the focus shifts entirely to human nature, specifically to human identity. The Enlightenment celebrated the emergence of the autonomous individual. Chapter 5 argues that this apparently autonomous individual is still being actively constructed today. Indeed, his or her individualism is taking increasingly extreme forms. The nature of this individual is better understood with the aid of modern-day psychology. Human beings' psychic nature has a potentially wide range of forms. In earlier societies relatively collective forms were the norm. But the dominant type of modern self is self-absorbed. This is one type of psychic structure, one very familiar amongst children. But it is now widely extended and realized in human adulthood. It is a particular kind of individualism generated not only by consumerism but also by new forms of information technology and labour markets. Self-absorption has been made the characteristic feature of the modern psyche. Furthermore, it is developed by the kinds of virtual environment now being made for people to observe and work on. The rift between society and nature has been made more extreme than Marx and Engels could have imagined.

Chapter 6

The book continues here with a consideration of 'internal nature', but now with particular reference to human biology. Again, Enlightenment ideals and values are alive and well. This is particularly the case with the new reproductive technologies, which promise that an improved human being is possible (one with fewer illnesses and greater intelligence) if only people will allow genetic science access to the human genome. In such a way, evolution can be 'progressed' still further. But here the 'shadow' of the Enlightenment is encountered again. Many see such developments as not representing great improvements and probably bringing considerable risks.

Chapter 6 also shows that biologically inherited powers of human development are being transformed in a number of ways which are *not* intended. Modern epidemiology clearly shows, for example, that children who are poorly treated are likely to suffer a range of problems later on in their lives. These include health risks and problems of cognitive ability. Typically, these are children from low-income families. This is another instance of how, in transforming nature, *internal* nature is itself changed. Furthermore, the internal nature of particular classes of people is transformed in particular ways. Chapter 6 also offers an instance of how modern science can still be profoundly helpful in understanding the powers of human nature and how they are transformed by their environment.

Chapter 7

This Introduction and chapters 1–6 allow a critical assessment of modern politics as it affects our environment and ourselves. Chapters 7 and 8 consider new kinds of politics aimed at developing better relations with our environment and new, enlightened, social and ecological selves. These difficult projects are addressed, initially at least, by reconsidering the Enlightenment's 'scientific' politics. The engagement of individuals into parliamentary politics now extends well beyond the property-owners celebrated by John Locke. Even non-human animals are finding their rights protected and strengthened via parliamentary politics. Nevertheless, many people are now profoundly disillusioned with the kind of 'scientific politics' invented and promoted 200 years ago. It seems to offer rather little influence over how society works. Even assuming that the autonomous individual were possible, it is not bringing about the kinds of freedom hoped for by Enlightenment philosophers. This has led to demands for more diverse and thoroughgoing kinds of politics, which would enable people to fully relate to one another and to control the institutions where they work and the communities in which they live. 'Scientific' parliamentary democracy is replaced by forms of politics which allow people to regain control over the institutions which necessarily influence their lives. In this way people's capacities, their needs for human association and association with their environment are more likely to be realized.

Chapter 8

Following on from the arguments of chapter 7, this chapter discusses what are called the new social movements. These include the peace movement, the women's movement, movements demanding the rights of racial and sexual minorities, as well as movements concerning the environment. They are very diverse, but there are, nevertheless, some connecting similarities. Many of them, for example, explore new cultures and values. But even so, they are rehearsing many of the debates that have taken place between Enlightenment and Romantic ways of thought. Furthermore, the differences between 'old' and 'new' movements are often exaggerated.

Jürgen Habermas, perhaps the leading social scientist of our day, was optimistic about the Enlightenment. He envisaged it as 'an unfinished project'. This book is similarly optimistic. Science must still be embraced, but in a more critical, less deferential way than that proposed by the Enlightenment philosophers. Furthermore, the sciences of the natural world need to be combined with those of the human social world. Scientific knowledge needs to be developed in relation to the practical, everyday kinds of understanding of those who are seldom listened to. Enlightenment science needs transforming, not rejecting.

FURTHER READING

The Enlightenment

The literature on the Enlightenment is very considerable. The following are especially helpful:

P. Gay, *The Enlightenment: An Interpretation* (2 vols). London: Weidenfeld, 1967.

N. Hanson, *The Enlightenment. An Evaluation of its Assumptions, Attitudes and Values.* Harmondsworth: Penguin, 1982.

D. Outram, *The Enlightenment.* Cambridge: Cambridge University Press, 1995.

D. Porter, *Enlightenment. Britain and the Creation of the Modern World.* Harmondsworth: Penguin, 2000.

D. Porter, *The Enlightenment.* Basingstoke: Palgrave, 2001.

A flavour of continuing debates on the meaning of the Enlightenment to modern society can be gained by reading:

S. Ashenden and D. Owen (eds), *Foucault Contra Habermas.* London: Sage, 1999.

P. Hulme and L. Jordanova, *The Enlightenment and its Shadows.* London: Routledge, 1990.

On rationalization and the environment see:

R. Murphy, 'Ecological Materialism and the Sociology of Max Weber', in R. Dunlap, F. Buttel, P. Dickens and A. Gijswijt (eds), *Sociological Theory and the Environment. Classical Foundations, Contemporary Insights.* Boulder, CO: Rowman and Littlefield, 2002.

The development of a new, non-human-centred social theory

Riley Dunlap and Bill Catton were amongst the first modern sociologists to recognize the importance of a new kind of sociology which could see the importance of the environment to human society. They argued against what they call the 'human exemptionalism paradigm'. For a discussion of the history of environmental sociology since the 1970s, see:

R. Dunlap, 'Paradigms, Theories and Environmental Sociology', in R. Dunlap, F. Buttel, P. Dickens and A. Gijswijt (eds), *Sociological Theory and the Environment. Classical Foundations, Contemporary Insights.* Boulder, CO: Rowman and Littlefield, 2002.

R. Dunlap and W. Catton, 'Struggling with Human Exemptionalism: The Rise, Decline and Revitalization of Environmental Sociology', *The American Sociologist*, 25/1 (1994): 5–30.

Further very useful introductions to the development of a social and political theory which takes environmental questions seriously include:

J. Barry, *Environment and Social Theory*. London: Routledge, 1999.

M. Bell, *An Invitation to Environmental Sociology*. Thousand Oaks, CA: Pine Forge Press, 1998.

M. Jacobs (ed.), *Greening the Millennium? The New Politics of the Environment*. Cambridge: Polity, 1997.

L. Martell, *Ecology and Society*. Cambridge: Polity, 1994.

J. O'Neill, *Ecology, Policy and Politics*. London: Routledge, 1993.

M. Smith, 'Green Sociology', *Sociology Review* (1997): 129–33.

M. Smith (ed.), *Thinking Through the Environment*. London: Routledge, 1999.

A recent text which readdresses questions about the usefulness of 'universal' knowledge is:

S. Yearley, *Sociology, Environmentalism, Globalization*. London: Sage, 1996. (*Very generalized forms of understanding, he argues, serve to 'conceal political assumptions and mask self-interest' (p. 140).*)

A useful general reference on contemporary rationalization is:

G. Ritzer, *The McDonaldization of Society*. Thousand Oaks, CA: Pine Forge Press, 1996.

The Enlightenment, contemporary society, nature and the making of new selves

This is a very large literature, and one that is gaining increasing prominence. Of particular interest in the context of this chapter are:

N. Abercrombie, S. Hill and B. Turner, *Sovereign Individuals of Capitalism*. London: Allen and Unwin, 1986.

E. Bragg, 'Towards Ecological Self: Deep Ecology Meets Constructionist Self-Theory', *Journal of Environmental Psychology*, 16 (1996): 93–108.

G. Cohen, *Self-Ownership, Freedom and Equality*. Cambridge: Cambridge University Press, 1995.

K. Dean, *Capitalism and Citizenship: The Impossible Partnership*. London: Routledge, 2003.

G. DiZerega, 'Empathy, Society, Nature and the Relational Self: Deep Ecological and Liberal Modernity', *Social Theory and Practice*, 21/2 (1995): 42–75.

J. Henriques, W. Hollway, C. Urwin, C. Venn and V. Walkerdine, *Changing the Subject*. London: Routledge, 1998.

R. Keat and N. Abercrombie, *Enterprise Culture*. London: Routledge, 1991.

S. Kroll-Smith, 'Toxic Contamination and the Loss of Civility', *Sociological Spectrum*, 15 (1995): 377–96.

M. Redclift, 'Environmental Security and the Recombinant Human: Sustainability in the Twenty-first Century', *Environmental Values*, 10 (2001): 289–99.

C. Taylor, *Sources of the Self. The Making of the Modern Identity*. Cambridge: Cambridge University Press, 1989.

P. Wehling, 'Dynamic Constellations of the Individual, Society and Nature: Critical Theory and Environmental Sociology', in R. Dunlap, F. Buttel, P. Dickens and A. Gijswijt (eds), *Sociological Theory and the Environment. Classical Foundations, Contemporary Insights*. Boulder, CO: Rowman and Littlefield, 2002.

See also Further reading sections to chapters 5 and 6.

Note that the rapidly developing field of postcolonialism is throwing new sociological and historical light on the incorporation of nature into processes of economic development and the simultaneous making of new kinds of 'self'. See, for example:

M. Davis, *Late Victorian Holocausts. El Niño Famines and the Making of the Third World*. London: Verso, 2001.

F. Driver, *Geography Militant. Cultures of Exploration and Empire*. Oxford: Blackwell, 2001.

C. Hall, *Civilising Subjects. Metropole and Colony in the English Imagination, 1830–67*. Cambridge: Polity, 2002.

R. MacLeod (ed.), 'Nature and Empire. Science and the Colonial Enterprise', *Osiris*, 14, 2nd series (2000).

Colonization in turn led to early concerns with impacts on tropical societies. For a useful introduction to how Enlightenment science combined with more Romantic, less rationalistic, visions see:

R. Grove, 'Origins of Western Environmentalism', *Scientific American* (July 1992): 22–7.

Other historical studies of the relations between social and climate change include:

R. Couper-Johnston, *El Niño. The Weather Phenomenon that Changed the World*. London: Hodder and Stoughton, 2000.

M. Glantz, *Currents of Change. El Nino's Impact on Climate and Society*. Cambridge: Cambridge University Press, 1996.

H. Lamb, *Climate, History and the Modern World* (2nd edn). London: Routledge, 1995.

The Enlightenment: for and against

T. Adorno and M. Horkheimer, *Dialectic of the Enlightenment*. London: Verso, 1979 (first published 1944).

S. Ashenden and D. Owen (eds), *Foucault Contra Habermas*. London: Sage, 1999.

J. Habermas, *The Structural Transformation of the Public Sphere: An Enquiry into the Category of Bourgeois Society*. Cambridge, MA: MIT Press, 1989.

Much contemporary social science on postmodernity has taken the supposed failings of the Enlightenment as its starting point. Science, scientific politics, rationalism and universalism, it is argued, have resulted not in certainty and reason, but in ambiguity, uncertainty and irrationality. See also Appendix and, for a modern example, see:

Z. Bauman, *Modernity and Ambivalence*. Cambridge: Polity, 1991.

Social constructionist approaches to science

B. Latour, *Science in Action*. Cambridge, MA: Harvard University Press, 1987.

B. Latour and S. Woolgar, *Laboratory Life*. Princeton: Princeton University Press, 1979.

Latour's approach has been developed as 'actor network theory', particularly by geographers. See, for example:

J. Murdoch, 'The Spaces of Actor-Network Theory', *Geoforum*, 29 (1998): 357–74.

S. Whatmore and L. Thorne, 'Wild(er)ness: Reconfiguring the Geographies of Wildlife', *Transactions of the Institute of British Geographers*, 23 (1998): 435–54.

Society, nature and Foucault

Foucault in particular applied himself to 'internal nature', especially to sexuality. Heterosexual sex is categorized as 'natural', while other forms are abnormal. These constructions lead, Foucault argues, to the self-policing subject regulating his or her behaviour in supposedly 'natural' ways. See:

M. Foucault, *The History of Sexuality*. Harmondsworth: Penguin, 1978.

Critical realism

T. Benton, 'Realism and Social Science: Some Comments on Roy Bhaskar's "The Possibility of Naturalism"', in M. Archer, R. Bhaskar, A. Collier, T. Lawson and A. Norrie, *Critical Realism. Essential Readings.* London: Routledge, 1998.

T. Benton and I. Craib, *Philosophy of Social Science. The Philosophical Foundations of Social Thought.* London: Palgrave, 2001.

A. Collier, *Critical Realism. An Introduction to Roy Bhaskar's Philosophy.* London: Verso, 1994.

B. Danermark, M. Ekstrom, L. Jakobsen and J. Karlsson, *Explaining Society. Critical Realism in the Social Sciences.* London: Routledge, 2002.

T. Lawson, *Economics and Reality.* London: Routledge, 1997.

A. Sayer, *Method in Social Science. A Realist Approach.* London: Routledge, 1992.

A. Sayer, *Realism and Social Science.* London: Sage, 2000.

K. Soper, *What is Nature? Culture, Politics and the Non-Human.* Oxford: Blackwell, 1995.

There are several ongoing debates within critical realism. One of the most important is that between humanism and naturalism. Humanists (see, for example, Soper 1995) treat humans as a highly distinctive species, in fact so distinctive as to be incapable of explanation by the natural sciences. Naturalists argue that despite humans' distinctive qualities, including their cultures, the natural sciences remain helpful. Humans are doing similar things to other species (eating, reproducing and so on) but of course these practices are overlaid with a vast range of cultural forms and values. See, for example:

T. Benton, 'Environmental Philosophy: Humanism or Naturalism? A Reply to Kate Soper', *Journal of Critical Realism*, 2/4 (2001): 2–9.

Also, a number of texts claim to be setting aside the supposedly 'tired' debate between critical realism and social constructionism. See, for example:

K. K. Burningham and G. Cooper, 'Being Constructive: Social Constructionism and the Environment', *Sociology*, 33/2 (1999): 297–316.

A. Franklin, *Nature and Social Theory.* London: Sage, 2002.

P. MacNaghten and J. Urry, *Contested Natures.* London: Sage, 1998.

They have not, however, addressed the central assertion of critical realism: that, independent of people's construal of the environment, there exists an independent reality, one composed of causal, generative mechanisms. These mechanisms and powers are addressed by the natural sciences, areas of understanding remaining largely uninterrogated by social and cultural theorists.

Le Corbusier and Frank Lloyd Wright

Those interested in the social and philosophical background to Le Corbusier and Frank Lloyd Wright will find the following useful:

J. Sergeant, *Frank Lloyd Wright's Usonian Houses. Designs for Moderate Cost One-Family Homes.* New York: Watson-Guptill, 1984.

R. Walden (ed.), *The Open Hand. Essays on Le Corbusier.* Cambridge, MA: MIT Press, 1977.

Introducing Key Themes

Overview

This chapter introduces some of the main ways in which the relations between society and nature have been understood. It is a trailer for the rest of the book, introducing themes and ideas that will be much developed later. Particular attention is given here to the four lenses outlined earlier (evolution, industry, community and risk).

The application of evolutionary ideas to human society has not only been widespread, but also highly influential. Yet in many ways it has been problematic. Later in this book, we will look at evolutionary ideas that stem from modern biology. These are more helpful than the evolutionary ideas developed by social scientists. Industry is essential to our concerns, because it is industry which transforms the natural world into the things we consume. 'Community' can actually mean a number of things. It broadly refers to human association, but it can also have other connotations such as association in particular localities. Especially important to our concerns is the extension of community to include humanity's relations with the environment. Yet few people in modern industrial societies have direct, working contact with their local environment. Their concern with their environment tends to be of a different kind; they value it as something to be viewed and protected but not as something to be worked on. Risk most often refers to the unintended effects of the application of science and of industrial development to the environment. More literally, it has recently been used by some social scientists to suggest that a wholly new 'risk society' is developing. There is a vast range of activities that are risky to human beings, it is argued, this being the result of a decline in tradition and established ways of proceeding. Thus forming a relationship or getting married nowadays is a distinctly 'risky' business in a society where there are few rules governing how families are made or unmade. Getting a job is a risky business, in a society where 'a job for life' is virtually unheard of. These second types of risk are all leading to increasing individualization. To an increasing extent, people are their own individual experts. They regularly conduct experiments, any number of which may end in disaster. This may be disaster for the environment, but, equally, it may be disaster for their private and social lives.

Contributions from Evolutionary Thought

Evolution is one obvious place from which to start. It is important to us in a number of ways. Evolutionary thought, particularly as developed by Charles Darwin (1809–92), is concerned with the relationships between organisms (including 'man') and their environment. Darwin and many other evolutionists have also been particularly concerned to see human beings as themselves part of nature. They have an evolutionary history like any other species. And this history must in some way throw light on human beings' behaviour and on the ways in which humanity has slowly changed itself as it struggles for survival. Darwin himself was quite cautious about exactly what kind of light our evolutionary past throws on our behaviour. But, as we will see, Darwin's interpreters, and indeed some evolutionists today, have not been as cautious as Darwin himself. Many would argue that they have over-emphasized the importance of our evolutionary past.

A harsh environment and the struggle for survival

Although Darwin himself did not express much concern about the relations between people and their environment, his evolutionary theories and ideas strike us as in many ways familiar today. The general picture, as articulated by Alfred Russel Wallace (1823–1913) as well as by Darwin, is that of organisms struggling for survival under conditions of resource scarcity (see box 1.1). Evolutionary thought was therefore claiming to have uncovered a basic mechanism underlying the rise and fall of individuals and species. But note, as many authors have suggested, that the theory can be seen as very much a product of its times. (For an example, see box 2.3 on p. 64.) Important to us is the fact that both Wallace and Darwin were inspired by Malthus's *Essay on Population*, published in the late eighteenth century. This argued, again in ways that seem familiar to us today, that population tends to rise at a much higher rate than do the resources available for its sustenance. This was the primary cause of poverty. Unless some catastrophe such as a war, mass famine or mass disease intervenes, there will simply not be enough resources to go around.

Darwin himself admitted that Malthus's ideas were the part of the jigsaw which brought his theory together. The harsh limitations of the environment themselves make people develop and behave differently. Shortages might mean that people have fewer children or, equally, they might lead to governments stepping in and providing resources for those unable to thrive in the struggle for survival. Note, however, the views of Wallace, co-discoverer with Darwin of the theory of natural selection. Like Darwin, he stressed that Malthus had been important to the

Box 1.1   Darwin and Wallace's theory of natural selection

Most living creatures produce many more offspring than are needed to reproduce their numbers. Yet, despite this, the number of any one species tends to remain much the same from one generation to the next. A struggle for survival and reproduction into future generations is taking place within the context of limited resources. No two individuals are alike, all show variations in some form or other. These variations are random. Those variations which give advantages for full development and reproduction of future generations will tend to prevail. Those individuals without these characteristics will fail.

Charles Darwin, c.1875   Alfred Russel Wallace

Photo AKG London   © The Natural History Museum, London

creation of the theory. On the other hand, Wallace had a socialist background. He also felt that resources are not inevitably in short supply; they only become so because of the fact that they are in private ownership. (Wallace was an active proponent of the public ownership of land.) So he had real reservations about the idea that environmental shortages and limitations are inevitable. To him, these problems were, to a large degree at least, 'man-made'.

Darwin's theory, and his understanding of resource shortages, is controversial when applied to human beings. Similar controversies continue today. Is it right to believe that resources are inevitably dwindling in our society? To talk about dwindling misses the point when private property is the cause of such scarcities.

Applying evolutionary ideas to human society

Further controversies surround Darwin's theory when it is applied to human nature and the idea that those with special mental and physical characteristics survive into future generations. The controversy became particularly heated when social scientists applied Darwinism to human society. Wallace once asked Darwin whether he was thinking of extending his theory of natural selection to the human race. Darwin replied:

> You ask whether I shall discuss 'man'. I think I shall avoid the whole subject, as so surrounded with prejudices; though I fully admit it is the highest and most interesting problem for the naturalist. (Cited in Hawkins 1997: 20)

Evolution and the emergence of the best people

Before continuing with Darwin, it is worth considering how his ideas were translated into human society by some social scientists. Herbert Spencer (1820–1903), a leading sociologist of his day, actually coined the term 'the survival of the fittest' some ten years before Darwin published *The Origin of Species*. He also developed his own version of evolutionary thought before Darwin, one that argued that human beings struggle for survival. As box 1.2 shows, he even developed his own understanding of social evolution.

Of particular relevance to us, however, was Spencer's conviction that, in the struggle for survival, it is the weakest *humans* who die out and it is the strongest who survive and reproduce into future generations. And, in terms which also strike many of us as familiar today, it is the weakest *races* that are most likely to die out:

> The average vigour of any race would be diminished did the diseased and feeble habitually survive and propagate; and . . . the destruction of such, through failure to fulfil some of the conditions to life leaves behind those who are able to fulfil the conditions of life, and thus keeps up the average fitness to the conditions of life. (Spencer 1898: 532–3)

The human struggle for survival inevitably leads, then, to the rise and rise of superior kinds of people, according to Spencer. And they will propagate their

---

Box 1.2   Herbert Spencer's theory of social evolution

Herbert Spencer's evolutionary theory owed as much to physics as to biology. He envisaged the whole of the universe as in a state of constant flux, claiming a general tendency, one which extended across the physical, biological and social worlds, for a transition from unstructured homogeneous forms towards structured homogeneous forms.

Herbert Spencer, 1888

Mary Evans Picture Library

In the case of organic nature, for example, he argued that organisms are constantly struggling to survive and, in attempting to survive in a hostile environment, they become increasingly differentiated and composed of connected parts. The transition over time from amoeba-like organisms to complex yet structured organisms is paralleled in the social world by the transition from 'simple' homogeneous societies to far more complex, heterogeneous and differentiated societies such as our own. Spencer argued that the tendency was for simple societies to be increasingly integrated with one another, albeit with powerful central leaderships. He also argued that there was a more recent tendency towards a transition from 'militant' to 'industrial' societies. The former are characterized by the extreme centralization of power, with people compelled and disciplined into supporting such power. Industrial societies are characterized, he believed, by the decentralization of power, by democracy and with governments working to support the individual.

Note that Spencer saw social evolution as linear. It has a definite direction with one kind of society evolving into another. The implication is that this is both a universal and an irreversible sequence. Spencer broadly approved of what he saw as this long period of social evolution. Its great benefit, he believed, lay in the increased realization of individual liberty. On the other hand, with the rise of state intervention and the growing number of military employed by the British government, he detected the unwelcome return of older 'militant' forms of society. Overall, however, he saw social evolution as bringing social *progress*. Partly because of this, Spencer's evolutionary ideas were even more influential than those of Darwin in the Victorian era.

Box 1.3 No gain without pain: William Sumner on hardship and the emergence of superior people in the struggle for survival

William Sumner (1840–1910), Professor of Political Economy at Yale, greatly approved of Spencer's perspective and is often seen as the main American proponent of Social Darwinism. Humans, like all other species, are struggling for survival. Intense hardships would be endured in the human struggle for survival. But, he said:

> we cannot blame our fellow-men for our share of these. My neighbour and I are both struggling to free ourselves from these ills. The fact that my neighbour has succeeded in this struggle better than I constitutes no grievance for me. (Cited in Hofstadter 1959: 56)

The implication, directly stated by this follower of Darwin, was that the richest and most successful people have become richer as a result of their superior characteristics. This is again a question of the laws of nature working themselves out in human society. The best will rise to the top. Furthermore, this should not be regretted or reversed. The best rising to the top leads in the long run to social betterment.

---

characteristics into future generations. Society is thereby seen as steadily changing itself for the better as competition for scarce resources continues. And this view led to a particular perspective on how society *should* be organized, one that is, again, familiar today. For Spencer, the implication was that governments should stand back. While he approved of charitable activity and gifts to the poor, major government interventions in the form of, for example, extensive health or education services could only serve to hold back the processes of human evolution. It would no longer be the best who survived and reproduced future generations; social progress would not be made. This was a philosophy that was well received in the United States of America. Human society is itself part of nature (see box 1.3). The best rise to the top as a result of their inherited biological and mental characteristics; the weakest are meanwhile eliminated. These processes are beneficial in the long run since they can only strengthen civilization as a whole.

Problems of 'progress', 'direction' and 'purpose' in evolution

Spencer's theory brings us to three more general ways in which the application of evolutionary ideas to the understanding of human society has been made. Since the days of the Enlightenment they have been extraordinarily influential in their effect on the social sciences and on popular opinion. At the same time they are increasingly seen as problematic.

The essence of Darwin's theory was that evolution is random. It should not be possible to say that any stage of evolution is 'better' than any other. Similarly, the theory implies that there is no direction to evolution, social or otherwise.

Furthermore, there was no inevitable end to which evolutionary processes were developing. Again, evolution is random. There is no end result which was built into the start of the evolutionary process. Rejection of religious accounts of how humans and other species have developed on earth should imply that there was actually no purpose, direction or God-given end to which either nature or society is evolving. But evolutionary thought, whether that expressed by Darwin or by writers such as Spencer, found it difficult to completely overthrow these notions. Here again, evolutionary ideas, particularly as they developed in the early days, were a reflection of the society in which they were created.

Progress As Darwin himself admitted, it is difficult to avoid the idea that the emergence of humanity (or 'the Descent of Man') in the long evolutionary process does indeed represent some kind of progress over the very basic kinds of organism with which evolution started. (Hands up those who would say humanity is not progress beyond amoeba!) Furthermore, if we believe that fully evolved human beings are capable of producing increasingly rational, scientific understandings of the world, then progress becomes equated with 'science'; including, of course, evolutionary science. Here again we find dominant nineteenth and indeed eighteenth-century values penetrating what might seem relatively objective accounts of the world. 'Science' is the way human beings understand nature. It uncovers the mechanisms on which humanity works to improve themselves. Humans are not just developing an understanding of nature through science, they are actively developing themselves in developing their understanding of the surrounding environment.

Furthermore, this is progressive. Greater scientific understanding entails greater realization of human capacities. Humanity is in effect improving itself as it works on revealing nature's secrets. Science, seen in this positive light, therefore has to be a progressive and good thing. Science, and evolutionary science in particular, is often considered to have replaced religion and God as an explanation of the world. But it can also be seen, perhaps with the benefit of hindsight, as a God-substitute, a largely untouchable item in which humanity should keep faith. In the light of the number of forests felled, the number of species wiped out and the number of seas polluted in the name of 'progress', there are now growing arguments against this view. We will return to these shortly, but note, in boxes 1.2 and 1.3 and in the following chapter, examples of 'progress' being built into earlier theories of social change.

Direction As regards direction, it has again been difficult for many social scientists to avoid making the assumption that there is a definite way in which both nature and society are developing. The evolutionary process, for example, seems to be producing ever more complex kinds of animal. Similarly, society (with its shift away from very simple tribal societies based on increasingly complex divisions of labour) seems to be on a general path away from one kind of society to another. Furthermore, applying evolutionary ideas to human societies can easily suggest that *all* societies are destined to develop in the same direction. There is, therefore, a definite evolutionary line (from simple to complex societies via feudalism) down which all societies must develop. The proposition sounds quite doubtful, even mystical. The implication is that what we call 'advanced' Western-style capitalist democracy is the 'end' towards which all societies must be developing (note the examples in boxes 1.2 and 1.3).

Purpose Linked to questions of progress and science is the idea of a predetermined end state to which evolution is leading (this is known as a 'teleological' explanation). Again, Darwin would have strongly resisted such an idea. But, as applied by many social theorists in the nineteenth and twentieth centuries to human society, the tacit assumption is that humanity has reached an end point to which social evolution had all along been developing. In a way similar to a seed developing into a plant, the end result was always potentially present, potential in the origins and waiting to be realized (see, for example, box 1.3). Again, one assumption easy to make in transferring the idea of evolution to human society is that the 'end' to which Western societies have been evolving was pre-set, and indeed it is pre-set for other societies still evolving. Western capitalist democracy is not only the end towards which all societies are tending, but it is also an end which finally fulfils the purpose for which humanity was created.

Human nature, sexual selection and the inheritance of acquired characteristics

Such are some of the ways in which evolutionary thought has been extended to the study of human society. They are, as suggested, quite problematic. The connection is largely based on apparent similarities and metaphors. But note that Darwin himself was much more cautious about these controversial matters. Furthermore, he was keen to explore other sources of evolution besides natural selection. This caution and openness to a number of processes underlying evolution is a warning to social scientists and others in our own day who remain committed to simple and single types of explanation.

Darwin had little time for analogies of the kind suggested by Spencer. As regards people, he certainly insisted that human beings are a natural sort, they had 'descended' from some other ape-like species and have an evolutionary inheritance which still affects their behaviour today. Furthermore, he recognized that human beings' distinctive capacities for reasoning and for communicating complex ideas led to their triumph over other species. On the other hand, he stressed that 'struggling for survival' does not necessarily entail outright competition between individuals. One significant feature of human beings, he believed, was altruism: their capacity to think and act on behalf of other human beings. Those who possessed this capacity for sympathy might do much to protect the tribe of which they were a part. Using evolutionary thought, Darwin argued that the capacity for thinking about other people might be useful in the struggle for survival.

> The difference in mind between man and the higher animals, great as it is, certainly is one of degree and not of kind . . . The senses and intuitions, the various emotions and faculties, such as love, memory, attention, curiosity, imitation, reason etc., of which man boasts, may be found in an incipient, or even sometimes in a well-developed condition in the lower animals. (1901: 13)

Furthermore, although Darwin's work on 'races' certainly betrays some of the influences of his day, he actually declared himself 'baffled' in accounting for 'the differences between the races of man' (ibid.). And this led him, especially in thinking about human beings, to modifications of evolutionary thought. The first such development is known as 'sexual selection'. In all animals, he believed, some physical forms and behaviours could be best explained as courtship displays and the exhibition of physical features which attract the opposite sex. If it is intelligence and muscular power in human beings that attract the opposite sex, then these attributes are likely to continue to be prominent in humanity. This is linked to an even earlier feature of evolutionary thought in biology, one which is no longer mainstream, even though it still finds minority support amongst some biologists. Darwin relied on what is known as a 'Lamarckian' understanding of human evolution, one named after an earlier nineteenth-century biologist. The idea is that it is possible for one generation to inherit the capacities which have been developed by a previous generation. It is now finding some limited application in modern biology (see box 1.4).

Box 1.4 Evolutionary thought after Darwin: the wisdom of the genes and the possibility of acquired characteristics being inherited after all

'Lamarckism' is associated with the idea that offspring can inherit the acquired characteristics of their parents. The blacksmith's child inheriting the blacksmith's muscles is the example usually given, but Darwin also attributed some of the differences between humans' developing mental capacities in attempting to overcome his 'bafflement' over human differences. Lamarckism is nowadays given little attention by mainstream evolutionary thought. On the other hand, there are some biologists who do claim that acquired immunity to diseases can indeed be passed on to later generations (Steele et al. 1998).

Another recent development in evolutionary thought looks similar to Lamarckism, but it is actually quite different. Wills (1989) refers to 'the wisdom of the genes'. This refers to the fact that humans and other animals have a genetic constitution which is not always realized. But when organisms encounter environmental or social 'shocks' they are able to realize a genetically-based potential which they had acquired during their long evolutionary history but had so far had no cause to use. All organisms are 'robust' in this sense, humans perhaps more so than other animals. This argument may look 'teleological' in that the argument may seem to be suggesting they are finally realizing potentials which they have long had. But evolution, according to this picture, still remains a largely arbitrary process.

These are two still controversial areas of evolutionary biology. They suggest, however, that, although the theory of natural selection as originally set out by Darwin and Wallace is now widely accepted, there may still be evolutionary processes at work which would help in the development of the theory.

Evolutionary thought and the social sciences: the debates continue

We will return to Darwin and evolutionary thought, particularly in terms of so-called 'evolutionary psychology', the relation between biological and social evolution, people's health and the general question of 'human nature'. But we should note here two issues pertaining to contemporary applications of evolutionary thought to the study of society and nature.

First, as regards biologically-based understandings of human behaviour, social scientists will note with some alarm that these accounts give little significance to the institutions and power relations which are the concerns of social theorists. Biologically-based accounts give undue prominence to the evolved or acquired characteristics of individuals. They reduce understanding to biological mechanisms. Little is heard here of the social relations and processes in which individuals are inevitably caught up. Evolutionary thought on its own is unlikely to be adequate as regards understanding the complex relations between society and nature. However we use such ideas, they will need combining with a concern for social and power relations.

Second, there is a continuing influence of functionalism on the study of human social structure. A strong theme in social theory, one going back at least as far as Herbert Spencer and Emile Durkheim, is to envisage human society as like a biological organism. It is closely allied to 'functionalism' in social theory, a view which envisages society as a system of collected parts, each connected to and supported by the others. These parts are capable of adaptation and they modify themselves. They do this in such a way as to ensure that society has the necessary natural resources, is able to reproduce itself and holds together in a relatively stable way. One of the most influential examples of functionalism is that adopted by Durkheim (1954). Religion, he argued, holds society together, to ensure its continuing structure and reproduction. Others have argued that the changing form of the family (from the extended family to the small independent family) functioned to support changing forms of industry. Smaller families are more mobile and hence able to fit in with industry's needs.

Functionalism, and its emphasis on society as a connected organism-like system serving certain underlying needs, is still a feature of social and political thought today. An example is Niklas Luhmann's recent use of this strategy in examining 'ecological communication'. He argued that the structure of modern society, its division into many separate units, has been important in decentralizing power, but that it is dysfunctional in the sense that there are no ways in which societies can be steered in a mutually agreed direction (see box 1.5). Perhaps the application of biological analogies to human society throws up new questions and helps to build up new theories. Nevertheless, analogies between biological and social structures seem to have had their day.

**Box 1.5 A biological metaphor today: the problem of
'ecological communication'**

Luhmann (1989) has roots in the functionalist tradition. By this is meant that he continued to envisage society as an interconnected set of parts, analogous to a biological organism. One question arising for him was whether the particular kind of social structure we have inherited does or does not encourage environmental sustainability.

Luhmann believes it did not. It undermines 'ecological communication'. He argues that the structure of contemporary society is such that it is divided into relatively *separate* parts. It is constituted by an array of relatively independent and 'self-referential' sub-systems: the economy, science, the law, the political system. This is beneficial insofar as people are not controlled by some hierarchical and overweaning system of power. But it is also socially and environmentally dangerous, Luhmann argues, because it means that contemporary society is drifting. There is no centralized and controlling system which can 'steer' society in a direction which is environmentally sustainable.

This application of the biological and functionalist idea to social-cum-environmental questions points to some real problems of management and control. It is questionable, however, whether the biological metaphor remains helpful in terms of explanation and political policy.

The Decline of 'Community'?

One of the big themes in social theory is 'community'. More particularly, for those early social scientists, living in a period which saw the arrival of industrial capitalism and momentous social change, the big concern was with the decline of community and its possible renewal. The concept is broad and amorphous. It can be unpacked to mean four quite distinct things (Bell and Newby 1976):

- it can simply be used in a commonsense topographical way, referring to a particular place;
- it can refer to a degree of social engagement in a locality;
- it can allude to 'communion', a sense of association based on personal ties, family and kinship links;
- it can be used in a confusing and ideological fashion, one in which a 'community' is asserted by dominant institutions (such as the European Community) but which has little meaning to most people's everyday life.

All these definitions and distinctions have been conflated. They are worth separating out, however. The 'decline' of community can be used to refer to all four of these subdefinitions. It is rarely, however, extended to our association with biological connectedness and relations between humans and the non-human world. An exception can be found in the work of Ferdinand Tönnies (see box 1.6).

Box 1.6 Ferdinand Tönnies on social evolution and community

Social transformation entails not only the separation of people one from another (including members of their own families); it also entails the separation of people from the environment on which they depend. Ferdinand Tönnies (1855–1936) was one of the few sociologists sensitive to both such forms of separation and to the relations between them. His picture of community and its breakdown would probably appeal to many environmental activists.

He made the famous distinction between *Gemeinschaft* and *Gesellschaft* (1887). The former is seen as the old and traditional order, albeit one which still exists in many societies in the modern era. Under *Gemeinschaft*, people are bound into an intimately shared order. Kin, family and neighbours work together, experiencing the common joys and sorrows of regular association within a shared, known and familiar territory. People work and live on the basis of shared values and a shared view of authority. This sense of communality is promoted through living in localities which are not only shared but which have been tended and passed down by past generations and which will be inherited by future kin and friends.

Tönnies argued, in a way unusual amongst social scientists, that human beings are themselves a kind of animal. They have, for example, a well-developed capacity for enjoying a sense of communion or association with other people and with the natural world. Also important to them is memory, learning values from others and incorporating them into their own beliefs.

Gemeinschaft, or early forms of community, fulfils these human needs well. It satisfies people's emotional needs. The same cannot be said of *Gesellschaft* or modern society, one which is seen by Tönnies as largely artificial and imposed on human nature. Impersonality, competition and individualism are seen as thriving under *Gesellschaft*. Tönnies nevertheless hoped that new forms of collective relations (including new forms of management techniques and emergent kinds of social security) might eventually help to recover older forms of community existence. But of particular interest to us in this picture is the relation between society and nature. Living on the same land, ploughing it, domesticating animals, handing down the land from father to son are all an integral part of *Gemeinschaft* and these relationships and processes are lost under *Gesellschaft*.

Tönnies was writing of links with nature under *Gemeinschaft* which were not only direct but which, it was assumed, people had the responsibility to maintain for the sake of future generations. His message is particularly relevant to today's concerns with environmental sustainability. But does it idealize early kinds of community life? There have been a number of instances in which tribal peoples have been responsible for environmental disasters. The giant Moa (an ostrich-like bird) became extinct 100 years after the arrival of the first people in New Zealand. In North America, elephants, anteaters, deer, antelopes and rodents were lost on a massive scale after people were able to cross the Bering Strait between 10,000 and 12,000 years ago. Furthermore, could such sustainability be gained without the same kind of work on the land and sense of intergenerational responsibility which remained a central feature of older forms of society? To put this another way, is it possible to imagine strong community relations (including strong relations with the land and with the natural world) in modern societies?

His account of the earliest forms of community quite deliberately includes land and blood (or kin) as constituting the kinds of close association that were being lost with the advent of modern society.

Durkheim offers a parallel picture of the transformation of human association, one which distinguishes between 'mechanical' and 'organic' solidarity (see box 1.7). His model is packed with biological and evolutionary metaphors. The idea of society 'progressing' in a linear way from one stage to another is one (inaccurate) interpretation of Darwin's theory of evolution. And his picture of a transition from simple 'mechanical' solidarity to an 'organic' solidarity based on people recognizing the associations between the parts of a complex modern society is again using a biological metaphor. It is somewhat paradoxical, therefore, that he does not pay substantial attention to the environment itself and to people's relationship with it. Nevertheless, his account (like that of Tönnies) remains very useful. He is also describing the transformation of *human* nature which he believed was accompanying the rise of modern society.

Box 1.7 Durkheim on the decline of community and the rise of individualism

Human beings have lived most of their lives in small-scale communities. Durkheim argues that much of their lives are controlled by such communities. Religion and tradition are dominant, with the individual's life subordinated to a strong sense of collective sensibility. The will of the community therefore prevails over the individual. They are homogeneous societies, in the sense that they are characterized by low divisions of labour. Property is communal. Durkheim distinguished the kind of social solidarity in such societies as 'mechanical'.

Now, however, as people live more in societies with high divisions of labour, the individual person is indeed treated by society as an individual. Writing in the late nineteenth century, Durkheim argued that egoism, impersonality and competition promote such individualism. Furthermore, modern society no longer presents norms, values or traditions which would help to limit people's desires. In these circumstances, Durkheim believed, people become unhappy. Left to themselves, people have, on the one hand, an unbounded array of wants. And yet they have limited means to realize these wants. Societies in the past have imposed norms as a way of dealing with this problem. But in modern society there are no such constraints. Anything is, in theory at least, possible. The result is 'anomie', a condition which, at worst, can lead to suicide.

All this brings considerable difficulties in maintaining a sense of community, at least in its old form. This new kind of society is termed 'organic' by Durkheim. It is analogous to a more advanced organism, one composed of a number of interconnected specialist parts. This kind of society is also based on private property and the division of labour. And this undermines the sense of collective solidarity felt in older kinds of society. At the same time, individuals are no longer repressed and made uniform by the laws and traditions of society. People may still be living quite peacefully with one another, but solidarity is now based on recognizing the necessary interdependence between different elements of the division of labour: companies, trade associations, unions, the state, households and so on. Such recognition is difficult to sustain, particularly given the levels of individualism and 'anomie' characterizing modern society. Nevertheless, Durkheim believed that a new kind of solidarity was likely to develop, one based on organic society. And sociologists as 'scientists of society' can do much to ensure that the new kind of society holds together, not least through education and the promotion of more collective forms of morality.

Durkheim exemplifies the themes of progress, direction and purpose in social evolution. He believed that sociology could, and should, be made into a science; one analogous to the sciences of physics and biology but one in which society could be studied as a separate entity. The methods of Enlightenment science – creating theoretical models and testing them with evidence – were appropriate to the social as well as to the physical and natural worlds. Making a new social science would bring understanding and hence 'progress', especially if the knowledge developed by social scientists could form part of the educative process.

Durkheim's model, like that of Tönnies, is linear, in the sense that he was arguing that one type of society developed from the previous one. (There is, for example, no possibility of a reversion from organic to mechanical solidarity.) It arguably contains a sense of purpose or 'teleology'. Modern society, for example, is seen as self-balancing in the same way as organisms which adapt and self-adjust so as to ensure their own survival.

Early sociologists such as Tönnies and Durkheim were therefore tracking important changes in people's identity and forms of consciousness. Tönnies was making some very suggestive interventions as regards the changing association between society and the environment. But what might a modern social science more sensitive to environmental considerations have looked like?

Such a social science would certainly pay attention to globalization and the extension of society over space. This again has major implications for small-scale community life and human association. Transnational corporations, the global market and the mass media are all combining to make society into an international phenomenon. A stock-market crash in Japan impacts on job opportunities in Europe. An event in Middle East is known about in Britain or the USA at the same time as it is known about in, say, Israel.

Society, it can be argued, has long been organized on an international basis. Perhaps what is most important now is that the societies which were previously at the centre of empires and markets are now being subjected to the same kinds of pressure (foreign imports of goods, immigration, consumerism, armed interventions) which they previously exercised over other societies.

Globalization and the 'disembedding' of social life

The kinds of interpretation offered by the older, classical social theory as represented by Durkheim and Tönnies can still be useful if they are combined with an understanding of contemporary globalization. The beginnings of an intellectual project of this kind are suggested by the contemporary social scientist, Anthony Giddens (box 1.8). He argues strongly that local community life has now lost the kinds of significance it used to have. Bearing in mind the many relationships and processes impacting on our lives which have their sources far-removed from us,

---

Box 1.8   Society spread over time and space: anxiety and the 'disembedding' of community

Modern society is becoming 'disembedded', to use a word adopted by Giddens and others. Human interaction in small-scale settings obviously still takes place but, in the context of globalized trade and communications, it does not have the same meaning or significance it once had. Many of the important institutions and processes affecting our everyday lives and interaction are located well beyond our community. This leads, Giddens and others believe, to a new form of human anxiety (one they term 'ontological insecurity') in which everyday life has lost much of its meaning. The interactions we have with one another are still important to us, but they have a decreasing significance in terms of the processes and institutions actually affecting our lives.

---

day-to-day interaction is left relatively empty. This has profound, even disturbing, implications for human identity.

But in contemporary society, humanity is separated from external nature as well as from its own species. In this respect, too, most people are being disengaged from immediate, sensuous engagement with the materials provided by nature which we need for survival. Food and raw materials now often travel thousands of miles to the place where they are finally consumed. At the same time, inputs to farming processes, such as phosphates and manure, are also transported around the globe rather than made and used locally. People have little direct understanding of the inputs to economic activity and consumption. The same applies to outputs. We also have little direct experience of what happens to the so-called waste products of our lives – these too are intangible, often affecting people far distant from ourselves. These kinds of detachment have been assisted by new technologies. Our understanding of ecological systems, of the way things grow, and indeed of the seasons, has been supplanted by new refrigeration techniques, by vast greenhouses and by the transportation of goods on a global scale.

Disengagement therefore extends to humanity's separation from the very environment which we inhabit. Arguably, this very separation and the lack of understanding it brings are important, largely unexplored, factors lying behind contemporary 'food scares'. Most food is actually quite safe to eat, and environmental crises are nothing like as threatening as is often maintained. Perhaps a central worry now concerns not only the real problems that stem from misuse of the environment, but also from the fact that most of us simply fail to understand the nature of the environment, the nature of the ecological systems of which we are a part. All this leads to further profound psychological disorientation. Knowledge of 'food', for example, is reduced to understanding gleaned from indecipherable additive numbers on packets in supermarkets and making uninformed judgements about the alternatives. At one level knowledge has never been so complete. The problem is to know what to do about it. The result (as box 4.1 point 2 illustrates – see pp. 120–1) is stunned confusion in the supermarket aisle.

Knowledge based on direct experience has given way to knowledge created by scientists (what Giddens calls 'abstract systems') in laboratories. Distrust of them, their apparently frequent changes of mind and of the impact of vested interests on knowledge is a key result. But so too is failure of confidence in our own, relatively unscientific, knowledge and our own abilities for critical engagement.

But, before we become completely mired in gloom, note the contemporary and ongoing attempts to re-engage with the environment. We must remain alive to continuing attempts at self-determination and the *re*-establishment of personal relations and direct relations with external nature. These are attempts to restore older (or what are assumed to be older) forms of social relation. Here, for example, is an interpretation of the contemporary allotment garden. It is one example of how the development of a new kind of self has been envisaged, one actively engaged in directly relating not only to the environment but also to other people.

> It is possible to buy a packet of frozen food and cook it instantly without knowing where or how or by whom it was produced. And this is less expensive than seeding, nurturing and harvesting the food yourself. Why, then, does the allotment garden continue to flourish? The answer must lie in its image, in the role of communal effort, in the feelings growers have in feeding a family through their own efforts. Our image of the allotment turns out to be not a matter of the way we glimpse its landscape from the train but a reflection of our image of the world as a whole and the social relationships we make in our small part of it. (Crouch and Ward 1988: 14)

The allotment is, therefore, one attempt to regain a sense of community and personal identity through interacting directly with people and nature. Note that the form of such interaction entails a reassessment of the way *production* is organized.

Industry and Production

It is sometimes said that we now live in a 'consumer society'. It is argued that the main way in which social relations, forms of status and human identities are now formed is in the sphere of consumption. Thus, what people buy (hence eat, drive, live in, dress in) has replaced other factors such as work and class in the way they think about themselves and their relations to others. People are, in effect, what they buy, consumption realizing the Enlightenment ideal of individual fulfilment.

This argument receives wide support. It has something to recommend it and we will return to it in chapter 4. But it is important to be cautious at this point. First, in Western societies, 'consumption' means rather different things to different people. Consumption, and the idea of making identities and relations through consumption, perhaps has a particular significance for the middle classes and for wealthy people – those with high levels of disposable income. But even amongst the middle classes, consumption is an important way by which one group can distinguish itself from another. Academics, for example, are prone to conspicuously underconsume, thereby distancing themselves from more affluent people and, in particular, from the values of these more affluent people. Other relatively wealthy people may engage in forms of consumption which appear to resist the mainstream. Green consumerism is an important case in point. In this case, relationships and forms of identity are made through, say, the consumption of organic foods or purchases made at the Body Shop. But, meanwhile, less wealthy people might well be wondering whether they are even part of contemporary 'consumer culture'. Many poor people in Western societies would still not really feel themselves part of this culture, though they may well aspire to it.

Again, we will return to these matters in more detail later. They are important for two reasons. First, new 'Western' lifestyles are having significant, sometimes disastrous, effects on people's health. Second, new kinds of identity based on consumption would seem to have implications for environmental sustainability. But the main point to be made here is that these arguments about a new kind of society based on consumption systematically fail to recognize the continuing importance of industry or production. Someone, somewhere, must still be *making* all these commodities which the more affluent people are consuming. This suggests that the idea of a 'consumer society' is simplistic and somewhat premature. It is perhaps an idea particularly linked with an emergent 'Western' way of life. But in so doing, it fails to recognize the broader, global picture (see box 1.9).

Box 1.9   Production and consumption: making the links

Dependent societies have always been subject to the changing consumption habits of dominant nations. A fashion for calico in eighteenth-century Europe, for example, led many Indian peasants to stop growing food and take up growing, or weaving, cotton. Many of these peasants starved when the fashion for calico changed. Nowadays, there is considerable awareness of these global connections. Before the 1992 Rio Conference on Environment and Development, delegates from developing countries asked for consumption in Western societies to be placed on the agenda for debate. This was partly because high levels of consumption and, as a result, high levels of *production* in the West are seen by many as the underlying cause of, for example, global warming, the thinning of the ozone layer and many other kinds of environmental degradation. But also, like the eighteenth-century Indian peasants, the delegates from third world societies did not want to be dependent on rapid shifts in patterns of consumption in the first world (Miller 1995).

In the end a compromise was reached in setting the conference agenda. It was agreed that the subject of levels and forms of consumption would not be raised by third world delegates if those from the first world did not raise the issue of population control. Nevertheless, as the following press-cutting shows, the underlying importance of considering Western industrialization remains:

Revealed: How the Smoke Stacks of America have Brought the World's Worst Drought to Millions of Africans

To those who live there, it is as if the rich have stolen the rain. For more than 30 years, the Sahel region of Africa has suffered the longest sustained droughts in the world. In some places, rainfall has fallen by between 20 and 50 per cent. As a consequence, crops have failed on a huge scale; in the worst years, between 1972 and 1975 and between 1984 and 1985 up to a million people have starved to death.

New research indicates that pollution from factories and power stations, especially in North America and Europe, have exacerbated drought in countries South of the Sahara. (*Independent*, 13 June 2002)

It is, to say the least, a pity if industry and production do not figure in social sciences' understanding of the environment. There is now considerable debate over the role of industry in affecting social change; the central question being 'is capitalism consistent with environmental sustainability?'

Competing scenarios of industry and the environment

(1) Business as usual: industry as the solution   There are those who remain fairly relaxed about the relation between industry and the environment. According to this view, industry is not the bogeyman which it is often made out to be. Power lies in the hands (or pockets) of the consumer. If consumer demands change (if, say, there is massive demand for electric cars), then firms will compete with one another to satisfy them. Those companies that fail to meet the changing demands will simply go to the wall. Those on the political Left have the picture entirely the wrong way round, goes the thinking. It is not industry which is in charge, but masses of individuals attempting to meet their needs. Industry, tied to the buying and selling of goods in the marketplace, itself operates rather like an ecological system, adapting itself to the signals generated by the costs people are prepared to pay.

The same applies to the resources which form inputs to production systems. As one set of resources becomes scarce, it will become more expensive. Industry needs to avoid such extra expense, so it will turn to other cheaper resources. Silicon, used in the making of electronic chips, is often given as an example. It is no accident, according to this perspective, that new forms of industry are based on silicon chips. Sand is available in vast supply. Again, industry will create new products once the nature and extent of global environmental change becomes clear. There is no need for heavy-handed state intervention, the market being the best means of coping with heatwaves, droughts, floods and famines as and when they occur. As one pro-market commentator puts it, 'Adaptation to climate change, when it happens, is undoubtedly the most rational course, for a number of reasons. Most countries will be richer then, and so better able to afford to build sea walls or develop drought resistant plants' (*The Economist*, cited in Foster 2002: 65). The main role for governments is to ensure and enhance the principle of private property-ownership. This allows for enhanced economic growth and accurate price signals to be made to the owners of industry regarding the availability of resources.

In an echo of the Enlightenment arguments encountered earlier, private ownership is also sometimes seen as the solution to environmental problems. If, for example, there was a real and sustained demand for rhinoburgers, then the owners and breeders of rhinos would make sure that this species did not become extinct. Environmentalists often say they would like to maintain a diversity of species. But are they prepared to pay for the survival of these species? The best way forward is via the market (see box 1.10). There have been a number of objections to this position. Perhaps chief amongst them is the argument made by many environmentalists that the value of the environment cannot be simply equated with the valuation it may acquire during a market transaction. According to this position, reducing value to market value is a moral crime. Owning and selling buffalo,

---

Box 1.10   Consumption as directing industry:
the case of animal consumption

Peter Saunders is one of the most active proponents of the promotion of consumption as a means of ensuring that species survive. This entails making rare breeds into commodities. As regards industry, consumers are dominant. Producers (such as producers of rhinoburgers) are seen as simply responding to consumer-demand:

> When resources have a market value and can be bought and sold as private property, they tend not to disappear, for owners then have an interest in maintaining and reproducing them. It is this that explains why free-roaming American buffalo was wiped out while cows graze on the same land today in their thousands, or why crocodiles (which governments allow to be farmed for their skins) are in plentiful supply while rhinoceroses (which roam free in reserves and are poached for their horns) are on the endangered species list. (1995: 70)

---

crocodiles, rhinos and other endangered species have all the morality of selling your grandmother to the highest bidder. But, for some, the criticism goes even further than this: the real problems start not with the exchange of commodities for money, but in the *production* of commodities. Furthermore, those who believe this remain unrelaxed about the wait-and-see pro-market philosophy.

(2) Capitalism as the problem   Second, there is the radically opposite position. This argues that an adequate understanding of environmental degradation must recognize that it is capitalist industry which is the key culprit. This is the dominant force in the land, not only generating ecological crises but actively moulding consumer demand. Consumers, therefore, are actually not in charge. Their tastes, and their demands of industry, are shaped by industry itself. Advertising and the manufacturing of false needs has a key role to play in the creation of these needs. According to this perspective, the record of recent history shows that capitalist industry ruthlessly undermines and wrecks the environment on which it depends. The costs of such destruction are borne by the whole of society, including those dependent on welfare. Furthermore, industry wrecks human nature, undermining the health of its workers and not paying the full costs of the damage it causes (see box 1.11).

Waiting for industry to appreciate its self-destructive tendencies and adapt is a hazardous undertaking. Many people, animals, resources and ecosystems will meanwhile have been wasted. Some forms of environmental change, such as global warming, may well be irreversible. What is to be done? Governments, if they are no longer in a position to own and control industry, must take extensive powers to regulate it. Such regulation is not only in the interest of people and 'resources' but in the interest of industry itself. 'Industry', after all, is only a set of largely unrelated firms interested in making a profit. Government intervention needs to save industry from itself; from, that is, collapse due to its own short-sightedness. But few on the political Left would nowadays suggest that extensive central government intervention or ownership is the answer. They would also point to forms

---

Box 1.11   The second contradiction of capitalism

James O'Connor is the leading proponent of the theory of the 'second contradiction of capitalism'. He bases his arguments on a reading of Marx. The 'first' contradiction in Marx's work is that for which he is best known: the conflict between capital and labour and a range of crises stemming from that conflict which, Marx believed, threaten to overthrow capitalist society as a whole. The 'second' contradiction was not given a great deal of prominence by Marx, but it seems particularly relevant in our own era. It consists of the tendency of capitalism to ruin the natural conditions of its own survival. These include the resources it needs and the health and well-being of its workers. O'Connor locates the second contradiction in our own era in the following way – note that 'socialized reproduction of laborpower' refers to the various ways in which the capacity of people to work is constantly reproduced in the home, in schools, in the health service and so on:

> Global capitalist development since WWII would have been impossible without deforestation, air and water pollution, pollution of the atmosphere, global warming and the other ecological disasters; without the construction of megacities, with no regard for congestion, rational land use and transport systems, and housing and rents; and finally, without the reckless disregard for community and family health, physical and emotional, education and other 'components' of the socialized reproduction of laborpower – not to speak of the welfare of future generations. If global capital had bothered to reproduce or restore the conditions of production as these presented themselves at the end of the post-WWII reconstruction period, world GNP growth probably would have been no more than one-half recorded rates, perhaps only one quarter of recorded rates. (O'Connor 1988: 10)

---

of collective ownership and control at a local level, forms which are largely the result of spontaneous actions by people with little or no support from governments. We will later meet some examples of these industries which are owned and controlled by the people who work in them.

What are the difficulties with this position? Most obviously, this emphasis on industry can be seen as neglecting the role of consumption. Marxists, like many other environmentalists, would point to excessive consumption as a major contributor to environmental problems. But they would point to an industry-driven form of over-consumption. In other words, it is industry, with the aid of carefully planned mass advertising, which tries to convince the population that it needs to consume in order to find satisfaction. Over-consumption, and aspirations to consume even more, can therefore largely be attributed to the powers of capitalist production. But note also that many today would not wish to limit 'work' to industrial work alone. Domestic work, with women still making the greatest contribution, can also entail interaction with the external environment. Marxism has been lax in recognizing the importance of this kind of work and interaction.

(3) 'Ecological modernization'   A final position comes between the above two. 'Ecological modernization' suggests that contemporary society can be made

---

Box 1.12 'Ecological modernization': a South-East Asia case-study

The German sociologist, Joseph Huber, invented the idea of 'ecological modernization' in the 1980s. As he wrote in 1985: 'the dirty and ugly industrial caterpillar transforms into an ecological butterfly' (cited in Spaargaren and Mol 1992: 334). Production – incorporating new forms of technology – is linked to other forms of restructuring (including transformation in forms of consumption and new government practices) in a more environmentally sustainable direction.

The 'ecological modernization' thesis has led to a number of case-studies. One of these concerns pulp and paper manufacturing in Indonesia, Malaysia and Thailand. It argues that ecological modernization is indeed proceeding. Modifications to old and new pulp mills are extensive, leaving them 'amongst the most efficient in the world'. New mills in South-East Asia 'show remarkable achievements in the reduction of the amount of water used per ton of pulp produced'. On the other hand, ecological modernization is uneven. It is well advanced in large-scale, export-oriented and modern parts of the economy in this part of the developing world. It is nothing like so well advanced in small-scale enterprises aimed mainly at the domestic market (see Sonnenfeld 2000).

---

ecologically acceptable. There are some variations within this position, but in general it is not prepared to adopt such a 'hands-off' approach as the first perspective outlined above. To go back to our evolutionary themes, we are now witnessing another stage in the linear and progressive development of modern society. Society, it is argued, has gone through 'traditional' and 'modern' stages, the latter being linked with an industry informed by a science in which there was a good deal of public trust. We are now moving into a new period. It is one in which the consequences of modernity are being assessed. And, most importantly, the lessons of modernity (including the environmental lessons) are being built back into modernity itself. Thus, as envisaged in this scenario, there is no need to give up on the development of the modern age in the light of environmental crisis. There is certainly no need to revert to pre-industrial forms of society. Capitalism can be 'greened', even if the process is slow and uneven (see box 1.12).

In particular, there is no need to give up on science or technology simply because they have in the past led to environmental degradation. New technologies can make production processes environmentally sustainable. New kinds of more flexible government, interacting with the private sector, and in some instances handing over management to non-government agencies, are now emerging. Such new alliances are ensuring that the pessimistic, almost apocalyptic, vision, as outlined above in the second scenario, does not transpire. Non-governmental organizations, which might in the past have been quite hostile to government and business, are now included in the decision-making process in a major way. Their capacity for generating ideas and forging links between the public and private sector is seen as a formidable means by which a dynamic green capitalism is brought into being.

Box 1.13 'Ecological modernization' in Holland

Arthur Mol is one of the leading proponents of ecological modernization theory. He is optimistic about the capacity of modern capitalism to reorganize itself in ways which are environmentally sustainable (Mol 1994). The Dutch chemical industry (entailing the production of paints, plastics and pesticides) is, Mol says, already restructuring itself to deal with environmental crises. This is just one example, he argues, of how economic institutions, governments, science and technology are diverging from the way in which their predecessors focused wholly on achieving high levels of productivity. A green capitalism is therefore being developed.

Finally, ecological modernization is seen as possessed of new cultures, new ways of seeing humanity's relations with nature. So-called 'green consumerism' might be seen as one feature of this new type of modernity. But proponents of 'ecological modernization' take a much wider view of this new kind of modernity. They refer, for example, to new 'storylines', which interrogate scientific ideas and pursue them to uncover their social and political consequences (see box 1.13). In short, the great emphasis on progress via increased productivity is questioned. New ways of achieving progress are found, with new technologies and new attitudes leading the way.

What are the difficulties here? 'Ecological modernization' finds few friends either from the proponents of 'business as usual' or from those who argue that industry is almost bound to wreck the environment. For the former it is a tinkering with the market in such a way as to stop the market operating properly while allowing bureaucratic states too much influence. For the latter it contains an insufficient understanding of how capitalist societies operate and, on the basis of some successful modernization in affluent societies and some industrial sectors, draws over-optimistic conclusions for industry's relations with the environment as a whole. Too many lessons are being based on the practices and experiences of affluent societies. Holland and Germany, for example, are sufficiently affluent (and sufficiently composed of ecologically conscious middle-class people) to be able to afford and indeed demand ecological modernization. Perhaps, at the same time, they have managed to ensure that toxic and other dangers are located in other parts of the globe besides theirs. On the other hand, as we have seen, there may be evidence of this tendency spreading to less developed and less affluent societies.

These are some of the central areas of debate around the role of industry in affecting the relations between society and nature. We might note that national governments in some societies, but not yet the USA, appear to be on the point of transforming their outlook from a 'business as usual' to an 'ecological modernization' perspective. On the other hand, the popular, locally based, forms of cooperative organization outlined under scenario 2 often find support from national governments of different political persuasions. 'Self-help' often appeals both to those kinds of politics supportive of individual freedom and to those supportive of people owning and running the organizations in which they work.

A Risk Society

The notion of ecological modernization closely links up with another influential theme in contemporary social theory. It is one developed in rather different ways by two contemporary theorists, Ulrich Beck and Anthony Giddens. There are differences in their accounts, but also close overlapping similarities.

Central is the notion that we live in a new kind of society. It is one characterized by high levels of risk, new kinds of social relations and new forms of politics. Not only is this assertion influential, but it also closely links to a number of the well-established themes we have developed in this chapter. Let us take the 'risk society' hypothesis and assess it in the light of some of our earlier points.

Manufactured risk

The argument here is that society has gone through a number of stages. Note the idea of a progression between different types of society, one similar to that identified in the 'evolution' section earlier. There was, according to Beck's understanding, a 'pre-modern' stage in which risks were largely external to society. Thus drought, famine and earthquakes then just 'happened'. They certainly constituted massive hazards to human populations and people perhaps felt that, by behaving differently and perhaps praying to deities, they could influence the extent of these disasters. Nevertheless, they were not usually a direct consequence of what society had undertaken.

This has all changed under conditions of 'modernity'. Now, the intervention of science and technology creates risks which are directly made by society itself. Global warming, environmental devastation, threats to human and animal health of all kinds are now of a distinctly 'man'-made kind. Furthermore, the spread of these risks is changing. There is now a sense in which risks generated in one part of the globe (Severe Acute Respiratory Syndrome (SARS), for example, or the generation of gases trapping heat in the atmosphere) are, as we discussed earlier, experienced by people far away from where the problem actually starts. According to this argument, there are important implications here for social stratification. In earlier forms of society the rich were able to buy themselves out of environmental threats by, for example, moving towards more healthy parts of town. Now this is no longer possible. Global threats (including threats to the food chain) are more likely to affect us all.

More generally, what earlier appeared to be wholly rational and inevitably progressive interventions based on science are no longer so unproblematic. The dark, and unanticipated, side of modern existence becomes disastrously apparent, and uncertainty makes a comeback. This, combined with a loss of faith in virtually all kinds of authority and certainty, leads, it is argued, to another kind of modernity, namely 'reflexive modernity', one in which people create their own biographies and identities, independent of class, regional origins or family circumstances. At the same time these people construct their own knowledge. Science can no longer be relied on: it now spends much of its time apologizing and clearing up the results of earlier 'scientific' interventions.

Social relations and the risk society

A related feature of the 'risk society' as outlined by Beck and Giddens concerns the relations between people. Taking up a theme which we have already identified in our discussion of 'community', the assertion is that society is increasingly constituted by autonomous individuals. We are treated as, and treat ourselves as, separate people. This makes the modern family particularly problematic. It is becoming 'an association of individual persons who each bring to it their own interests, experiences and plans and who are each subjected to different controls, risks and constraints' (Beck and Beck-Gernsheim 2002: 97).

Furthermore, people are treated and indeed treat themselves as clever, proactive individuals. The opposite side to the coin of a widespread distrust of science and other forms of authority (such as governments, teachers and parents) is that each individual becomes an independent expert. This means that individuals are made into, and make themselves into, their own scientific consultants. People ask themselves why, for example, weather patterns are changing or what are the most healthy ways of living. Not only science, but also tradition has broken down as a source of guidance. Tradition, like authority, has constantly to justify itself. It, too, is up for grabs. Indeed, the Enlightenment has prided itself on dismissing tradition as a source of reference for understanding the world.

Changing forms of economy, with high levels of self-employment, constant moves by individuals between firms and high levels of individual assessment *within* firms, contribute to this individualization (see box 1.14). The idea of a lifetime career within a single firm is breaking down. Individuals are now determining their own careers, often consulting themselves as to how they should run their lives. The consumerism discussed earlier also contributes to these new kinds of social

---

Box 1.14 The individualization of work

Ulrich Beck argues that we are moving into a new kind of modern society, characterized by 'the individualization of work'.

> Linda's new working life is not without its drawbacks. Chief among them is a constant cloud of anxiety about finding the next job. In some ways Linda feels isolated and vulnerable. Fearful of the stigma of having been laid off, for example, she doesn't want her last name to appear in this article. Linda gets to build her schedule around her son's. She gets to find her own assignments. And she gets to be a pioneer of the new work force. (*Newsweek*, 14 June 1993, cited in Beck 2000)

Such individualization at the workplace, Beck argues, combines with the individualization of life more generally. Society, he believes, 'is in danger of falling apart'. Flows of capital continue to move around the world and the working class is split up into bodies of individual consumers. Far from resisting capitalist society, their values and priorities are caught up in supporting it.

relation. The traditional ways of classifying people (with, for example, concepts of class and gender) are no longer appropriate. We are categorized, and categorize ourselves, more by the kinds of product we purchase (and eat, drive, dress in, live in) than by our class as defined by, for example, our work position.

Nothing can be taken on trust in the 'risk society', and it is up to us as individuals to be constantly monitoring the enormous amounts of information available to us and to make our own decisions on that basis. These include our own decisions regarding the risks we are taking. Nobody, and no institution, is going finally to assure us that we are doing the 'right' thing to minimize risk, improve our own life chances or act in ways that will secure an environmentally sustainable future.

All this is simultaneously liberating and oppressive. There is much to be said for not having authority constantly breathing down our necks. On the other hand, having all courses of action as equally open can lead to a considerable sense of personal anxiety and uncertainty. This is one of the big problems of our age, one analogous to the kinds of anomie of which Durkheim originally wrote (see box 1.7 above). With no standards, norms or external advice, we are again, in the end, left in a position of insecurity.

The politics of the risk society

For both Beck and Giddens, this emergent kind of society is linked to new forms of politics. Distinctions between Left and Right are no longer relevant. They are remnants of an old kind of class society, another set of traditions which is no longer justified. If identity is largely individualized and if the whole notion of scientific 'progress' is being undermined, so too are forms of politics that are based on such assumptions. People have, according to this thesis, given up on all such forms of authority. This includes government and the large-scale, reforming projects which governments used to pursue. Instead, we look to our own, mainly *personal*, forms of politics, salvation and progress, and these include self-care. Governments (and still less government scientists) are seen as being unlikely to help us in any attempt to avoid global warming, food risks, skin cancers and so on. It is up to us individually to come up with a conclusion and to act accordingly. The same kind of individualized politics applies to life more generally. Politics is a hedonistic concern for the present, one which positively welcomes and consumes the products of corporate capitalism (see box 1.15). A recurrent theme of the environmental movement is that we should think and act on behalf of future generations. Perhaps hedonistic concern for the moment is itself a product of not knowing what the future holds. But it is difficult to see how an immediate interest in the present squares with any concern for future generations.

Central, particularly to Giddens, are 'life politics'. These are essentially about gaining control over your own life, empowering yourself in relation to your environment. Part of such empowerment is knowing yourself, becoming aware of yourself. And new scientific developments in the form of genetics and *in vitro* fertilization are becoming new means to this end. Why should this be? It is because they appear to offer an understanding of the self and, through the possible

---

Box 1.15   Individualized 'life politics' in the contemporary risk society

They used to want a revolution. Now they just want money.

Meet Ade, Danielle, Ryan and Lisa. They look like any other streetwise teenagers. It is 10 am and they are heading off to meet their friends for a Saturday in town. But this is no ordinary weekend – they are going to Britain's first teen lifestyle 'exhibition'.

Far from rebelling against corporate success, youngsters cannot get enough of it. Those who know them say teens cleave to consumer icons as badges of identification. 'Young teens do not use politics, religion or class to express themselves; they speak a new language – consumerism,' says Sean Pillot de Chenecey, a marketing consultant who has worked for Levi's, PlayStation, and Coca-Cola. 'They understand that products have personality and they use those products to help them see their own identity and to communicate that identity to their peers.' Forget Reclaim the Streets, Prague, Seattle and the 'No Logo' rebellion, today's teens are growing older younger and getting on with the all-consuming business of consuming. (*The Observer*, 19 November 2000)

---

manipulation of the body and the genetic code, further insight and even speci-fication of the self. While these technologies and techniques bring risks, they also bring forward the possibility of new relations to, and understandings of, nature. Note here a link to our central theme. Again, the suggestion is that in better appreciating nature, we start to know ourselves better. And there is even a strong notion of purpose here, one described earlier as 'teleological'. Humanity is seen as constantly understanding itself better as it becomes more knowledgeable. The emergent forms of science (including genetics and cloning) are just further means by which we gain an insight into ourselves.

There is another element to contemporary politics as envisaged here, and one which again has links to some of the ideas reviewed earlier. For Beck in particular, there are real problems in steering modern society. In a way similar to the bio-logical analogies adopted by some of the early Social Darwinists (see pp. 32–6), society is envisaged as increasingly fragmented into separate units. This fragmen-tation makes modern society very difficult to steer – it is not easy for separate units to adequately communicate with each other, and it is almost impossible for a government to attempt to direct the society for which it is responsible. It becomes increasingly difficult to envisage the idea of a government steering a society towards some 'end' or 'purpose'. Given such fragmentation, how can a society be led towards environmental sustainability, for example? This difficulty contributes to the destabilization of government authority itself. If governments cannot guide societies, what are they for? Why do they make claims and promises which they are incapable of delivering? Governments therefore join other kinds of authority and tradition as constantly needing to justify their existence.

Such are some of the key arguments of the thesis of the 'risk society'. Whether proponents of this thesis have adequately understood the phenomena they are describ-ing is a matter to which we will return in some detail. Suffice it to say here that much of the autonomy apparently gained by these independent, tradition-free individuals may be more apparent than real.

Summary

This chapter has introduced four core themes: evolution, community, industry and risk. These might seem like four relatively separate concepts, yet we have uncovered a number of connecting ideas that span them. These include the idea that societies are evolving in discrete stages and that 'progress' is being made during this evolution. This theme, and continuing problems with the notion of 'progress', will make a reappearance later, especially in chapter 2. Most applications of evolutionary thought to the understanding of society have tended to be of a largely metaphorical kind. Analogies are made between social and biological development which are not always helpful in understanding social change. Biological science, as such, is rarely used. Chapter 6 will address some contemporary ideas in evolutionary science and the study of disease in an attempt to understand human nature and human health. A further theme has been the collapse of community and factors, including globalization, which underlie detachment both from other people and from non-human species. 'Community' is also a political rallying-cry, one we will come across again. Other processes underlying people's separation from one another and the environment can be considered, and these will shortly be addressed. Closely linked to community is individualism. This issue (and the making of individuals with apparently little attachment to one another or to the environment) will also be revisited. Chapter 5 will suggest that it is possible to understand individualism (and its problems) in ways which are better informed than much of the literature covered here. The claim that we are becoming an increasingly individualized society also has major implications for contemporary politics. Chapter 7 discusses the development of an Enlightenment type of politics which focuses on individual rights. These are widely seen as an inadequate way of ensuring that people develop an understanding and control over their lives, their relations with others and with their environment. Chapter 8 will discuss alternative forms of politics which are more collective and which explore alternative values and social forms.

FURTHER READING

Evolution and its relation to social theory

This is a very large topic. A very helpful introduction to evolution as the organizing principle of modern biology (by one of the leading contemporary biologists) is:

E. Mayr, 'Evolution', *Scientific American*, 239/3 (1978): 39–49.

One attempt at a brief review of how social scientists have used evolutionary ideas is:

P. Dickens, *Social Darwinism. Linking Evolutionary Thought to Social Theory*. Buckingham: Open University Press, 2000.

Further useful references include:

T. Ball, *Reappraising Political Theory*. Oxford: Clarendon, 1995. (Note in particular Chap. 10, 'Marx and Darwin: A Reconsideration'.)

P. Blackledge and G. Kirkpatrick (eds), *Historical Materialism and Social Evolution.* Basingstoke: Palgrave Macmillan.

J. Domingues, 'Evolution, History and Collective Subjectivity', *Current Sociology*, 47/3 (1999): 1–34.

J. Durrant, 'Scientific Naturalism and Social Reform in the Thought of Alfred Russel Wallace', *The British Journal for the History of Science*, 12/40 (1979): 3–58.

K. Eder, 'Societies Learn and yet the World is Hard to Change', *European Journal of Social Theory*, 2/2 (1999): 195–215.

P. Hirst, *Social Evolution and Sociological Categories.* London: Allen and Unwin, 1976.

G. Jones, 'Alfred Russel Wallace, Robert Owen and the Theory of Natural Selection', *The British Journal for the History of Science*, 25 (2002): 73–96.

M. Kottler, 'Alfred Russel Wallace, the Origin of Man, and Spiritualism', *Isis*, 65/227 (1974): 145–92.

N. Luhmann, *The Differentiation of Society.* New York: Columbia University Press, 1982.

J. Mingers, 'Can Social Systems be Autopoietic? Assessing Luhmann's Social Theory', *Sociological Review*, 3 (2002): 278–99.

J. Offer (ed.), *Herbert Spencer. Critical Assessments.* London: Routledge, 2000.

S. Sanderson, 'Evolutionary Materialism: A Theoretical Strategy for the Study of Social Evolution', *Sociological Perspectives*, 37/1 (1994): 47–73.

S. Sanderson, *Social Evolutionism. A Critical History.* Oxford: Blackwell, 1990.

P. Taylor, 'Natural Selection: A Heavy Hand in Biological and Social Thought', *Science as Culture*, 7/1 (1998): 5–32.

B. Trigger, *Sociocultural Evolution.* Oxford: Blackwell, 1998.

R. Young, 'Malthus and the Evolutionists: the Common Context of Biological and Social Theory', *Past and Present*, 43 (1969): 109–45.

Industry and consumption

T. Benton, 'Beyond Left and Right? Ecological Politics, Capitalism and Modernity', in M. Jacobs (ed.), *Greening the Millennium?* Oxford: Blackwell, 1997.

Community

For a modern discussion, and one which links community to environmental ethics, see:
M. Smith, *An Ethics of Place. Radical Ecology, Postmodernity and Social Theory.* Albany: State University of New York, 2001.

Another contemporary discussion on the theme of community's decline is:
D. Putnam, *Bowling Alone.* New York: Touchstone, 2000.

Risk

U. Beck, 'Global Risk Politics', in M. Jacobs (ed.), *Greening the Millennium?* Oxford: Blackwell, 1997.

A. Elliott, 'Beck's Sociology of Risk: a Critical Assessment', *Sociology*, 3/2 (2002): 293–315.

Students interested in a critical survey of the 'risk' question (in the context of a wider discussion of social theory and the environment with particular emphasis on Beck and Giddens) should turn to:
D. Goldblatt, *Social Theory and the Environment.* Cambridge: Polity, 1996.

The following is useful for a re-statement of Beck's theory, plus criticisms of the theory and Beck's responses:
B. Adam, U. Beck and J. Van Loon, *The Risk Society and Beyond. Critical Issues for Social Theory.* London: Sage, 2000.

Students will also find very useful in this context:

B. Turner and C. Rojek, *Society and Culture. Principles of Scarcity and Solidarity*. London: Sage, 2001. (*They argue, inter alia, that Beck is wrong to conflate environmental risk with the cultural risk, individualization and so on. The connection between these two types of risk is not adequately made.*)

Students may well wish to monitor the 'risk society' thesis in relation to ongoing events. The exceptionally hot summer of 2003 in France, for example, resulted in more than 15,000 deaths. This disaster can be seen as an example of what Beck calls, somewhat chillingly, 'the democratization of risk'. Note also the blame being shifted away from the underlying social and economic causes of climate change and towards the more visible sphere of national politics.

Journals

Note the following journals, which are consistently helpful in dealing with the issues raised in this chapter and, more generally, in all matters relating to the society–nature links.

Science as Culture
Capitalism, Nature, Socialism
Journal of Critical Realism

A helpful website on the theme of evolution is available at: <http://science.kennesaw.edu/~matson/evolutionlinks.html>

2

Work and Environmental Transformation

Overview

Industry, its use of resources, the things it makes and the waste it produces, is a common feature of environmental debate. Yet the activities and processes that take place between the inputs of raw materials and the outputs of waste and commodities do not often feature in considerations of the relations between society and nature. This is surprising. Every society is engaged in some kind of interaction with nature. The resources and powers of the non-human world have to be used and changed to make the things that a society needs and wants. Anthropologists have stressed this process for some time, but it was Marx and Engels who first fully recognized the fact that the transformation takes place via a *labour process*. Social relations are formed in the process of working on nature's powers to produce commodities. And in contemporary societies the levels of waste used start to overload the ecological systems which might be expected to absorb waste products. One result is global environmental change. We will take the four basic themes of this book, industry, evolution, risk and community, as a means of producing an account of Marx and Engels's work and in order to develop their approach.

Industry and Humanity's Metabolism with Nature

Metabolism is a concept employed most often by biologists. They use the idea to refer to the basic processes of life: the conversion of matter into energy, the latter being central to the growth and reproduction of an organism. A cell in a living being carries out thousands of biochemical reactions each second. Metabolism is the sum of all these reactions. Why do all these reactions take place? Raw materials from the environment are converted during the process of metabolism. They are made, in the case of a typical cell, into the building blocks of proteins and other compounds unique to organisms. All this is the key way by which living things grow and reproduce themselves. Lost materials are constantly being replaced by new ones; the raw materials are being converted into energy.

Yet the notion of 'metabolism' can be extended. It can quite easily be widened to include the relationship between organisms. (An organism, once eaten or turned into inorganic matter, becomes 'raw materials' for another.) But the notion can be extended still further to refer to the kind of relationship all societies have with nature. People work on nature and transform it to make the things they need. They do this by growing plants and breeding animals. They then output a range of materials, producing what we typically call 'waste'. Societies thereby reproduce themselves.

Society's metabolism with nature: contributions from anthropology

There are self-evident pressures on all kinds of society to be socially and politically organized in ways which allow a relatively constant throughput of matter and energy. And, while there is absolutely no guarantee that this will happen, it might be expected that the metabolism of nature by society is organized in ways which allow the continued reproduction of people and social systems. It must provide them with enough resources to live and reproduce future generations.

The discipline of anthropology has often been to the fore in setting out the connections between society and nature. In many respects it has been ahead of other social sciences in terms of understanding the interaction between humanity and its environment. Given anthropology's traditional concern with small-scale societies and the very identifiable ways in which societies metabolize nature in such societies, it perhaps comes as no surprise that this discipline should have pioneered such an approach (see box 2.1 for examples).

Box 2.1   Humanity's metabolism with nature: case-studies from anthropology

Julian Steward, one of the most influential anthropologists of the modern era, developed the notion of 'cultural ecology'. He specified this discipline as the study of the processes by which a society adapts to its environment. His work with Robert Murphy compared small-scale rubber-tapping societies in Brazil with North-East American Indians, based on animal-trapping (Murphy and Steward 1955). In both cases they were examining shifts of small-scale societies based on the immediate expropriation of their natural environment to societies based on more complex divisions of labour, in which people no longer depended on their immediate environment for social systems based on trade with neighbouring tribes and villages. The picture offered for both types of society was therefore one of an increasing division of labour between neighbouring societies and, in the case of native Indians in the USA and Brazil, acquiring 'a seemingly insatiable appetite for the utilitarian wares and trinkets of civilisation' (Fischer-Kowalski 1997: 125). Paradoxically, the precise kind of metabolism between society and the environment seems, according to this research, to be of relatively minor significance to the inner workings of these societies. In both cases a similar kind of social development (one based on an increasing division of labour and trade) developed and undermined local cultures.

A contrasting anthropological example of humanity's early metabolism with nature comes in Harner's famous discussion of Aztec cannibalism (Harner 1977). Pre-conquest Mexicans conducted some 20,000 human sacrifices a year. According to Harner, this phenomenon can be understood as a response to an ecological problem. Population pressure in the Valley of Mexico meant that wild game supplies were 'no longer adequate' to provide the necessary protein for a human diet. Herbivorous animals could in theory be used for eating, and this occurred in many societies in the West. But in the Mexican case, Harner argued, ancient hunters had made such animals largely extinct. All this meant, according to Harner, that human sacrifice was a thinly veiled form of cannibalism. The sacrifice of 5–20 prisoners per 100 inhabitants a year was little more than a major contribution to the human diet. Once a particular territory had been conquered, the Aztecs always moved on to another area. They did not colonize them in the way practised in the New World. Again, such a practice could be explained by using the vanquished as food in hostile environmental circumstances. In this case, therefore, the metabolism between human society and nature not only mattered for society. It also mattered, with a vengeance, for those particular members of society being metabolized by their fellow human beings.

Anthropology and functionalism

Ecological anthropology has often been developed from a 'functionalist' viewpoint. Anthropologists adopting this starting-point viewed the environment apropos its function in terms of supporting human society.

To put this another way, social systems (including households, tribes or communities) are unable to function if the ecological system on which they depend is not adequately operating. If this happens, then the social system needs to adapt itself or its environment accordingly. An unspoken assumption in much of this functionalist work is that social systems and ecological systems are in some kind of self-adjusting balance or harmony. The research task for the anthropologist working within this framework is to examine how social and environmental systems interact in such a way as to allow the society in question to go on reproducing itself.

This view of society–nature relations as an integrated and functioning whole has some parallels with the perspective adopted by Durkheim, the underlying issue again being what keeps society holding together and 'functioning'. (For Durkheim, a large part of the answer was ritual and religion.)

Metabolism between industrial societies and nature

Contemporary commentators who have recognized and used the concept of metabolism have particularly emphasized the use and misuse of raw materials and the production of waste by modern industrial processes (Fischer-Kowalski 1997; Schandl and Schulz 2000). For an example of this approach, see box 2.2.

Box 2.2 Society's metabolism with nature

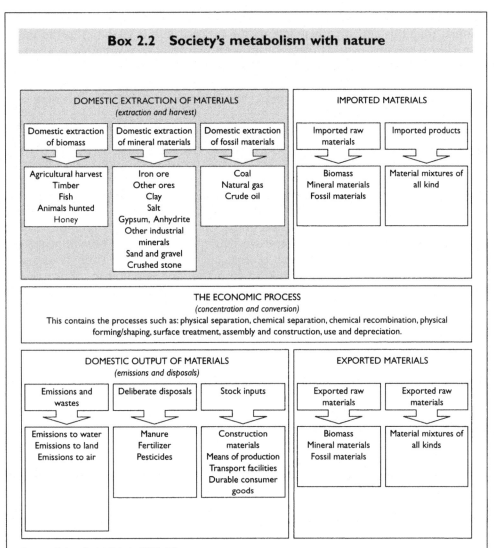

Source: Schandl and Schulz 2000: 34

This diagram shows the enormous array of inputs involved in society's relations with nature. These include the extraction of materials needed for food, energy, building construction and so on. Some of these materials are of course imported from outside the society in question. In the centre of the diagram is 'The Economic Process'. This is the process involved in converting the domestic and imported materials. Finally there is a range of emissions, wastes and disposals. These can be classified as 'domestic' and 'exported'. The tons of biomass, minerals and fossils consumed per person per year is actually quite similar across all the developed societies. Total domestic consumption (for 1991) is 18.5 tons for Austria, 19.5 for Germany, 16.6 for Japan and the Netherlands, 18.7 for the United States.

This perspective on humanity's metabolism with nature is clearly helpful. For the first time it is actually documenting the process with hard data. Furthermore, historical work on society's metabolism with nature is very valuable in showing the massive rise in the use of energy that has accompanied industrialization. Particularly important has been energy based on the fossil fuels, primarily coal and oil. In Austria these contributed 1 per cent of energy input in 1830. It is now over 50 per cent (Weisz et al. 2001).

But, comparing this perspective with the anthropological perspectives outlined earlier, this account leaves a key set of relationships unexplored. In particular 'The Economic Process' section of box 2.2 needs opening up to explore a range of social relationships and processes which are involved in the conversion of inputs into outputs. Such a consideration would be central to many social and political scientists.

It is at this point that Marx, Engels and the historical materialist tradition becomes especially helpful. The transformation of the environment (or 'external nature') is accompanied, they argued, by the transformation of society and human beings (or 'internal nature'). Important as the 'ecological' half of metabolism between society and nature has now become, the transformation (or metabolism) of people and their social relations is just as important. The two are very closely related.

Marx, Engels and nature

Marx and Engels are particularly well known for their emphasis on the economy and on class struggle in the industrial workplace as the main forces generating social change. They are not well known as contributors to environmental debates. Yet their interventions are critical.

The key point about Marx and Engels is that they saw industry as the way to understand modern humanity's metabolism with nature. On the one hand, people form relationships and work processes. They combine with the resources and powers of nature to produce the things their societies need. But new kinds of social relations and new kinds of person are made in the process. The following was Marx's way of articulating this important, wider position.

> Labour is, first of all, a process between man and nature, a process by which man, through his own actions, mediates, regulates and controls the metabolism between himself and nature. He confronts the materials of nature as a force of nature. He sets in motion the natural forces which belong to his own body, his arms, legs, head and hands, in order to appropriate the materials of nature in a form adapted to his own needs. Through this movement he acts upon external nature and changes it, and in this way he simultaneously changes his own nature . . . It [the labour process] is the universal condition for the metabolic interaction between man and nature, the everlasting nature-imposed condition of human existence. (1970: 177)

This transformation of external and internal nature can, however, be seen as a continuous process. Human beings are also able to monitor how they have made both themselves and their environment. And this in turn means they can readdress both themselves and their impacts on nature, including even the meanings they give to their environment. This means that humanity can work on nature in different ways and further change its concepts of nature. Arguably, parts of humanity are now developing new attitudes and interpretations of the natural world. They are no longer visualizing it as an inanimate thing just to be conquered in the interests of 'progress'. Increasing concerns for non-human animals are now advanced, for example, and there is a growing insistence that their lives and powers of growth must be respected.

Nature and industry: debates over the relevance of Marx

Insofar as Marxism has been considered in our own era in relation to environmental questions, it has a reputation for adopting a cavalier attitude towards nature. In line with classical Enlightenment philosophy, the powers of nature are again there to be subdued and controlled in the interests of making a communist society. Communist societies which have actually been brought into being, such as the Soviet Union and in Eastern Europe, strongly enhance such a reputation. To many environmentalists, communism values nature in the same way as capitalism. They are both dedicated to the Enlightenment project. Capitalism and communism (at least the kinds of communism so far encountered) are both committed to full-scale production with external nature being fully subjugated to that end. For many interested in environmental questions, the choice between capitalism and communism is about as attractive as choosing between Tweedledum and Tweedledee. Both are committed to unfettered growth without concern for the environment.

Marx was writing at a time when ecological issues did not loom large in social and economic debate, so he did not pay much attention to them. But his view is actually much more complex and subtle than the stereotypical position often attributed to him. Friedrich Engels, Marx's great colleague, made even greater efforts to link the insights of the sciences with those of politics and philosophy. The experience of the actual forms of communism which developed during the twentieth century has blinded us to the interests and insights of this partnership.

Marx's intellectual development

Marx's intellectual origins demonstrate that he was highly sensitive to ecological questions. They informed much of his social, as well as his environmental, analysis. As box 2.3 shows, for example, he was well aware of Darwin's perspective on the relations between species and their environment. At the same time, he was cautiously critical about the extent to which Darwinism could be directly introduced into the kind of social and economic theory which he and Engels were developing.

Recent research on Marx's intellectual development shows him to have been sensitive to ecological questions in further ways. He was indeed someone who could, in today's parlance, lay reasonable claim to being 'green'. After finishing his doctoral thesis, for example, he went to work as a journalist in what is now Germany. As well as actively engaging in leftwing politics there, he used his job with a newspaper to start supporting the remnants of the peasantry. They were still being expelled from common land and were collecting dead wood for shelter, cooking and food.

Box 2.3   Marx on Darwin's theory of evolution

Marx, less so Engels, was ambivalent about Darwin. He was exceptionally wary of Darwin's adoption of Malthus as part of his conceptual framework. Malthus had argued that the growth of human numbers inevitably outstripped the supply of food necessary to feed them. He hoped that such inevitability would lead the poor to recognize the admonitions of God to lead a Christian existence and, more specifically, to stop having so much sex. Marx thought all this was humbug and that any notion of 'shortages' of food had to be seen in the light of property relations. Who actually *made* these shortages through the ownership of land and the means of production? Shortages are socially produced.

Marx was also suspicious of Darwin's transposition of English society on to nature. As he wrote in a letter to Engels: 'It is remarkable how Darwin rediscovers among the beasts and plants, the society of England with its division of labour, competition, opening up of new markets, "inventions" and the Malthusian "struggle for existence." It is Hobbes' *bellum contra omnes*' (quoted in Schmidt 1971: 46).

On the other hand, Marx was enthusiastic about Darwin, writing in a letter to Engels that 'It is the basis in natural history for our view.'

Marx's ambivalence over Darwin again draws attention to how theories are often made. They are socially constructed. They are a product of their society, but they can indeed refer to something real.

The Prussian authorities were passing laws against these people, forbidding them from encroaching on private land. The young Marx stood up for the rights of those 'stealing' dead wood, while at the same time realizing that his understanding of environmental issues was 'embarrassing', that political debates were at too philosophical a level and that he needed to get involved in political economy as represented by, for example, Adam Smith.

Marx was an 'ecologist' in yet more ways. He was fascinated, for example, by the work of Epicurus, an early Greek philosopher who believed that 'nature never reduces anything to nothing'. Epicurus is nowadays seen as an early propounder of our modern-day theory of thermodynamics and the conservation of energy. He was also an early 'Darwinist', recognizing evolutionary processes of species variation and the adaptation of species to their environment. Epicurus insisted on understanding the material processes of the world, which has led some to call him 'The Great Enlightener of Antiquity' (for discussion, see Foster 2000: viii).

The point is, then, that Marx was both highly influenced by environmental and evolutionary thought and well aware of developments in these areas. The same applies to an even greater extent to his co-worker, Engels, who went so far as to envisage a single theory, one linking the physical, natural and human sciences (1969a). Perhaps most important, these concerns were built into both men's social and economic theory.

Marx and Engels therefore continue to be explored by contemporary scholars interested in the relations between society and nature. They are still accused of being

Box 2.4 'Human centredness': an area of debate

It is often argued by environmentalists that our society is too 'human-centred' or 'anthropocentric'. Human freedom consists of the domination of nature and the subjugation of non-human species. 'Anthropocentric' is usually contrasted with 'eco-centric', this being a consciousness which is aware of ecosystems as a whole and of the rights and independence of non-human species. However, what does 'anthro-pocentricism' actually entail? And is it necessarily different from 'ecocentricism'?

There are at least three understandings of anthropocentrism and not all of them necessarily entail environmental destruction.

1   Human needs could be met without necessarily wrecking ecosystems or other species. It is possible to envisage a supply of food, sufficient shelter or reason-able levels of health which respect the needs of ecosystems and other species. 'Anthropocentrism' of this kind, therefore, may not necessarily be a problem.
2   Humans could, however, try to overcome natural limits in the attempt to increas-ingly realize their capacities. Human freedom is envisaged as the fulfilment of human needs through the conquering of the environment. Therefore humans become more free to the extent that they conquer external nature and use it to meet their ends. Some of Marx's writings make this argument as do many supporters of capitalist production. This is probably what most environmentalists mean when they refer to 'anthropocentrism'.
3   Another understanding of anthropocentrism, however, might seem more satis-factory. It would be possible to envisage a new kind of human centredness which finds fulfilment in recognizing the independent qualities of the environment and non-human species. It would also recognize the rights of other species and the fact that humans must live within natural limits. Indeed, it would revel in such independence, finding spiritual and aesthetic pleasure in, for example, an uncaged animal. Such a view is simultaneously anthropocentric and ecocentric. It entails a new view of human flourishing. This understanding of anthropocentrism is pre-sent in some of Marx's work, especially that written when he was a young man.

very human centred. Even this accusation, however, needs some serious discussion. 'Anthropocentrism', or human centredness, is not necessarily bad. It depends on what is meant by the term. Being concerned for human beings does not neces-sarily preclude being concerned for non-human species (for further discussion, see box 2.4).

Society, nature and the 'second contradiction'

As we saw in the previous chapter, James O'Connor argues that an ecological Marxism must recognize a 'second contradiction', one outlined by Marx but hardly developed since Marx's day. The first contradiction according to this view is that of over-production. Capitalism, it is argued, is consistently unable to realize the value incorporated into commodities because the wages of labourers are so tightly controlled. This leads, it is argued, to the rise of increased competition, aggressive marketing and the creation of elaborate credit structures in an attempt to overcome so-called 'crises of realization' in which manufacturers cannot sell what they have produced. In due course, according to the 'first contradiction', massive and climactic social upheaval develops. And this situation, Marx and Engels predicted, would prefigure a transition to communism. In short, capitalism has an inbuilt tendency towards crisis. It stems from the struggle at the heart of capitalism, that between capital and labour. Marx and Engels believed (and hoped) that the first contradiction would destroy this struggle and generate a new kind of classless society.

But as O'Connor and other contemporary Marxists have stressed, capital also tends to dig its own grave in another way (Benton 1996; Burkett 1999). At this point the so-called 'second contradiction' is encountered, that of capitalist industry almost literally undermining the conditions necessary for its own continuation. These conditions include the environment (see box 1.11 on p. 48 for details). Today's global warming, for example, is in large part a product of capitalist industry, but the exceptional weather patterns it generates are damaging factories and workplaces.

This contradiction may not necessarily take especially dramatic or apocalyptic forms. More typically, it takes the form of extra and continually growing costs of production imposed on capitalist enterprises. Whether these are 'fatal' to capitalism remains to be seen. It depends on how the costs of the metabolism process are dealt with. Who pays for the production of wastes and their overloading of ecological systems? Possibly, the outcome is some kind of 'green capitalism'. Just as likely, people in developing countries will pay.

Social Evolution, Biological Evolution and Labour

Two concepts from the life sciences influenced Marx's thinking about how societies develop. One was metabolism. The other was evolution. And, as social evolution led to capitalism, he believed, so humanity's metabolism with the environment was being destroyed.

As box 2.3 showed, Marx was well aware of contemporary evolutionary and environmental thought, especially that of Darwin. Like many others of his day, Marx remained strongly influenced by Darwin. As regards *social* evolution, *Das Kapital* strongly suggests that his extension of evolutionary theory entailed examining how humans as a species were able not only to work on nature but to work on it with a preconceived purpose. To this extent it was a 'teleological' theory. In this case it was the human purpose of human self-realization.

This was one way in which Marx extended Darwinism into the human social realm. But Marx (and Engels to an even greater extent) was later to envisage a single science, one linking 'philosophy' and the emergent physical and evolutionary sciences. They were trying to forge the links between the sciences, links which seem increasingly necessary today.

Social evolution and metabolism with nature

Marx, again like other social scientists of his era (some of whom were explored in the last chapter), was therefore deeply influenced by a notion of *social* evolution. And this led him, again like many others, to suggest that society was itself evolving in a linear way through a series of stages. The final stage, according to Marx, would be communism, evolving out of the wreckage of capitalism. This was his idea of social progress.

What is the link between social evolution and metabolism with external nature or what we call 'the environment'? For Marx, there was a pressing need to understand the form of this metabolism in the contemporary stage of social evolution. This is because the particular form of metabolism in modern societies was generating new threats and risks. These were, both Engels and he believed, coming to haunt capitalism in much the same way as the over-exploitation of humanity was itself generating new kinds of social risk. Environmental upheaval, as well as social upheaval, were in prospect. Engels, in his incomplete book, *The Part Played by Labour in the Transition from Ape to Man*, fully recognized the risks stemming from the transformations to nature attempted in modern society (see box 2.5).

Box 2.5 Friedrich Engels on 'the risk society'

Arguably, Engels was one of the first social scientists to recognize that the ways in which modern society worked on the environment could cause impact on human beings themselves. He called these impacts 'revenges':

> Let us not, however, flatter ourselves overmuch on account of our human victories over nature. Each victory, it is true in the first place brings about the results we expected, but in the second and third places it has quite different, unforeseen effects which only too often cancel the first . . . Thus at every step we are reminded that we by no means rule over nature like a conqueror over a foreign people, like someone standing outside nature – but that we, with flesh, blood and brain belong to nature, and exist in its midst. (1969a: 12)

Marx on social evolution and detachment from nature's metabolism

The 'metabolism' between society and nature was, for Marx and Engels, more than just a concept borrowed from biological science. It was used for distinct analytical and political purposes. Marx was monitoring the development of new social forms; specifically, the emergence of private property and its implications for people and the environment. He argued strongly that the type of metabolism developing in modern capitalist societies was potentially and even actually disastrous.

Modes of production and nature

In a number of texts Marx and Engels describe types of society, or modes of production, and their relationships with nature. 'Modes of production' refers to the ways in which people work with the forces of production (machinery, the powers and resources of nature and people's own capacities) and the forms of specialization and divisions of labour to make the things that society needs. A change in the mode of production might therefore include a change in forms of technology or a change from strip farming to enclosed fields. Marx was further concerned with whether the product was being made for direct use by the producer. For example, is a self-sufficient peasant producing food for her or his own consumption? Or does the landowner consume part of the product? Alternatively, is something being made for exchange-value, for its exchange for money?

Again with evolutionary ideas informing him, Marx set out a linear process whereby each mode of production transformed into the next. Each stage, according to this model, contained the kernel or seed of the next social formation. They took the following sequence:

1 Primitive communal
2 Advanced communal
3 Feudalism
4 Capitalism
5 Communism

Each mode of production is seen as organized around the division of labour, the ways in which human beings have organized themselves and their property to produce the things they want. But note again the central theme of humanity's exchange or metabolism with nature in a labour process. Producing the things needed for society remains central to all these understandings of 'social formation'. This is the necessary and underlying condition for all social formations, even though it takes very different forms during the process of social change (see also Wolf 1982). The point about this scheme is that humanity's relations with nature took, in Marx and Engels's view, a less alienated, less estranged form than they do in modern society. A rift has now opened up between humanity and nature, one which endangers humanity and limits human beings' aesthetic capacities.

(1) **Primitive communal** The first stage in Marx and Engels's evolutionary scheme was a 'primitive' communal form. The word 'primitive' is now considered problematic, of course. It perhaps suggests that today's tribal peoples are somehow undeveloped simply because they have not been caught up in Enlightenment forms of modernization and rationalization. And of course 'primitive' tells us rather little about how they are organized. For Marx, 'primitive' is associated with communal ways of life or early forms of collective ownership, which were later to be dispensed with by capitalist forms of private ownership.

The German tribes An example of these early primitive societies is what Marx called 'the German tribes'. These people now have legendary status. They included the

---

Box 2.6   Early communal ownership: the German tribes

Marx cites the early German tribes as an example of a primitive form of communism. The people lived with their animals in small settlements or villages, usually surrounded by strong timber defences against animals and potential enemies (see illus. 2.6A). Land was collectively owned. No less a person than Julius Caesar wrote of the German tribes that 'no land is the property of private individuals and no one is allowed to cultivate the same land for more than a year' (in Todd 1972: 36). Leaders of the community met each year to decide which pieces of land should be ploughed and planted. This area was divided into equal plots and distributed among all the households making up that community. The following year, these plots of land were allowed to lie temporarily fallow and new areas were parcelled out. Clearance of forest or scrub, ploughing and harvesting were carried out collectively.

The Romans commented on the huge size of these people, their powerful limbs, blue eyes and reddish or blond hair. The size of these people is confirmed by corpses which have been well preserved in peat bogs (see illus. 2.6B). The Germans were considered fearsome opponents by the Romans.

Visigoths, the Huns and the Vandals, and they were at least partly responsible for the collapse of the Roman Empire. Production at this stage was, and in a few extant cases remains, relatively undeveloped. People engaged with external nature in a range of ways in order to sustain themselves. These would typically include 'bands' of food collectors who do not transform nature in a fundamental way. They meet human needs simply by acquiring what Marx called 'the spontaneous productions of nature'. The people therefore work on nature without thoroughly transforming it (see box 2.6).

Hunters, farmers and fishers   Later, humans in these collective forms of production and consumption started to sustain themselves by hunting, fishing, cattle-raising or farming. They used the powers of nature (for example, the powers of animals or plants to grow) as a means of creating more food, clothing and so forth. And they remained severely limited by ecological and other environmental constraints. Kinship groups or 'families' tended to dominate at this stage, with people exploiting the environment in a direct way for their own direct use. But co-residence was often just as important amongst such groups as were blood relations (Wolf 1982). Similarly, work might have been done by groups of non-relatives and the products caught or made may have been shared between non-relatives as well as relatives.

An emergent class system   Out of this group there developed a class system. This is one in which the chieftains came to dominate and one which used slaves, perhaps captured from neighbouring tribes. 'Metabolism with nature' in these instances largely took the form of hunters and gatherers collecting what nature had spontaneously produced. Again, this is in contrast to later forms of metabolism in which, through agriculture, horticulture and the domestication of animals, humans started to 'colonize' nature, to make it more fundamentally their own.

Illustration 2.6A   Reconstruction of Zeijen (Drenthe) village, early Roman Iron Age

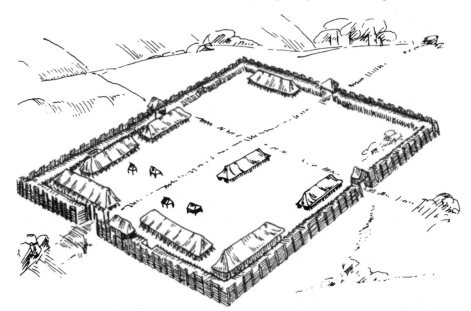

In M. Todd, *Everyday Life of the Barbarians*, p. 48. © B. T. Batsford (Chrysalis Books)

Illustration 2.6B   Face of man from Tollund Bog, Jutland

Photo Silkeborg Museum, Denmark/Munoz-Yague/Science Photo Library

(2) **Advanced communal**   A second stage in the metabolism between humanity and nature, according to Marx and Engels, entailed a further division of labour. It involved the separation of industrial and commercial production from agricultural labour. And this in turn led to the historic distinction between town and country. This was linked to another phase in the development of property relations. Cities were constituted by the linking of tribal groups, either by agreement or conquest. The cities were themselves composed of different economic divisions – industry, for example, and those promoting trade outside the city. At this stage communal city property became the dominant form, though dependence on slavery could still be (as in Rome) part of this type of economy. Marx notes, incidentally, that slaves in Rome were seen as, and were conceived of and treated as, little more than 'beasts'.

(3) **Feudalism**   The Roman conquests and the spread of agriculture provided the seeds, almost literally, for a third phase. This was feudalism. New types of property relation developed, particularly in the countryside. A new type of class structure and class struggle developed, one in which feudal nobility was opposed to serfs. Meanwhile, in the towns the most basic form of property was simply individuals' own labour. But at the same time there was a range of social organizations, including the guilds, which ensured a strong sense of solidarity and community. Central power in this type of social formation was often weak and was by no means guaranteed. In particular, the surpluses made in the countryside did not necessarily flow directly and completely to the city. On the other hand, class alliances even in the countryside could be fragmented, and this in turn could weaken the position of the primary producers on the land, meaning that they might have to seek out central authority (for further discussion, see Wolf 1982).

Marx's notion of the Asiatic mode of production should be mentioned here. In India, China and elsewhere, he argued, there had emerged a mode of production in which the unity of manufacture and agriculture within the village commune was especially well organized and difficult for later colonizing powers to break down. Again, there was an absence of private property. The main difference, according to Marx, between this mode of production and the feudal mode was the existence of an exceptionally strong and centralized group of power-holders. Access to resources was again the key, but the central rulers had their own armies which curtailed the power of local sects and lords. Furthermore, they laid on strategic public works (such as waterworks) which enabled them to control and direct the surpluses being made in the countryside. Later scholars have questioned the idea of an 'Asiatic' mode of production. But note here that Marx and Engels were using the concept to develop a political point about private property being the key issue underlying the destruction of working people and the environment.

(4) **Capitalism**   Out of feudalism, Marx and Engels argued, there evolved the capitalist mode of production. This started in the cities, with the further division of labour between production and trade, but also with the further specialization of production. Capital began to develop outside the guilds and provided an opportunity for the peasants who had previously been out in the countryside and excluded from the guilds. At this point private property begins to hold sway, as all forms of property, including capital and land, became owned by commercial

or industrial interests. At the same time, the holders of wealth acquired the necessary means of production and denied access to the proletariat. The latter now depend wholly on the owners of the means of production for work and are rewarded with wages which gave them the means to survive. In this way a new class system was created, based on people's access to land and resources.

People now tended to be treated as individuals – they were paid wages for their work and, indeed, they competed in the search for work. In short, they became alienated from each other, from their own species. This was catastrophic for humanity since human beings are, according to Marx, an overwhelmingly social species; they need to associate with one another in order to become fully human.

Meanwhile, the resources of external nature now become inputs into the production system. They are made mere commodities, rather like the people working on them. The proletariat has little or no control or even understanding of the powers of nature or of ecological systems. His or her internal nature is just another input into the production process, one which, again like external nature, is consistently *over*-exploited. Once more, capitalism and private property are the overarching villains of the piece. A mode of production that is based on private property is the chief culprit in the wrecking of external nature. Capitalism and private property are also seen as undermining human nature, again separating human beings from the environment on which they depend for their material and spiritual well-being. Internal as well as external nature is suffering.

From this perspective, we can see that pre-capitalist modes of production were based on some form of collective or community ownership and control. This applied, for example, to the extensive common ownership of land in feudal societies. In his earliest writings Marx referred to nature as 'man's inorganic body', meaning that external nature has to be seen as integral to humanity itself. In order to thrive and survive, humanity must associate with nature, understand it and actively engage with it. With the emergence of private ownership under capitalism, however, this close link between humanity and nature is severed. The sense of continuity with external nature is lost, as is humanity's understanding of its relations with nature.

Capitalism, as Marx and Engels were the first to admit, has achieved great things. This includes a degree of control over nature's powers, meaning that humanity is no longer subjected to the vagaries of the natural world and that nature has been to a large degree harnessed in an attempt to create better standards of life. But in the process capitalism has severely disrupted human beings' relations with one another and with nature.

Note here the extent to which changing images of construals of nature simultaneously generated and were generated by new kinds of social relations and industrial processes. These have been traced in an important study by Carolyn Merchant (see box 2.7).

(5) **Communism** Marx and Engels believed it would take communism and new forms of communality based on collective ownership, developed out of the advances of capitalism, to regain the lost relation between humanity and nature, the latter actually being part of the former, its 'inorganic body'. As noted, this inorganic body was envisaged as having an aesthetic and spiritual dimension, as well as providing for the more obvious needs of physical survival.

Box 2.7   From organism to mechanism: historical shifts in people's views of nature

People in different historical periods 'construct' or 'construe' the environment in different ways. These constructions help people to make sense of their world. And they can have real, material impacts.

In *The Death of Nature* Carolyn Merchant argues that, with the rise of modern Baconian science and during the Enlightenment, a profound change took place in Europe in people's image of the natural world. The image of a cosmos with a living female earth at its centre was supplanted with an image in which nature is conceived as a dead mechanism. The first image commanded respect and demanded limits to the use of the earth for new human needs. The second image encouraged dominion over the earth, one supported by new discoveries being revealed by Enlightenment science. Porter, as we saw in chapter 1, argues that Enlightenment philosophy saw humanity as in broad balance with the earth. Merchant, on the other hand, argues that a rapacious attitude towards the earth emerged out of this era.

Merchant argues that a further transformation is happening in the present day: 'The machine image that has dominated Western culture for the past three hundred years seems to be giving way to something new. Some call the transformation a "new paradigm"; others call it "deep ecology"; still others call for a postmodern world view' (1990: xvii). Note that James Lovelock's so-called 'Gaia Hypothesis' can be seen as a recovery of older types of image, this time based on the chemical and ecological sciences. Lovelock argued in the early 1970s that we live 'on the best of all possible worlds'. The earth, and its delicate and unstable mixture of gases and ecosystems, is envisaged as itself a living being, one which industrial activities are fouling up. The new image owes a lot to Romanticism, to a recognition of external nature's own independent qualities. The pendulum is swinging back.

Marx and Engels's political message

The above sequence of modes of production is obviously a considerable simplification of Marx and Engels's view of social evolution, one based on different forms of property and social relations. It is one which both these authors, and Engels in particular, continued to develop during their working lives and which takes varying forms in their writings.

The result was a strong idea of social change, which would have a directional sequence and would eventually result in 'progress'. But Marx and Engels's view of history has a clear political point, one which still needs serious debate. As society develops away from communal forms of ownership and towards private property and capitalism, people have become progressively estranged not only from one another but from the very environment on which they depend. This estrangement means that humans now have little understanding of, or engagement with, the environment. The great majority do not appreciate how it operates and how they are dependent on it. Enjoyment of its aesthetic and spiritual capacities has been separated from an understanding of its actual use.

Updating Marx and Engels

Marx and Engels's work has recently been a powerful inspiration to contemporary understandings of society–nature relations. And their work can be greatly updated with the aid of new historical and anthropological evidence.

'Go home, my friend': famines and the making of the third world

The period of industrial capitalism covered by Marx and Engels can be better understood. Davis (2001), for example, is an historical materialist who has made the crucial links between climatic and economic change. During the last quarter of the nineteenth century some 50 million people died as a result of drought and famines in India, China and Brazil. Some of these were due to the El Niño phenomenon, when the Pacific Ocean, operating as a generator of planetary heat and combining with the trade winds, affects rainfall patterns in the tropics and even in the temperate regions. But the deaths were also the result of massive economic disruption as these societies were made part of an international trade system. The price of corn, for example, escalated very rapidly and communally organized stores that were being held in case of harvest failure were incorporated into the market.

So while it is tempting to ascribe massive humanitarian disasters in the so-called third world to severe forms of climate change, the fact is that complex interactions are involved between social and political programmes on the one hand and the powers of nature on the other. These interactions are still not properly understood. It seems clear, however, that central government in India (under the leadership of Queen Victoria) considerably exacerbated the effects of climate change by refusing to interfere in any way with 'free trade'. Controlling prices or providing emergency supplies were anathema. Such interference was seen, in line with Social Darwinist theory, as in the long run undermining Indian society. Interventions of these kinds would only mean that the least 'fit' would survive. Sir Richard Temple, the Lieutenant Governor of Bengal in 1874–7, was the enforcer of the free trade credo on behalf of the then Viceroy, Lord Lytton (for more details, see box 2.8). His advice to an applicant for assistance is not only chilling but resonates with the free trade solutions to poverty which persist today: 'Go home, my friend, and come back to me in three weeks or a month, when you have eaten the proceeds of your hut, your plough, and your ploughing cattle' (in Couper-Johnston 2000: 14). With society combining with the powers of nature in these ways, what we now call 'the third world' was actively made; great wealth being accumulated in the imperial societies (with Britain then in the lead) while millions of people were left to starve.

Pre-modern societies and domestic work

Other researchers since Marx's day have developed forms of historical materialism which revisit some of the so-called 'primitive' societies and extend 'production' to that conducted in the household.

Box 2.8   Changing nature, changing ourselves: late nineteenth-century famines

Alfred Russel Wallace, the explorer and co-discoverer of the theory of evolution, was one of the few people to make the connections between the riches being accumulated in Britain and other imperial societies during the late nineteenth century and the great famines in India, China and South America. The slums, on the one hand, and the millions of people dying from hunger, on the other, were, he wrote, 'the most terrible failures of the century' (in Davis 2001: 8). A new set of social relations was being formed as the economies and cultures of these societies were bound into this early phase of globalization. In the Indian case they were presided over by Lord Lytton, Queen Victoria's favourite poet and enthusiast for free trade versions of Social Darwinism. But social history needs to be combined with an understanding of environmental mechanisms. In this instance, Social Darwinism was being combined with the El Niño phenomenon: a combination that resulted in massive drought and famine. Between 12 and 30 million Indian people starved to death during the last quarter of the nineteenth century.

Distribution of relief at Bellary, Madras, 1877

Mary Evans Picture Library

The anthropologist Marshall Sahlins presents the idea of a 'domestic mode of production'. He writes: ' "The economy" of a primitive society is an exercise in unreality'. The notion cannot be transferred to pre-industrial societies, since it is 'something that generalized social groups and relations, notably kinship groups and relations, *do*' (Sahlins 1974: 76; emphasis in original).

Sahlins argues that a number of non-industrial social forms, such as agriculturalism, pastoralism and hunter-gatherer societies, can all be seen as variants on this 'domestic mode of production'. The basic unit of all these societies, he suggests, is the family group or household. Such a group has a tendency to under-produce. They had, in modern terms, large amounts of leisure time. However, the tendency was for these small domestic groups to combine, with 'higher level' social structures, trading systems and forms of political authority all increasing the overall level of social production. These larger groups, Sahlins argued, then produce contradictory tendencies. They can be used to mediate between households and prevent social conflict. Alternatively, they can actually generate social conflict.

Modern societies and domestic work

The question of divisions of labour other than those in industrial production arises in studies of modern kinds of society. The social divisions of labour, especially those between men, women and children in the home, have often been neglected by social scientists sympathetic to Marx (for discussion, see Sayer 1995). These divisions, and their distinctive interactions with the environment, largely escaped Marx and Engels's analysis. Unless food was prepared and cooked and unless people were brought up and cared for in the home, there would be no fresh supplies of labour to work in the factories. Unless work of an emotional and caring kind was conducted in homes and communities, capitalism in its present form would break down. These kinds of work outside the formal place of work are still overwhelmingly done by women (Parker 2001).

This important argument is often made by feminists, and in particular by feminists working in developing countries (Mies and Shiva 1993). Furthermore, these kinds of care in the home and community can entail constant interactions with the environment. Making shelter and goods such as baskets and clothes is often, for example, done at a community level. And they may well be exchanged on a reciprocal, non-cash basis within communities or kin networks (Redclift 1987). Furthermore, interactions with external nature may be of a distinctly dangerous kind if caring work is undermined by interaction with industrial waste. Human beings in developing and developed countries alike are now routinely exposed to toxic metals, organic solvents, pesticides and endocrine disruptors, many of which are having serious effects on people's reproductive and developmental health (Schettler et al. 1999). In short, there are many kinds of work and interactions with external nature outside the formal workplace. A focus on formal 'industry' has left these activities and interactions largely ignored.

On the other hand, note that the domestic sphere itself is increasingly commodified and industrialized. Activities previously conducted in the home are now carried out by industry, with people being obliged to buy commodities such as food which they were previously responsible for growing and preparing. In a way analogous to that in industrial work, domestic production has thereby been increasingly deskilled. This is an important tendency, even if it has not yet fully penetrated developing societies to the extent outlined in box 2.9.

Box 2.9   The domestic sphere and society's metabolism with nature: Lenin versus McDonald's

To an increasing extent, society purchases ready-made food. According to one estimate, 90 per cent of food now comes in part-prepared forms. To an increasing extent, therefore, our 'metabolism' with nature is done only indirectly. And, even when it comes to daily activities such as cooking food, we are again being 'deskilled'. It may be that soon very few people will know how to cook at all. A survey of 7–15-year-olds in Britain found that barely half could boil an egg. Nevertheless, 75 per cent of the children did want to learn more about cooking.

Percentage of British children able to perform certain tasks in 1993

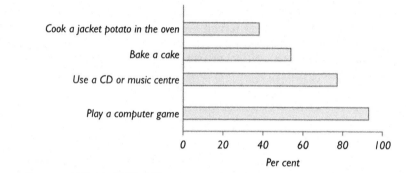

Source: Tansey and Worsley 1995: 163.

But this deskilling is in part replaced by commodified food production in the form of frozen and take-away meals. And these have also enabled more women to join the labour force. One hundred years ago Lenin said he would release women from the drudgery of cooking. But it has taken modern supermarkets and McDonald's to realize Lenin's promise. (For further discussion, see 'Food as a Cultural Barometer', chapter 4, p. 141.)

Family groups and the noble savage fallacy

A somewhat similar focus on households has been profitably used to examine environmental risks in pre-industrial societies (Spence 2001). Where family groupings are dominant and where levels of production are relatively low, levels of environmental damage also tend to be relatively low. Where households are subsumed into larger units and where levels of production are higher, Spence argues, environmental degradation tended to be more prevalent.

Contemporary research on early societies in Australia and America suggests, however, that it cannot be assumed that any of these earlier societies either produced or avoided environmental destruction (see box 2.10). In some circumstances the impact has been devastating and in other instances it has not. The arrival of

***

Box 2.10   Are environmental crises new?

It is often assumed that pre-industrial societies lived in close harmony with nature and never created environmental problems. Unfortunately, according to commentators who focus on the material ways in which ancient civilizations have interacted with their environment, this was not the case. Studies of ancient Mayan civilization have shown, for example, that pressures of population growth and agricultural intensi-fication resulted in deforestation and 'catastrophic soil erosion' (Hughes 1999a,b). As Ancient Rome expanded territorially during the first and second centuries BC, agri-culture was changed from a mixed and diversified system based on a peasantry to a plantation agriculture which 'mined rather than farmed the soil, deforested the hills and created the downward spiral of flood and drought that has been the death of more than one culture' (O'Connor 1998: 26). In the sixteenth century, and in the context of an economic boom created by the inflow of New World gold and silver, land held in common was increasingly turned over to commodity production and this 'destroyed the integrity of the land and accelerated the enclosure movement' (ibid. 27). Earlier civilizations did not live in timeless harmony with nature. They were easily capable of making catastrophic mistakes, not least because they could not predict the consequences of their actions.

***

the first humans in America severely disrupted ecological systems. But this was because of their omnivorous diet, use of fire and hunting of the fittest animals. It had little to do with private or communal property as such.

People in earlier kinds of society neither systematically destroyed their environ-ment nor lived in perfect harmony with it. Marx and Engels were, arguably, in danger of romanticizing ancient societies, one in which humans were in complete harmony with their environment.

Industry, knowledge and power

In Marx and Engels's picture, new kinds of social relations are formed in the devel-opment of capitalism with, on the one hand, a massive deskilled working class and, on the other, powerful groups of people who benefit exceptionally well from the work of others.

Managers do not necessarily control in direct, overt, ways. Rather, they mani-pulate and retain knowledge. Modern scholarship indicates that since at least the eighteenth century onwards power has been exercised by elites constructing abstract forms of knowledge and ensuring that they are the ones who have con-trol over this type of information. As science and industry are developed to better exploit the powers of nature, new kinds of social relations are therefore made. Again, these are made by the creation of an apparently unchallengeable science. Old labour processes are analysed, taken apart and reconstructed, an exercise which allows some classes of people to exert control over the labour process. The other side to

Box 2.11   The circuit of capital

The circuit of capital (M_1 = money invested, LP = labour power, MP = means of production (including raw materials from nature), P = labour process, C = exchange of commodities, M_2 = profit)

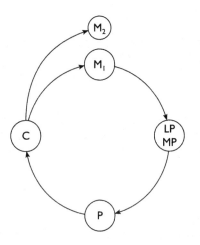

This diagram shows the role of external nature in capitalist economies. Money (M_1) purchases technology, or the means of production, and labour power (people's capacity to work). These are combined with the raw materials taken from nature and with other commodities into a labour process which produces commodities for sale. The resulting money is either recycled into another labour process (purchasing new labour power, raw materials, new machines) or generated as profits for company shareholders. This diagram is at the heart of Marx's understanding of how people are estranged or 'alienated' from the environment. It continues to be helpful to understand modern people's relations with external nature. The environment, 'man's inorganic body', still tends to be treated as a mere input into a labour process.

this same coin is the downgrading of more localized, immediate and unquantifiable kinds of understanding. In these ways abstract forms of knowledge are used as a way of managing and degrading other types of understanding.

Marx's perspective on the circuit of capital, the labour process, on the social relations and forms of knowledge associated with the labour process, still offers a very precise understanding of the context in which power is exercised through the control and management of knowledge (see box 2.11 for discussion). It is a process of alienation which has continued today. It even extends to labour processes in the so-called 'service' industries (Braverman 1974). An emphasis on power, knowledge and industry has a particular resonance today for much work in less developed countries. In agricultural work in India and elsewhere, women often have a particular knowledge of seeds and ecological systems.

Yet, according to radical feminists such as Maria Mies and Vandana Shiva (1993), they often find themselves marginalized by agricultural development. Enlightenment-style 'progress', they argue, actually consists of the imposition of regimes of high productivity and crop uniformity, often by Western companies. The impact of this progress on the environment, and in particular on biodiversity, can be devastating. But, as Mies and Shiva in particular argue, it can be equally devastating for those women whose work and knowledge is often of a complex, often non-codified, form. They find their skills and livelihoods consistently undermined. This is a contemporary version of the kind of deskilling and 'alienating' processes originally discussed by Marx.

Risk and the Metabolic Rift

The discussion above of metabolism, community and industry links to Marx, Engels and their understanding of risk stemming from ecological change. Note that this is 'risk' in its environmental sense. It is not of the broader kind referred to by Beck in which people experience risk in all aspects of their lives.

Environmental risk stems directly, according to the position originally sketched out by Marx and Engels, from the rise of capitalism and private property. The plundering of labour power, or the capacity of people to work, as a result of the industrial labour process is a central and well-known feature of *Das Kapital* and of contemporary concerns with the health and safety of industrial workers. A less well-known aspect of Marx's work – but as central – is his argument that capitalism also plunders ecological systems. Yet Marx's early background led him to undertake no less than an analysis of what would now be called 'environmental sustainability'. In particular, he developed the idea of a 'rift' in the metabolic relation between humanity and nature, one seen as an emergent feature of capitalist society. Early, pre-capitalist societies were closely integrated with their environment. This was important in two ways. It meant that people had a clear understanding of their relations with the environment, the external nature on which they depended and which they necessarily transformed. It also has a more material meaning. In earlier societies the wastes which people produced were returned to the soil, recycled in ways which were not damaging to people or to other species. By contrast, Marx argued, the tendency under capitalism is for society to violate these connections between humanity and nature. Also violated are the conditions for ecological systems to reproduce themselves. As Marx put it, 'capitalist production turns towards the land only after its influence has exhausted it and after it has devastated its natural qualities' (cited in Foster 2000: 163). Marx intensively studied the work of industrial chemists of his day and built their analysis into the heart of his work, including *Das Kapital* itself.

Like Engels in *The Housing Question* (1969b), Marx documented at great length the implications of large numbers of people living in towns and the systematic failure to recycle the nutrients that had been removed from the soil. Urban pollution and irrational sewerage systems were all part of the metabolic rift generated by industrial capitalism. Marx noted: 'In London . . . they can do nothing better with the excrement produced by 4.5 million people than pollute the Thames with it, at monstrous expense.'

The notion of an ecological rift, one separating humanity and nature and violating the principles of ecological sustainability, continues to be helpful for understanding today's social and environmental risks. These risks are becoming increasingly global in extent. This is partly because they directly impact on environmental mechanisms operating at a global scale. Examples include the depletion of the ozone layer and Arctic meltdown which now appears to be affecting the Gulf Stream and the temperate and stable climate on which European societies depend (Brown 2001). They are also becoming global because local environmental change is having global implications. Examples of the latter include groundwater pollution, deforestation or soil depletion on prime agricultural lands (Goudie 2000).

But the nature of these violations is difficult to determine. Concerns about the global environment have for some time been concentrated on the *absolute* depletion of resources (Meadows et al. 1983). The fear has been that society would simply 'run out' of resources and that cataclysms of many kinds would be likely to follow. The resulting picture was a 'Doomsday Scenario'. There are now developing, however, more sophisticated understandings of natural limits, albeit understandings which leave us with more uncertainties than the earlier approach. The issue is not just about a finite supply of resources but also about the laws of nature themselves and precisely how humanity should organize itself with respect to these laws (Hughes 2000). The extent to which ecosystems 'bite back' at humanity depends on the causal mechanisms within the physical and biological worlds and precisely how humanity attempts to control them.

Global environmental change: from absolute to relative limits

This new approach is typified by the historical work on El Niño covered earlier (Davis 2001). It certainly consists of incorporating an understanding of the underlying, extraordinarily well-established, largely unchangeable causal mechanisms affecting the world's climate and resources. But it is also trying to appreciate how humanity is both using and impinging on these mechanisms (Benton 1996; Hughes 2000). Again, the underlying mechanisms are very much considered to be in place, but the question is whether and precisely how a particular kind of society is affecting them. The outcomes are not only unpredictable but variable. There may be devastating results for some groups of people and other species in some contexts. They may be only minor irritants to other settings. Again, the effects are relative to how these underlying natural mechanisms are being combined with social relations and social systems.

Land and farming

The same approach can be extended to contemporary concerns. Figure 2.1 shows the ways in which humans, animals and plants have been gradually separated over the past 300 years or so (Foster 2002). Early agriculture entailed the recycling

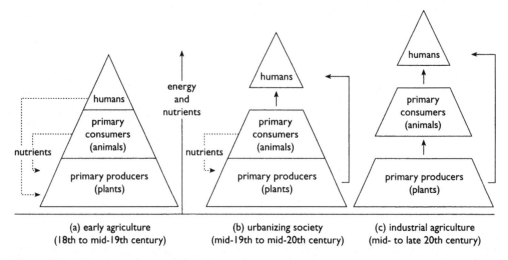

Figure 2.1 Agriculture: the metabolic rift over three centuries
Source: Foster 2002: 162

of organic matter from people and animals to 'primary producers' in the form of plants. By the mid-nineteenth century (the period of capitalism to which Marx was referring) humans were no longer integrated into this process, and artificial rather than natural manures were used to supplement soil fertility. By the mid- to late twentieth century, however, this process had been continued further, as nitrogen fertilizers were introduced to overcome still more declines in soil fertility. Meanwhile, a 'rift' was opening up between animals and their environment – animals were being raised near to animal processing facilities, and relations between humanity and external nature became, as a result, further stretched and even broken. But this is not simply an aesthetic matter of urbanized people being disconnected from the natural world. The decline of nutrient recycling is now having a number of severe outcomes, many of which extend well beyond their original source.

Nitrogen is very energy-intensive, being by far the largest component of the energy needed to produce an acre of corn. Nitrogen contaminates groundwater and high concentrations of animals generate more nutrients than the soil can absorb; they also require high levels of antibiotics to counter disease. These medicines contaminate food and encourage bacteria which are antibiotic-resistant and potential hazards to human health. Finally, and as Foster (2002) describes in detail, the mining operations undertaken to supply nutrients can themselves generate environmental damage.

Risk and the ozone layer

Understanding contemporary global environmental risk therefore entails knowing how human production processes are organized, as well as the technologies that are required, and also being aware of what kinds of metabolism with the underlying mechanisms of nature are involved and how humanity's activities are in turn affected. One example of global risk is the thinning of the ozone layer.

Ozone is found throughout the earth's atmosphere. It was formed about a billion years ago and, since it absorbs most of the sun's ultraviolet light, is essential to human life and health. Chlorofluorocarbons (CFCs), found in refrigerators and certain forms of packaging, accumulate in the stratosphere and are broken down by the sun's ultraviolet light. This releases chlorine atoms which attack the ozone layer. As a result, extra high levels of ultra-violet light are reaching the earth's surface. One of the ensuing threats is to phyto-plankton, the single-cell plants on which marine life depends, and this has worrying implications for the whole of the ocean food chain. Outcomes more widely discussed, however, are increasing levels of skin cancer, cataracts and infections through the skin. A set of nature-imposed mechanisms essential to human life, production and consumption has still not been thoroughly transformed. Like the conditions that generate El Niño, it has, however, been impinged on and made to work in different ways, and these have dangerous implications for humans and other animals. As regards humans, this may be one instance of Beck's 'democratization of risk' with some of the wealthier groups (such as those in Australasia) being most prone to skin cancers and other problems stemming from the depletion of the ozone layer.

Weather extremes: greenhouse risks

Similar arguments can be made as regards the greenhouse effect, though in this case the impacts are far less 'democratic'. Greenhouse gases have for several million years been reflecting part of the earth's heat back to the earth itself. Without this process, the planet would not have been warm enough to support life in the form we now know. The fear now is that particular kinds of human activity are exacerbating this exceptionally well-established process, making it work in new ways. Carbon dioxide (CO_2) emissions (which stem from the burning of oil, coal and other fossil fuels) combine with deforestation to generate what appear to be real threats to humanity and other species. The potential threats include a rise in the sea-level that will particularly affect coastal areas and river estuaries such as Bangladesh and the Nile Delta. Severe droughts, increased water shortages and more 'extreme' weather events such as intense hurricanes and cyclones seem to be quite likely outcomes. But all these processes are taking place in an 'open system', one that involves complex feedback processes. Half of the released CO_2, for example, is absorbed by the oceans. But, as the earth heats up, the oceans will be less efficient in absorbing CO_2, leaving more in the atmosphere and further adding to global warming. Similarly, it is believed that increases in temperature may be liberating large quantities of methane stored in the frozen tundra of the north. These in turn may cause further warming.

Understanding the key underlying natural causes of global warming, therefore, is only the start of unravelling the problem. Understandings are needed which probe the complex reactions between the still-intact mechanisms that cause global warming and other, more local, conditions, and the kinds of lifestyle which people in different localities are leading. Many of the critiques of science imply that it should be omniscient, when in fact social relations and practices are deeply implicated in science's supposed failures.

Cities and the metabolic rift

The notion of an ecological rift, one that violates the principles of ecological sustainability and has a particular impact on human life, has a particular significance for today's mega-cities (Davis 2002). Their great concentrations of people mean they pose some of the greatest challenges to ecological systems. Nowhere is this more true than in large industrial cities. Here the 'metabolic rift' (the overloading and exhausting of ecological systems) is often most apparent.

The metabolic needs of a city consist of the materials and commodities needed to sustain that city's inhabitants. They even include the construction materials needed to build and reconstruct the city. The metabolic cycle is only completed when the wastes and residues produced by the city have been removed and disposed of without creating health and other hazards. But in many instances this has proved very difficult to achieve. This does not, however, mean they are absolutely impossible. It means that no one has picked up the bill for dealing with these wastes. Their elimination has not appeared as part of the costs of their production, the prices at which they are sold or the level of profits enjoyed by shareholders.

Three metabolic problems have developed in the modern city. These are the provision of an adequate water supply, the effective disposal of sewage and the control of air pollution, problems not unknown before the present time (see box 2.12). This is another instance, therefore, of humanity's metabolism with nature not being

---

Box 2.12   Megacities and the metabolic rift

Cities, as great concentrations of producers and consumers, pose particular problems as regards the 'rift' between humanity and nature. One historical example of the metabolic rift is industrial Chicago in the mid-nineteenth century. There, the pollution of the water supply became a major problem: 'The stench that hung over the South Branch [of the Chicago River] and the filthy ice harvested from it were clear signs of its pollution. Decaying organic matter, whether in the form of packing wastes, manure or raw human sewage, was the chief water supply problem the city faced by mid-century' (Cronon 1991: 249). One 'solution' was to reverse the Chicago River. But this led to more problems. As one downstate resident wrote: 'Ever since the water from the Chicago River was let down into the Illinois River, the stench has been almost unendurable. What right has Chicago to pour its filth down into what was before a sweet and clean river, pollute its waters, and materially reduce the value of property on both sides of the river and canal, and bring sickness and death to the citizens?' (in ibid. 250).

New forms of environmental overload have been created in contemporary cities. Unburned hydrocarbons and carbon dioxide released from automobile exhausts leave Los Angeles, for example, shrouded in smog for up to 100 days per year. New York City has long had a problem in ensuring regular water supplies. Lake Erie has long been polluted along three miles of its industrialized shoreline, with the city of Cleveland having much to be responsible for. (For further discussion of the metabolic rift in the modern city, see Wolman 1965.)

Los Angeles shrouded in smog

Photo © Nik Wheeler / CORBIS

An example of the metabolic rift can be seen above. There are topographical and meteorological reasons why Los Angeles suffers from so much smog, but the prime cause is the hydrocarbons and carbon monoxide produced by car exhausts. Exhaust-control systems are one obvious way forward in an attempt to reverse the situation.

ultimately destroyed but being overloaded in the context of a particular kind of social and spatial organization. The important social and political implication is that in a different social and political context the metabolic rift could be healed. These new ways of understanding Marx's metabolic rift (one prefigured by Marx himself) demonstrate that the matter is a fundamentally social and political issue. It seems unlikely that the rift can be healed by the middle classes retreating to cultivate their gardens in the suburbs.

Science, practical knowledge and risk

Science has been relatively good at offering an understanding of the key, under-lying, causal mechanisms affecting environmental change. But it is less good at predicting the risks. This is because the mechanisms that affect processes such as global warming and the depletion of the ozone layer combine with other, often more localized, processes. Furthermore, they combine with different kinds of society and metabolism in complex ways. As a result, it is currently difficult for science to determine the precise ways in which people are being affected and changed. Environmental injustices are clearly linked to social and economic injustices, but science needs to be combined with knowledge of a more practical, everyday, local and 'non-scientific' kind. Such a combination would help establish how the generative mechanisms of nature are impacting on people and other species, while also keeping a check on whether these generative mechanisms are themselves properly understood.

Community: A New Basis for Industrial Production

Marx was highly critical of contemporary forms of politics and briefly proposed new forms. These criticisms have considerable significance today.

Communities of producer-consumers

The so-called 'freedom' to choose a government – one of the outcomes of the Enlightenment – actually amounted, Marx argued, to choosing between different fractions of the ruling class every five years. This did not constitute, in his view, human emancipation. It offered no serious possibility for workers to grasp substantial power to run their own lives or avoid the kinds of alienation from nature of which Marx wrote. This position was shared with Engels in *The Communist Manifesto*. Meanwhile, the rapid development of capitalist society, both these writers believed, was turning out to be ruinous, not only to the environment but also to the health of the workers.

To develop more meaningful forms of politics and to counter the way in which these might be debilitating to both humanity and the environment, workers must, Marx argued, 'associate among themselves . . . in the form of combinations'. 'The associational imperative' was a key feature of his understanding of the transition to communism. The combinations that workers found themselves in as a result of industrial labour and their living conditions took, Marx believed, largely defensive forms. 'Community', that is, remained the enforced community of the oppressed. It must be replaced under communism by new forms of combination which would go beyond the wage–labour relation and defend the principle of association as a key mechanism in creating new conditions for the development of human beings.

Furthermore, and most importantly, such associations would not be focused on industrial production alone. These new kinds of association would link community with industry. In a new kind of communist society:

> What he has given to it is his individual amount of labour. . . . The individual labour time of the individual producer is the part of the social labour day contributed by him, his share in it. He receives a certificate from society that he has furnished such and such an amount of labour (after deducting his labour for the common fund), and with this certificate he draws from the social stock of means of consumption as much as the same amount of labour costs. The same amount of labour which he has given to society in one form, he receives back in another. (Cited in Burkett 1999: 233)

There is a strong sense here of community as 'communion', with association being based on consumption of collectively made products. Here, in Marx's *Das Kapital*, is a vision of how a future association of producers might operate. It sounds remarkably like an account of some cooperatively-based systems of production today. The individual producer receives back from society – after the deductions have been made – exactly what he gives to it. Industry is combined with community via a system of loosely linked networks.

Marx intended that these new fusions between work and non-work life would allow narrowly conceived and industrialist visions of a future communism to be superseded. Popular and self-activated struggles in such areas of culture and domestic life join industrially based politics, with the common and unifying theme of reorganizing not just industrial relations but the whole range of social and environmental conditions surrounding production. It would be a form of association which avoids the market and overcomes the sense of alienation from the product and from people. Collective and communal ownership would be a way of overcoming the disruption between humanity and ownership, overcoming the 'metabolic rift' and recovering the connections between humanity and nature.

Associations of producer-consumers today: theory and practice

The idea of community-based associations of producer-consumers remains alive today. André Gorz, for example, is a 'green Marxist' who emphasizes the importance of social life outside of work as a form of emancipation. He turns Marx's arguments on their head. He agrees that work, at least for the great mass of people, is always going to be subject to control by capitalists and, as such, is almost bound to be unfulfilling. By contrast, leisure time is the arena of a future political freedom and autonomy, the zone of social life to be celebrated.

Gorz (1994) recognizes, however, that this is not a genuine zone of freedom if it is simply the setting in which people endlessly buy and consume commodities (see box 2.13). Ways need to be found, he believes, of making leisure independent of the market and more fulfilling to human beings. This includes small-scale, community-based enterprises in which new technologies and new kinds of labour process can be developed which are not harmful to the environment. So, although rejecting industry as the place where people find fulfilment, Gorz is implying associations of producer-consumers outside capitalist production. Despite his differences with Marx, he shares much of Marx's vision.

Meanwhile, there are actually now developing important new 'associations of producers' in the form of vast numbers of small-scale 'third sector' organizations such as self-build groups, organic food delivery groups, community banks and local exchange trading systems (LETS). The focus of the latter is still on the production of goods and services. But these are acquired not with conventional cash, but through local forms of 'currency' specifically designed for the people involved in the schemes (for more detail, see pp. 132–6). The environmental importance of LETS is that they start to overcome the 'metabolic rift' between humanity and nature that was outlined by Marx.

These locally created exchange systems (which are increasingly combined into regional, national and even international networks) also escape, at least in part,

---

Box 2.13   André Gorz: a contemporary 'green Marxist'

Gorz is a French 'Marxist' who has often drawn conclusions from Marx which do not endear him to other Marxists. Marx was right, he argues, to suggest that capitalism alienates people and is environmentally destructive. The solution is to focus on areas outside industry and production as sites of freedom and environmental sustainability and alternative forms of politics. Gorz argues for the development of voluntary cooperation and human freedom outside production, and for the development of new technologies and ways of working which:

- can be used and controlled at the level of the neighbourhood or community;
- are capable of generating increased economic autonomy for locally and regionally-based groups;
- are not harmful to the environment;
- are compatible with the exercise of joint control by producers and consumers over products and production processes.

Box 2.14   Foodsheds: linking localities, consumers and producers

'Foodsheds' are described by Jack Kloppenburg as 'self-reliant, locally or regionally based food systems comprised of diversified farms using sustainable practices to supply fresher, more nutritious food stuffs to small-scale processors and consumers to whom producers are linked by the bonds of community as well as economy' (1991: 56).

---

the dictates of the market and the social relations imposed by capitalist society. Kloppenburg (1991) coins the term 'foodshed' to capture the idea of a network of producers and consumers (see box 2.14). This is another way in which individuals, farmers and local food are combined in an attempt to recover a community of people and nature. The same can be said of other kinds of practical utopia, such as ecologically conscious self-build producer-consumers (see box 2.15). They too are attempting to heal the rift between societies and their environment and between individuals and members of their own species.

Such emergent social forms perhaps herald a new kind of society, which is developing within the capitalist system. They can arguably be seen, again using the Marxian metaphor, as seeds or kernels developing in the heart of society and perhaps representing new, more autonomous and environmentally sustainable ways of living in the future. These groups are small and hardly visible but, taken together, they represent important forms of resistance to developing trends. In particular, they can be seen as actively creating new kinds of producer and associations of producers in the context of the growing concentration and centralization of power which has developed since Marx's day. The revival of small, cooperatively based

The Hedgehog Self-Build Housing Cooperative has erected ten homes in Brighton, England (Sharp 2001). Organized as an unhierarchical association of producer-consumers, the group adopted an anti-market, pro-ecological set of values. Nevertheless, this entailed some compromises. Companies were, for example, approached for extra resources. Ten cordless power drills and overalls and protective clothing were acquired in this way. The firms supplying the equipment insisted on placing advertising for their products on the site. This was especially important as a television programme was shortly to be made on the project, providing good publicity. The Hedgehog Cooperative acceded to their demand. But, in a gesture of defiance, some members of the group erected a black flag with skull and crossbones on one of the houses (see illus. 2.15A), which countered a nearby flag advertising the clothing firm (see illus. 2.15B). The company's money had been accepted but, it was felt, the Hedgehog Cooperative's values had remained intact.

Illustration 2.15A   Resistance from the Hedgehog Cooperative

Illustration 2.15B   The clothing firm's flag

Photos taken by Graham Sharp

food production, for example, is specifically aimed at local, rather than global, markets. These developments are the first signs of a new, less alienated relation with external nature, one that is emerging from the seeds of an older type of society. Their multiplication, however, cannot be relied on to produce a more socially just and environmentally sustainable society. More profound and general social transformations are still needed, such as the placing of industry in collective hands. These issues will be further discussed in chapter 8.

Summary

This chapter has focused on the ways in which societies engage in an exchange with nature, extracting resources and using these resources in work processes. It began by addressing anthropological work which focused on small-scale pre-industrial societies. We then turned to Marx and Engels, who emphasized the importance of *production* processes in the formation of people's relations with one another and with their environment under industrial capitalism. The effect, Marx argued, was to alienate people from their environment. We have also addressed some criticisms and developments of Marx's approach. Modifications to this approach are important, particularly as regards understanding forms of work in the home and community. Marx and Engels's perspective is nevertheless a good illustration of the perspective being developed in this book: in using the powers of external nature, people also transform the nature of their own, internal being.

FURTHER READING

Historical materialism

Key texts written from an historical materialist perspective include:
  R. Eckersley, *Environmentalism and Political Theory. Toward an Ecocentric Approach.* London: UCL Press, 1992.
  J. Foster, 'Marx's Theory of Metabolic Rift: Classical Foundations for Environmental Sociology', *American Journal of Sociology* (Sept 1999): 366–405.
  D. Harvey, *Justice, Nature and the Geography of Difference.* Oxford: Blackwell, 1996.
  D. Pepper, *Eco-Socialism. From Deep Ecology to Social Justice.* London: Routledge, 1993.

Two early and influential texts were:
  M. Redclift, *Development and the Environmental Crisis. Red or Green Alternatives.* London: Routledge, 1984.
  M. Redclift, *Sustainable Development. Exploring the Contradictions.* London: Routledge, 1987.

Students interested in ongoing debates should read the journal *Capitalism, Nature, Socialism.* It was in this journal that the 'second contradiction' argument was first laid out and debated. See, in particular:
  J. O'Connor, 'On the Two Contradictions of Capitalism', *Capitalism, Nature, Socialism,* 2/3 (1991): 107–9.

More recently, this journal has started critically to assess the relationships between 'actually existing' socialism(s) and environmental degradation. See, for example, the collection of papers in the September 2002 issue. J. Foster's *Marx's Ecology. Materialism and Nature* (New York: Monthly Review Press) is critically assessed in a 'symposium' in *Capitalism, Nature, Socialism*, 12/2 (2001): 46. It is argued, for example, that the theory of the metabolic rift needs considerable development to take account of advances in the ecological sciences since Marx's day. Students wanting a very readable account of this position by an activist (who has run for President of the United States) may wish to read:

J. Kovel, *The Enemy of Nature. The End of Capitalism or the End of the World?* London: Zed Books, 2002.

Other useful texts written from this perspective include:

P. Dickens, *Reconstructing Nature. Alienation, Emancipation and the Division of Labour*. London: Routledge, 1996.

P. Dickens, *Society and Nature. Towards a Green Social Theory*. Hemel Hempstead: Harvester, 1986.

J. Foster and P. Burkett, 'The Dialectic of Organic/Inorganic Relations', *Organization and Environment*, 13/4 (2000): 403–25.

R. Grundmann, 'The Ecological Challenge to Marxism', *New Left Review*, 187 (1991).

T. Hayward, *Ecological Thought. An Introduction*. Cambridge: Polity, 1994.

One response to the 'second contradiction' would be the commodification of outer space – converting, for example, solar power into electricity. This, plus using lunar and asteroid materials to power satellites, is canvassed in:

J. Lewis, *Mining the Sky, Untold Riches from the Asteroids, Comets and Planets*. Reading, MA: Addison-Wesley, 1997.

Research in this area is being conducted by James Ormrod, Dept of Sociology, University of Essex, UK.

Marxists who argue that Marxism needs to be fundamentally transformed to deal with contemporary ecological issues include:

R. Bahro, *Avoiding Social and Ecological Disaster: the Politics of World Transformation*. Bath: Gateway, 1994.

Links between internal and external nature using a broadly historical materialist approach are developed in:

P. Dickens, *Social Darwinism. Linking Evolutionary Thought to Social Theory*. Buckingham: Open University Press, 2000.

Also relevant here are lively debates within biology as the relations between organisms and environment. Those who promote a focus on the organism (rather than on the genes) and the role of organisms in actually making their environment tend to be sympathetic to Marx and Engels's position. See, for example:

R. Lewontin, 'Organism and Environment', in H. Plotkin (ed.), *Learning, Development and Culture*. Chichester: Wiley, 1982.

There is, of course, no real substitute for reading Marx and Engels themselves. Particularly inspirational are Marx's writings as a young man, especially:

K. Marx, 'Economic and Philosophical Manuscripts', in L. Colletti (ed.), *Karl Marx. Early Writings*. Harmondsworth: Penguin, 1975.

See also:

H. Parsons, *Marx and Engels on Ecology*. Westport, CT: Greenwood Press, 1977.

Students wishing to follow up the idea of the transformation of humanity and labour should turn to Hegel, who exercised much influence over Marx's early thinking. Hegel believed that in labouring on nature humans develop new needs and desires. And in making new divisions of labour, they realize fresh human potential and different forms of social interaction. See Appendix and:

F. Hegel, *The Philosophy of Right*. Oxford: Clarendon Press, 1945.

R. Plant, 'Hegel and Political Economy: 1', *New Left Review*, 103 (1977): 79–92.

Such a view has some similarities with the considerably later work of André Gorz:

A. Gorz, *Farewell to the Working Class. An Essay on Post-Industrial Socialism*. London: Pluto, 1982.

A. Gorz, *Paths to Paradise: on the Liberation from Work*. London: Pluto, 1985.

Society's metabolism with nature

M. Fischer-Kowalski, 'Society's Metabolism. The Intellectual History of Materials Flow Analysis. Part 1: 1860–1970', *Journal of Industrial Ecology*, 2/1 (1998): 61–78.

M. Fischer-Kowalski and W. Huttler, 'Society's Metabolism. The Intellectual History of Materials Flow Analysis. Part II: 1970–1998', *Journal of Industrial Ecology*, 2/4 (1998): 107–36.

H. Schandl and N. Schulz, 'Changes in the United Kingdom's Natural Relations in Terms of Society's Metabolism and Land-use from 1850 to the Present Day', *Ecological Economics*, 41 (2002): 203–21.

H. Schandl and N. Schulz, 'Industrial Ecology: The UK', in E. Ayres and W. Ayres, *A Handbook of Industrial Ecology*. Cheltenham: Elgar Press, 2002.

An excellent text which argues that the relations between humanity and nature have been a regular, if suppressed, theme in the social sciences is:

J. Martinez-Allier, *Ecological Economics. Energy, Environment and Society*. Oxford: Blackwell, 1987.

Students interested in the impact of imperialism on external nature should turn to:

A. Crosby, *Ecological Imperialism. The Biological Expansion of Europe, 900–1900* (2nd edn), Cambridge: Cambridge University Press, 1993 (1st edn 1986).

Constructions of 'nature'

On 'constructions' and 'construals' of nature, see in particular:

P. MacNaghten and J. Urry, *Contested Natures*. London: Sage, 1998.

Like C. Merchant (*The Death of Nature*. New York: Harper and Row, 1990), they argue that there is no one single understanding of 'nature'. Most obviously it is the 'countryside'. But it can also be construed as a landscape handed down through many generations or, most recently, as ecosystems and resources that need to be treated in a sustainable way.

The intrinsic value of nature

'Intrinsic value' has a number of interpretations. These include (1) the idea that an object cannot be used towards some other end, (2) the idea that 'intrinsic' refers to an object's inherent properties and (3) the idea that an object has a value independent of the valuations made by valuers. These, and other, interpretations are discussed in:

J. O'Neill, 'The Varieties of Intrinsic Value', *The Monist*, 75/2 (1992): 119–37. (*This issue of* The Monist *contains a number of other papers concerning intrinsic value.*)

Debates surrounding the labour process

D. Spencer, 'Braverman and the Contribution of Labour Process Analysis to the Critique of Capitalist Production: Twenty-Five Years On', *Work, Employment and Society*, 14/2 (2000): 223–43.

P. Thompson, *The Nature of Work: An Introduction to Debates on the Labour Process*. London: Macmillan, 1983.

The journal *Work, Employment and Society* is always useful in this area and on debates surrounding the labour process.

Ecological modernization

A. Mol and D. Sonnenfeld (eds), *Ecological Modernisation Around the World. Perspectives and Critical Debates.* London: Cass, 2000.

M. Andersen and I. Massa (eds), Special Issue on Ecological Modernization. *Journal of Environmental Policy and Planning*, 2/4 (2000).

Contemporary accounts of functionalism and its relation to environmental sociology

E. Papadakis, 'Social Theory and the Environment: A Systems-Theoretical Perspective', in R. Dunlap, F. Buttel, P. Dickens and A. Gijswijt (eds), *Sociological Theory and the Environment. Classical Foundations, Contemporary Insights.* Boulder: Rowman and Littlefield, 2002.

Local exchange trading systems (LETS)

D. Boyle, *Funny Money. In Search of Alternative Cash.* London: HarperCollins, 1999.

B. Bowring, 'LETS: An Eco-Socialist Initiative?' *New Left Review*, 232 (1998): 91–111.

T. Fitzpatrick and C. Caldwell, 'Towards a Theory of Ecosocial Welfare: Radical Reformism and Local Exchanges and Trading Systems (LETS)', *Environmental Politics*, 10/2 (2001).

J. Ford and K. Rowlingson, 'Low-Income Households and Credit: Exclusion, Preference and Inclusion', *Environment and Planning A*, 28 (1996): 1345–60.

R. Lee, 'Moral Money? LETS and the Social Construction of Local Economic Geographies in Southeast England', *Environment and Planning A*, 28 (1996): 1377–94.

D. Purdue, J. Durrschmidt, P. Jowers and R. O'Doherty, 'DIY Culture and Extended Milieux: LETS, Veggie Boxes and Festivals', *The Sociological Review*, 45/4 (1997): 645–67.

A useful website on El Niño (in the context of global warming in Oceania) is: <http://www.climatehotmap.org/oceania/html>

3

Commodifying the Environment

Overview

The selling of nature has become a popular rallying cry. Indeed, it has become a dominant theme in contemporary politics. Those with faith in the role of markets in bringing social and environmental benefits fully endorse the commodification of nature in its many forms. This is progress. Nature needs to be privately owned and made into a commodity for its potential to be realized and for the common good to be served. Those without such faith see the division of nature (in the form of, for example, plots of land and separated seeds and genes) as another example of the way in which humanity attempts to treat nature as a mere object for its own use. Furthermore, the process of commodification separates humanity from the natural world, alienating it from the very thing upon which it depends for survival. Enemies of commodification also see nature as bringing considerable profits to a few people while at the same time generating a wide range of risks. This chapter addresses some of these issues. It does so by looking at them in the light of the four sub-themes of this book: industry, community, evolution and risk. Knowledge – its acquisition and its use – emerges as a key theme.

Commodification and Industry

All societies must produce and consume the resources offered by the natural world. If they did not do so, they would become rapidly extinct. Societies of all kinds must use the powers of nature to their own ends, converting the raw materials of nature into the energy that people need in order to survive and reproduce. Such is the everlasting requirement of all societies. But how is this achieved in our own society?

Commodification and privatization

Our social system is organized around the production of the things needed for its own reproduction. But, more particularly, a production process is created by investing in the people and machines that make the necessary commodities.

Our society is based on private ownership and the production and exchange of commodities. Privatization and commodification are not the same thing, although they are often linked. Privatization means a change of ownership: it always involves commodification but the reverse is not the case. For example, the introduction of user charges for access to government land and services amounts to commodification. But it is clearly not privatization. Privatization therefore entails a transfer of property rights, while commodification refers to a change in the nature of the contract or transaction.

Commodities are things that provide for some human need or want. They have, in other words, a 'use value'. A piece of land may be used for enjoyment of the landscape or for skateboarding. Commodities also have an 'exchange value' built into them, a result of the amount and type of work which has gone into making them. 'Commodification' entails the extension of the 'commodity form', or exchange value, to a new sphere such as land and facilities previously owned in common or by government. Note that labour power (the capacity to work) can also be commodified. This has been one of the defining features of capitalist development. It does not, however, mean that labour is privately owned. Indeed, the development of capitalism created the 'free' labourer, someone not beholden to a master as was a slave or serf. On the other hand, the commodification of both labour and land means that people are left primarily with their own labour to sell.

The processes of privatization and commodification have fundamentally changed the connection between people and the land and other means of production they need to sustain themselves. They must now earn sufficient wages to buy the food, clothes and so on which they need to survive. These goods have been privatized and commodified and must be paid for rather than simply used. The overall value of commodities becomes visible through the medium of money – cash, that is, which has paid for the goods in the market.

Privatization and commodification have resulted in subtle shifts in humanity's relations with nature. Nature is now something to be invested in and consumed. Modern industrial societies have brought many gains, including much-improved material well-being for many people. But a major downside to this progress is that people have lost an understanding of their relationship with the natural world, one based on direct engagement. Cash and commodities are prized so much as things in themselves that people in modern society have lost an understanding of the ecosystems of which they are a part. They have also lost an understanding of the complex social relations involved in bringing them into our homes. In pre-industrial societies, and in parts of many developing countries, a more thorough understanding of the relations between society and nature remains intact. It is based on working on the land. In short, to use Marx's word, people have been 'alienated' from nature in modern, capitalist society.

Commodification and private ownership continues

Given that commodities and private ownership are central to the way in which contemporary society is organized, it comes as no surprise to find both commodification and privatization of the environment as dominant processes. These two processes combine therefore to entail the conversion of common property into 'things' produced and created during a labour process. They are eventually sold via the exchange of money for the items people want. These processes are still extending to areas of the world which have not yet seen major human intervention in the form of private ownership (see box 3.1). But they are also extending to features of internal and external nature with which we are becoming familiar. These include rice, for example. And, as box 3.2 indicates, the genetic structure of rice

---

Box 3.1 Commodification at work: the Arctic National Wildlife Refuge

The debate over the Arctic Wildlife Refuge is reminiscent of the old debates between the Enlightenment rationalizers and the Romanticists (see Introduction). On the one hand, industrialists are claiming that, with the aid of private ownership and new technologies, significant economic benefits will accrue to society at large. On the other hand, those protecting the Refuge emphasize its wild, untainted and sublime nature. These qualities, they argue, are worth retaining and valuing for their own sake. (See also box 3.8.)

OIL INTERESTS EYE CRUDE IN ARCTIC REFUGE

Conservationists believe that setting value on the Arctic National Wildlife Refuge in Alaska is inconceivable. This week, however, a government group put a price tag on the pristine wildland. The Energy Information Administration, an arm of the US Department of Energy, released a report Monday that details different production scenarios for extracting oil from the coastline of the refuge, which is believed to hold the largest supply of untapped oil reserves in the United States.

The EIA team estimates that the refuge could generate 1 million to 1.4 million barrels of oil per day during peak production. According to the analysis, oil sucked from the rocks below the refuge could inject anywhere from $125 billion to $350 billion into the US economy over a 60-year period.

'We developed scenarios based on US Geological Survey estimates of the amount of technically recoverable undiscovered oil in the refuge, which should give some indication of what the production could be over the next 50 to 60 years', said Floyd Wiesepape of the EIA.

EIA, an independent, non-partisan agency within the DPE that performs statistical analyses, conducted its research at the bidding of Senator Frank Murkowski (R-Alaska), chairman of the Senate Committee on Energy and Natural Resources.

Murkowski, who is in favor of drilling for crude in the refuge, liked what he read. (Environmental News Network. <http://www.enn/news/enn-stories> 26 May 2000)

Box 3.2 Commodification at work: plant biotechnology

The sequencing and eventual privatization and commodification of genes for food is seen by its proponents as having the potential for solving mass hunger. For those opposed to these developments, the genetic modification of plants (and animals) with the transfer of genes from one species to another poses a large number of risks.

RICE GENOME WORK CREATES HOPE

According to columnist Smith from CNEWS Science, the sequencing of the rice genome – which may turn out to be even more important than the sequencing of the human genome in some ways – has passed almost unnoticed. Smith says that because of genetic similarities, discoveries made using the rice genome will translate with ease to wheat, barley, sorghum, millet and a host of others. We might, in fact, begin to speak of a cereal grain genome. In the short term, though, it's rice that's important, because rice feeds an inordinate number of us. Since 1965, in fact, the world's rice production has been growing at 2.5 per cent a year – enough to keep pace with humanity's hungry bellies.

That miracle, says Smith, has been wrought using standard breeding techniques to produce high-yield varieties. But standard breeding is your classical black box – you cross some plants, observe their characteristics and then cross some more, hoping to come up with an improvement. You don't know what's going on inside the plant. In the short term, says Steve Briggs, knowing the rice genome will let standard breeders peep inside the black box and guide their efforts more efficiently.

Briggs is head of the Torrey Mesa Research Institute in La Jolla, California, which, for the record, sequenced the rice genome. Also for the record, the Torrey Mesa Research Institute is the genomic research centre for a company called Syngenta, which was formed last November when Novartis Agribusiness and Zeneca Agrochemicals merged.

So – Smith says he can hear this now – one more big international biotech company has a proprietorial interest in something of vital interest to small farmers in Asia. But Syngenta has learned a lesson or two from the past few years. The rice genome will be available without fees or royalty payments to research centres in the Third World. It will also be available free to academic scientists. That should mute any protests of the 'big bad multinational' variety.

Now, rice breeders in the Third World will have a powerful new tool at their disposal. For the first time, Briggs said, they'll know 'at the DNA level' what's going on when they make a cross. And, with any luck, they may be able to come up with varieties that will continue to fill those billions of stomachs. (Excerpted from Biotech Knowledge Center Web Site. <http://www.biotechknowledge.com> (sponsored by Monsanto Company) 19 February 2001)

---

has been sequenced, with the same happening to many other types of food being a real possibility. Industry sees such scientific discoveries, once harnessed in private ownership and incorporated into an industrial production process, as the solution to world hunger.

Commodification, then, is proceeding rapidly. The process has been paralleled by a steady industrialization of the farming process, one which first of all took agricultural processes as they stood and improved them, and which has more recently moved on to substitute the farming process with a large-scale *agricultural industry*.

Commodification and 'the tragedy of the commons': competing interpretations

There are many who actively support the parcelling-up and privatization of land and other resources held in common. They believe this to be the best way of ensuring economic progress and environmental sustainability. This is one interpretation of Garrett Hardin's famous thesis of 'the tragedy of the commons' (see box 3.3). There are competing interpretations of Hardin's thesis. It is an argument which can be aligned with, and used to justify, different types of politics. One interpretation is that extended private ownership is the answer to environmental degradation. However, this picture is based on an image of society and economy which perhaps existed in eighteenth-century Britain. It takes no account of the concentration and power of agricultural interests in today's society and their hold over landed interests and farmers.

Box 3.3   The tragedy of the commons

It is rational, Garrett Hardin (1968) argued, for each of us to maximize our own gain through the use of land and other natural resources. But, he argued, major problems start with massive population growth and the unrestricted use of land, air and sea for food, production of waste and so forth. Under such conditions a crisis of survival will soon be upon everybody, as individuals rationally maximizing their own gain bring dire results for everyone. Individual freedoms therefore need constraining, decisions need making which restrict the rights and freedoms of people to use resources. 'I believe it was Hegel', wrote Hardin, 'who said "Freedom is the recognition of necessity".' The solution, often an unpalatable one, was 'mutual coercion, mutually agreed upon by the majority of the people affected'.

However, there have been a number of competing reactions to Hardin's argument. There are four basic positions here (see Eckersley 1992 for details and further references and Saunders 1995):

1   The problem Hardin is really referring to is the absence of clearly defined property rights. If the commons are broken up (as occurred with the enclosures) and private property was the norm, this would resolve the problem. 'Green consumerism', charging for access to common resources or, most radically, privatizing or commodifying public goods, would be the best approach to preventing the 'tragedy of the commons'. This is the 'minimum state' solution.
2   Only a full-blown, centrally planned and autocratic authority can arrest the crisis of survival which Hardin described. This might be considered undesirable, not least because it leaves open the possibility of a malign dictatorship, which would be socially disastrous. But it might have to be an at least temporary solution in the wider interest of long-term human survival. This is the 'maximum state' solution.
3   Neither Hardin's position nor the two arguments above sufficiently recognize social divisions. 'Spaceship Earth' is composed of captains and crew and some are in a better position to make sacrifices than others. Neither the 'minimum state'

solution (maintaining property rights and social order) nor the 'maximum state' solution (maintaining a strong, directive, government authority) recognizes the potential of small, locally organized political institutions.

4   Hardin and his critics are all arguing within narrow limits. They are all premised on the notion that the environment comprises, simply, 'resources' to enable human beings to survive and that human nature is essentially self-seeking. More generally, it is an evolutionary picture which is too close to nineteenth-century (mis)interpretations of Darwin. The idea of people struggling for limited resources and of the 'best' people surviving from this struggle and reproducing is no longer intellectually or politically acceptable.

Changes to Farming

Self-contained farmers of the past

Before the development of today's agricultural industry, farmers largely retained all they needed to keep the farm going from one year to the next. They grew the crops for their own livestock. Dung was recycled as the main input to fertilizers. Ploughs and other pieces of equipment were frequently bought from the local blacksmith. An example of such an early farm was documented in the early 1930s by a group of economists (see box 3.4). Note in particular the extent to which the farm was relatively self-contained and the farmer had a good deal of autonomy as to how it should be run. None of this should be understood as a 'golden age' of farming. Farm incomes were remarkably low and life was undoubtedly hard for many of those working on such farms. The position of women and children, often obliged to work on the farm, would not be acceptable today. Nevertheless, this is a good base-point from which to compare the industrialized food system today.

Box 3.4   Hooten Pagnell Farm, Yorkshire

A study of a dozen farms in Hooten Pagnell in the early 1930s brought out the following characteristics.

1   A system of land husbandry existed which still followed organic cycles and the limitations imposed by seasons and physical distance.
2   Links between the farm and the outside market were relatively weak. Links with industrial suppliers and processors were poorly developed.
3   Tenancy dominated over ownership. This restricted the possibilities for modernization through capital investment.
4   The labour process was based on the family.
5   There were few contacts with government as regards the regulation of markets for farmed products.

One of the most notable features documented in this study was a much-prized 'freedom to farm'. Part of this freedom was a result of farming being a relatively diversified activity. Farms were less specialized than they are now, with farmers growing crops to feed the cattle as well as raising the cattle themselves. This was the era before the introduction of highly intensified farming based on each farm being highly specialized. The authors of the report (Ruston and Witney) wrote of the 'freedom to farm' in the following terms:

> If there is one thing which differentiates the modern farmer from his forerunners, it is his freedom – freedom to crop the grounds as he wills, freedom to market his produce when, where and as he wills, freedom to devote his time and money and energies to furthering his own interests as he thinks fit, although signs are not wanting that this 'freedom' may not last forever. (Cited in Goodman and Redclift 1991)

Box 3.5   The trivialization of agriculture: an early example

In the late nineteenth century the process of industrializing food was already well established, particularly in the USA. Previously 'rural' products such as flour became mere inputs into a centralized, large-scale, manufacturing process. This is a process which has rapidly escalated over the past century.

> Marketed in standardised blends from large mills situated mainly at the ports, this new flour suited the needs of large bake-houses, which employed kneading and other processing machines and the steam-heated ovens that began to appear after 1850. The use of machinery to produce standard quantities and qualities of flour and other ingredients was even more important to the biscuit-maker – of whose services to the housewife even Mrs Beeton approved – for his reputation depended upon maintaining an absolutely uniform product. (Derry and Williams 1973; cited in Goodman et al. 1987)

The development of an agricultural industry

Over time, the picture for farmers has become one in which the 'freedom to farm' has been greatly reduced (Goodman et al. 1987; Goodman and Redclift 1991). To an increasing extent, and for a long period, competing companies have appropriated processes which previously took place on farmland. Fertilizers, specially bred seeds, are now, along with machinery, generally made in factories and sold to farmers. Chickens and other 'farm' animals are produced and reared in circumstances resembling factories. Other goods that might in the past have been produced in homes or in scattered small-scale premises are made in increasingly centralized or concentrated factories (see box 3.5).

However, farmers now have decreasing control over, and understanding of, the whole process of which they are part. Farming, in the form of land-management, is now largely divorced from the pre-industrial society presented by both Hardin and by those presenting privatization as the solution to environmental degradation. Seed companies, for example, make new seeds in enterprises which combine plant breeders, laboratory technicians, warehouse workers and so on. Control, as with the production of food for farm animals, has moved to large, concentrated and centralized corporations, with farmers becoming little more than piecework labourers, producing predetermined numbers of goods, at predetermined weights, to organizations over which they have no influence and using cattle-feed which is also produced by outside interests. Farmers are increasingly obliged to buy seeds annually and responsibility for developing new strands has passed from them to large, corporate concerns such as Monsanto. Seeds, like genes, are now mostly patented and commodified. All this is a long way from the pre-industrial vision to which Hardin seems to be alluding.

For thousands of years seeds have been, as the first link in the food chain, a key symbol of food security. And free exchange of seed amongst farmers has been the basis of food security and the maintenance of biodiversity. Now that these most basic forms of external nature have been commodified, influence and control have shifted to major corporate concerns. Farmers are mere adjuncts to production processes that are run elsewhere. These are some of the procedures underlying the critique of commodification. Ecological systems are undermined, animals are treated as machines and people's own skills and capacities are ignored or badly developed.

The growth of an 'agri-industrial complex'

The problem with arguments in favour of increased commodification is that they systematically neglect questions of economic, social and political power. Society is no longer made up of individuals selfishly seeking their personal good. It is doubtful whether any society was constituted in this way. What we term 'the market' is to a large degree dominated by powerful producer interests. These interests organize, and constantly reorganize, the labour processes and social relations involved in the production of commodities, and are highly influential for the rest of society. In the agricultural industry, therefore, commodification is not simply a question of dividing up and privatizing land and other forms of collective resource. It necessarily brings with it a range of profound *industrial* changes. Such changes are particularly significant for agriculture, entailing nothing less than the radical transformation of older, 'traditional' ways of doing things. They also involve a number of important transformations in the links between agriculture and industry.

Biotechnology and the trivialization of farming

The overall effect of the commodification of agriculture is that farming becomes trivialized and that farming processes and localized forms of production are incorporated within an organized capitalist industry. Food production is thereby slowly replaced by an 'agri-industrial complex'. The tendency is to mass-produce standardized products such as a few kinds of patented 'super-seeds', made by seed companies using another labour process that involves plant-breeders, laboratory technicians, warehouse facilities and so on. In modern industrialized agriculture the commodity seed is then sold to the farmer and becomes part of her or his means of production.

The regulation of animal biology is similarly likely to result in the standardization of animals which can grow faster, produce greater yield and apparently withstand environmental stresses. Industrial organizations compete with one another to own and control the biological science necessary to substitute food created by conventional farming with food of all kinds made by what has been termed 'the life industry' (Yoxen 1983). As Goodman et al. put it:

> The ultimate prize is domination and proprietary ownership of the scientific knowledge and process engineering technology required to control the complex biological reactions and microbial activities involved in food manufacture. These technical changes and their repercussions on industrial structures and agro-food chains are aptly described as bio-industrialization. (1987: 138)

Along with the *appropriation* of processes which used to take place on farms and land is the increasing *substitution* of farm-based products (ibid.; Goodman and Redclift 1991). What is produced on farms becomes at this stage just one input amongst many to the production of food. It must compete with, for example, other chemical inputs which have had nothing whatsoever to do with conventional 'farming'.

The development of biotechnology has strengthened this substitution process and dramatically hastened the long-term trend towards erasing distinctions between agriculture and industry. It has hastened the development of fabricated foods, often with very standardized basic components such as soya beans. (This industrialization and homogenization is, of course, in great contrast to the *apparent* great variety of food products seen on supermarket shelves and the apparent contemporary interest in real cooking via televized 'celebrity chefs'.) Biochemistry has greatly improved processes of industrial fermentation and this has direct implications for many of the traditional industries such as baking, brewing, winemaking and food preservation. The effect of this is further industrialization. And this further trivializes agriculture in the form of field crops associated with particular types of food.

Yet, for all these developments, the problems of food poverty remain dominant. Massive gains in production and productivity have taken place yet they have only brought small reductions in the incidence of hunger (Pretty 2002). The problem is that people in the better-off societies (and, as we will see in the next chapter, some people more than others) tend to eat greater amounts of the available food. This especially applies to meat. The increased productivity resulting from industrial transformation is going into the production of greater amounts of food, and especially into the production of livestock feed. Annual food demand in industrialized societies is 550 kilograms of cereal and 78 kilograms of meat per person. But in developing societies it is just 260 kilograms of cereal and 30 kilograms of meat per person. In short, the massive gains have not solved the problems of world hunger (Pretty 2002). Indeed, they have increased the disparities between rich and poor.

Arising from all this is the need for social scientists of all kinds to get behind some of the rhetoric and politics surrounding commodification and to start exploring how this process fits into industries and industrial complexes seeking profitable markets. Placing land and genetic structures in private hands is important, but it is just part of a wider process of production and consumption. Food, oil and so on are not just things that are bought in markets. They are also made by powerful agro-industrial combines. Furthermore, this act of production entails the making, and constant remaking, of relations between people.

Commodification and Community

The implications of commodification for community life are already becoming clear from the above discussion. Industrial change is having very substantial, even devastating, implications for farms and for the people associated with agriculture. Farmers are being dispossessed of the knowledge and control over their lives which they once had. Here is another instance of people being separated, or alienated, from the land on which they work and depend. This is not just a question of people having decreasing control over the use of land but also the fact that they have decreasing *understanding* of their relations with the environment. New kinds of genetically altered crop still depend on herbicides, but these too are often provided by a parent chemical company such as Monsanto. Such increasing concentration of economic power runs alongside the popular constructions and mythologies of community and farm life which are still based on field-type agriculture which many of us still hold dear.

Community as an idyll

In *The Country and the City*, a path-breaking study of English literature, Raymond Williams makes it is clear that there are many myths and interpretations surrounding the notion of 'community' (1973). Nobody would wish to deny the devastating impacts on people as societies have been transformed from pre-industrial and rural ways of life to industrial and urban ways of living. Similarly, no one would wish to deny the impacts of industrial change on people living in farms and rural areas today. Many of these are being violently experienced in so-called third world societies. Here, the 'second agricultural revolution' has paralleled developments in Western agriculture. Changed labour processes, replacement of biological with chemical pest control, creation of monocultures and creation of enclosed rearing of stock-animals have had far-reaching and often grievous implications for local social relations and links to ecological conditions.

The difficulty is, however, that many people (including many early sociologists such as Durkheim and Tönnies) refer to 'the decline of community' when they are really referring to forms of separation (from land, animals and other people) resulting from new kinds of industrialization and the developments of new kinds of labour process. 'Community' becomes a shorthand, a relatively straightforward way of responding to massive economic change and new types of social relation, often with reference to a mythical golden era, an 'organic' or 'natural' society. The rise of industrialization and the decline of community are therefore made to look like a fall from grace, a decline into misery equivalent to the dispelling of Adam and Eve from the Garden of Eden. Community as an idyll remains a long-standing and powerful myth.

Community can also, however, be 'the mutuality of the oppressed', a defensive gathering-together under a perceived threat. Again, there can be strong mythical elements to this kind of community. They perhaps hark back to a time when, like the 'free' farmers in 1930s Yorkshire, people retained a good deal of control over and understanding of their circumstances. Unfortunately, appeal to a lost 'community', and attempts to recover this loss, may do little justice to the concentrations of economic and political power which are the sources of the problem. We should also note that many hardships and lack of freedoms in 'the good old days' tend to be forgotten.

Commodification, community and the 'second contradiction'

The development of the modern economy and society could be written around the commodification of common property. The process began as early as the 1500s with the enactment in Tudor England of the famous 'enclosure acts'. This was the beginning of the end for the feudal era, as land previously held in common was transformed into a set of small units and turned into private estates. 'Enclosure' therefore entailed surrounding a piece of land with hedges, ditches and so on, the idea being to stop the passage of humans and animals between areas of 'real estate'. Government-appointed commissioners arrived in English villages, dividing up the commons into units, assigning them to distinct owners and attaching monetary value to them.

Up until this time much of social and economic life had been focused on village commons. These were owned by feudal landlords but were leased to peasant farmers. The latter had to commit themselves either to working on some of the landlord's own fields or to turning over some of their produce to the landlord. As the money economy developed in the late medieval period, peasants were obliged to pay rents to the landlords in return for the rights they had acquired to farm the land.

These arrangements were far from idyllic. On the one hand the feudal period was communitarian in the sense that agriculture was collectively organized and village life revolved around shared experience and some degree of collectively owned land. But, on the other hand, the peasant farmers often lived unpredictable and harsh lives, while the landlords, the monarch and the church authorities kept an often oppressive control over them. Yet, as the enclosure movement gathered pace from the 1500s into the early 1800s, a fundamental transformation did take place in relations between people and nature (see box 3.6). People became commodities, selling their labour to the new landowners. A whole set of customs, traditions and obligations, which had been passed down many generations over several hundreds of years, were no longer appropriate to the arrival of a new form of property-

Box 3.6 Commodification, community and the 'second contradiction': a Fenland case-study

The commodification of land via enclosure has been taking place at least since the medieval period. It is also closely linked to the 'second contradiction', whereby capitalism tends to systematically undermine the natural conditions necessary for its own reproduction. A short-term, rapacious outlook can be disastrous for capital itself, while generating appeals to lost 'community'.

Examples are legion. One comes from an area near where I live, 'The Fens', an area of land which people have attempted to drain and make productive at least since the Middle Ages. From the early seventeenth century onwards many hundred thousand marshes were recovered. But this was not only enclosure. It was the making of land which could be actively used for agriculture. The Fenland was to see the most spectacular transformation of land in the country and spectacular opposition to this process.

This was a very early form of enclosure and commodification. In 1607 the King induced thirteen 'adventurers' to pay for the drainage of this common land. It was agreed they would receive two-thirds of the reclaimed land in payment for undertaking these works. Cornelius Vermuyden, a Dutch engineer with an established reputation, was hired to plan and execute the drainage, making the land suitable for intensive agriculture. The excess of water in The Fens had two causes: rivers draining into the area continually overflowed their banks after heavy rains; second, the land is so low and flat that the rain cannot drain away. So the priority for Vermuyden was to build the river banks higher. In this way, they would be of sufficient height to keep the water in check even at flood times. Next, he cut drains throughout the Fenland to collect the rainfall from the fields and send it into the larger channels, which in turn carry all the water out to sea. Much of the Fenland so exposed consisted, and to some degree still consists, of peat. This could be up to 6 metres thick, being the relics of ancient forests, and was excellent both for agricultural purposes and for providing fuel.

Note the way in which The Fens were socially constructed as part of this draining. The Anti-Projector, a contemporary anti-draining and pro-Fenman tract, pointed out that 'the undertakers have always vilified the Fens, and have misinformed many Parliament men, that all the Fens is a mere quagmire and that it is a level hurtfully surrounded, and of little or no value: but those which live in the Fens, and are neighbours to it, know the contrary'. Note that the people of the Fens were also construed as in a state of unimproved nature. A contemporary pro-draining pamphlet wrote that 'the generality of the fen people are very poor, lazy, given much to finishing and idleness, who were very much against the draining because they feared their condition should be worse, which truly was almost impossible' (Lindley 1982: 3). Another contemporary account described them as 'a rude and almost barbarous sort of lazy and beggarly people'. These people, like the land they occupied, had still not been civilized.

However, the drainage operation set in train another long, and ultimately destructive, process. First it encountered major opposition from a large number of local people, who formed what Williams (1973) calls 'the community of the oppressed'. And this greatly held up the works. In 1650 Sir John Maynard articulated the feelings of those who were resisting the drainage, arguing for retaining the Fens as a relatively closed ecosystem. It was not the swamp which the pro-drainers had claimed.

Our Fens as they are, produce great store of Wooll and lambe, and large fat Mutton, besides infinite quantities of Butter and Cheese, and do breed great store of Cattell, and are stockt with Horses, Mares and Coltes, and we send fat Beefe to the Markets, which affords Hides and Tallow, and for Corne, the Fodder we mow off the Fens in summer, feeds our Cattell in the winter: By which meanse wee gather such quantities of Dung, that it inriches our upland and Corne-ground (which are contiguous halfe in halfe). Besides, our Fennes relieves our neighbours in a dry summer, and many adjacent Counties: So thousands of Cattell besides our owne are preserved, which otherwise would perish. (Cited in Darby 1956: 69)

Hostility to the draining continued even after the work had been started. In some instances the banks made by the drainers were thrown down and subsequently needed guarding with armed force. Oliver Cromwell, later to be the leader of the English Civil War, supported the resistance movement. Meanwhile, 'The Gentlemen Adventurers', who had bought large sections of the Fens on a speculative basis and had set Vermuyden to work, called on the state authorities to prosecute those engaging in such sabotage. The latter were popularly, and improbably, known as The Fen Tigers. But it was not easy to discover who or where these Tigers were. As contemporary state papers put it, 'the business is so much in the dark, and so subtly and cunningly carried out by the country, that no considerable discovery could be made'. One favourite way of conducting sabotage was for the peasants to pretend to be playing games of football while covertly seeking opportunities to throw down the ditches.

Destruction of the drainage system, however, actually took a different, and unexpected, form. Withdrawing water from peat and consequently exposing it to the air sets in train a set of new chemical processes known as 'oxidations'. The result is bacterial and fungal attack and the breakdown of the peat by animal organisms. Thus, over the long term the peat becomes wasted. Being an essentially organic product, it virtually disappeared into thin air. These organic processes, combined with shrinkage stemming from the withdrawal of water, meant that the surface of the peat rapidly became lower. The outcome was that the peat surface soon fell below the levels of the channels into which it was supposed to drain. Flooding became a constant source of concern and this was worsened by another circumstance which Vermuyden had failed to see. Much of the Fens lay below sea level, so there was no natural fall to the ground. The slow-moving rivers started to fill up, and the flow of water slowed down. In all, to use Darby's words, 'what had seemed a promising enterprise in 1652 had become a tragedy by 1700' (1976: 34).

These problems were, however, partly dealt with by windmills. Until the early eighteenth century they provided power to the pumps that drained the fens. Indeed, windmills became a distinctive feature of the Fen landscape. But even this palliative was unsatisfactory by the late eighteenth century. The peat continued to sink – indeed, the more effective the windmills were, the lower the peat fell away. Furthermore, the windmills were subject to damage by frost and high winds. By the same token, there were long periods when the wind was insufficient to make them adequately do their job. By the end of the century observers were shocked to see the 'misery and desolation' and 'waste and water' which confronted them (ibid. 34). Further 'solutions' consisted of steam-driven pumps and, eventually, electrical pumps. Diesel pumps in the end became the longer-lasting solution to the problem of the sinking peat.

Vermuyden, the great Dutch engineer, became the subject of much criticism at the time. One of his contemporaries, an engineer who believed Vermuyden should have

> used existing rivers rather than new straight cuts to drain the land, remarked drily: 'Vermuyden began badly, progressed ignorantly and finished disastrously.... The object Vermuyden had in view was to show how much better he could drain the land than nature could, by doing all in his power to abstract the wealth of water from her works and pour it into his own.'
>
> Today's intensive farming methods have further hastened this process of wastage. The black, highly productive peat is slowly disappearing and being replaced by brown soil. This is a result of ploughs biting into the underlying clays. In line with the 'second contradiction' thesis with which we started, the conditions necessary for continued profitable farming are being undermined by farming itself. The original peat is running out, while the dykes needed to drain it need continual deepening.
>
> Finally, and ironically, many contemporary observers see the whole area as a candidate for flooding should global warming continue. One option being seriously considered is partial or total abandonment; leaving the Fens to the sea in a form not dissimilar to their original, predrained state. The 'communities' now living in the Fens are meanwhile constituted by a declining number of agricultural workers combined with workers attracted to the area by the high-tech microelectronic and biotechnology industries which have grown around the University of Cambridge.

ownership and the beginnings of industrial capitalism. For example, there was no longer a need for neighbours to reach mutual agreements whereby they would plough each others' fields or collaborate in the grazing of animals on collective land. People and land were thus both made into commodities. Land became an item with a monetary value, and the close, working links between people and land were undermined. The links between people, society and nature were reforged in rational, bureaucratic forms that were based on the market.

Environmental Politics as Anti-Commodification

Commodification is central to many contemporary political struggles. Water, land, air, seeds, genes and so on all properly belong, it is argued, in collective ownership, to 'the community' (see box 3.7). In the present day resistance to commodification takes a number of forms. At one end of the spectrum are views sometimes characterized as 'deep green' or 'deep ecology'. These tend to operate on the principle of 'biospherical egalitarianism' – recognizing, that is, the importance of all forms of life in addition to humanity. The focus tends towards a romantic view of nature: protecting, indeed celebrating, a supposedly pristine and untouched nature, one to be preserved for its contribution to the spiritual well-being of humanity. Commodifying it, and integrating it into an industrial process, is anathema to such a position. Here, then, is a direct attempt to create a less alienated, more connected relation with the environment. It is one which no longer treats the environment as a set of separate objects to be invested in and bought.

Illustration 3.7 Politics as anti-commodification

Poster courtesy of *New Internationalist*
Photo © Sebastiao Salgado / Contact Press Images, New York

Box 3.7   Resistance to commodification and contemporary politics

Resistance to commodification is a common theme in environmental politics. Land, water, air, seeds and so on belong, it is said, 'to the community' (see illus. 3.7). Meanwhile, proponents of commodification argue that collective ownership results in over-intense usage and waste. Capital investment, on the other hand, will result in generally rising living standards, and private ownership is necessary to ensure that owners of capital get a return on their investment.

It is often forgotten that commodification is usually part of a labour process, commodities being inputs into a process involving human labour and the production of new commodities. This is the value of the Marxian analysis as outlined in chapter 2.

The Wilderness Society

The Wilderness Society in the USA is an example of this tendency. See box 3.8 for a description of its attitude to the proposed development of the Arctic National Wildlife Refuge. 'Nature' in this case is no longer a mere 'resource' to be bought and sold; it is something to be cherished and conserved in its own right. As discussed in box 3.1, this is a version of the Romantic reaction to Enlightenment. But note also the concern with native people, the suggestion being that their older kind of relationships with nature are more fundamental and more valuable than those of people in the industrialized world. They should be recovered and retained.

Box 3.8   Wild Alaska

AMERICA'S SERENGETI

Spring arrives late on the coastal plain of the Arctic National Wildlife Refuge. Long Arctic days coax rich sedges and grasses from the tundra, a nutritious feast for some 150,000 hungry caribou that have migrated from their wintering grounds in Canada to their calving grounds on the coastal plain. Millions of migratory birds are also heading for the coastal plain. Oldsquaw, eiders, snowgeese, tundra swans, and some 130 other species use the refuge for resting and nesting.

Very soon, the sunlit plain will be bursting with life. Attracted by the possibility of a square meal after a long winter of fasting, grizzlies will amble down from the foothills. Wolves, arctic foxes, wolverines, even golden eagles also will converge on the coastal plain in search of food for themselves and for their young. Their primary food source: the ground squirrel, fondly called 'tsik-sik' by native people.

This dance of life and death has been going on for tens of thousands of years.

WHAT WOULD DEVELOPMENT MEAN?

The oil industry claims it can develop the Arctic Refuge in an 'environmentally sensitive' manner. They point to Purdhoe Bay. Yet there, oil spills have averaged 500 a year, and permitted emissions of air pollutants exceed the total emissions of at least six states. Here's what can be expected if the oil industry is set free in the coastal plain:

Hundreds of miles of roads and pipelines leading to dozens of oil fields, blocking the free movement of wildlife.
Toxic wastes leaking from pipelines onto the fragile tundra, contaminating wetlands.
Rivers and streambeds – key habitat for wildlife – stripped of millions of tons of gravel for road, airstrips and drillpad construction.
Living quarters for thousands of workers and air pollution rivalling that of a small city.
Smoky oil flares extending for miles across the arctic horizon.
Helicopters, cargo planes, dump trucks and bulldozers; the sights and sounds of heavy equipment would at times be almost constant.

(Wilderness Society: 'Stand By Your Lands' <http://www.wilderness.org/wildalaska/anwr.htm>)

Resistance in action

Resistance to commodification, however, does not necessarily take an overtly 'political' form. At the other end of the spectrum it can be built in a more material and rational way into people's everyday lives. It need not, therefore, take the form adopted by those attributing special aesthetic and mystical value to an untouched 'nature'. As discussed earlier, in the United States, Europe and many other societies there exist a large number of so-called 'third sector' organizations which aim deliberately to avoid the processes of commodification. Especially notable is the fact that they all value small-scale locality. Their intention is to attempt to restore people's relations with their immediate environment, including land, food supply and, indeed, other people. The following represent some of the ways by which this is being done:

1 Locally created money systems are becoming quite commonplace, as people borrow and lend money at interest rates which are determined locally and not by the global market. Such schemes represent an at least partial attempt at decommodification.
2 Farmers' markets, where local producers sell direct to the public, are currently proving popular in many advanced capitalist countries. These can be seen as attempts to resist the centralized, globalized and industrialized nature of contemporary food production. The market is still in place, but innovations of this kind partially circumvent it and offer a more direct understanding of where food comes from and who produced it. Such markets short-circuit the 'trivialization' of agriculture by a centralizing and increasingly concentrated and anonymous

agricultural industry. Here you can actually meet the people who have been involved in producing the food.

3   In the case of Local Employment and Trade Systems (LETS), commodification processes are bypassed altogether. But the implications of such schemes are even more far-reaching. Their working practices also represent a major challenge to those in the mainstream economy. They operate in a relatively unhierarchical way, thus challenging the normal social relations of a modern workplace. Of course, there are divisions of labour in terms of who produces and sells what. But these are based on skills and interests rather than on divisions imposed by managements. Indeed, these developments can often be seen as forms of 'reskilling': recovering and realizing the capacities and personal forms of knowledge and understanding which are often neglected or lost in a capitalist economy. Finally, they can convincingly claim to be ecologically benign, in the sense that they are operating at a wholly local level, and do not involve goods and people being transported over long distances.

It is easy to dismiss all these developments as mere pin-pricks in the global capitalist economy. In some instances too they can be seen as self-serving middle-class institutions. Their importance, however, is that they are miniature utopias, not only challenging commodification and the concentration of economic and political power, but also advancing alternative ways of relating to the environment and alternative ways of people relating to one another. They are alternatives which perhaps prefigure possible future forms of society (see also chapters 2, 7 and 8).

Commodifying Evolution?

New kinds of 'enclosure' are now being created, which are associated not so much with pieces of land as with the appropriation of gene sequences and genetically modified organisms. Arguably, the result should be that humanity, or at least certain groups of humanity, will be able to take charge of evolution via the privatization of genes and the manipulation of animals and humans by means of biotechnology. However, this picture of human-directed evolution is less clear than it would seem. This is because commodification is affecting the deep-lying structures and causal mechanisms affecting the growth of animals and other organisms. The results are unpredictable.

Genetically modifying and improving animals

The genetic engineering of animals takes three main forms:

1   Biotechnology is used to create animals which assist in the development of an understanding of disease. An example is the 'cancer mouse', a patent for which was granted in April 1988. Human cancer genes were introduced into the 'oncomouse' as a means for understanding how breast cancer develops and in

order to test new drugs and therapies that might be used for the treatment of cancer in humans. These patented mice are now on the market.

2   A further application of biotechnology to animals has been the production of pharmaceutically useful human proteins. An example is the attempt to make sheep lactate Factor IX, which is the blood-clotting factor missing in one type of haemophilia. If sheep could also be made to lactate Factor VIII, this could be of even greater benefit to haemophiliacs throughout the world.

3   Applications 1 and 2 demonstrate the extent to which modern industry is attempting to improve on evolution. A further application of biotechnology, however, may have even further-reaching implications. This is the production of 'improved' organisms. In the case of animals, for example, the fusion between genetic engineering and the new reproductive technologies is allowing farmers to mass-produce creatures with genetic traits considered more desirable from a commercial perspective. A single cow, for example, can be made to produce twin calves five times a year. Pigs are being genetically modified in ways which enable them to reach the size of an adult pig at an earlier stage. This would make them more tender for eating. Similar experiments are under way for other farm species such as chicken, as are attempts to produce fish that will achieve five times their normal size. The overall objective is to alter not only speed of growth but also levels of weight and fat. These all make the commodities more marketable.

Super-seeds and other transgenic activity

'Transgenics', the transfer of genes from one species to another, forms part of this type of intervention. And it is at that stage that humanity seems to be radically departing from evolutionary history and from classical breeding techniques. The making of patented 'super-seeds' is an example of what one author refers to as 'outdoing evolution' (Kloppenburg 1988). Animals are being 'improved' in similar ways. They have long been selectively bred in ways designed to amplify or eliminate certain traits. The practice goes back to the domestication of animals in prehistoric times. But the making of transgenic animals means that evolution as we understand it seems once more to have been overcome. Until recently, genetic material has never been deliberately transferred between species.

Alternative ethical perspectives

Ethical attitudes to biotechnology vary considerably (Wheale and McNally 1990). For some people, biotechnology is 'tinkering' with evolution, meddling with something which is naturally given or even God-given, and doing so without taking account of ecological systems as a whole. Genetic engineering is seen as a 'magic bullet' in dealing with world hunger, but it is shot into complex systems with the result that the wider consequences are as yet unknown.

For others, these interventions actually *are* evolution. Human beings are a highly intelligent species. Their new biological knowledge, combined with actual

---

Box 3.9   Biotechnology: an area for continuing debate

Supporters of biotechnology see the opposition as engaging in 'ecological horror stories' and 'hyping eco-scares'. Movies such as *Jurassic Park* simply feed (and feed on) these scares. Biotechnology enthusiasts are up-beat about the new technologies. They argue that problems of population growth and possible environmental impacts of the new technologies can be offset by:

1   Biotechnology being made ecologically advantageous. It can, for example, be actively used to *make* greater levels of biodiversity with key genetic interventions. And, for example, by building pest-protection into crops, it can be used to reduce the need for chemical sprays.
2   Biotechnology being made socially advantageous. It offers a solution to problems of world hunger while generating economic growth, especially in the third world.
3   Biotechnology improving on standard selective breeding. The latter crosses two organisms, each of which possesses thousands of genes. There is no way of predicting which characteristics will be expressed in the offspring. In genetic engineering, by contrast, the breeders work from gene maps of each organism, taking exactly the genes they need for selected purposes. The engineered organisms are thoroughly tested before they are allowed out into the open world. For further discussion see Avery (1993, 1998).

Biotechnology tends to generate extreme reactions. Those in favour tend to be excessively 'gung-ho', seeing very few problems and largely ignoring the sphere of production. Those against are likely to be extremely pessimistic and often prey to scare stories of the 'Frankenstein Foods' variety. They look back to older forms of production (such as those based on organic farming) as the only viable way forward. But can there be a middle way? Can we envisage future applications of this technology which really do offer major food or health benefits or which allow farmers to save their seeds for future ways?

---

ownership of animals and gene-sequences, means they are making evolution happen. Furthermore, they make evolution happen in improved ways. Biotechnology is actually an improvement over the traditional ways (see box 3.9).

Risk of unanticipated consequences

The use of genetics in an 'Enlightenment' way to improve the qualities of plants and animals has not always been the unmitigated success story hoped for by its proponents. This has proved to be the case when combined with the new reproductive technologies to make better, more profitable, animals (see box 3.10). The fast-growing pig, for example, is:

Box 3.10   Some unanticipated consequences of 'playing God'

The 'Beltsville' pigs were genetically engineered at a research institute in Beltsville, USA, in the 1980s. The pigs had bovine or human growth hormones built into the DNA which caused severe health problems. Some of the pigs were unable to stand due to arthritis.

Beltsville pig, genetically engineered in the USA, 1980s

Photo CIWF / Compassion in World Farming

grossly deformed, and even before reaching the age of two years is crippled by arthritis. It is a boar with extremely short legs, crossed eyes and has a strange wrinkly rust-coloured skin. However, it is capable of breeding and its meat is low in fat. Indeed, the fast-growing pig produces so little fat that it is at risk of dying from the cold. (Wheale and McNally 1988: 164)

A technical fix to an organism, made to generate a particular beneficial outcome, has therefore had disastrous consequences for the organism as a whole. A pig's long evolutionary history has left it with genetically inscribed causal powers to grow and develop. These powers have actually not been overridden by genetic engineering. They have been left intact, though interfered with. These powers of development inherited via evolution are, in the case of the Beltsville pigs, expressing themselves in disastrous ways, especially for the animals concerned.

The conclusion here must be that commodification in the form of genetic manipulation may have massive and unforeseen risks. These are the downsides of any attempt to make evolution happen in human-directed ways. Furthermore, we humans sometimes consider ourselves immune to the kinds of problem experienced by the Beltsville pigs. But, as will be discussed in the next chapter, such an assumption could prove unwise.

Commodification and 'Manufactured Risk'

According to Beck and others, we live in an era of 'manufactured risk'. The foregoing discussion helps elucidate what the nature of this manufactured risk really is. It is not part of a secular trend, a long-run tendency or aberration with no real explanation. Rather, it is the product of a relatively recent set of circumstances stemming from the reorganization of the food industry. Such reorganization takes place in the context of a growing political emphasis on deregulation and the commodification of the commons – which now includes not only land and plants but the genetic structure of organisms such as pigs.

The rise of monocultures and the decline of biodiversity in both crops and animals are designed to create not only standard products but also cheaper products. Farmers under increasing financial pressure are likely to grasp any opportunity to buy apparently more reliable products at lower prices. But such cost-effectiveness is probably a short-run solution. A decline in biodiversity leaves agricultural products at increased risk to the spread of disease. Populations of animals and crops without diversity are left vulnerable to epidemics such as BSE and foot-and-mouth disease. A cheap, short-run solution has been bought at the expense of long-term security. Furthermore, an over-myopic concentration on the genetic modification of plants tends to overlook the possibility that genes in plants may 'escape' into local ecosystems, perhaps generating weeds that are able to resist herbicides. In short, 'the risk society' can be best understood as part of a continuing process of commodification, one that started as early as the seventeenth century.

Commodifying scientific knowledge

Underpinning these developments has been the reorganization of knowledge. On the one hand, large corporations have been competing with one another to control the food industry. This has placed an extra premium on scientific understandings of a kind which can be quite easily transformed into marketed products. This particularly applies to genetic knowledge. Here are individual parts of an organism which can be readily identified, patented, invested in and used for commercial purposes. Branches of scientific knowledge have themselves, therefore, been commodified. But such knowledge has been systematically detached from knowledges of a more practical, local and everyday kind. Farmers and farm workers, whether in Yorkshire or India, have found themselves deskilled. Their particular knowledge

---

Box 3.11   Women: custodians of biodiversity

The growth of monocultures in many third world countries has, according to Maria Mies and Vandana Shiva, been particularly devastating for many women. Mies and Shiva argue that the denigration of women's knowledge and work is part of a wider process by which they, and their reproductive capacities, are construed and exploited as 'nature':

> In most cultures women have been the custodians of biodiversity. They produce, reproduce, consume and conserve biodiversity in agriculture. However, in common with all other aspects of women's work and knowledge, their role in the development and conservation of biodiversity has been rendered as non-work and non-knowledge. Their labour and expertise has been defined into nature, even though it is based on sophisticated cultural and scientific practises. But women's biodiversity conservation differs from the dominant patriarchal notion of biodiversity conservation. (Mies and Shiva 1993: 168)

---

of local conditions, local ecological systems and older forms of animal husbandry has been progressively marginalized. This has often had a devastating effect on some third world farmers (see box 3.11). This is not to argue, however, that all forms of abstract knowledge are easily commodified. Understandings of organisms as a whole (as distinct from the genetic make-up of organisms) and their complex relations to the environment can be quite abstract and scientific without being easily codified and made into simple, easily marketable, types of information.

But, at the same time, care must be taken not to romanticize or overestimate local and practical knowledge. This can also be wrong and dangerous. Both kinds of understanding are needed, especially where technologies based on science are being applied to 'open systems' of landscapes and organisms in which the parts relate to the wholes in complex, not always well-understood, ways.

The enforced division between abstract, laboratory-based knowledge and knowledge based on direct experience may well result in short term and even dangerous solutions. Abstract scientific knowledge constantly needs criticism and development. As discussed in the Introduction, doing this requires constant interaction with knowledge of a more practical kind, especially if this helps to locate the impacts of technological innovation on local conditions and ecosystems. Making and testing scientific knowledge depends on the kinds of understanding which are to an increasing extent demeaned.

So in addition to marginalizing populations such as the third world female farmers to which box 3.11 alludes, the result of a science based on results in insulated test-tubes can generate considerable risk when released into the environment. This is another critique of the kind mounted by Beck and others against Enlightenment rationalization. The practical application of rational science can result in highly irrational outcomes.

Summary

This chapter has focused on the process of commodifying the commons. It is a process that is often closely linked with the extension of private ownership, that entails subdividing both internal and external nature and selling it on the market. Commodification is a historically very significant process. It has brought considerable material benefits, such as the creation of cheap food and medicine. On the other hand, it is often achieved at the expense of people failing to understand the complex relations between themselves and their environments. Furthermore, it has become a major area of debate between different types of politics. For some people, commodification and the market are seen as beneficial, solving world hunger, regenerating national economies and even assisting the development of an environmentally sustainable society. For others, the commodification of the commons is to be resisted. Capitalism and the market has already led to a widespread view of nature as a mere resource to be rapaciously exploited. Encouraging commodification, they say, is like asking a burglar to revisit your home.

There are some lessons in this chapter for both points of view. 'Commodification' needs placing in a wider context. The battle between commodifiers and anti-commodifiers does not touch on many of the key issues. It needs locating in the context of how industry as a whole is reorganizing, how systems of production are changing and how the use of land and resources is caught up in these processes. It also needs relating to risk and the ways in which some forms of science are being used, while other kinds of knowledge (particularly those of a more practical and local kind) are denigrated or ignored. Commodification also closely links to mass-consumption and the making of new human identities or 'selves'. This important matter will be discussed in the following chapters.

FURTHER READING

Note that the literature on the commodification of the commons tends to be highly polarized. The sociological literature tends on the whole to be antagonistic. For the arguments in favour, see:

D. Avery, *Biodiversity: Saving Species with Biotechnology*. Hudson Institute Executive Briefing, 1993. Available from Hudson Institute, Herman Kahn Center, P.O. Box 26–919, Indianapolis, Indiana 46226, USA.

D. Avery, 'Feeding the World with Biotech Crops', *The World and I*, special edn of *Natural Science at the Edge* (May 1998): 154–61.

For the arguments against, see, for example:

F. Magdoff, J. Foster and F. Buttel (eds), *Hungry for Profit*. New York: Monthly Review Press, 2000.

S. Nottingham, *Eat Your Genes. How Genetically Modified Food is Entering Our Diet*. London: Zed Books, 1998.

N. Perlas, *Overcoming Illusions About Biotechnology*. London: Zed Books, 1994.

J. Rifkin, *The Biotech Century. How Genetic Commerce Will Change the World*. London: Phoenix, 1998.

V. Shiva, *Stolen Harvest*. London: Zed Books, 2000.

B. Tokar (ed.), *Redesigning Life*. London: Zed Books, 2001.

Nevertheless, the critical literature in this area still downplays the importance of the sphere of exchange (of, that is, the sphere of life in which commodities are bought and sold) and stresses the sphere of production, the social relations formed in this sphere and the social and environmental damage that may be caused. On the industrialization and 'trivialization' issues, see:

T. Benton, 'One More Symptom: The Foot and Mouth Crisis in Britain', *Radical Philosophy* (Nov/Dec 2001): 7–11.

Nanotechnology – offering control over the atomic structure of matter – seems likely to generate new concerns with risk, analogous to those currently expressed over biotechnology. Self-replicating 'planet-mending machines' are currently suggested as one application. But the ecological and social risk implied by this technology may be considerable. See, for example, <http://www.nanospot.org/> and:

C. Dyson, *Darwin Among the Machines*. London: Allen Lane, 1997.

Relevant websites relating to the genetic modification of crops and food include the following:
<http://www.genewatch.org>
<http://www.isis.org>
<http://www.purefood.com>
Like the sociological literature, this material can also take extreme positions, sometimes verging on an anti-science stance.

On animal welfare, see, for example, the websites of Compassion in World Farming and Viva:
<http://www.ciwf.co.uk>
<http://www.viva.org>

4

Consumption, the Environment and Human Identity

Overview

The last two chapters have been about society's relationship with the environment, with 'external' nature. This chapter is followed by two concerning human or 'internal' nature. In the centre of this sandwich is the present chapter, which is about both external *and* internal nature. The theme here is human consumption. It is often argued that environmental crises stem from high levels of consumption of limited resources by increasing numbers of people. This chapter begins by assessing this argument. It argues that environmental problems do not, as is often supposed, simply stem from more and more people making demands on the earth's resources. Instead, the problems start with high levels of consumption by specific classes of people. This links to this chapter's second theme: that of *human* nature. Consumption is one of the main ways by which human identity is made in modern society. It offers, or appears to offer, high levels of autonomy to individuals and households, giving them a sense of self and, depending on what they consume, a sense of association with others who consume in similar ways. Taking this chapter as a whole, therefore, consumption can be seen as an environmental problem, but in a more complex way than is often suggested. It is a problem because it is now a key way in which influential social classes are forging their personal and collective identities. These arguments regarding the link between consumption and human identity are developed with the aid of the four central themes encountered earlier: community, industry, evolution and risk.

Society and Nature: Over-Consumption as the Problem?

Consumption at large is, for many environmentalists, at the heart of the environmental problem. The consumption of a rapidly rising world population is often taken as the central starting-point for understanding environmental crisis. Furthermore, it looms large in many environmentalists' solutions to global environmental change. If only we in the North could somehow learn to consume less, the problem of the over-use and destruction of nature would start be reversed. 'The solution to the greenhouse effect', it is argued, 'needs a radical rethink of the entire Western industrialized lifestyle – and of the financial interrelationships between North and South' (Elsworth 1990: 235).

The critique even extends to so-called 'green consumption' in which people buy products which are in some way good for the environment. This kind of consumerism leads to many arguments. Some would say, for example, that any form of 'environmentally friendly' consumption is still consumption. Green consumption simply encourages us, particularly those of us in the North, to consume more (see box 4.1). Again, what is really needed is for human society to scale down its consumption as a whole.

Box 4.1   Green consumerism and its critics

Green consumption, or the purchase of commodities which are supposedly 'good for the environment', is where many of us confront the environmental question at an everyday level. This relation to the environment may still prove important in dealing with environmental questions but critics raise a number of questions:

1   'Green consumption' is still consumption. The priority, many argue, is to reduce level of consumption as a whole. The 'green' version still does not address this issue.

> The record shows that if everyone in the United States recycled 100 per cent of what now constitutes their personal solid waste, 99 per cent of the nation's solid waste would remain. Industry would still be dumping upwards of 4.6 million pounds of toxic chemicals a year into the air, water and soil; the military would still be producing more than 500,000 tons of hazardous wastes a year; plants would still be emitting more than 281 million pounds of known carcinogens into the environment. The solution does not lie with individual consumers changing their individual habits. (Plant and Plant 1991: 7)

2   In practice it is not so obvious what to do in the supermarket. The following scenario is quite familiar:

> Now, even if you've actually been an environmentalist for a decade or more, you find yourself standing in the supermarket aisles racking your brains over whether

you should be buying straight recycled toilet paper, or searching vainly for non-chlorine bleached toilet paper, or rejecting the otherwise perfect recycled, non-chlorine
toilet paper because it was trucked in from two thousand miles away. (Plant and
Plant 1991: 2)

3   Information and labelling remains a highly fraught issue. Labels on products are
    unhelpful and we are being led astray by industry. Note for example the follow-
    ing remarks on waste-disposal using 'degradable' plastics:

> [Degradable bags] are not the answer to landfill crowding of littering. . . .
> Degradability is just a marketing tool. . . . We're talking out of both sides of our mouths
> when we want to sell bags. I don't think the average customer knows what degrad-
> ability means. Customers don't care if it solves the solid-waste problem. It makes
> them feel good. (Spokesperson for Mobil Chemical Company, manufacturer of Hefty
> degradable trash bags; Greenpeace Report, cited in Plant and Plant 1991: 12)

> You are being duped. Most of the products hailed as biodegradable in the
> marketplace today are little better than their 'non-biodegradable' counterparts.
> Biodegradability means one thing: the material is capable of being broken down by
> natural processes into pieces small enough to be consumed by micro-organisms in
> the soil. Plastics, as petrochemical products, are not the outcome of biological evo-
> lution, so living things lack the enzymes that can break them down to a molecular
> level where they can be taken and incorporated into living things. (Plant and Plant
> 1991: 12)

Modernizing Malthus

Yet human society is growing at an alarming rate. This links us to a familiar
argument concerning rising population levels in relation to global resources. The
nearly fourfold expansion in human numbers at a global level over the past century is also often linked to drastically increasing demands on natural resources.
Increasing pressures on forests, water, energy, food and materials are all attributed
to this unprecedented expansion in human numbers, combined with rising levels
of expectation and consumption (Brown 2001). Environmental limits, as a result,
are seen as increasingly tested by this population pressure.

But note that this argument can be seen as a re-run of the arguments around
Malthus (see chapter 1). Absolute numbers could be the problem. But equally, social
relations, property-ownership and questions concerning different levels of consumption by different classes hardly come into the question. The neo-Malthusian
argument may have some validity, but it raises few issues about social power
and who is doing all the consuming. Absolute numbers throw little light on these
matters.

According to the popular picture, therefore, we have a twin problem leading to
environmental crisis. Rapidly rising populations are consuming more. But we can
get beyond this somewhat simplistic picture by exploring in more detail actually
who is consuming what and precisely *why* they are doing all this consuming.

Consumption and the Making of Community

Who exactly is doing all the consuming? What forms does consumption take and what are the social and environmental implications? What is the personal and social significance of consumption in modern societies? These are questions not often asked by those concerned with humanity's relations with nature. Tables 4.1 and 4.2 go some way towards answering these questions.

Who is doing all the consumption globally?

Table 4.1 shows vast disparities in global consumption levels. Purchasing power per person per year varies between, for example, $29,240 in the USA and $2,060 in India. But of course there are vast disparities in consumption levels within societies. The share of the top 10 per cent of the population's consumption varies between 47.6 per cent in Brazil and 21.7 per cent in Japan.

As regards environmental as well as social implications, table 4.2 divides the planet into three 'consumption classes'. These are the comparatively rich consumers who make up the majority in the North and the elite in most of the South; the global majority who are poor by Northern and Western standards but are well above those living at subsistence level; the one billion or so of the world's poorest people. A number of social and environmental features stand out. The more affluent people are likely to eat processed, industrialized foods. Most important to us, they are also more likely to generate higher levels of waste. Furthermore, as people get richer they tend to replace old commodities. Unlike the poor, they do not spend time repairing them. The richer people draw resources from further away. Poorer people tend to live off local resources. They tend to be herbivores, living off their local or regional ecosystems.

Table 4.1   Consumption trends in nine societies

Country	Purchasing power per person 1998	Share of consumption by highest 10% of population 1993–8
Japan	23,592	21.7
United States	29,240	30.5
Germany	26,570	23.7
Brazil	6,460	47.6
South Africa	8,296	45.9
Russia	6,180	38.7
China	3,051	30.4
Indonesia	2,407	30.3
India	2,060	33.5

Source: Brown 2001

Table 4.2 Consumption classes: the global picture

Category of consumption	Richest consumers	The global majority	The poor
	1.1 billion	3.3 billion	1.1 billion
Diet	Meat, processed food, soft drinks	Grain, clean water	Insufficient grain, dirty water
Transport	Private cars	Bicycles, buses	Walking
Materials	Throw-aways	Durables	Local biomass
Status	Carnivores	Omnivores	Herbivores
Commodities	Replace	Repair	Re-use

Source: Redclift 1996

These consumption patterns and levels of individual consumers have major implications for the environment. If we equate high levels of personal consumption with demands in the form of increased energy consumption and levels of waste, it seems clear that some people in the most advanced capitalist societies are having by far the greatest impact on the environment and natural resources. But, as table 4.2 suggests, not all those in the affluent Northern and Western societies are over-consuming.

This raises further important questions. Who, within these advanced capitalist societies, are the heaviest consumers? Instead of talking about 'North' versus 'South', it is better to start talking of high consuming classes in both the North and the South and the extent to which consumption has become a central way of creating identity in modern society. Social relations and well-engrained ways of making the self in modern society are therefore at the heart of global environmental change.

Consumption, the Self and Social Identity

Consumption has become one of the growth areas in the social sciences and a number of useful and provocative debates have developed around the subject. Not least is the argument over whether consumption really has taken over from production in the formation of human identity (Crompton 1996). Does consumption, with the apparent triumph of choice that it offers, finally represent the Enlightenment ideal for the individual? This and related matters will be discussed in some detail later. But few researchers have addressed the issue of consumption in connection with environmental questions and the whole over-consumption thesis.

A key writer for such a study might be the French sociologist Pierre Bourdieu. His contribution is to link consumption to the making of social classes. In other words, consumption has not necessarily 'taken over' from class in the formation of identities. Rather, consumption patterns are ways in which social classes (and of course parts of the middle classes in particular) are able to form themselves as identifiable communities.

Consumption and the self

Bourdieu has not written particularly about green consumption, but his work has been developed to include the newer forms of 'healthy' consumption which now characterize many of the advanced capitalist countries. He offers some insights and some good working methods for our area of interest. Consumption for Bourdieu is above all generated by the quest of individuals and social groups to distinguish or differentiate themselves; to distinguish themselves from others as social groups. He uses the term 'symbolic violence' (1984) to describe how commodities and their meanings, especially in a Western society such as France, the USA or Britain, are key means by which groups of people distinguish themselves. In effect, they are making new kinds of 'community', though this refers to community in a purely social and associational sense. People in modern, Western societies identify themselves and their communities largely via the purchase and display of the goods they consume.

Who has what taste in what is the key means by which individuals define themselves and their community of like-minded people. They do this by buying certain goods and, in the process, using the knowledge and skills which they have picked up during their lives. Clearly, people's own family background and education will be important in developing these characteristics. Forms of acquired knowledge are known by Bourdieu as 'cultural capital' – capital which has been accumulated in the process of education or family upbringing but which can also be acquired by money, by economic capital.

The significance of cultural capital is that it offers powerful signals between people, especially between relatively affluent people. It demonstrates in modern societies what is supposedly 'tasteful' or 'tasteless', thereby drawing one social group together and excluding another. Culture, according to this view, is therefore a relatively gentle or genteel form of class struggle, one that is conducted at the level of signs, again entailing 'symbolic violence' in the making of sub-communities of people. It is also a way in which further economic gains can be made. Knowledge, however gained (through formal education or in the home, for example), can therefore be used to further increase levels of well-being. As a result we become involved in a circular process, with education or culture being a means by which further economic capital or assets are made.

Using Bourdieu: a case-study of consumption and identity-making

Using information based on the British Market Research Bureau 'Target Group Index' (TGI), we can begin to approach some of the difficulties associated with the loose notion that 'we' need to consume less (Savage et al. 1992). It turns out that this exhortation should be particularly extended to some groups. TGI is an annual survey of 24,000 adults carried out by the British Market Research Bureau; respondents are asked to provide details of a large range of consumption habits. In addition, an annual survey is made of the upper 'AB' social groups (they are, of course, given special attention since they are the big spenders in whom market research is especially interested).

The data here must be considered as simply indicative for our purposes. When my colleagues and I analysed it, we were particularly interested in the British middle classes. Therefore the evidence outlined below does not touch on the consumption habits or identity formation of semi- or unskilled manual workers. Nor does it touch on what the survey called 'those at the lowest level of subsistence': state pensioners and widows, casual and lower-grade workers. Finally, it touches only on some elements of what might be called 'green consumption', in particular people's commitment to 'healthy' lifestyles in the form of sports and the consumption of certain goods such as mineral water. The objective here, however, is less to consider green consumption in any detail than to address consumption as a whole, linking the entire question of consumption to the human need for identity and answering our earlier question, 'who is doing all the consuming?' Nevertheless, we gain some indication here of how 'green' consumption relates to the bigger picture. The survey and our use of it begins to address from a sociological angle some of the critique of over-consumption in the environmental literature. It also offers some insights into who are the most likely supporters of contemporary environmental politics, a point to be taken up in chapter 8.

When analysing this data, we focused especially on those in the AB social group, the As being the so-called 'upper-middle class' (higher managerial, administrative or professional) and the Bs the 'middle class' (intermediate managerial, administrative or professional). We focused on two years' worth of around 11,000 people's consumption habits. The TGI index itself is a measure of the extent to which a particular group within the AB category in the survey is distinguished, or distinguishes itself, from the category as a whole. In the data that follow (see figures 4.1–4.3), the number 100 is the average for the population as a whole. A figure of 500 would indicate that the group in question is 50 per cent more likely to engage in that particular kind of activity. Note also that the band between 80 and 120 is omitted, our purpose being to draw attention to the really distinctive consumption patterns of the group being considered.

Figure 4.1 offers a preliminary overview of the links between levels of income and forms of consumption. Consumption starts to emerge as a subtle way by which groups of people (and again some people more than others) distinguish themselves from each other. Most importantly from our viewpoint, it shows that the new culture of health and body maintenance is very much associated with the higher income groups. It is closely linked, in other words, with the development of an important kind of 'self', especially amongst a distinct group of middle-class people. (Note, for example, their especially high attendance at sports clubs, repeated vacations and their well above average consumption of mineral water.)

We might note, however, that this 'healthy' lifestyle is in contradiction to a much more extravagant lifestyle. The high earners, for example, are also the heaviest drinkers and attenders of restaurants. The important fact is that the wealthy engage in a fantastic range and extent of lifestyles, not all of which are necessarily compatible with one another. More affluent people engage in a greater variety of lifestyles. In an important sense, they 'consume everywhere'.

This becomes clear when we consult figure 4.2. There are three groups here, all quite distinct from one another. Government workers (civil servants and those working for government at local and central levels) do not seem to have a particularly distinct way of life. They are a relatively stolid group of people whose excesses

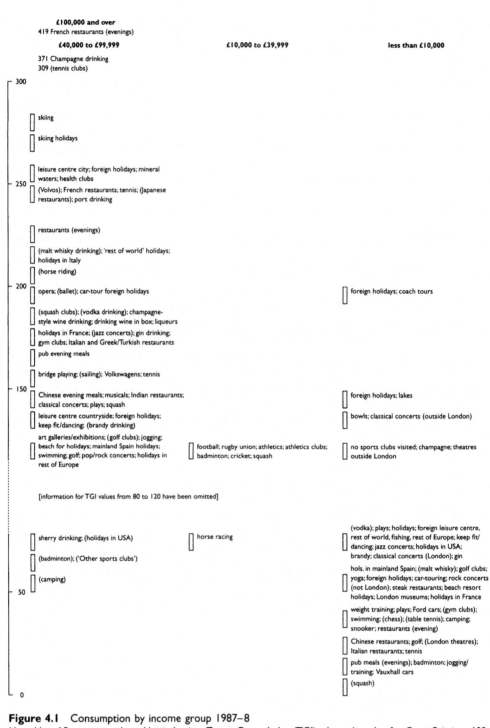

£100,000 and over
419 French restaurants (evenings)

| **£40,000 to £99,999** | **£10,000 to £39,999** | **less than £10,000** |

371 Champagne drinking
309 (tennis clubs)

300

skiing

skiing holidays

250   leisure centre city; foreign holidays; mineral waters; health clubs

(Volvos); French restaurants; tennis; (Japanese restaurants); port drinking

restaurants (evenings)

(malt whisky drinking); 'rest of world' holidays; holidays in Italy

(horse riding)

200   opera; (ballet); car-tour foreign holidays   foreign holidays; coach tours

(squash clubs); (vodka drinking); champagne-style wine drinking; drinking wine in box; liqueurs

holidays in France; (jazz concerts); gin drinking; gym clubs; Italian and Greek/Turkish restaurants

pub evening meals

bridge playing; (sailing); Volkswagens; tennis

150   Chinese evening meals; musicals; Indian restaurants; classical concerts; plays; squash   foreign holidays; lakes

leisure centre countryside; foreign holidays; keep fit/dancing; (brandy drinking)   bowls; classical concerts (outside London)

art galleries/exhibitions; (golf clubs); jogging; beach for holidays; mainland Spain holidays; swimming; golf; pop/rock concerts; holidays in rest of Europe   football; rugby union; athletics; athletics clubs; badminton; cricket; squash   no sports clubs visited; champagne; theatres outside London

[information for TGI values from 80 to 120 have been omitted]

(vodka); plays; holidays; foreign leisure centre, rest of world, fishing, rest of Europe; keep fit/dancing; jazz concerts; holidays in USA; brandy; classical concerts (London); gin

sherry drinking; (holidays in USA)   horse racing

(badminton); ('Other sports clubs')

hols. in mainland Spain; (malt whisky); golf clubs; yoga; foreign holidays; car-touring; rock concerts (not London); steak restaurants; beach resort holidays; London museums; holidays in France

(camping)

weight training; plays; Ford cars; (gym clubs); swimming; (chess); (table tennis); camping; snooker; restaurants (evening)

50

Chinese restaurants; golf; (London theatres); Italian restaurants; tennis

pub meals (evenings); badminton; jogging/training; Vauxhall cars

(squash)

0

Figure 4.1   Consumption by income group 1987–8
Note: Uses AB survey as a base. Vertical axis = Target Group Index (TGI) where the value for Great Britain = 100. Brackets are used when cell counts are too low to produce reliable data.
Source: British Market Research Bureau (also see Savage et al. 1992)

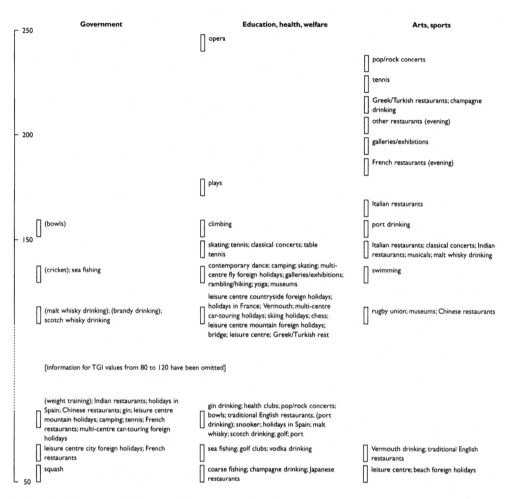

Figure 4.2   Consumption by type of employment 1987–8
Note: Uses AB survey as a base. Vertical axis = Target Group Index (TGI) where the value for Great Britain = 100. Brackets are used when cell counts are too low to produce reliable data.
Source: British Market Research Bureau (also see Savage et al. 1992)

include little more than an above-average propensity to play bowls. This is their distinctive way of keeping fit.

There is another particular group here whose lives are quite distinct from those of the AB category as a whole. These are people labelled by the British Market Research Bureau as 'Education, health and welfare'. Clearly their work is closely related to their leisure activities. They engage, for example, in a considerable number of pursuits designed to cultivate their spiritual and physical well-being. These include climbing, skating and camping. They also do more yoga than those in the AB group generally. The body is of key importance to them. They are pioneering newer, 'green' forms of consumption – 'green' in the self-centred sense of engaging in body-centred and supposedly healthy lifestyles.

In an influential argument, Inglehart (1997) suggested that as a society becomes more affluent, its thoughts, actions and politics turn towards 'postmaterialist' values. They turn, that is, to questions of quality of life and self-expression, as distinct from the grubby business of merely staying alive and holding on to a job. Environmental questions can include, of course, both kinds of priority. They can be about 'staying alive' as well as being an added extra for wealthy people who have already achieved a relatively high standard of well-being.

Clearly we are more concerned with those in the group in our survey of middle-class behaviour. Operas and theatre loom fairly large in their lives, though to a lesser extent than another group shown in figure 4.2: those categorized as working in arts and sports. This group comprises what Bourdieu calls 'intellectuals', people with high levels of what he calls cultural capital but with rather little economic capital. In fact, much of their lives can be seen as rationalizing the fact that they have little economic capital and claiming that those owning large amounts of cash have sacrificed the civilized ways of life of which humanity is capable. The leisure practices they choose entail relatively low costs and they are more concerned with keeping physically fit. But they would also claim to be in touch with 'higher things', with aesthetic matters and with ways of life which those with high levels of income and spending would hardly appreciate. Here again, the postmaterialist thesis has a particular significance. The choice of consumption style does much to distance this group of intellectuals from others, as Bourdieu originally suggested.

This brings us to figure 4.3. The managers shown here make up a culturally conservative group, albeit highly represented in relations and attitudes to nature which hark back to those of the now largely defunct landed classes. These relations and attitudes are summed up by their distinctive commitment to shooting and fishing. 'Symbolic violence' has been made into real violence at this point, with birds being shot out of the sky and fishes caught from the water, as this group attempts to recover its lost association with nature. The professionals shown in figure 4.3, however, form an exceptional and dominant group. They work at the upper levels of companies in financial services, law, personnel management, marketing, advertising and information technology. They have exceptionally high levels of income, or economic assets, and pursue an extremely wide range of consumption patterns.

The 'Education, health and welfare' and 'Arts and sports' groups shown in figure 4.2 are important, particularly in terms of developing new lifestyles and alternative kinds of environmental politics. Their position is nevertheless contradictory. On the one hand they pursue 'Romantic' ideals of recognizing an external nature which is independent, something to be appreciated and loved in its own right (Eder 1993). In this respect they are likely supporters for many forms of contemporary environmental politics which are opposed to using the environment in a ruthlessly dominating way, appropriating animals and resources simply to further human 'progress'.

On the other hand, those shown in figure 4.2 are also acting as an intellectual vanguard for the professionals. The latter too adopt new anti-materialistic lifestyles, promoting a healthy body and espousing older forms of culture. Supposedly 'alternative' and 'healthy' ways of life are being extensively taken up and indulged in by the new dominant professional class. Romanticism has been made mainstream by them. But it is being combined, pick'n'mix style, with a great range of other practices and lifestyles. As figure 4.3 shows, they have picked up on and invested in the 'alternative' culture of health and well-being in a big way, from windsurfing through to jogging and gym clubs. It is they, with greater or lesser

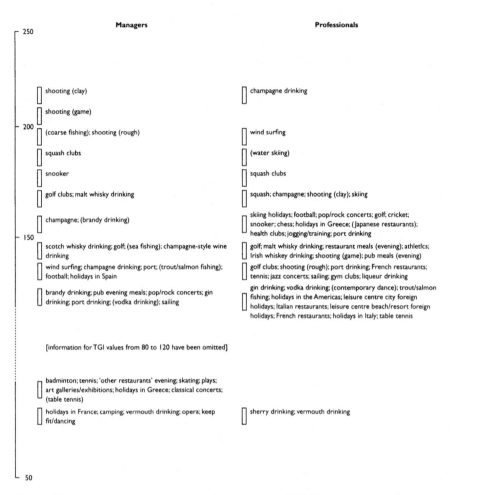

Figure 4.3   Consumption by managers and professionals 1987–8
Note: Uses AB survey as a base. Vertical axis = Target Group Index (TGI) where the value for Great Britain = 100.
Brackets are used when cell counts are too low to produce reliable data.
Source: British Market Research Bureau (also see Savage et al. 1992)

success, who are attempting to ensure that the biological body is fit for the rigours
of their high-earning lifestyle. Arguably, they are adopting a healthy lifestyle in order
to perpetuate their income-earning capacity over a relatively long time. Unlike the
'vanguard groups' represented in figure 4.2, they are dominating their *own* nature,
making it serve material, economic ends.

They key point, however, is that calls for a general slowing down of consumption and tightening of belts in the interests of stopping environmental degradation
need to be addressed specifically to the professionals. They have an especially important causal influence on the practices of others, including many young people. To
a large degree, the professionals are role models for society as a whole.

Nevertheless, as figure 4.3 also shows, the professionals do lead a contradictory
lifestyle, also engaging to an above-average extent in a number of potentially
*un*healthy practices, including high intakes of alcoholic drink. Here the biological

Box 4.2 The contradictory body-centred lifestyle of the professional classes

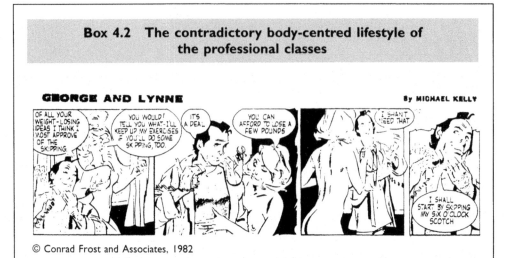

© Conrad Frost and Associates, 1982

'George and Lynne' is a comic strip in the *Sun* newspaper documenting the practices of an affluent couple living in a spacious home. George is a young executive and Lynne stays at home. Featherstone and Hepworth (1991) use the cartoon to illustrate the body culture led by this couple. 'Both George and Lynne are at home with their bodies, they generally like the way they look and Lynne especially' (1991: 202). They are dedicated to sex, self-surveillance and their own bodies. They even decorate their homes with pictures of themselves in an undressed state.

Featherstone and Hepworth's acute discussion of George and Lynne does not, however, give adequate stress to the undoubted pain associated with such self-absorption. Living the body-centred lifestyle entails, as the cartoon reproduced here suggests, not only non-stop exercise but also endless anxieties about having over-indulged in food and drink. The body remains an unfinished project. Self-surveillance of this kind therefore entails inordinate levels of guilt as well as constant and unmitigated pleasure.

body is being submitted to competing demands. This particular group consumes at a high level in the evenings, perhaps, while retiring to the gym or jogging off the excess in the mornings (for further discussion, see box 4.2). Meanwhile, we might note that they even indulge to a considerable degree in many of the older forms of consumption. These include shooting as well as relatively high levels of alcohol-intake, as indulged in by the managers. Our survey also showed that it is the relatively *young* and college-educated middle classes in particular who are engaging in the high-living but health-conscious culture we have been describing here. College students may feel impoverished now, but the high levels of economic capital they are investing in culture and education now will, they hope, pay off in the form of high incomes and an impressive array of consumption practices later on.

The young professional classes are also engaging in *many* and *diverse* kinds of consuming. They are involved in all kinds of sport, while still indulging in just about every way of life, from eating exotic foreign foods, to driving exotic foreign cars, to drinking exotic foreign alcoholic drinks. Sociologists of consumption, and social science more generally, refer to a postmodern way of life. It is one in which people sample all kinds of cultures, dipping into them, taking them out of their social and cultural contexts and engaging (perhaps in a necessarily superficial way) in an enormous variety of ways of life. The picture is therefore one of diverse cultures, which undermine and destabilize the single, dominant, 'high' culture which was previously the province of the dominant classes. But if sociologists often refer to postmodernity, they say less often where it came from and how it came about. Figure 4.3 and box 4.2 show from whence it is coming: from a dominant and extremely influential class. There is a major significance of all this for the development of a particular element of human nature, that of psychic structure. It is a structure now particularly associated with this dominant class and it will be further considered in the next chapter. The new high-consuming and diversely consuming dominant class tends to act as a beacon to the less economically successful. It is these groups in particular that need to confront the popular image of 'high-consuming Western societies', consuming high levels of energy on the one hand and producing high levels of waste on the other.

Bourdieu gives little attention to gender, an area that is partly dealt with in figure 4.4. This compares the consumption practices of men and women. Note the

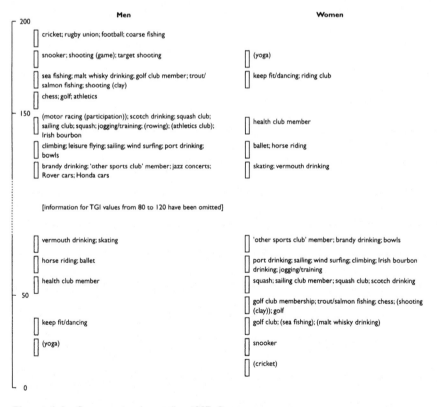

Figure 4.4 Consumption by gender 1987–8
Note: Uses AB survey as a base. Vertical axis = Target Group Index (TGI) where the value for Great Britain = 100.
Brackets are used when cell counts are too low to produce reliable data.
Source: British Market Research Bureau (also see Savage et al. 1992)

extent to which women in particular are amongst those who help to pioneer new lifestyles based on health and well-being. They are especially above-average when it comes, for example, to keep-fit classes and gym attendance. At the time of our survey, women were also less likely to indulge in the contradictory 'health with champagne' lifestyle engaged in by their male counterparts. This may, however, be changing, as women now appear to be drinking (and smoking) on a larger scale. At the same time, men are perhaps becoming more body-conscious.

Bourdieu's general scheme, which explores the relations between economic and cultural capital, attempts to distinguish between dominant and subordinate class fractions and is helpful in allowing us to understand the contemporary role of consumption in the important process of identity-formation in modern societies. It is easy enough to make assumptions about who is engaging in 'green' or 'alternative' lifestyles and what these practices actually mean in this context. But there is still little hard empirical evidence to support such assumptions. When we start looking, we find the picture becoming somewhat less clear and more contradictory than might be expected. Nevertheless, this discussion of contemporary consumption patterns suggests two things: that consumption can indeed be seen as a crucial way by which to distinguish identities, and that appeals to reduce levels of consumption should be particularly addressed to the wealthy, educated and young middle classes. This is not just for the obvious reason that they are engaged in high levels of consumption. Their apparently successful ways of life powerfully influence the goals and values of other people.

Subcultures and enemies of consumerism

The picture outlined above focuses wholly on middle-class groups. It gives little sense of how people with less economic power act in relation to consumption. It would clearly be wrong to suggest that consumption choices are easily chosen and indulged in by all groups of people. Those living on the margins of society, who barely scratch a living, may not in any serious sense be adopting any particular lifestyle or identity in the realm of consumption. Still less are they suffering agonies of choice in supermarket aisles or, as risk society theorists suggest, intense angst about the range of lifestyles open to them. If anything, they are having their identities imposed on them by the failure to fully engage in the new world of commodities. For these people the world of goods and consumption is of the 'company store' variety. That is, they are given a limited amount of money with which they are then obliged to buy a limited array of items in the marketplace (Harvey 2000).

But if this sounds over-pessimistic and constrained, it should be remembered that creative forms of opposition or resistance can also take place amongst the dispossessed and indeed parts of the middle classes (Hall and Jefferson 1976). In particular, the institutions of the market can be adapted to create new, alternative forms of consumption and production. Consumption, and its close link with production, can, in short, be made into an area of struggle and contest.

New forms of self-provisioning discussed earlier (local exchange trading systems, credit unions, self-build housing groups and the like) attempt, for example, to resist

---

Box 4.3   Society and nature: alternative forms of production and consumption

In chapter 3 (pp. 110–11) we encountered a variety of locally based schemes intended to promote the direct connection between producers and consumers. One example are farmers' markets, where food is sold by the producer directly to the public in the area close to where it was grown or produced. The distance of the farm from the market is usually limited and the food must be sold by the people producing it. Further examples are local exchange trading systems (LETS), in which goods are traded, using a locally invented currency and thereby evading the market altogether. Another way of interpreting these schemes is that they are attempting to overcome the separation between production and consumption which has become such a dominant feature of contemporary society.

---

dominant forms of consumption with the aid of products readily available on the market. These alternatives offer new combinations of production and consumption and new kinds of relation between people. They are a radical alternative to those which currently dominate, overcoming many of the forms of alienation between production and consumption and between people and nature which are a central feature of modern society.

The people involved in these alternative schemes frequently try to emphasize or realize new forms of human association or 'community'. In this sense they can be seen as attempting to bring about a recovery of community, one of the oldest themes in the sociological tradition. As box 1.6 showed (see p. 40), a prime example of such recovery is the work of Ferdinand Tönnies.

Environmental-cum-social subcultures are, in effect, asking whether, and how, consumerism can be contained and older forms of more collective living and relationships between the land and people can be recovered (for examples see boxes 2.15 and 7.14). But note again that the market is not being wholly rejected by these alternatives. Rather, it is attempting to make a social and environmental recovery within modern capitalist society and often using the resources of local, national and even transnational government agencies.

These often subordinated groups of people are therefore harnessing well-established forms of economic and political power and bending them to form new relationships between people and the environment. They are again trying to link consumption back to production. And, looking ahead to our concerns in the next chapter, they are perhaps the first signs of a new human identity. Experiments of this kind enable people to become much more conscious of the social and ecological systems on which they depend for food, shelter and other resources.

Locality-based experiments such as local currency schemes and community banks still incorporate the buying and selling of commodities and, as such, make an important political statement (see box 4.4): they are in immediate opposition to the globalization of trade and to the sense that association with locality is being lost. But, just as important, they are making a social statement, one which

---

Box 4.4   Seikatsu: Japanese housewives organize

Motivated by the fundamental need to combat rising prices, in June 1965, one housewife from Tokyo's Setagaya district organized 200 women to buy 300 bottles of milk. Though it was not founded until 1968, in a sense it was the Seikatsu Club's first collective purchase.

What started as a strategy to save money, however, gradually developed into a philosophy encompassing the whole of life. In addition to cost-effective collective purchases, the club is committed to a host of social concerns, including the environment, the empowerment of women and workers' conditions.

The primary function of the Seikatsu Club is not to sell but to buy. Unlike most Japanese coops which distribute merchandise through their stores, the club delivers goods directly to its members. Primary products like rice, milk, chicken, eggs, fish and vegetables make up 60 per cent of our total stock. Seasonings such as miso and soy, processed food and general merchandise like powdered soup, clothing and kitchen utensils are also available
. . .

We believe that our business should be run by our own investments. This is part of the club's vision to reduce the division between producer, consumer and investor. When members join the coop, they make an initial investment of 1,000 yen. This, supplemented by monthly contributions of 1,000 yen, brings the average investment to roughly 47,000 yen per person, which is returned whenever a member leaves the coop. Our investment strategy has been highly successful: although the membership (15,000) ranks ninth out of Japan's 700 coops, for instance, we are fourth in terms of investment capital which totals 7.5 billion yen.

We stand by the belief that housewives can begin to create a society that is harmonious with nature by 'taking action from the home'. (Maruyama 1991)

---

promotes relative self-reliance, resisting the often individualistic nature of 'green consumption' and enabling new social relations to be made. Such ventures can perhaps best be seen as mini-utopias, examples of how society as a whole might in the future be organized. To borrow a word used by some early feminists, they are 'prefiguring' future societies, future ways of producing, consuming, living together and relating to their environment in ways which challenge the globalized nature of world trade.

These experiments still run the risk of being subsumed within the wider social and political culture. (Some LETS schemes, for example, are dominated by the middle classes, others are being promoted by governments as a means by which the poor can simply service themselves.) Whether they really can challenge and successfully resist dominant forms of market provision remains to be seen. And, if they are indeed successful, a very likely outcome might well be that dominant companies, farmers, food-suppliers and so on will adapt themselves to take account of the priorities and practices of these subcultures. The demands of 'alternative' lifestyles, or at least versions of alternative lifestyles, can be quite readily met and commodified. Pallid and unchallenging versions of the original movement may be the result.

'The Consumer Society': The Final Stage of Social Evolution?

The sphere of consumption, it is often now argued, is particularly important in terms of realizing people's personal liberty. Achieving such liberty is partly a political project, with governments guaranteeing the legal and social conditions necessary to ensure that people retain a strong sense of autonomy and an ability to develop themselves. But those within this philosophical tradition (broadly known as the liberal or neoliberal traditions stemming from the Enlightenment era) especially point to the economic freedom of the consumer as finally providing the way of allowing individuals to realize their ambitions *as* individuals. The market is flexible and open to changes in people's needs. It is also impersonal, allowing people to be independent of outside authority while allowing them to use their full rational faculties in deciding how they are to choose their commodities and lifestyles. Self-interest is assured, and without damaging the interests of others.

Neoliberals therefore welcome the advent not only of privatization and commodification but also of wide-scale consumption. All these developments are seen as ways in which individual freedoms and capacities can finally be realized. It is the development of a final stage in social evolution, one which started in the Age of Enlightenment. And all this is now being achieved without the heavy-handed incursion of governments.

Seen in this light, the creation of new kinds of community and social definition can be seen simply as people defining their selves and realizing their individual potential according to their habits of consumption. The middle classes, as examined by Bourdieu and his followers, are rationally creating particular kinds of selves through the purchase of particular kinds of food, drink, exercise and so on. Meanwhile, some of the developments outlined earlier (for example, 'green consumers', farmers' markets and locally based food networks) are means by which certain groups realize *their* objectives through the market. What we call 'society' is made up of millions of people rationally consuming in these particular ways. Freedom, via the exercise of self-interest in the market, is finally being achieved.

However, some of the other experiments discussed above raise certain questions about this glowingly optimistic picture. The Japanese cooperative cited in box 4.4, for example, is resisting the idea of personal freedom and autonomy being made in the market alone. Privatization and commodification are actually not being given a free run. The coop is turning its gaze to the sphere of production and starting to define what it makes and whether or not it is damaging to the environment. LETS schemes in many instances successfully resist the separation between producers and consumers. (Producers actually are consumers, and vice versa.) They resist privatization and commodification altogether. The freedoms promoted here are of a more collective kind. All this suggests that social evolution may not have reached a final terminus with extensive privatization, commodification and consumption. Shopping may not be the prime way of achieving personhood, autonomy and fulfilment after all.

As regards identity, recent work on the relations between people and commodities suggests that the picture offered by the neoliberals may be far too simplistic. It does not recognize the complex, often contradictory, relations between people and commodities.

Commodity fetishism

As many of those opposing the development of alternative systems of consumption argue, commodities in contemporary society have been separated from the conditions of their creation too, and as a result tend to get treated as mere objects; the separation only promotes this process. And not only do they get thought of as separate items, they also become actively worshipped or, to use Marx's word, 'fetishized' as such. Like gods, commodities have attributed to them mysterious powers, values, properties and lives of their own. The advertising industry is clearly in the business of promoting these deity-like, detached properties and meanings. It attempts to persuade people that to purchase a brand means they are buying into an image and identity (one of, perhaps, sophistication, fitness and sexuality) to which people (young people in particular) are drawn (see, for example, box 4.5).

Box 4.5   Marketing through brand images

Nike, for example, is leveraging the deep emotional connection that people have with sport and fitness. With Starbucks, we see how coffee has woven itself into the fabric of people's lives, and that's our opportunity for emotional leverage.... A great brand raises the bar – it adds a greater sense of purpose to experience, whether it's the challenge to do your best in sports and fitness or the affirmation that the cup of coffee you're drinking really matters. (Tom Peters, 'What Great Brands Do', *Fast Company*, August/September 1997; cited in Klein 2000: 21)

The divided identity

Furthermore, the separation of production and consumption has important, even dangerous, implications for human consciousness. As human existence is split into two spheres, the pleasures of consumption perhaps offer a zone of fun, diversion, perceived control and apparent self-realization which is not enjoyed in the zone of paid work.

   Those opposed to unrelenting consumerism point to the enormous psychological as well as social implications resulting from the separation of production and consumption. And there are a number of arguments surrounding the sociological implications of living in a society in which commodities come to dominate many people's lives and thoughts. First, there is the suggestion that people become swamped by all the purchasable items with which they are surrounded. Minds become riddled, dominated, even wholly absorbed and infested, with consumption as a way of life. People are virtually trapped by a world of commodities and, more specifically, in a world where *simulations* of reality become dominant. In fact, as will be discussed in more detail later, their whole psyches are adapted to their commodified environment.

Consumption of a Disneyfied nature

Perhaps the ultimate extension of the commodification of nature is that 'nature' is itself perceived as a mere object or commodity. This has happened as human society has come to dominate the environment, a point to be developed later. A plastic or Disneyfied nature is a key example of how commodification results in people not recognizing the material and environmental reality of which they are a part. Everyday life becomes merely the consumption of a series of images, pictures and simulations rather than an active engagement with either the social or natural worlds. Producer interests provide a form of 'nature' which we are told we need. The result is still further alienation of 'man' from 'nature', from what Marx called his 'inorganic body'. As box 4.6 implies, nowhere does this seem clearer than in the booming tourist industry, where constructions of nature and our experiences

---

Box 4.6   Disneyfication: the case of Sea World

In modern capitalist society the individualistic self is promoted by, amongst other means, the commodification of nature. Commodified nature reinforces a person's sense of all-powerfulness. Sea World (a theme park, the theme being life in and around the ocean) is an example. 'Wild' and 'fierce' animals feed human narcissism. The tourist experience is another kind of mirror, apparently confirming humanity's all-conquering powers. The central problem with this kind of consumer-oriented all-powerfulness is that it actually leaves people largely uninformed as to their interaction with both the social and natural worlds. (See Davis 1997.)

Sea World: consuming a commodified nature

Box 4.7   Disneyfying the environment: colonizing the imagination?

Theme parks and the heritage industry are amongst the classic instances of the commodification of nature. Not only is nature commodified but it is also constructed and packaged to represent different kinds of 'authentic' experience. They are the product of a globalized tourism industry in which people are seen as anxious to capture as many different types of experience as possible in a short space of time. But this is difference with a difference. Consumption of this kind also seems to demand a lack of danger, dirt and anything too reminiscent of the original circumstances in which these environments were made.

In Britain (the first industrialized society) there are now more than forty heritage centres, including Ironbridge Gorge near Telford, Wigan Pier Heritage Centre, Black Country World near Dudley and Lewis Merthyr coalmine (Urry 1990). Meanwhile, in the USA other forms of authentic experience are available. As Cypher and Higgs write of Disney's Wilderness Lodge in Orlando, Florida:

> While other Disney hotels offer guests an 'authentic' Polynesian experience, or a taste of turn-of-the-century Floridian elegance, the Wilderness Lodge is billed as a 'tribute to the great lodges of the early 20th century' with the motto 'don't just stay, explore.' The Lodge and its surroundings, which most closely resemble the northwestern United States, are entirely human-created, offering the visitor a natural experience in an artificial setting. (1997: 108)

Note, however, that this interpretation of 'Disneyfication' suggests the largely successful attempt to 'colonize the imagination'. People believe they are experiencing something representing reality and are not trying to resist it. But an alternative response is boredom, alienation and the attempt to find an alternative that is *really* authentic. But what is really authentic in a modern society? Perhaps the modern condition is one of a completely manufactured nature with *everyone* as tourists within it. As Baudrillard writes, 'It is Disneyland that is authentic here!' (1998: 104).

---

of nature seem wholly orchestrated by the private owners of that part of the world we happen to be visiting (see also box 4.7).

Separation via technology

The creation of an inauthentic reality to be simply consumed seems further advanced by new electronic forms of communication. Theodor Adorno and others in the Frankfurt School of sociology argued, for example, that the media (especially film and news media) turn people into passive consumers and consequently subject to domination by those who own and control these forms of communication. The 'culture industry' offers apparent choice to people, but really it is an organized form of choice, one that is again wholly based on consumption

– it consists, for example, of pressing buttons to receive only marginally different television programmes. Watching, say, a social or ecological disaster on a television screen is little more than being involved in a form of detached entertainment, an alternative to becoming actively involved.

The Frankfurt School's somewhat bleak diagnosis of the role of the media therefore suggests that individual potentials for understanding and action are suppressed or unrealized by the consumption of images. Arguably, however, some of these problems are overcome with the new media, especially the internet. This is a matter considered in more detail later, but it is clear that there are at least competing opinions about whether the new media do indeed represent a major challenge to established forms of social and political power and whether they do enable a passive population to gain more than a superficial understanding of society–nature relations. Some competing opinions, particularly as applied to understanding relations between society and nature, are given in box 4.8.

Box 4.8 Society, nature and the media

Does the internet encourage environmental degradation or is it leading towards an environmentally sustainable society? There are at least five arguments here; some pessimistic, some optimistic:

1 Cultural sociologists point to the imaginary world that the internet offers. As a wholly simulated world it further separates people from the environmental and social consequences of their actions. This applies to e-consumption or shopping on the net.
2 The kind of information passed through the internet tends to be of an arcane, 'clubby' kind. The big social, political and environmental issues get forgotten in the welter of 'chat room' trivia and exchange of information of interest only to the participants concerned.
3 The new technologies can easily be used to develop new social and political strategies. They might, for example, accelerate environmental sustainability by enhancing the capacities of relatively powerless people (for example, indigenous farmers) to use local resources in ways they feel most appropriate.
4 The technology itself, being dependent on sand for the making of silicon chips, seems relatively sustainable. Presumably the supply of sand is virtually unlimited. It is an example of producers shifting their form of production in the light of the changing availability and costs of raw materials.
5 As a mobilizing tool for environmental activists, the internet can lead to new kinds of environmental and social consciousness of many new ways of living. Most of the main players in the anti-capitalist movement, for example, publicize websites and appear to use the internet as a way of coordinating local resistances, starting in Seattle in November 1999. See chapter 8, 'Further reading'.

Perhaps the key point is not so much the technology itself but what kinds of information and knowledge are being transmitted and the ends to which they are being used. This matter is further considered in chapter 6 (see also Castells 2001; George et al. 2001; Murphy 2000).

The search for authenticity

The simulation of external and internal nature can be further theorized, a point to which the next chapter returns. But note the counter-argument here. All these simulations of reality, including the relations between society and nature, remain in the end superficial and fundamentally unsatisfying. They are even unsatisfying for affluent middle-class people buying their great range of commodities. They too are alienated and unhappy. Human beings are less taken in by producer interests than the latter would like to think. These forms of pseudo-authenticity might satisfy for a while, but in the end they leave people feeling devoid of meaningful experience. The tourist experience in the 'wildernesses' of Alaska, Florida or the Lake District may at first seem fundamentally distinct, for example, but they remain inauthentic and a knowing public becomes fully aware that they are being taken in.

Given that people are not such dupes as the Frankfurt School and others might imply, these simulations actually therefore generate a counter-demand to find something *really* meaningful and less rationalized. For a few, this might, for example, mean down-shifting and moving to a simpler and supposedly more genuine way of life in the South of France with a few chickens. For a larger number, it might mean shifting to more active kinds of consumption rather than continuing to take further mind-numbing family holidays to yet another theme park. Such resistances take the form of a search for a more authentic, 'organic' way of life – 'organic' in the sense not just of organic food bought from small-scale farmers' markets but a community-oriented, *Gemeinschaft* kind of life as outlined by, for example, Tönnies (see box 1.6).

The argument that people remain fundamentally unsatisfied and bored by consuming simulacra, including simulations of the environment, stems from assumptions about what really constitutes human nature. According to the situationists and those trying to recover and celebrate the spontaneity of everyday life, all such packaging and superficiality is anathema. Commodification makes those putting up a shelf into 'do-it-yourselfers' (one supported by a booming Do-It-Yourself industry), those pottering in the garden into Gardeners (backed up by the out-of-town garden centre), travellers into Tourists (backed up by the 'package' holiday industry). The argument is that humans are essentially creative creatures who find fulfilment through actively *making* things, whether physical objects, their food or relationships with other people and the environment. Consuming simulations and preconstructed images remains, therefore, not only a tedious, irritating and unfulfilling activity but one which leads to the search for opportunities to realize an essentially creative human potential. No doubt, however, the pessimists in the Frankfurt School tradition would argue that the continuing search for authenticity and spontaneity has already been spotted and orchestrated by powerful economic interests. Nike's catch-phrase 'Just Do It' comes to mind.

Industry and Consumption

As the above examples suggest, the liberal or neoliberal view of individual freedom via consumption neglects the commodification of human activities by powerful industrial interests. This particularly applies to activities taking place within the home, an important example of which is the making of food.

Food as a cultural barometer

Much food preparation has been taken out of the home and placed in factories. In Britain, for example, there are now around three million people working in the British system of food production, distribution and retailing. Of these, only about 300,000 work in agriculture. Food production is highly industrialized. Furthermore, women have a central role in this kind of production. Around 40 per cent of food manufacturing is currently carried out by women, 35 per cent of distribution, 63 per cent of retailing and 67 per cent of hotel and catering (Goodman and Redclift 1991).

Food production and distribution by women has in large part passed from the home to the factory. This is a massive and relatively recent social change, one encouraged by a number of related processes. It has been generated by the rise of 'white goods' (refrigerators, freezers, washing-up machines and the like) and by the mass-production of frozen foods made available in packaged form by the rapidly growing supermarkets. In the British case the percentage of households owning deep freezers or fridge freezers rose from 49 to 93 between 1981 and 1999 (*Social Trends* 30, 2000). This is a two-way process. Women joining the paid workforce more generally has itself helped to spawn the 'white goods' industry and new industries creating instant meals.

The outcomes are complex and are again not adequately explored by enthusiasts for the freedoms offered by the consumer society. The demand by women for paid work can bring greater financial autonomy (though it is also generated by the need of many families for two incomes to bring in an adequate domestic income). But women gaining paid work by no means results in their loss of dependent status in the home. As time-budgets consistently show, women often finish up doing two workloads, one paid, the other not. As table 4.3 shows, women still predominate in the areas of domestic food production.

One impact of industrial change in the food-production system has been the deskilling of domestically based skills. A range of skills previously used in the home and community have largely disappeared. These include the full range of food production and consumption, including the growing, preparation and cooking of foods. Furthermore, a form of alienation has occurred. Industrialized food production, combined with the globalization of the industry, has resulted in a form of estrangement from the cycles of the seasons and from the ecosystems necessary for their production. Here is another instance of what Marx called the 'metabolic rift' between people and their environment.

Table 4.3   Division of household tasks in Great Britain: by gender, May 1999

	Minutes per person per day		
	Males	Females	All
Cooking, baking, washing up	30	74	53
Cleaning house, tidying	13	58	36
Gardening, pet care	48	21	34
Care of own children and play	20	45	33
Maintenance, odd jobs, DIY	26	9	17
Clothes, washing, ironing, sewing	2	3	4
All	142	235	191

'Household tasks' are main activities carried out by individuals who are married and living together or co-habiting couples
Source: Social Trends 32, 2001

Consumer demand and post-Fordism

Finally, an overemphasis on consumption per se and 'the consumer society' can also ignore other important developments within industry. Contemporary industry is increasingly sensitive to changing consumer demand and to demands of different kinds from particular *segments* of the population. It comes as no surprise to find market-research bureaux taking a very active interest in the consumption patterns of the wealthy middle classes. It is the central way of indicating to industry what they should be producing. Modern, consumer-oriented industry has been termed 'post-Fordist', a phrase which denotes a shift to making commodities of many kinds which are not standardized, or which do not appear standardized. Short runs of particular items are produced, the idea again being to keep very close tabs on changing consumer demands and to change forms of output accordingly. This even goes to the extent of production being directly linked to sales tills, the latter being the ultimate way in which changing tastes and fashions are monitored. Food and the fashion industries are some of the areas where this post-Fordist phenomenon is most advanced. The differences between the products made under a post-Fordist system are not always fundamental. The differences between one type of packaged meal and another or one sweater and another are often more apparent than real. But that is not the issue. Consumption cannot be clinically divorced from industrial production and from the creation of consumption patterns by industrial interests.

The Risk Society: Poverty and Industry

As we saw in chapter 1, there is now considerable discussion of the 'risk society' in which we are said to live. This, according to Beck and Beck-Gernsheim (2002), is part-social, part-environmental. On the one hand, it is argued that we live in a society which is increasingly insecure. For better or worse, people are increasingly obliged to make their own lives, to construct their own biographies. There is no tradition, company career, religion, science or other form of authority to guide our lives. Humans now, it is argued, are very much constituted as individuals with little in the way of a guarantee as to how things will turn out. We therefore live in a society which is socially 'risky'. On the other hand, risk is also of an environmental kind. We live, it is argued, in an era of 'manufactured' risk, one in which risk is not so much an unfortunate accident which inflicts itself on people, but one which is made by industry itself. Furthermore, the argument goes, there can be little escape from environmental risk, whether you are wealthy or poor. A food scare, like a cloud from a nuclear reactor, affects all social classes equally.

The risk society for some

What kind of light does the foregoing discussion of consumption throw on the risk society thesis? We have indeed started to encounter some of the themes developed by Beck and other risk society theorists. Individuals are creating their own lives and self-identities by, amongst other means, choosing particular forms of consumption. This is a significant way in which a sense of self is forged in modern society. There is an important sense, however, in which the social and environmental aspects of the risk society are actively made *for* these individuals by industrial combines. Powerful interests make products for these supposedly independent individuals and, through advertising, persuade them that they need to engage in particular kinds of consumption to become genuine, successful people. The risk society incorporates the idea that people no longer have their lives and careers made for them by governments, companies and handed-down tradition. Instead, it is argued, they construct their own biographies. This has some basis in reality but it is also succumbing to the individualistic, self-serving and logically impossible dream-world promoted by corporate interests.

Furthermore, despite Beck's argument that environmental risk is 'democratic', it seems clear that some classes of people are actually able to avoid the worst excesses of such risk. By consuming healthy food and engaging in exercise, for example, they are actually able to avoid the kinds of risk which Beck believes to be universal. Or, by buying out of the city centre and into the suburbs, they can still escape many of the worst kinds of pollution. The 'risk society' continues to inflict itself on the already-poor as it has done for at least two centuries. Some risks, like a nuclear cloud, may be universal, but many, such as the risk stemming from the consumption of cheap food or from exposure to toxic chemicals, are not.

Beck is right to emphasize the role of industry in actively *making* risk. Human behaviour in the field of consumption (including, for example, the driving of cars or the recycling of domestic wastes) is clearly an important part of generating climate change and the overloading of ecological systems in ways that result in risk. The 'Zero Waste' movement, for example, attempts to address the problems of global environmental change through preventing toxic releases and atmospheric damage (Murray 2002). It resists the incineration and burying of waste and aims to treat

Table 4.4 Emissions of carbon dioxide in the UK: by source (million tonnes)

	1971	1976	1981	1986	1990	1991	1994
Industry	72	64	52	49	47	47	46
Power stations	56	56	56	54	54	54	44
Transport	21	22	23	28	33	32	33
Domestic	25	22	23	25	22	24	23
Other	—	1	3	2	2	2	2
All emissions	173	165	157	157	157	159	149

'Industry' includes commercial and public services, agriculture and refineries
'Transport' includes road and other
Source: Social Trends 30, 2000

it as a resource and valuable material which can be used as a source of energy rather than just being dumped or burned. Its aim of recycling the majority of waste is no less than an attempt to mend the 'metabolic rift' between society and nature.

Such developments are important, not least because they attempt to make manufacturers financially responsible for materials that cannot be recycled or re-used. They are also important in terms of developing consciousness regarding the links between personal actions and environmental change: householders sorting out their own wastes into different categories in preparation for their collection, for example. Yet many of these experiments still focus on domestic waste, even though it is industry which has the greatest impact on the environment. Toxicological studies indicate that the sources of the problem are still overwhelmingly industrial (Schettler et al. 1999). Lead, mercury, manganese and pesticides, for example, all have primarily industrial sources.

Furthermore, as table 4.4 and box 4.9 show, other kinds of environmental risk also largely stem from industry. This includes, for example, emissions of carbon dioxide in Britain, which is the main greenhouse gas contributing to global warming. Industrial outputs appear to be in steady decline, though the decline now seems

---

**Box 4.9   Water companies and farms singled out as
Britain's worst polluters**

The agriculture and water industries were named yesterday as the two chief culprits in a report detailing levels of environmental pollution in Britain last year. Barbara Young, the Environment Agency's Chief Executive, said 'Most regulated emissions from industry continue to go down and air and water quality continue to improve. But there is no room for complacency. The increase in the number of serious pollution incidents affecting water bucks an encouraging trend of improvement over the past decade. Contamination of water takes many forms – noxious effluent, raw sewage, silt and oil – but it had one single cause. Management failure.' (*The Independent*, 25 July 2002)

to have flattened out (perhaps this indicates limits to the extent of 'ecological modernization'). However, outputs of carbon dioxide from transport (of all kinds) increased by more than half between 1980 and 1994. 'Domestic' sources are significant, though they are greatly outweighed by industry. All this is further reason for not losing a focus on the manufacture of risk by industry and production. On the other hand, the risk society thesis ignores the extent to which the affluent middle classes are able to escape from such growing risks as increased air pollution stemming from traffic. The problem is not therefore universal. The rich and powerful are more able to flee to the countryside, while the poor are still subject to such risks as air pollution and toxic pollution.

Consumption, risk and the civilizing process

The 'risk' stemming from increasing domestic consumption is not, however, inconsiderable and needs some kind of sociological explanation. In modern societies people are increasingly detached from ecosystems and the effects of their own waste on these systems.

'The civilizing process' offers one explanation (Elias 1978, 1982). This process has been affecting modern societies since the late medieval period. It is one in which people repress confrontation with their bodily functions. Personal restraint in the interest of 'manners' characterized the civilizing process. It culminated in the courtly aristocracy of Western Europe, with Paris being its focal point. Yet it is a process which has gathered pace ever since. It is now a regular feature of middle-class norms and behaviour and one which has long helped the middle classes to distinguish themselves from the lower orders. The rise of the civilizing process means, amongst other things, that humanity in modern societies makes itself deliberately unaware of the wastes he or she is making. This means, however, that transformations to ecological systems remain something of an unseen 'black box'. In other words, the downside to the civilizing process is that growing numbers of civilized middle-class people have deliberately ignored the vulgar business of their own waste products. This is yet another instance of the 'metabolic rift' between humanity and nature; one misleadingly suggesting that risks stemming from personalized waste can be safely ignored. Being civilized can be bad for your health.

Summary

This chapter has been about human consumption. It has had a double emphasis. On the one hand, it has been concerned with the consumption of resources in the environment. On the other, it has been concerned with the role of consumption in the making of new kinds of human identity or self. Over-population and over-consumption are often advanced as the prime causes of environmental degradation and the generation of risk. This chapter has argued that this picture is useful but far too simple. It neglects the extent to which certain classes of people in modern societies are engaging in high levels of consumption (and, it might be added, the extent to which some people in developing countries are hardly able to adequately consume at all). It also underestimates the role of industry and the remarkable ways in which industry is generating new forms of consumption. None of this is to say, however, that the rise of the 'consumer society' is unimportant. Perhaps its main significance lies in the transformation of human nature: modifying, that is, people's sense of self-identity in a particular, consumerist and individualist way. These are matters to which we now turn with reference to areas of social life other than consumption. Meanwhile, it has been noted that converting more people into freedom-loving shoppers may not be the last word in human emancipation. The process has clear downsides which cannot be ignored and this has led to practices and social movements which attempt to link consumption to production and take more care in the use of environmental resources.

FURTHER READING

Consumption

Consumption is currently a major growth area within sociology. In addition to the works referred to in the text, the following are some of the most important texts:
    R. Bocock, *Consumption*. London: Routledge, 1993.
    T. Edwards, *Contradictions of Consumption*. Buckingham: Open University Press, 2000.
    M. Lee (ed.), *The Consumer Society Reader*. Oxford: Blackwell, 2000.
    H. Mackay (ed.), *Consumption in Everyday Life*. London: Sage, 1997.
    D. Miller (ed.), *Acknowledging Consumption: a Review of New Studies*. London: Routledge, 1995.
    D. Miller, *Material Culture and Mass Consumption*. Oxford: Blackwell, 1987.
    S. Slater, *Consumer Culture and Modernity*. Cambridge: Polity, 1997.

The extension of consumer studies to humans' relations with external nature is less well developed. For an important exception, however, see:
    E. Shove and A. Warde, 'Inconspicuous Consumption: The Sociology of Consumption, Lifestyles, and the Environment', in R. Dunlap, F. Buttel, P. Dickens and A. Gijswijt (eds), *Sociological Theory and the Environment. Classical Foundations, Contemporary Insights*. Boulder, CO: Rowman and Littlefield, 2002.

A European Commission website giving special emphasis to over-consumption as the source of environmental degradation is: <http://reports.eea.eu.int/92-9167-078-2/en/tab_content_RLR>

Consumption in the study of society and nature has tended to be equated with marketing strategies, eco-labelling and clean technologies, as distinct from consumption by individuals and households. See, for example:
    ESRC Global Environmental Change Programme, *Producing Greener, Consuming Smarter*. Brighton: University of Sussex, 2000.

An exception is the consumption of food. This has become a topic of central interest to sociological and cultural studies. This is partly a result of so-called 'food scares' but it also relates to contemporary sociological interest in the body and its relation to human identity. It also parallels contemporary middle-class fascinations with food as discussed by Bourdieu and others. Examples of texts in this area include:
    A. Beardsworth and T. Keil, *Sociology on the Menu*. London: Routledge, 1997.
    W. Belasco and P. Scranton (eds), *Food Nations. Selling Taste in Consumer Societies*. New York: Routledge, 2002.

N. Fiddes, *Meat. A Natural Symbol*. London: Routledge, 1991.

P. Kaplan (ed.), *Food, Health and Identity*. London: Routledge, 1997.

D. Lupton, *Food, the Body and the Self*. London: Sage, 1996.

G. Tansey and A. Worsley, *The Food System*. London: Earthscan, 1995.

A. Ward and L. Martens, *Eating Out. Social Differentiations, Consumption and Pleasure*. Cambridge: Cambridge University Press, 2000.

The Malthusian argument

For the (Malthusian) argument that environmental crises are a product of too many people consuming too much, see for example:

J. Cohen, *How Many People Can the Earth Support?* New York: Norton, 1995.

And for a major reassessment of this argument from social scientists working within the historical materialist position, see:

T. Benton, 'Marxism and Natural Limits: An Ecological Critique and Reconstruction', in idem (ed.), *The Greening of Marxism*. New York: Guilford Press, 1996.

D. Harvey, 'Population, Resources and the Ideology of Science', *Economic Geography*, 50/3 (1974): 256–77.

Further references

T. Adorno and M. Horkheimer, 'The Culture Industry: Enlightenment or Mass Deception?' in *Dialectic of Enlightenment*. London: Verso, 1997 (originally published 1944).

S. Plant, *The Most Radical Gesture. The Situationist International in a Postmodern Age*. London: Routledge, 1992.

5

Industrial Change, the Network Society and Human Identity

Overview

This chapter further examines human psychic structure and its contemporary transformation, turning to theories which may help in understanding such changes. It starts by examining influential understandings of human nature based on the theory of evolution. These depend too much on evolutionary and biological theory to understand human behaviour. They fail to explore the relations between human psyche and broader social change. The chapter then explores an alternative approach, starting with an examination of contemporary industrial change. Particularly important are new kinds of industrial relations, new forms of information technology and the rise in 'virtual reality' made possible by these innovations. All these changes, in conjunction with the extension of consumerism, are associated with the rise of increasingly individualistic and narcissistic personality structures. These developments are psychically disabling in that they reduce society to individuals with a decreasing understanding of real social relations and links between social and environmental systems. Like undeveloped infants, they remain disastrously unaware of the resources and kinds of society needed to satisfy their demands. New technologies, however, can be used to develop stronger senses of identity and understanding.

An Evolved Human Nature?

The previous chapter opened up the issue of human identity and self, linking the development of a certain kind of self with consumerism. However, more can be said about this matter. Consumerism is not the only process leading to a new kind of human identity. Before developing this argument, however, we should confront some of the debates within this complex area. What, in particular, does evolutionary theory claim to tell us about human nature?

What human nature actually is and how this relates to the social order and social stability has long been of central concern to philosophers and social scientists. The debates continue today. Does the evolutionary history of human beings offer, as evolutionary psychology claims, an explanation of a wide range of human behaviour? Does it, as some social scientists argue, imply that humans are essentially individualistic creatures? Or perhaps our evolutionary inheritance tells us, as other social scientists and students of animal behaviour suggest, that humans are an essentially collaborative kind of animal. And, given these different types of understanding, how are these types of human nature seen as meshing with, or failing to mesh with, social change?

Evolutionary psychology

Evolutionary psychology is the natural heir and successor to sociobiology. This latter kind of biology argued that animal and human behaviour can be explained in terms of its reproductive success. This means 'success' in spreading its genes into future generations. Animals and humans are therefore what Dawkins (1976) referred to as 'survival machines', programmed to spread their genetic material (see box 5.1).

Box 5.1   Sociobiology and science as a social product

The distinguished biologist, J. B. S. Haldane, was once asked in a bar whether he would lay down his life for his brother. After an extended pause, he replied: 'not for one brother. But I would for two brothers or eight cousins.' This sums up the central idea of sociobiology. It was a gene-based biology, one which was largely developed to deal with 'the problem of altruism' by arguing that humans are basically reproducers of genes. If sufficient genes are passed on to later generations, organisms are reproductively 'successful'. Humans and other animals are therefore altruistic if by so doing they finish up reproducing their genes in future generations. Altruism towards kin is an obvious way of achieving this. Altruism towards your children or cousins, for example, is a way of ensuring that your genes do indeed get transmitted to future generations.

Richard Dawkins, one of the chief proponents of sociobiology, explained gender relations in terms of human beings as machines for reproducing their genes. Given the millions of sperm produced by males, it is in their reproductive interests to fertilize as many females as possible. Females, on the other hand, seek males most likely to assist them in caring for the product of their rare egg. 'Sex inequality', argued Dawkins in *The Selfish Gene*, 'begins here.'

Sociobiology is now mainly interesting as an historical phenomenon. As Sahlins (1972) and others argued, it reproduced many of the entrenched ideologies of its era, including not only patriarchy but 'selfish' genes and altruism as 'problems'. These critiques, plus the 'genetic reductionism' of sociobiology, led to the decline of the discipline.

More recently, alternative types of biological thought have focused on the relations between the organism and the environment. The focus is therefore not on genes per se. These later developments can also be seen as a reflection of human concerns, particularly with human relations and the environment.

This suggests that science is a social product. It reflects the priorities of its time. Nevertheless, it does not have to be *only* a social product. Good science (including that conducted by many geneticists) is seeking to understand *real* relations and processes in nature. Sociobiology was not good science. Its overemphasis on genes limited its prospects for understanding why humans are altruistic. Today the emphasis would be more likely to shift to human development, to the ways in which children are parented, schooled and employed. Genes lay down the basic plan of people and other organisms. They also generate general forms of development. On the other hand, they do not directly programme people and animals as 'machines'.

From sociobiology to evolutionary psychology

Sociobiology commands declining support nowadays. But, despite the many critiques to which it has been subjected, its main themes have been taken up and developed by evolutionary psychology. One of the subject's chief exponents is Pinker. He describes the mind as: 'A neural computer, fitted by natural selection with combinatorial algorithms for causal and probabilistic reasoning about plants, animals, objects and people. It is driven by goal states such as food, sex, safety, parenthood, friendship, status and knowledge' (1997: 524). Pinker goes on to explain almost all types of human practice in terms of our evolutionary development. Selfishness is a means by which we are assured of survival. So too is altruism, this being a means by which people ensure later assistance in the reproduction of their genes. Not only that, but human beings' liking for savannah-style landscapes is a product of their evolutionary inheritance – they offer possibilities for seeing your enemy coming from a distance. The fact that children are more likely to be killed by step-parents than by genetically related parents can also be explained by evolutionary psychology. Humans are programmed to protect copies of their own genes, not those of other people. People are gene-reproducing machines constructed, evolutionary psychology argues, to ensure that it is their genes which are transmitted to future generations.

The list of human dispositions stemming from our phylogeny, or evolutionary history, is very large, at least according to the picture offered by evolutionary psychology. Our phylogeny is being made to do a great deal of explanatory work by this perspective. And the outcome can easily be seen, as one critical commentator argues, as a series of *post hoc*, non-falsifiable 'just-so stories' (Gould 1980). The most important underlying problem here is the tendency towards 'genetic reductionism', as discussed earlier. The attempt is to explain all human practices and indeed the whole of society in terms of our genetic inheritance and our supposed genetically based predispositions.

It is not clear why one discipline should make such extraordinarily large claims, particularly since it is by no means established that genes on their own actually do influence behaviour in the way suggested. Perhaps it is best seen as a kind of disciplinary imperialism which rashly attempts to reduce social life to a very simple explanation (Benton 1999a). Meanwhile, modern biology (especially biology which focuses on the developing organism) is now concluding that genes combine with each other to produce certain general forms of growth. But the developing organism is quite flexible and these forms can easily be influenced by environmental and social shocks. This is in line with the critical realist position advanced earlier. It is certainly a long way from arguing that humans are genetically programmed to behave in certain ways. Evolutionary psychology, like its predecessor of socio-biology, therefore looks like another over-ambitious attempt by a single discipline to encompass and understand the whole of human (and animal) behaviour. It resists sociological reductionism (whereby sociology manages to ignore biology almost completely) but goes to the other extreme of arguing that biology and evolution are *all* that matter.

Human nature and individualism

So sociobiology and evolutionary psychology run the risk of understanding human mental structure entirely in terms of biology. Such an approach has a long history. Ardrey (1961) and Chagnon (1992) argued in somewhat different but in influential ways, for example, that humans are essentially individualistic killer-apes. The underlying predisposition of human beings is to be aggressive, violent and out for other people's blood. These tendencies are again seen as a product of our long history as hunter-gatherers. Despite the fact that humans hardly need these capacities now in order to survive and reproduce, they still prevail and provoke wars and violence.

The struggle for survival

In similar vein, Wrangham and Peterson use a version of Darwinian theory to suggest that individual militancy is a product of the struggle for survival: 'Better fighters tend to have more babies. That's the simple, stupid, selfish logic of sexual selection' (1977: 173). War, slavery, colonialism, sexism and competitive capitalism are all, then, products of humanity's inbuilt predisposition to fight for survival, the 'fittest' and the best breeders being the best fighters.

Humans as naturally individualistic

A similar position comes from Maryanski and Turner (1992; see also Maryanski 1992). But there is an important difference between this and earlier accounts. Here the argument is that humans are essentially individualistic, a position close to Locke's Enlightenment view that people are naturally individualistic. The problem is that they have been caught up in a society which insists on them being collectively and communally oriented. Marriage, domestic relations, kinship units, monarchies, companies and state bureaucracies all form part of a 'social cage' into which we are trapped, our predisposition being to escape from such social confines and become free individuals. Tension, aggression, competition for territory and so on, therefore, are not so much a part of human nature per se but a human nature which is frustrated by the particular kind of society in which it now finds itself. The picture is not, however, all bad. Modern forms of society, incorporating forms of individual citizenship and the development of consumerism, all promise to unlock and realize the individualism that humans have inherited during the evolutionary process.

Interestingly, such a picture turns much of early sociological theory on its head. Durkheim, Marx, Tönnies and others all in different ways mourned the decline of community and the rise of individualism. They looked forward to alternative ways in which a sense of community and collectivity could be restored. But for Maryanski and Turner, this would be a false move. The individualism associated with capitalist modernity is to be celebrated.

A collaborative human nature?

Anarchism is a philosophy which appeals to many in the environmental movement, not least because it promotes the vision of decentralized community life in which work, leisure and the land are combined. It is a vision in which all kinds of authority and hierarchy are resisted. Class authority, as attacked by Marx, is seen as just one form of oppression amongst many. Authority based on gender and species is just as significant. The state, in protecting these forms of authority, hierarchy and power, is seen by many anarchists as the first institution requiring attack and removal. Note that some anarchists look back to the pre-modern era as a time to be emulated in the new kind of anarchist vision (see box 5.2).

Box 5.2   Anarchism in the USA

John Zerzan doesn't have a car, a credit card or a computer. He lives a quiet life in a cabin in Oregon and has sold his own blood plasma to make ends meet. So why does corporate America think he is the Antichrist?

John is an anarchist author who believes that our culture is on a death march and that technology in all its forms must be resisted. He corresponds with Ted Kacazynsk, the Unabomber. He believes that civilization has been a failure and that the system is fast collapsing and he has been blamed by some for the mayhem at the Battle of Seattle in 1999.

He is often portrayed as part of the 'hunter-gatherer' wing of anarchism, so how would he describe his views?

It's the effort to understand and do away with every form of domination, and that involves questioning very basic institutions, including the division of labour and domestication upon which the whole edifice of civilization and technology rest. ... If you took away the division of labour and domestication you might have something pretty close to what obtained for the first two million years of the species, during which there was leisure time, there was quite a lot of gender equality and no organized violence – which doesn't sound too bad. They say 'Oh, you want to be a caveman.' Well maybe that's somewhat true. (Duncan Campbell, *Guardian*, 18 April 2001)

Anarchy and cooperation

But for some in the anarchist movement hierarchy is resisted because it is seen as conflicting with human nature. Humans, like most other species, are seen as having evolved as collective and communal creatures. They are predisposed to help their own species.

In the early years of the twentieth century Kropotkin made just such an influential suggestion. Cooperation, rather than individualism and competition, is the fundamental byword throughout the animal kingdom (Kropotkin 1987). Kropotkin appealed to Darwin himself in making such a suggestion. It is, he believed, precisely those species which know how to avoid damaging competition which stand the best chance of survival and further development. They are the ones who prosper while the unsociable or uncooperative species decay. Kropotkin's book, *Mutual Aid*, is a fascinating study not only of human beings but, as he saw it, of the fundamental principle of cooperation extending across all species.

Later anarchists also claim an inherent biological basis to human beings' supposedly cooperative nature. Bookchin remains an influential figure in this respect. He believed, however, that the human propensity to combine and collaborate comes not from long-term evolution but from early human development, in particular from females nurturing their young. The modern problem, according to Bookchin, is that this skill and propensity for caring has been relegated and repressed by modern, male-dominated civilization. Meanwhile, the courage to go out and kill an animal to feed a family has been perverted by modern society into (male) aggression and domination. Athleticism 'is directed increasingly to the arts of war and plunder' (Bookchin 1982: 80).

This picture, therefore, represents a completely opposite view to many of the accounts offered earlier. Humans are not inherently individualistic and competitive but cooperative and communal. The problem is that they are living in a society which does not welcome the traits they inherit, whether this is a result of their biological dispositions or the form of care they received as infants. It is a picture which has some resonance with our final evolutionary account of 'human nature'.

A collaborative human nature trapped in an individualistic society?

Recent research on hunter-gatherer societies and some theorizing about the evolution of early human beings can be seen as supporting some of the assertions made by the anarchists. Erdal and Whiten (1996), for example, have carried out a detailed comparative survey of behaviour in existing hunter-gatherer societies. They claim that the predominant behaviour is egalitarian. A form of primitive communism consistently prevails in all such pre-modern types of civilization.

Such a finding does not necessarily suggest that these forms of behaviour were engaged in by earlier hunter-gatherers. But if it did, it would help explain what proponents of this view call 'the egalitarian puzzle' (Knauft 1991). Chimpanzees are our closest living relatives. They are the primates with whom we share our most recent common ancestor of about 6 million years ago. Bearing in mind that chimp societies remain characterized by hierarchies of dominance, why should hominids have started to develop more egalitarian predispositions during their early evolution?

The answer according to contemporary cognitive ethologists and others is that humans 'got clever'. Early human beings in hunter-gatherer societies, it is argued, increasingly realized that collaboration rather than conflict was the best way to ensure survival. Primitive communism developed not because these people instinctively loved one another but because collaboration (allowing, for example, the best hunter to be the hunter for everyone else) conferred distinct evolutionary advantages. Rather than waste time and energy in a futile effort to compete and dominate, it was preferable for those not hunting to be getting on with the equally important work of foraging, bringing up future generations and so on.

Therefore the growth of the human brain and the extension of intellectual skills in the early days of hunting and gathering came to replace primitive competitive behaviour. However, the picture goes beyond this. These extended intellectual capacities were, according to this view, further used to develop an understanding of not only their own selves but also of other people's selves. Intellect, in other words, allowed humans to start getting inside other people's minds and understanding them. Such understanding allowed early people to detect deceit amongst others and also to think what they were thinking and, if necessary, to manipulate them. According to this view, the development of the mind at the earliest stages of human evolution enabled the development of self-identity and understanding of others. At the same time, a form of egalitarianism evolved, one in which developing intellectual capacities enabled early human beings to engage in collaborative forms of behaviour.

However, this is not the end of this particular story. The argument is that human beings developed relatively egalitarian, or sharing, mentalities during a period between points B and C as shown in figure 5.1. Although it is not clear exactly when B was, it is presumed to have been long enough ago for humans (who some 6 million years ago split from chimpanzees) to have evolved their egalitarian dispositions, as are arguably still displayed amongst modern hunter-gatherers. However, they are seen as having been incorporated into hierarchical behaviours in the relatively recent past. From about 10,000 years ago until the present day they have been part of hierarchical societies, first of a pastoralist and most recently of a capitalist kind.

But the central point, according to Erdal and Whiten, is that their brains and behavioural predispositions have not had time to evolve to deal with the new social

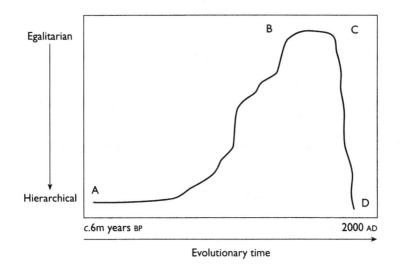

Figure 5.1   Social structure and human evolution
Source: Erdal and Whiten 1996 (repr. in Dickens 2000)

and political circumstances. So whereas Maryanski and Turner argue that people are essentially individualistic and frustrated by hierarchy, Erdal and Whiten say that humans are essentially egalitarian types hampered by modern individualism and competitiveness. These are complex and contentious matters. It is clear, however, that evolutionary and biological accounts of people's behaviour and identities seem to be coming up with very mixed results. Too much is being expected of 'evolution' and humans' evolutionary inheritance in the attempt to achieve an understanding of people's behaviours and identities.

One lesson, given the very diverse findings about human nature, is that there is actually rather little that we can describe as humans' 'essential' nature. Clearly there have been certain basic continuities over the ages in terms of sexuality, basic bodily functions and needs and the development of people from infancy through to adulthood. But, beyond this, it could be argued that humans are, above all, an extremely flexible sort, adapting to changing conditions in many ways. This flexibility has resulted in their survival as a species for so long and in their domination of other kinds of animal. This means that their minds, as well as their bodies, are probably nothing like as 'hard-wired' as many of the above accounts suggest.

As regards their psyche, it can be argued that humans are not 'essentially' anything; that their behavioural predispositions are to a very large degree moulded by the kind of society of which they are part. 'Evolution', 'evolutionary inheritance' or 'genetics' must therefore be prepared to take a back seat in the attempt to understand people's behaviour dispositions. This is not to say that evolutionary explanations are wholly worthless, as we will see. Rather, that they cannot be relied on to give us a full account, that they combine in many complex ways with the social circumstances in which people are living. Let us now explore these circumstances.

> ### Box 5.3   The subsumption of humanity to capitalism: developing Marx's view
>
> Marx argued that the recent history of humanity is the history of people's incorporation (or 'subsumption') into capitalist social relations. The first stage, he argued, is the 'formal' process of subordination of labour to capital, i.e. the incorporation of work processes despite the fact that they may well be technologically undeveloped and that the workers are not fully under the control of capitalists. A second stage is the 'real' subordination of labour by capital, i.e. the complete transformation of labour processes by capitalist industry. Marx hints at a third stage when the worker's internal nature is itself transformed. The worker is made into not much more than an extension of the capitalist's machine (Marx 1976: Appendix).

Industrial Development, the Network Society and Changes to Human Nature

One useful starting point for discussing the development of new types of human identity is the realm of paid work. This was the starting point for Marx about a century and a half ago (for further discussion, see box 5.3). Modern forms of industrialization are important, along with the consumerism discussed in the previous chapter, in forming new types of personality. As the next chapter will report, a stage is probably now being reached in which people's biologies are being formed in ways which make them appropriate for the particular social position in which they find themselves. And, as discussed here and in the previous chapter, a particular kind of individualistic psyche appropriate to contemporary capitalism is now being forged. On the other hand, it is clear that people are being moulded not just by their work processes but by the forms of *consumption* in which they engage. Furthermore, these changes are costly to capitalism, not least in terms of the costs imposed on systems of public health.

A commonplace observation is that an increasing number of people are working on a part-time basis. The 'Brazilianization of the economy' refers to a process in which a vast percentage of the population works on a part-time basis (Beck 2000). Figure 5.2 gives an account of Brazilianization as it is affecting Beck's own society in West Germany. Between 1970 and 1995 the number of dependent employees in 'normal work situations' declined from 84 per cent of the population to 68 per cent. The other side to this coin is the increasing numbers of people working on a subcontracted or part-time basis. This is a general tendency spreading across all industrialized societies. As might be expected, and as figure 5.3 confirms, this picture varies between societies. It depends, not least, on the kinds of protection which people in 'normal work situations' enjoy. This is one reason why Britain has such high levels of part-time employment. People in this country enjoy relatively

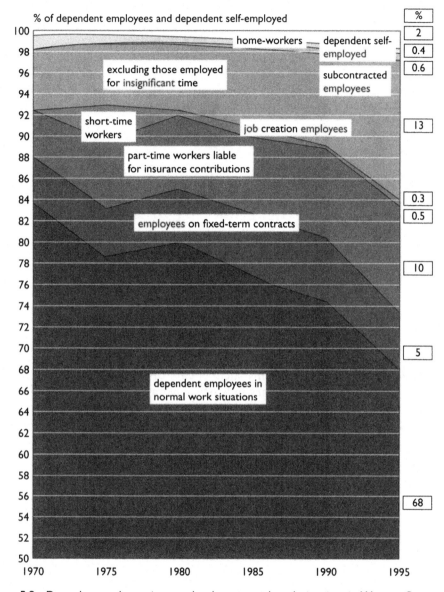

Figure 5.2 Dependent employees in normal and non-normal work situations in Western Germany, 1970–95

Source: Beck 2000: 105

few forms of employment protection. But it is important to probe into the reasons for these changes to find out how it is that large numbers of people are being peripheralized and are becoming separated from large industrial combines. A particular type of individual is, as a result, emerging. They have few, if any, associations with others in the workplace and they are flexible and ready to enter the workforce if needed.

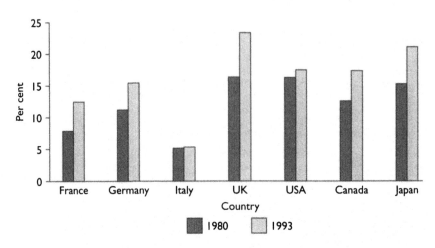

Figure 5.3 OECD countries: part-time employment, 1980–93 (% of total employment)
Source: Employment Outlook, 1994. Cited in Castells 1996

From 'just in case' to 'just in time'

The giant enterprise, employing thousands of workers and mass-producing thousands of standardized physical items such as cars or washing machines, remains the dominant image of contemporary industry. The rationale for this image is familiar. Economies of scale, high volumes of production and the continuous speeding up of the production process bring ever lower unit costs and competitive advantage. Long production runs are also the familiar hallmark of the pre-assembly production of components, the overall objective being to minimize the length of time during which machinery is not being used. To this end, large stocks of components and materials tend to be built up in anticipation of actual demand.

In 'just in case' or Fordist modes of production, key workers, such as those with particular skills or in key organizational positions, are protected (or protect themselves). Trade unions, incorporated into the firm itself, were the original means by which this protection was created. Meanwhile, 'peripheral' workers are treated in a distant, even cavalier, way. They are usually unskilled or semi-skilled. Management exercises 'direct control' over their work as they are brought in to (and expelled from) the production process in line with fluctuations in demand. The same applies to subcontractors. Centralized hierarchies treat them as largely disposable. Relations between the large centralized companies and peripheral firms are often antagonistic.

There are still many companies organized on this Fordist, just in case, basis. Two kinds of important change are now, however, being introduced into a number of companies. First, since the 1970s there has been a move to a 'just in time', sometimes called post-Fordist, type of production. A combination of crises in profitability, the weakening of labour, high levels of unemployment, lessons on industrial organization from Japan and increasingly globalized competition have all led to a questioning of the 'just in case' model.

The rise of the flexible workforce

Conventional Fordism is not at all good at being responsive to changing and varied patterns of consumer demand. Post-Fordism, or 'just in time', industrial organization is therefore tuned to changing and rapidly increasing levels of consumption, what some would call 'the consumer society'. The key word is 'flexibility', organizations with more flexible technologies and, most importantly, more flexible workforces, standing by to respond to changing forms of consumption. They may well be included in temporary 'teams', developed for a particular piece of work.

The workforce is flexible in another way. Somewhat like Fordism, the new system depends on a number of farmed-out workers. Again, they are not incorporated into a factory where they might gain a sense of how labour processes are made and the types of power relations involved in factory life. Instead, they too are individuals on the periphery of organized work, drafted in as and when fluctuations in demand take place. But such 'peripheralizing' of the workforce takes an even more dramatic form under the new regime. A central workforce is maintained (one composed of people not just with distinct skills but also with the 'correct' flexible attitudes to work) and is looked after in a rather different way. Typically, its members accrue benefits (such as paid holidays, private health provision, sickness benefits, pension contributions by firms, training or a contribution towards house-removal costs), but these take the form of personalized 'packages'. Trade unions have a relatively minor role. Meanwhile, a great range of activities which would previously have been part of the firm are now conducted by small autonomous firms or by separated individuals living and working in their homes. Relations with subcontractors tend, however, to be more collaborative and responsive.

This is a relatively new type of capitalism, one sensitive to changing consumer demands. The new emphasis on flexibility, the flexible firm and the flexible workforce have direct implications for our particular interest in human nature and the human psyche. The emphasis is also increasingly on the *flexible, independent, autonomous* and *responsive* individual.

To an growing extent people are made into what Dean (2003) calls 'self-programmable workers'. Figure 5.4 shows the kind of workforce the new kind of flexible firm might have. It is the kind of workforce which is beginning to dominate in many industrial societies. At the centre are the core groups of workers and managers. The group works flexibly and is instantly responsive to changing conditions. It often contains a small number of trainees who are, to an increasing extent, graduates. This core group may be protected by a union, but it is not a union of the old sort that safeguards skills. Its role is more to create the kind of team which modern companies are looking for. There is no room here for workers who wish to stick to a particular task or to a particular skill they may have developed. Rather, they need to be flexible and proactive and to adapt to, even predict, changing circumstances. Distinct personal qualities are at a premium. They are treated as, and treat themselves as, autonomous and flexible individuals, and this is the case despite the fact that they are actually employees and totally dependent on their companies for their livings. They are not really the separated and self-programming individuals that they, and many social scientists, might like to think they are.

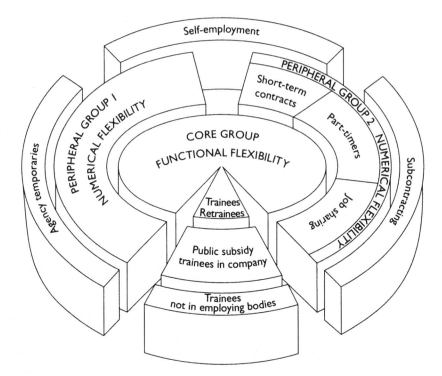

Figure 5.4 Brazilianizing the economy: the flexible firm
Source: J. Atkinson and N. Meager, 'Flexibility – Going the Distance?' *Personnel Management*, Aug/Sept 1986; cited in Dickens 1988: 50

Around the core, however, is a wide range of even more peripheral people, some hired directly by the flexible firm, others not. Group 1 in figure 5.4 includes people who are simply hired and fired and are unlikely to achieve career status within the firm. Then there are the employees in Group 2: they are hired on short-term contracts. Other kinds of peripheral worker include casuals or part-timers as well as trainees paid for by the public sector. Note again the increasing individualism of the workplace, people being made (and making themselves) into *apparently* individualized, autonomous workers.

Meanwhile, further towards the periphery of the flexible firm are the people not directly employed by the core company. These are subcontractors, specialists and independent self-employed, often employed to work on particular projects for a fixed fee. Outsiders may include people working for specialist agencies such as cleaning or catering staff. These peripheral people are clearly a very mixed set of workers. Many work in what is called the service sector of the economy. An increasing proportion are self-employed. They depend on the large organization for their income. They may not be able to rely on a regular income from a given company, but this is not to say that many of them (especially those with high levels of training) are not able to lead good lifestyles. Very few of them, however, can rely on the kinds of company-provided benefit enjoyed by the central workers in the large organizations. They must make their own health and pension arrangements.

The overall view here, therefore, is a picture of an industrial society largely populated by apparently self-programming, self-interested individuals. A special premium is placed on their personal qualities, on the capacity to be self-maintaining, to adapt to changing conditions. They are required to be fully developed individuals, despite the fact that this involves active engagement in social relations, something which this kind of atomization consistently denies (Dean 2003).

An 'informational' society

These forms of industrial change and transformation to the human sense of self have been paralleled, supported and extended by important new developments in the area of electronic communications. All companies are attempting to increase their productivity and profits. The stereotypical industrial enterprise does this by processing resources and energy into making physical commodities. This of course still continues, but now extra sources of productivity and profits are created by making and processing information and knowledge.

An increasing proportion of economic value is 'weightless'. In other words, it can be transmitted over fibre-optic cable rather than transported in a container ship. Even those material goods which are managed in conventional ways are managed by technologies which allow information to be readily transferred and exchanged on a global scale.

These developments in communications have led to what Manuel Castells (1996) calls 'the informational society'. Flows of information are now taking place via many kinds of means. The sociologist John Urry uses the word 'scapes' to refer to many forms in which information can now be transmitted: satellites, radio, television, cellular phone and so on (see box 5.4).

The processes of decentralization, linking subcontractors with main companies, linking companies to decentralized workers of all sorts, monitoring sales on a global scale and adapting often multinationally organized production to changing consumer demands, are all greatly facilitated by computer-based information systems.

Box 5.4 'Scapes' and 'flows' in modern sociology

Castells's discussion of the flows of information in modern society can be generalized. Urry (2000) argues that 'society' has long been the central focus of modern sociology. Yet, given the characteristically borderless nature of the modern world, 'society' as an object becomes increasingly difficult to understand and theorize. In its place, Urry argues that sociology should focus on physical 'scapes' such as roads, air-routes, cables, satellites and so on, along which flows of people, money and information are made to pass. Such a recasting of sociology would be one way of combining an understanding of social processes with an understanding of the environmental. Clearly, 'flows' include inputs of materials and energy into a labour process and outputs of so-called 'waste'. And, as Urry suggests, these flows now very often transcend national boundaries.

High-speed computers and telecommunications are therefore ideal for developing and managing the flexible firm and its links to consumers and other organizations. Close collaboration between firms to achieve 'just in time' production is also enabled by advances in desk-top computers, the internet and so on. Often these firms are located within a geographical region around a manufacturing base. Nevertheless, instant communication remains highly valued.

However, Castells goes further than this. The making and transmitting of information is not just a means of making pre-existing firms work better. Powerful computers, communications technologies, new software and processing devices are all means of finding increased productivity and profitability. Stock markets extract the most obvious benefits from these technologies, but this process of generating and transmitting information is now of central concern to all economic sectors.

Castells is careful not to suggest an evolutionary industrial sequence, one which starts with agriculture, evolves into manufacturing and then service-based economies and culminates with an 'informational' society. Rather, he argues that all these different types of work or industry are being simultaneously 'informationalized'. Again, profits and extra value are being made through information, as well as physical commodities, being generated and transmitted. The 'network society' is therefore all-pervasive. And it is important to note that it relies and depends on people not just as physical workers but also as information-generators, receivers and communicators.

The Network Society and Virtual Community

What Castells calls 'the informational society', however, does not just apply to industrial enterprises and the sphere of employment. To an increasing extent the whole of social life is caught up in the process of making, selling and communicating information and images. And there are further implications here for human psychic structure.

In part, the making and communicating of images is the result of the industrial changes discussed earlier, the considerable growth of numbers of people who only work at home and who may be doing their work in their home. In theory, this leaves large numbers of 'subcontracted' workers staying in their houses with their computers and responding to central companies' requirements for work. It could also mean increasing numbers of people taking their work home, while keeping in touch with their organizations via the new technologies. In practice, however, these developments are not occurring on the scale which might be expected. Most important, at least in the United States, is the growth of work from 'telecenters', 'networked computer facilities scattered in the suburbs of metropolitan areas for workers to work on-line with their companies' (Castells 1996: 395).

But the extension of the network society outside the company is only part of the reason for the development of what some call the 'virtual society'. There has been an explosion in forms of communication over the last few decades. Starting with television in the 1950s, the process now includes the development of increasingly personal forms of communication. 'Discmen', mobile phones and lightweight computers are all ways in which people can readily communicate using combinations of text, sound and images and at a global as well as a local scale. To an increasing extent, human beings rely on 'virtual' images of the social and natural worlds.

A very large part of such information-processing now takes the form of one individual interacting with another. These forms of communication are what Dean (2003) calls 'disorganizing': not greatly helping people to develop the resources, relationships and understandings they need to become fully autonomous subjects. Social relations and relations with nature of the kind necessary to be adequately 'self-programming' are ignored. People just need to perform, not asking too many difficult questions.

It is also possible to argue that new forms of community are being actively made via the internet. Durkheim regretted the decline and fall of old-style community but hoped it might be discovered in the midst of an emergent capitalism. Although there are many arguments here, new forms of community can be made and are being made via the internet. A distinction needs to be made, however, between a community in which people simply perform and a community in which people experience an understanding of the whole picture, warts and all. In such ways stronger individuals are made (see boxes 5.5 and 5.6).

Box 5.5   New kinds of self and community on the internet?

Is the internet capable of creating new kinds of community life? Perhaps it can replace older kinds of 'community' which have been undermined.

Optimists claim that cyberspace networks are capable of generating new possibilities for social interaction, work and political participation. They can overcome some of the individualism and separation of modern life. They also bring all kinds of information to people and thus enable them to become better informed and politically active citizens. Other commentators are less optimistic. They suggest that the internet does not systematically challenge, and may even strengthen, already well-established centres of power. As regards the individual, it insulates people from the social and political relations necessary to enable them to become fully autonomous, confident individuals.

Finally, the internet encourages a new kind of individualism in which people can project selves other than their own. But this potential can be used for malign purposes such as the entrapment of children (for further discussion, see Smith and Kollock 1999).

Box 5.6   The sociology of technology: time for a rethink?

Social theory has so far adopted three main perspectives on technology:

1   Technology triggers new waves in economic profitability. They are invented in the lab, some are then introduced into the market leading to explosive economic growth and finally they are challenged by new technologies and their economic impact is weakened (see, for example, Freeman and Louca 2001).

2   Technology as 'socially shaped'. This perspective emphasizes the social and political relations surrounding technology, and variations in these relations over time and space. Typically, those in power tend to influence the development of new technologies and their applications – multinational corporations influencing the development of biotechnology is one example (see, for example, MacKenzie and Wajcman 1999).

3   Technology development as 'evolutionary'. In a manner analogous to the development of species, some technologies are 'selected' (that is, invented, invested in and allocated patents to), while others never see the light of day. The first groups survive and 'replicate' into future 'generations' as they are mass-produced (see in particular Ziman 2000).

These three approaches are all valuable. However, contemporary developments suggest they are in need of an up-date. For example, consumers and social activists are now having an increasing emphasis on the development of new technologies (the development of biotechnology is a topical example). And, as discussed in the text, there is a growing tendency for some technologies (such as the new information media) to be used and developed in ways not originally envisaged. Perhaps all these developments point to a need to distinguish between different technologies; one type of theory for technology as a whole does not necessarily apply to all forms of innovation.

From virtual to real community?

But there are ways in which the new technologies can be used to develop a thoroughgoing understanding of how the world is actually organized (developing what Freud called 'the reality principle' necessary for childhood development). These technologies can be developed in alternative, unanticipated and subversive ways. It is too easy to suggest that the new communications technologies are simply and inevitably a means by which masses of subordinated people are swept up into the capitalist order. These technologies can also be used to develop more fundamental understandings which could be associated with alternative kinds of social and environmental transformation (see boxes 4.8 (p. 139) and 5.6 for further discussion). As regards resistance to globalization and environmental degradation, for example, emergent social movements are proving extraordinarily adept at using and transforming new forms of media to organize themselves and capture public attention (see box 5.7). The kinds of society they propose and the kinds of social and environmental risks they are clearly trying to avoid all transcend the idea of a 'virtual society' in which people and their environment are only experienced on computer screens.

The new communications technologies:
remaking community and identity

For people in the anti-globalization movement the new media are often seen as being used towards radically alternative ends. They are not just something to be passively

---

Box 5.7 New media and anti-globalization movements

The Independent Media Center, commonly referred to as Indymedia, is the largest and most innovative of the alternative media groups. Originally established by various independent and alternative media organizations for the purpose of providing grass-roots coverage of the World Trade Organization protests in Seattle, Indymedia served as a clearing house for journalists, providing up-to-the-minute reports, photos, audio and video footage through its website. Since Seattle, Indymedia has become a global network, with twenty-six collectives in the USA and eight in Canada alone. Indymedia activists are found at all major protests and demonstrations, and its website is a rich source of camera footage and reporting, aimed at bypassing the 'corporate media's distortions' (for further discussion, see George et al. 2001).

---

consumed or goggled at, but are used to develop new kinds of social and environmentally conscious selves. There is, in other words, no necessary reason why a network society should automatically focus on depthless images and virtual realities. It can also be used to understand, and mobilize against, some of the big issues of the day, such as global environmental change and social injustice.

Such a philosophy can be applied in less spectacular, less overtly 'political' ways. A group of us at Sussex University, for example, encouraged people to use the new technologies in a rather different way, so that they could make their own information and develop more collective ways of making knowledge. We asked a sample of 430 schoolchildren (9- and 14-year-olds) to collect information about urban wildlife sites near their schools (Dickens and Parry 1998). They made flow charts, incorporating text and pictures, describing what they had found. With the help of a professional software specialist on the research team, the flow charts were made into compact discs which could be shown on new multimedia hardware and shared via the internet with other children in other schools, localities and, in due course, countries throughout Europe. We asked experts (on, say, global warming) to make taped or video contributions which would allow the children's own findings to be developed and set in more general and global contexts.

In these ways, the children themselves, in conjunction with adults such as their teachers and people with specialist expertise, are able to generate their own information, skills and judgements and combine these understandings with more abstract and global information about the environment and society in which they are living. All this information can be shared on compact discs and other forms of data-storage which, unlike 'read-only' prepackaged computer games, the children had themselves collectively made and, in a sense, 'owned'.

To assess the impact of this innovation, a 'conventional' class of pupils prepared descriptive wall displays or folders about their local wildlife areas. This latter process is the usual practice adopted in Britain for group fieldwork. The innovation showed what can be done if the new technologies are used in these more active, involved, ways. The pupils focused much more on what they were doing. They had to concentrate hard on planning the organization and content of their flow charts.

But the innovation was important from both an ecological and a social viewpoint. The children became, for example, more aware of the management strategies for the sites and this led many of them to feel more responsible for these sites themselves. Just as important, the innovation offered a way of avoiding social isolation, forcing much discussion, planning and interaction to ensure its effective use. The social value (as well as the value of pupils making their own knowledge and information) was particularly commented on by the teachers. As one of them said:

> [The flowcharting was] . . . very interesting. For them. You know, because it's a complete change from what they normally do. I mean I found mine, [her group of pupils] keeping on task with these [little booklets] was difficult – they weren't that interested. After they'd done all the Pit Hill [Bradford ecology centre] stuff, you know, and got there, it was like, 'eh, oh well I don't particularly want to do this', to write it up and produce a booklet, whereas going into this group [the flowcharting group] was like going into a different world. They were all gathered around; all putting work in; and all working extremely well, gelling really well, as teams, you know. Whereas mine were scattered – they might be chatting, time-wasting, wandering round the classroom, getting colours, you know. (Cited in Dickens and Parry 1998: 32)

The flowcharting experiment at Pit Hill showed that the new information technologies can still actually be used to reinforce existing forms of community, one in which a premium is still placed on people interacting with each other and with the strengthening of their public sense of self. As with the use of the new technologies by the anti-globalization movement, the new technologies are not being treated as ends in themselves, but are being used as a means towards distinct social and environmental objectives. The making and sharing of information also helps people to develop *themselves*; to recognize, that is, their relationships to one another and their environments.

Psychic Structure, the Network Society and Evolution

We are now in a position to return to our starting point: the psychic structures of people and their transformation. The alternative ways in which the informational economy and society can be subverted are important, not least because they open up possibilities for new, more holistic relations between humanity and its environment. But it would be wrong to suggest that these applications and understandings are becoming dominant. Individualization again has to be a central theme here. And it is a theme which has long been central to sociology.

Modern society and industrialization, according to almost all social theorists, does seem to entail the atomizing of communal and corporate entities (for a survey of the sociological literature on this topic see, for example, Nisbet 1966). For some, this is a progressive development to be celebrated, one that entails people's separation from oppressive religious and economic structures. For others, it is a matter of great regret, one that represents significant social decline. Richard Sennett, in his famous book *The Fall of Public Man* (1974), felt that the development was regressive but pointed to the fact that such atomism and individualization are in fact largely fictional. People in modern capitalist societies, he argued, are withdrawing from the public realm. But the reality is that they are still very much living in social and environmental relationships. This means people are still wholly dependent on the society in which they live. But meanwhile:

> the psyche is treated as though it has an inner life of its own. This psychic life is seen as so precious and so delicate that it will wither if exposed to the harsh realities of the social world, and will flower only to the extent that it is protected and isolated. Each person's self has become his principal burden; to know oneself has become an end, instead of a means through which one knows the world. And precisely because we are so self-absorbed, it is extremely difficult for us to arrive at a private principle, to give any clear account to ourselves or to others of what our personalities are. The reason is that, the more privatised the psyche, the less it is stimulated, and the more difficult it is for us to feel or to express feeling. (1974: 4)

Sennett's thinking on 'the privatized psyche' can, however, be improved on. This can be achieved with the aid of psychoanalytic theory. The psyche is indeed under reconstruction. And there are ways of understanding why this should be so.

'His Majesty the Baby': the culture of narcissism

The social and economic developments outlined above, combined with the consumerism discussed in the last chapter, suggest, despite the challenges from oppositional kinds of politics, that a socially and politically dominant psyche is being made by contemporary capitalist society. It is that of *narcissism*. At this point, Freudian psychology can be used to theorize what is taking place. Narcissism is a particularly extreme form of individualism, the ideal of an autonomous subject.

Narcissism, in classical psychoanalytic theory, has its origins in the newborn infant's sense of being at the centre of the world. The outside world is what Craib calls 'a magical extension of itself' (1989: 10). Thus, when a hungry baby cries, it is 'magically' supplied with food. Or, when it infuriatingly throws a plate of food on the floor, it 'magically' disappears. But as human beings grow up and develop, they are normally made aware of their relations with their environment and the distinction between themselves and others. A sense of well-being is made, one based on recognizing the reality of an independent world. This is the process of *anaclysis*, one facilitated by responsible parenting.

But the central point is that narcissistic behaviour can easily continue as a characteristic of adults. People, some people at least, are under the mistaken impression that they need never grow up. 'Narcissistic rage' is an important clinical phenomenon. It stems from a continuing demand that the world should provide us with exactly what we need if we make sufficient commotion. To use Freud's famous phrase, 'His Majesty the Baby' continues to expect the world to be organized around him or her even though they are supposedly grown up. Narcissistic bliss can be found, if temporarily, by a stream of courtiers or credit cards providing instant pleasures. Things which are out of sight, such as food production, waste and environmental degradation, remain firmly out of mind. Meanwhile, psychotherapists, confronted by extreme versions of self-centred narcissism, encourage sufferers in the belief that

---

Box 5.8 Contemporary media and the culture of narcissism

The media in Britain and other 'advanced' societies are currently concerned to promote the culture of narcissism. Self-obsessed people in 'docudramas', engaging in breast-beating studio debates and revealing their innermost secrets to the popular press, are the most obvious examples. These developments are paralleled in high culture by, for example, Tracey Emin, a leading 'Britart' representative. By publicly displaying her unmade bed or her tent naming 'everyone I have ever slept with', she has managed to turn self-centred narcissism into an exclusive and expensive art form. One of the most striking features of this particular kind of commodification is that it is democratic: anyone can be a celebrity.

---

they will be better as and when they can see how they are seen by others. Nevertheless, influential opinion-makers continue to promote, and invest in, this form of self-absorbed self-centredness (see box 5.8).

This brings us back to the social settings in which this characteristic form of contemporary psyche develops. Confidence in the self is one thing. Confidence in a self which can relate to the outside world is what would normally be expected from the process of development (see box 5.9). And no doubt such successful development is experienced by people from many different social backgrounds, particularly if they have been adequately guided during their early development. But egocentric, self-serving narcissism is another matter, one which can be damaging to the self, to society and to the environment.

Consumerism, post-Fordist work structures and the rise of the network society are creating individuals who are supposedly free, independent, self-reliant and flexible. They promote not only individualism but also its extension into a self-centred, adult kind of narcissism (Lasch 1979; Dean 2002). The independence is illusory because these individuals are still deeply dependent on other people and on their environment. But this reality does not stop the culture of narcissism developing. Lasch's work on the social origins of egoistic narcissism points to an array of characteristics typical of what he calls 'the culture of narcissism'. These include not only extreme individualism but also a disregard for others, preoccupation with personal relations at the expense of political activity, lack of concern with social

---

Box 5.9 Contrasting views of self-love

To refer to someone as 'narcissistic' is not necessarily to condemn her or him. Following the philosopher Rousseau, we can make a sharp distinction between two forms of self-love. He made the distinction between *amour-propre* and *amour de soi*. The former is an egoistic concern for one's actual, bodily self. The second refers to self-esteem. This is a necessary condition for self-empowerment and altruism towards others. (For further discussion see Rousseau 1979; Dent 1988; Bhaskar 1993.)

---

cohesion and, importantly in the context of any concern with the environment, an overarching lack of concern with future generations.

The network society of individuals communicating via computers and other electronic devices can be used to further promote a sense of the free, unattached individual. But, unless the new electronic networks are used for overtly collective purposes (their adoption by the anti-globalization movement would be an example), this is at the expense of depriving them of the resources and experience which they need to acquire a strong sense of self-identity.

These individualizing, infantilizing tendencies have been made even more pronounced by extremely high levels of commodified consumption. This includes the consumption of a commodified 'nature'. Guy Debord's 'society of the spectacle' is based, in his words, on 'an eternal present'. It is a manufactured present in which

> fashion itself, from clothes to music, has come to a halt . . . is achieved by the ceaseless circulation of information and always returning to the same short list of trivialities, passionately proclaimed as major discoveries. Meanwhile, news of what is genuinely important, of what is actually changing, comes rarely, and then in fits and starts. (Cited by Gray 2002: 29)

As regards the specific question of external and internal nature, the society of the spectacle includes the commodification of 'dangerous' experiences, in supposedly 'natural' settings, and further confirms a sense of all-powerfulness. A Disneyfied 'nature' constructed wholly for the tourist gaze has important implications for human identity. It reinforces the subject's sense of self-significance and power over the environment. His Majesty the Baby rules again. Everyone becomes a baby making demands for instant gratification through the market and other means such as the media and the internet. What Freud called 'the reality principle' (the recognition that the demand for pleasure must be tempered by the recognition of real external constraints) can be safely ignored. Or so it seems.

Narcissistic personality traits are nevertheless likely to be unevenly developed. They are most likely to be pronounced amongst, for example, high-consuming elites; specifically the professionals discussed in chapter 4 (see figure 4.3, p. 129). Such traits are likely to be less developed amongst other groups. These might include the unemployed and those on low wages. Perhaps here, more socially aware, anaclytic forms of self prevail. Other, less affluent middle-class groups (such as those referred to in figure 4.2) are also less likely to be high-spending, self-regarding, apparently autonomous individuals. Nevertheless, the professionals constitute a new ruling class, one that is economically and culturally dominant. The culture of narcissism associated with this class is most likely to be aspired to and imitated by others.

In both the spheres of industry and consumption, therefore, new and important kinds of individualistic and self-absorbed identity are being formed. Freud and others have given some insight into how they originate and how they might be extended in modern society. Nevertheless, none of this suggests that a growing number of people are simply and unproblematically parenting themselves and shaping their own lives (Giddens 1991; Beck 2000; Beck-Gernsheim 2002). People's biographies are still to a large extent being written for them.

Individualism, including its advanced narcissistic form, has been detached from material reality. People may be treated by employers, by the media and others as independent, proactive individuals. And they may well behave as though they are such, with their behaviour having significant material effects. Yet all these people actually still live in systems of power and ecosystems on which they are deeply dependent. Apparent autonomy has been bought at the expense of alienation from their social and natural environments.

A biological basis to narcissistic psychic structures?

Despite emphasizing the relations between human psychic structures and changing forms of society, it would be a mistake to ignore the biological bases of human subjectivity, including contemporary narcissism. The different ways in which human subjects sense themselves and their environments have some basis in the instinct to survive, as indeed Darwin suggested. Cunningham (1996), writing of human experience from a Darwinian and 'naturalist' perspective, argues persuasively that humans do not just perceive their environment in a raw sense. They, like other animals, are actively evaluating it, assessing it in terms of its potential for survival and reproduction.

A sense of value, in other words, is built into people's experience of their environment. Forms of identity (whether of an individualistic and narcissistic kind or of a more collective kind) are not only a product of consumerism, work relations, electronic networks and so on. They also stem from people trying to survive and improve themselves. Narcissistic self-engrossed individualism is one particularly desperate strategy to this end.

The biological and evolutionary work outlined at the start of this chapter may well overemphasize humans as a natural sort and their similarities with other creatures. But it can also be seen as a corrective to any attempt to over-emphasize the social bases of people's identity, including their narcissistic identity. Social scientists tend to ignore biology altogether, whereas there is likely to be at least some evolutionary basis to human behaviour.

This highlights the central point that human beings are an immensely flexible species. Their nature is not as 'hard-wired' into them as the biological and ethological literature examined earlier suggests. In ways analogous to the biological changes which they undergo (explored in the next chapter), they are also well capable of changing their identities and sense of self under changing social circumstances. Narcissistic egoism is the currently dominant, desperate expression of some people's attempts to thrive. But other kinds of more collective subjectivity could come to the fore under, say, conditions of war or environmental calamity. Historical work suggests that more anaclytic, collective forms of consciousness developed under conditions of stress (see box 5.10). Perhaps the rise of social and environmental threat will lead to a modern version of such awareness and human subjectivity.

In contemporary industrial society one understandable way of attempting to survive and thrive is to make oneself indifferent to the kind of society and environment in which one is born. As we have seen, this is a self-deluding strategy in the obvious sense that humans, like all other species, do still actively depend on their social and natural environment to survive, even if they think and act otherwise. It is also self-deluding and corrosive in the sense that the narcissistic personality can

---

Box 5.10   Society, nature and pre-capitalist forms of consciousness

Different kinds of human subjectivity prevail in different kinds of society. Chapter 3 discussed the process of commodifying the commons, dividing what was previously common property and treating the land and external nature as items to be bought and sold. One case-study was The Fens, in Cambridgeshire, England. Commodifying entailed an attack on traditional rights, on common property and on what Thompson (1991) calls 'customs in common'. What were these rights? They consisted not simply of common land but also of a kind of connectedness to other people and to the land. As regards the latter, it consisted of understanding the diverse ecological context within which they lived, even if this context was very harsh and often resulted in illness and short lives.

We also noted how The Fens and their residents were consistently vilified by those attempting the drainage as part of an uncontrolled 'Nature'. The 'Fen Tigers' also, however, pointed to the vast range of animals and crops being raised in The Fens and to the reed and sedge used for houses in these lands. Wild animals, in particular large flocks of geese, were known as 'the Fen-men's treasure'. 'The Fen-men's dowry' was 'three-score geese and a pelt', the latter being a sheepskin used as an outer garment. And as regards human association, the 1646 'Anti-Projector' pamphlet opposing the project pointed out: 'we have many thousand cottagers, which live on our Fens, which otherwise must go a-begging, so that if the undertakers take from us a third part our Fens, they destroy not only our pastures and corn ground, but also our poor and we are utterly unable to relieve them. What is cole feed and rape, they are but Dutch commodities and but trash and trumpery.'

Popular pamphlets give some sense of the collective consciousness of the time and of connectedness to the environment and survival of future generations. But it would be easy to romanticize this kind of consciousness. It stemmed from the simple need to stay alive and, in the case of the Fen people, under hazardous and highly unhealthy circumstances. Note also that resistance to these customs in common was often couched in parochial, defensive, conservative and nationalistic terms (see Smiles 1862).

---

never actually know her or himself. This is because they remain unable to take a position outside themselves and see themselves as they really are. This brings us to the question of risk, given the ways in which human personality is currently being restructured.

Post-Fordism, the Network Society and Risk

The diagnosis offered above first allows some critique and development of the 'risk society' notion. It will be recalled that, going well beyond environmental risk, Beck and Beck-Gernsheim (2002) argue that the whole of contemporary social life is becoming more 'risky'. How plausible is such a suggestion?

Modern human nature versus environmental sustainability

First, note that this is a critical moment in this book's discussion. 'The risk society', understood as the creation of environmental hazards, is not just a product of what humanity is doing to its environment. It is also a product of a particular kind of personality-type created by modern capitalism. A culture of narcissism is a remarkably unpromising basis for developing an understanding of the contemporary rift between humanity and its environment. Here is another contradiction at the heart of contemporary capitalism. Elites and others transfixed by celebrity and instant gratification combined with a commodified 'virtual nature' are fatal combinations. They are perhaps the least likely forms of personality and environment for developing an adequate understanding of global environmental change and social justice. Rising levels of risk are an almost guaranteed outcome; until, that is, the risks become so transparent as to create alternative types of identity and self.

Unpacking 'the risk society'

The label 'risk society' does not do justice to the complex range of processes involved. Beck and Beck-Gernsheim have pointed to the decline of tradition, the family, state institutions and well-established forms of community in which people live. These changes, they argue, are leading to new forms of individualism and risk. To an increasing extent people live in conditions of uncertainty. They are made into their own experts. They make their own understandings (including their own knowledge) and assert their own ways of life, all independent of any form of authority. It is the end of the Enlightenment dream, one of a detached, a-political science with society effortlessly developing in a simple, single, 'progressive' direction as a result of scientific intervention. Taken to its logical conclusion, Beck and Beck-Gernsheim's argument implies that in the future there will be almost as many directions and forms of 'progress' as there are people.

Individualization is certainly a feature of modern society. And Beck and Beck-Gernsheim are certainly pointing to some important contemporary phenomena. But there are three things to say about their assertion. First, the tendencies they outline are by no means as new as they suggest. They are a continuation of a phenomenon which many other sociologists (including, in particular, Durkheim and Marx) have commented on. Human society is now witnessing an especially 'advanced' version of individualization, especially amongst certain dominant classes.

Second, it is really surprising that the 'risk society' thesis does not allude more often to the social relations and economic processes underlying and underpinning these developments. These include, as discussed above, the development of new types of work structures, and forms of information exchange are combining with extensive commodification to generate just the kinds of insecurity and individualization to which Beck and Beck-Gernsheim refer. These changes are coming *from somewhere*, specifically from some very powerful social classes and forces. They are much less acts of God than Beck and Beck-Gernsheim imply.

This links to the final point. It is possible to understand the process of individualization even better by stepping outside sociology and borrowing from the neighbouring discipline of psychology. Pre-existing narcissistic tendencies in the human psyche are being activated by the kinds of social change (changing work structures, the retreat of collective state provision and so on) which characterize contemporary society.

Taking these points into account, these transformations to the human psyche and the resultant risks they generate cannot be easily lumped together with the risks generated by environmental degradation. Or, if there is a connection, it is that of modern forms of industrial capitalism. They are simultaneously transforming both external and internal nature.

Summary

This chapter has continued the discussion of human nature and its transformation. It has been about the human identity and psychic structure. It has argued that the changing nature of the self needs relating to its particular social and economic circumstances. More specifically, the development of new types of capitalist economy and the development of an 'informational society' are leading to the development of new kinds of human identity. Drawing on aspects of Freud's theory of the personality, on aspects of Marx and on contemporary interpretations of this work, this chapter has argued that a narcissistic 'self' is emerging from new forms of industry, new types of electronic communications and the extension of consumerism. At this point, the discussion of commodification in chapter 3 starts to pay further dividends. The rift between society and nature has become more profound. Not only are people alienated from the natural world in the sense that they have few working connections with it or understandings of it. They are now confronted by a 'virtual' nature which further estranges them from the environment on which they depend. More importantly still, their selves are being remade in ways that ensure they are fully and actively engaged in this commodified environment. These developments are not conducive to the creation of an environmentally sustainable society. The engagement is of a peculiarly passive, even unknowing, form. This chapter has, however, tracked alternative, less alienated, relations between society and nature which are currently under development. These alternatives represent important, more active engagements with external nature.

FURTHER READING

Debates within evolutionary psychology

For a summary of current, biologically based understandings of human nature, see:
P. Dickens, *Social Darwinism. Linking Social Theory to Evolutionary Thought.* Buckingham: Open University Press, 2000, esp. ch. 5.

For a full account of 'evolutionary psychology', see in particular:
C. Badcock, *Evolutionary Psychology. A Critical Introduction.* Cambridge: Polity, 2000.

Changing subjectivities

Texts which show very valuably how forms of subjectivity are modified in different epochs are:

R. Reiche, *Sexuality and Class Struggle*. London: New Left Books, 1970.
E. Thompson, *Customs in Common*. London: Merlin, 1991.

The sources of modern narcissism are still a matter of debate. One recent study argues that Beau Brummell, the early eighteenth-century 'dandy', was the original self-obsessed individual, the prototype for today's 'fraudulent democratic dandy' as exemplified by contemporary celebrities. See:

G. Walden, *Who's a Dandy?* London: Gibson Square, 2002.

Note also that personality disorders such as adult narcissism are unevenly developed in our own era. They are particularly prevalent in the USA but much less so in more collectivist societies such as Sweden and Japan. And in India and China these forms of psychopathy afflict only 1 in 1,000 people, compared with 20–40 per 1,000 in the developed world. The relevant surveys are summarized in:

O. James *They F*** You Up. How to Survive Family Life*. London: Bloomsbury, 2002.

At a more theoretical level there are important issues lurking here regarding relations between the human subject and the object being interacted with. These issues have been most thoroughly explored by Soviet psychologists and philosophers working in the Soviet Union. See:

D. Bakhurst, *Consciousness and Revolution in Soviet Philosophy. From the Bolsheviks to Evald Ilyenkov*. Cambridge: Cambridge University Press, 1991.

Early work on the self and society

Students interested in earlier work on the relations between the self and society should study the work of the Marxist Frankfurt School. Particularly recommended are:

H. Marcuse, *Eros and Civilization*. London: Ark, 1956.
E. Fromm, *The Sane Society*. London: Routledge, 1991, esp. ch. 3.

Note that Fromm argues that narcissism and lack of human relatedness stems from human separation from nature. Marcuse is often said to have heralded student-led sexual liberation movements in the 1960s. In fact, he was arguing for the *transformation* of sexual energy into emotional communication in social institutions. See:

A. Elliott, *Psychoanalytic Theory. An Introduction*, 2nd edn. Basingstoke: Palgrave, 2002.

More recently, Kovel has argued that narcissism under late capitalism is focused on the commodified family. Parents, themselves feeling powerless and inadequate, 'invest' in their children as a means of achieving long-term, narcissistic gratification. See:

J. Kovel, 'Narcissism and the Family', in idem, *The Radical Spirit: Essays on Psychoanalysis and Society*. London: Free Association, 1988.

The social implications of the new communications technologies

On emergent communications technologies and their implications for community life, see, in particular:

H. Rheingold, *The Virtual Community. Finding Connection in a Computerized World*. London: Minerva, 1995.
I. de Sola Pool, *Technologies of Freedom*. Cambridge, MA: Harvard University Press, 1984.

6

Modifying Human Biology

Overview

This chapter continues the emphasis on *internal* nature. How, as society adapts itself to exploit external nature, are people's biological and intellectual capacities being developed? Focusing first on industry, attention is given to the new reproductive technologies. These are sometimes claimed to offer the possibility of a full-scale transformation of human beings, their well-being and their intellectual abilities. This chapter argues that many of these suggestions exaggerate the possibilities for these technologies. Furthermore, they are often based on a misplaced confidence in genes and their supposed effects on human beings. Too many claims are made for genes when a greater emphasis is needed on human organisms as a whole and their relationship with the environment. The new technologies may still turn out to be significant for understanding human beings and 'the good life', but for now students would be wise to turn to the ways in which society is *actually* transforming human biology. Millions of people throughout the globe are suffering from so-called 'diseases of affluence' such as diabetes and cardiovascular disease. This is a result of the ways in which people have encountered modern ways of life. They are amongst the key ways by which not only are new social classes being made but also their internal characteristics and their fates are being determined.

Industrializing Birth, Improving Humans?

In July 1978 Louise Brown was born. She was the world's first 'test tube baby'. Ever since then a number of terms have become almost household words. These include not only genetic engineering but also *in vitro* fertilization (IVF), surrogate motherhood, frozen embryos and egg donations. The implications of all these developments are still not all that clear. It is nevertheless evident that an important development is now afoot: namely, the industrialization of human procreation.

IVF was first used as a last resort for treating women who could not conceive. Now it is used for a number of fertility problems, including help for those who cannot produce eggs and for women who may be carrying genetic disease. There are a number of different strategies here, the details of which are not central to our argument (for further information see, for example, Spallone 1989). They all centre on removing a woman's eggs and keeping them alive under laboratory conditions. This is particularly important for current developments since it is now possible to test an embryo for its genetic characteristics. This means that those embryos with 'incorrect' genetic characteristics can be rejected. Conception can proceed on the basis of what are seen as the 'best' embryos.

The point is that birth is now starting to be made into a fully commodified and industrialized process. It is a 'labour process' in the fullest sense. On the one hand, there is a range of companies marketing drugs and equipment, entrepreneurs who stock medical equipment, sperm banks and medical centres which form an 'input' into this new kind of labour process. On the other hand, there is the production of children. In the middle are embryos and women engaged in making the potential child grow. As regards the latter, here too it is possible to buy the services of certain selected women who act as surrogates (see boxes 6.1 and 6.2). In all, we are witnessing the development of a fully commodified process, with even the 'outputs' of the children having a monetary value for which some people are prepared to pay.

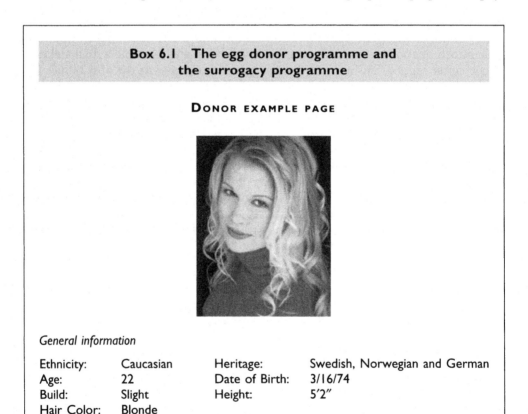

Box 6.1   The egg donor programme and the surrogacy programme

DONOR EXAMPLE PAGE

General information

Ethnicity:	Caucasian	Heritage:	Swedish, Norwegian and German
Age:	22	Date of Birth:	3/16/74
Build:	Slight	Height:	5'2"
Hair Color:	Blonde		

Academic information

Highschool:	3.9	ACT:	26
College:	4 years	Degree:	Bachelors

Career/goals

'To find challenge, knowledge and growth on my career path in media relations/ corporate communications. I hope to segue [sic] my experiences in the entertainment industry and corporate America into a collegiate teaching position one day.'

Personal information

Favorite movies: *Ferris Bueller's Day Off*, *The Breakfast Club*, *High Fidelity*, *Rushmore*
Favorite book: *Candide*, by Voltaire; *She's Come Undone*, by Wally Lamb; *The Grapes of Wrath*, by John Steinbeck; and *A Natural History of Love*, by Diane Ackerman
Hobbies/talents: Cardio workouts, weights, mountain biking, reading, movies, music, art, people, travel and being outside

Donor's message

'Love the child but don't smother and make sure you're ready to be parents. Make sure your relationship is strong because a child shouldn't be raised in a house of tears.'

Our message

Smart, creative and ambitious, this strong and independent woman is a ray of sunshine in the life of everyone who is privileged enough to know her. With her blonde hair, delicate features and ethereal good looks, she sometimes runs into resistance in her line of work from people who just can't believe such a young woman could be an extremely successful publicist for a television network. At the age of 27, she's not satisfied with a job level most never attain. She's just about to branch out with her business partner and open her own PR firm. Although she loves her work, she makes sure that it doesn't engulf her life entirely. A well-read woman, she's always got a book in hand and even organized a book club amongst her friends so she can share her love of literature with other women. A talented writer, she is currently working on her first novel. On the weekends she loves to get out of the city and you can find her hiking in Yosemite, camping in the desert, snow skiing, water skiing or any other outdoor activity she can get herself into. As though that were not enough, she has also just completed her first marathon and continues her training with regular trail runs and yoga. A definite leader, she is the one amongst her friends to plan all the camping trips and even organized a trip for her family to Hawaii for the holidays. Always ready to laugh, she's got a goofy, sweet sense of humour and intelligent sense of fun that will keep you laughing until your stomach hurts. A previous donor with successful cycle behind her, we were beside our-selves when she came to us about donating again. We cannot say enough about this woman. She's a giving and big hearted person who would give her friends the shirt off her own back. She is loved by everyone in the program as a daughter, sister, friend and sister [sic].

Additional information about our candidates is available after a phone or in-person consultation. Other information includes three generations of family medical and career history, complete details of educational background, aspirations, in-depth information on primary relatives, characteristics, additional photographs, essays, psychological test-ing and extensive personal interviews. <http://eggdonation.com/angel/example.asp>

Box 6.2   Creating Families Inc. A centre for surrogacy and egg donation

SURROGATE MOTHER/EGG DONOR SEARCH MENU

This page contains selection items you can click on that will help to narrow the number of surrogate mothers and/or egg donors that have the traits you prefer. To have your search return the most likely candidates, please specify as many of the choices that are available below, leaving blank only those that you have no preference for.

Choose the kind of profile you are looking for:

Age	Race	Ethnic Ancestry
20 years old or younger	White	Arabic
21–23 years	Black	Balkan
24–26 years	Asian	Basque
27–29 years		Belgian
		Black African
		Chinese
		Egyptian
		English
		French
		German
		Greek
		Hispanic

Height	Weight	Physical Build
Less than 5 feet	Less than 100lbs	Petite/fine boned
5 feet to 5 feet 7 inches	101 to 125lbs	Medium boned/average
5 feet 8 inches to 6 feet	126 to 150lbs	Big boned/heavy set

Natural Color of Hair	Texture of Hair	Eye Color
Blonde hair	Straight	Green eyes
Brown hair	Fine	Brown eyes
Red hair	Slightly curly	Black eyes
Black hair	Thick	Blue eyes
	Curly	
	Very curly	

Complexion	Tanning Ability	Hand Coordination
Fair	Easily tan	Right handed
Fair with freckles	Slight ability to tan	Left handed
Medium	Moderate ability to tan	Ambidextrous
Olive	No ability to tan	

Vision	Hearing	Blood Type
20/20	Normal	O positive
Mildly nearsighted	Slightly impaired	O negative
Mildly farsighted	Moderately impaired	A positive
Severely nearsighted	Severely impaired	A negative
		B positive

Education

Highest grade completed	High school grade point	College grade
Sixth grade or lower	A average	2.0 to 2.4 average
7th to 9th grade	B average	2.5 to 3.0 average
10th to 12th grade	C average	
Junior college		
Bachelor degree		

Approximate IQ score	Are you looking for a woman who has been one of the following in the past?
	Egg donor
Less than 75	Surrogate mother
76 to 100	Both a surrogate mother and egg donor
101 to 120	
121 to 140	

(Note that all boxes contain a 'No Preference' option).

Source: <//www.eggdonorfertilitybank.com/profiles/search.html>

'Designer babies'

This industrialization process shows signs of being taken still further. It may (the word 'may' is important) be possible to specify what child you wish to buy. Embryos are already being screened for the genes which make children more likely to have cystic fibrosis or muscular dystrophy, as well as for those that determine gender. Embryos may soon be tested for predisposition to other medical problems such as bowel cancers, Down syndrome and familial Alzheimer's. An obvious extension of such advances might include selection for, say, eye or skin colour, athleticism or intelligence. In this way we can envisage a kind of post-Fordist production process. In the same way as it is possible to specify what kind of car you want, it may be possible to specify the kind of child you want (see boxes 6.1 and 6.2).

The 'GenRich' and the 'Naturals'?

What are the social implications of such developments? Lee Silver is a microbiologist at Princeton University. Taking current trends to what he sees as their logical extent, he predicts that in three hundred years' time, the United States will be made up of two distinct biological classes (Silver 1998). These are the 'GenRich' and the 'Naturals'. Synthetic genes will have been incorporated into the GenRich, making them 'a modern-day hereditary class of genetic aristocrats' (ibid. 7). The GenRich will be quite diverse, some being excellent football players as a result of genetic modification, some being inspired scientists or excelling in the world of media. Meanwhile, the Naturals will have been reproducing themselves 'in the old fashioned way'. Their parents will have been unable to afford genetic enhancement. Nor will they have been given private education, even if they have received gene-enhancement.

In due course the GenRich and the Naturals will be two separate species. They will be unable to cross-breed and will be possessed with 'as much romantic interest in each other as a current human would have for a chimpanzee' (ibid. 7). Furthermore, Silver has few reservations about such polarizing. It is only an extension of what happens today. Humans have a right to do their best for their children.

The genetic modification of animals and people via the private ownership of bodies and genetic manipulation might make it seem as though evolution has been finally overcome. We are now moving into what Fukuyama (2002) calls a 'post-human' period of evolution in which humanity is finally able to manage its own evolution (see also Baldi 2001). Enlightenment-style self-improvement is carried to its ultimate extreme. However, the picture is unlikely to be as simple as this.

Is 'playing God' desirable or effective?

For most illnesses or characteristics it is unlikely that they will ever be directly attributable to particular genes or gene sequences. There are indeed some direct links of this kind. Silver himself mentions sickle-cell anaemia, cystic fibrosis, Tay–Sachs disease and Huntington's chorea. But making such connections for other diseases seems at the moment improbable.

It is even less clear that there are direct links between genes and such qualities as 'intelligence' or 'athletic ability'. Insofar as there are genetic links, they are likely to entail complex *combinations* of genes and even more complex interactions between genes and their environment. Much less of what Fox-Keller (2000) calls 'gene talk' is needed if even an adequate *understanding* of human development is to be acquired. And such understanding of the impacts of genetic modification is a still more distant possibility. The GenRich may easily feel they have been sold short when they realize they have not gained all the benefits promised to them.

The importance of the environment

Second, and closely related to the above, the picture derived from Silver as regards the GenRich takes little account of the environment. Here is another set of complexities which are likely to confound any tendency to reduce all understanding to microbiology and the 'magic bullet' approach to solving human problems. Someone's abilities or illnesses are likely to entail interactions between their bodies and their environment. Even if genetics are involved, it is best to think of there being genetically based propensities which may or may not be triggered by environmental factors. Again, these of course include the social environment (including the level of education someone receives) as well as physical circumstances.

Why the GenRich should insure themselves

Finally, remember the unfortunate Beltsville pigs. People with real or imagined genetically based problems, and those who are likely to lead short and unhealthy lives, may find it difficult to gain the kinds of insurance cover secured by the Normals. But the Beltsville pigs are a reminder that if people, in a true Enlightenment way, attempt to improve themselves by changing their genes, they could be letting themselves in for some very unpleasant unexpected consequences. They too should take out extensive insurance cover in case their hoped-for upgrading turns out to be disastrous. For people, as for other animals, introducing genes as magic cure-alls into complex organisms may be introducing longer-term serious problems.

Resistances to the industrialization of childbirth

The possibility arises of a kind of DIY eugenics, with wealthy households buying the 'designer child' they think will best succeed in the world. The result could in theory be what some commentators refer to as the 'Nazification of medicine', with the screening of embryos before they are implanted being equivalent to the mass euthanasia programmes in Germany in the 1930s and '40s. Experience so far suggests, however, that the characteristics looked for are most likely to be modelled on the parents who are paying for the surrogacy; a variant on adults narcissistically transforming the environment in their own image (Richards n.d.). 'The Nazification of medicine' represents the kind of sound-bite sensationalism which seems to surround these developments, a matter we will return to shortly.

Nevertheless, as Gimenez puts it, 'the mode of reproduction is in transition' (1991: 334). At first sight this looks very akin to other forms of production, with the 'commons' of the human body again becoming commodified and the 'consumers' being offered high degrees of market 'choice' as to the kind of child they would like for their money. However, a number of difficulties ensue. One is that some women feel the whole process has become over-rationalized and medicalized. People are being turned into 'baby-machines', with their emotional lives and connections to their children being ignored or overturned. This leads to resistance in the form of older forms of birthing being developed (see box 6.3).

Box 6.3   Irrational or rational childbirth?

Resistance to industrialized and over-medicalized childbirth is now emerging. This partly entails the recovery of older 'irrational' forms of knowledge. Independent birth centres are springing up in the USA, UK, Holland and elsewhere which are devoted to the needs of mother and child. Floor mats and cushions to kneel or squat on are provided, as are birthing rockers to support the mother's weight and to enable her to find a comfortable position. Hydrotherapy suites are provided, where two people can sit in a jacuzzi or just have a soothing shower or massage. Water is recognized as an efficacious pain-reducer. On the one hand, old and traditional ('irrational') practices such as birthing feasts are positively encouraged. On the other, midwives are often encouraged to become more 'scientific'. In Holland this is achieved by adding a postgraduate year to their three-year training course.

There are further, equally profound issues about whether the new industrialized forms of childbirth are really likely to deliver all they promise. In particular, the great emphasis on genes and their effects on people's well-being, levels of intelligence and so forth is open to considerable question. There is a looming problem of what is known as 'genetic reductionism' here: reducing the good and the bad life to the genes inherited from parents. It is reminiscent of some of the early extensions of Darwinian thought to human beings in which it was wrongly assumed that 'intelligence' and other attributes were biologically handed down from one generation to the next. In our own day too, and even given the insights of the new genetics, there is little evidence that this kind of inheritance is a serious possibility. It is still less clear that 'designer children' can actually be made with the aid of the new genetics. If parents do try making their offspring into model children, the chances are they will be disappointed.

Improving on Evolution: Genes and the Good Life

Oversold genes

The 'designer babies' vision makes good newspaper copy, but it does not accord with biological and social reality. The new reproductive technologies can be seen as an attempt to achieve the genetic optimization of offspring. And, as Beck and Beck-Gernsheim argue, there is every possibility that women who do not use them risk being labelled as 'selfish, ignorant or stupid' (2002: 145).

But the fact is that genes do not do all that is often claimed for them. Mutations in the same gene can, for example, lead to a number of different illnesses or syndromes. Conversely, mutations in a single gene have been attributed to a number of different syndromes (Ho 1999). Furthermore, genetic tests are often poor predictors of the condition of any one individual. Such testing remains largely blind to the very considerable variations within populations. A genetically standard individual seems to be assumed.

Genes and health

Disease is typically a product of highly complex circumstances. It is rarely the product of genes alone. The underlying cause and effect model (assuming that a gene causes a disease or a characteristic) is highly inappropriate. At 'best', in explanatory terms, a disease is a simultaneous product of underlying genetically based predispositions and the environment in which a person is living. In other words, it is usually unlikely that there is a gene 'for' anything. And, to the extent to which genes are important, the most likely process of causation will probably take the form of a cascade of genetic changes, one affecting a multiplicity of others.

> ## Box 6.4   Cracking the code of human life
>
> ### UNRAVELLING THE SECRETS OF CHROMOSOMES WILL CHANGE THE FACE OF RESEARCH INTO CURES AND TREATMENTS OF ILLNESSES FOR YEARS TO COME
>
> In human terms, the fact that chromosome 22, the second smallest of the human chromosomes, carries genes linked to schizophrenia, chronic myeloid leukaemia and a trisomy 22, the second commonest cause of miscarriages, as well as genes involved in congenital heart disease, mental retardation, breast cancer and cataracts, offers hopes for vast improvements in the way diseases and medical conditions are treated for hundreds of years. (*Guardian*, 2 December 1999)

Take, for example, the press report shown in box 6.4. Note the phraseology. A chromosome is said to carry genes 'linked' to schizophrenia and other diseases. Other genes are 'involved in' congenital heart disease. The 'fact' of these links and involvements 'offers hopes for vast improvements'. But what explanatory claims can be made here? A small number of illnesses, such as Huntington's chorea and cystic fibrosis, are indeed acquired by largely genetic means (Marteau and Richards 1996). But once more, the range of diseases connected to specific gene sequences (known as 'alleles') is small and highly variable between individuals. A disease such as Huntington's is therefore a 'freak' in these terms. And even with Huntington's, the age of onset is very variable, once more suggesting that other extra-genetic processes may be at work.

The connections between genes and illnesses are therefore far more complex than the publicity surrounding the human genome project might suggest. It is not at all clear, for example, whether such illnesses are a product of a number of gene combinations or of relations between the human body and the external social or even natural environment. Words such as 'linked' and 'involved in' seem at first sight to be saying much, but in explanatory terms they are saying rather little.

In short, it is almost certainly too early to say what can or cannot be achieved by these techniques. As in the case of animal experiments, genetic manipulation joins human cloning as practices that understandably attract much press speculation. But they still have to prove themselves as effective ways of dealing with medical 'problems' while avoiding any number of new hazards and risks.

All too often a dramatic announcement is made as regards finding a gene for a condition or illness. (As I write, a gene has recently been discovered 'for' asthma.) Such a claim may be successful in generating further research funds, but, as box 6.5 indicates, the claims frequently evaporate into thin air. This is again because the causes are likely to be far more complex than single genes 'for' any condition. A substantial part of this complexity lies in the fact that the condition may well be triggered off by the social and environmental conditions of the organism's environment.

Box 6.5   Behavioural genetics: a suitable case
for critical realism

Periodically, the association of genes with certain human behaviours and propensities is announced. But in all cases these claims have usually remained unsubstantiated and the links between animals and humans have not been adequately made. Here are some examples (taken from *Scientific American* 1992: 125):

Crime   In the 1960s researchers reported a link between an extra Y chromosome and violent crime in males. Follow-up studies found the association to be non-existent.

Manic depression   In 1988 a research group reported a gene associated with schizophrenia in British and Icelandic families. Follow-up studies reported no linkage. The initial claim has now been retracted.

Alcoholism   In 1990 a group claimed to have found a link between a gene and alcoholism. A later review of the evidence concluded that the link did not exist.

Homosexuality   In 1991 two groups claimed to have evidence of genetic heritability of 50 per cent for male or female homosexuality. These reports were, however, disputed. Another group claims to have preliminary evidence of genes linked to male homosexuality. But the data have not so far been published.

In all these instances it is being claimed that genes on their own are centrally important causal mechanisms. But this is very misleading. Only 3 per cent of human diseases, for example, are attributable to defects in a single gene (Rennie 1994). Genetically-based propensities (usually the result of combinations of genes) are much more likely to combine with environmental and social conditions to produce illnesses, alcoholism and so on. Critical realism, as discussed in box 1.8 (p. 20), offers a way of recognizing the causal powers of genes or clusters of genes while also acknowledging the key significance of environmental factors in activating biologically-based tendencies toward certain behaviours and illnesses. Human illnesses and behaviours, in other words, are rooted in, but not reducible to, the causal powers of individual genes.
    Critical realism also asks scientists and social scientists to be self-critical. What social effects are they having by, for example, insisting that single genes can have important effects on people's behaviour?

Genes and intelligence

The issue becomes still more complex and contentious when it is assumed that society, and people's success in society, is a product of their biologically inherited nature. The issue of 'intelligence' is especially germane here and it is one which gained particular prominence with the publication of *The Bell Curve* (Herrnstein and Murray 1994). The book has sold several hundred thousand copies, been the subject of a presidential press conference and of cover stories in many news and

> ## Box 6.6 Society as a product of human nature?
> ### *The Bell Curve* hypothesis
>
> A recurrent theme in much of social and political thought is that society is itself a product of human nature. It is the result of inborn human capacities and the striving of people to survive and be successful. Human fate is therefore a product of inborn abilities. Those who are intellectually 'fittest' are most likely to survive and reproduce. One of the most recent versions of Social Darwinism comes in *The Bell Curve* (Herrnstein and Murray 1994). In a society where the premium for successful and well-paid work is intelligence, people are increasingly getting the kinds of job for which they are mentally cut out. The intelligentsia of whatever class is being selected (and through interbreeding is selecting itself) to become a cognitive elite. They are the ones who find themselves at the upper levels of management or in education. At the same time, the argument goes, the same processes are leading to a rapidly increasing underclass. These are people with low IQ levels. And, unfortunately, they are breeding much faster than the elite. The logic of this position is that little can be done in the way of social or welfare programmes. Such interventions are likely to have little effect since the original causes of deprivation and disadvantage are lodged in human nature itself. The best way forward for those losing out in the struggle to be successful is for them to be happy with the jobs where they finish up. Many of these jobs have psychic rewards and are highly valued by society at large.

opinion magazines. And its authors have received the support of Robert Plomin, of whom more shortly. For all these reasons alone, it is worth taking seriously.

The book's central thesis has often been misrepresented. It is not primarily about the supposed inadequacies of black people. It is centrally about the class structure of modern America and, by implication, of other Western societies. The central thesis concerns what Herrnstein and Murray call 'cognitive ability'. Those who have this ability are most likely to rise into the elite well-paid jobs (see box 6.6). The authors of *The Bell Curve* strongly suggest that state schooling for the underclass would be a waste of resources. This is logical if we assume that intelligence is genetically bred into these people. The best that might be expected is for a lack of high IQ to be bred out. But this would mean that the underclass would have to stop interbreeding. Going back to our 'designer baby' discussion, the ideal infant might be one in which 'the gene for intelligence' has been inserted. Equally, those who do not possess the correct gene might be aborted at the embryo stage in order to enhance the success of a society and particular groups of people within it. On this basis, a technical, genetic fix is therefore likely to be more effective than a social fix.

Such a scenario might be deduced from the work of Robert Plomin. He is one of a number of scientists who claimed in 1997 (see box 6.7) to have made such a link between genes and intelligence and he has supported the work of Herrnstein and Murray. And yet in a later review of the field, Plomin (1999) is remarkably candid about these contentious matters. He shows that in fact there are so far very few, if any, established connections between genes and IQ. He remains confident,

---

Box 6.7 Scientists discover gene that creates human intelligence

The first gene that influences human intelligence has been found by scientists, a discovery with huge social and educational implications. The research could herald the development of genetic tests to target potential high-flyers, pave the way to IQ-boosting drugs and will raise fears that embryos that lack smart genes could be aborted. The gene, believed to be the first of many that contribute to normal intelligence, has been found after a six-year search by a team headed by Prof. Robert Plomin of the Institute of Psychiatry in London ...

'I really think this is a breakthrough', he said. Neuroscientists will now study how this gene works to affect the functioning of the brain, ending years of argument over whether genes can affect intelligence. 'It is hard to argue with a piece of DNA', he said. (*Daily Telegraph*, 31 October 1997)

---

however, that genes associated with a measure of intelligence (called 'g') will in due course be found. But he is much less confident about whether individual genes, as distinct from clusters of genes, will ever be closely related to a measure of intelligence. Perhaps, he believes, several hundred genes will be needed to account for special intellectual abilities.

So it seems that scientific endeavour is still a long way from providing the kind of simple genetic understanding that would be needed for modifying embryos in such a way that intelligence could be ensured. Similarly, it is unlikely to provide anything like an adequate basis for aborting embryos without the 'smart' genes, even if such a practice was deemed to be ethically acceptable. Trying to link specific genes to levels of intelligence is likely to be a fruitless enterprise.

Genetics and society: beyond reductionism

But there is an alternative form of biology, one which remained largely ignored for a long time. It emphasizes the human organism as a whole, its relationship to the social-cum-physical environment and the development of the organism within this environment. Such an explanatory strategy avoids the problems of genetic reductionism and starts to allow biological ideas to be adequately combined with social relations and social processes.

It also avoids 'sociological reductionism'. As box 6.8 discusses, an influential tendency in contemporary sociology is to argue that all knowledge, including all biological and evolutionary knowledge, is 'socially constructed'. All understanding, that is, is made in society and is the product of power relations and discourse. Such a view is useful, not least because it emphasizes the diversity of forms of knowledge. It is also helpful as a reminder that no knowledge has dropped from the sky with a label attached saying 'Unassailable Truth' and that power relations are critical in determining which kinds of knowledge prevail and which do not. All knowledge is indeed a product of the society in which it is made. And it can always be challenged and changed.

Box 6.8 Representing the body

Cultural sociology gives special attention to 'plastic', 'bionic', 'virtual' and 'interchangeable' bodies. All these are responses to recent developments in spare-part surgery, IVF, the new reproductive technologies and so on. Haraway (1991) is a particularly well-known contributor to this perspective. She argues that contemporary developments are leading to the development of 'cyborg' creatures, organisms which are half-human, half-machine. As a feminist influenced by postmodernism, she welcomes these developments, seeing them as heralding the end of oppressive dualism between 'man' and 'woman' as well as between races and even species.

How do these forms of social science link to a perspective which recognizes what contemporary biology has to say as regards the reality of evolution, of the body, of death and birth?

Clearly it is important to examine how the body is socially construed and how identities are made and remade via the body. It is also important to challenge, as does Haraway, what scientists say to be the truth about nature and evolutionary change. These construals or representations are also important because they clearly influence how illnesses, levels of intellectual ability and so forth are interpreted by people, and they may be vitally important in determining public health strategies, education policies and research funding.

But these representations must not be confused with the actual physical, bodily reality to which they refer. As Williams puts it in his discussion of human disability, 'diversity and difference . . . are rooted in real impaired bodies' (1999: 811). They are, to use his words, 'organically moored'. Cultural sociology, in short, runs the considerable risk of 'over-sociologizing' the body, birth, illness and death. This is another kind of reductionism, one equivalent to that adopted by some biologists.

The difficulties of sociological reductionism start, however, if the argument continues by insisting that knowledge is *only* socially constructed and there is no external reality to which knowledge can refer. There are serious arguments at the moment, for example, between those who think that illnesses are a product of genes and those who think they stem from the relationships between organisms and their environment. Whatever the disagreements here, however, no one is seriously saying there are no real mechanisms underlying illnesses. These are real, even if they cannot be easily observed. And they are having real, often devastating, effects. The strongest versions of social constructionism would not recognize that there are realities of this kind, realities which are clearly a product of scientific endeavour. No independent reality developed in this way is deemed possible.

Non-reductionist forms of biology

Returning to biology and the natural sciences, what are the alternatives? Holistic, non-reductionist, approaches to biology in fact go back to Darwin and to certain key figures in the early twentieth century (Dickens 2000). In our own era we should mention the highly influential figure of Conrad Waddington. He and later authors such as Wills (1993) and Maynard Smith (1998) suggest that organisms grow not only in relation to their physical and social environment but through realizing their new genetically based potentials. The perspective offered by all these authors places particular emphasis on the organism's *development*. It provides an ontology (an understanding of the nature of reality) which 'puts genes in their place' and allows a better understanding of the often complex relations between genes, organisms and the environment.

This explanatory strategy therefore recognizes the causal powers of the development of species while realizing that the context within which these powers develop is of crucial importance to the organism's lifetime development. Waddington outlined such a view as early as the 1950s. An organism can be likened to a ball, developing as it runs down one of a number of genetically influenced 'valleys', each one of which is different according to the genetic composition of individuals (see boxes 6.9 and 6.10). An organism is relatively robust and is not easily deflected from one 'valley' to another. But social or environmental shocks can flip the developing organism from one valley to another.

Importantly for Waddington, and for a small but growing number of contemporary biologists, 'ontogeny', or lifetime development, may have important

---

Box 6.9   The epigenetic landscape

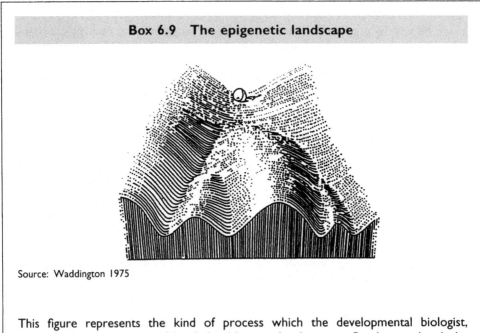

Source: Waddington 1975

This figure represents the kind of process which the developmental biologist, Conrad Waddington, argued lies behind human development. On the one hand, the organism (represented by a ball) is most likely to develop along a certain path or 'valley'. On the other, given external or environmental 'shocks', the individual can start developing in a different way, along other paths.

Box 6.10   The relations between genes and
the epigenetic landscape

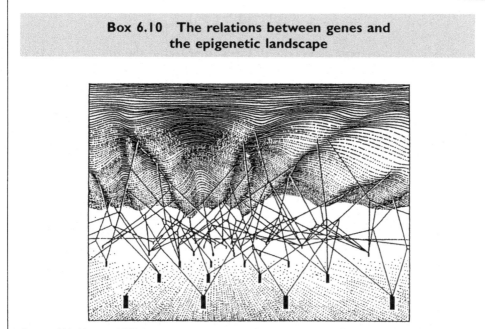

Source: Waddington 1957

Waddington proposed that the 'valleys' of an organism's development were linked to genes. But they are linked in complex ways. Like other biologists of his day, he had little understanding of genes (represented by the black cylinders at the bottom of the diagram), but he proposed that they are most likely to combine with one another in complex ways to effect the direction and form of an organism's development. The approach proposed by Waddington recognizes the significance of genes while avoiding genetic reductionism. It is an approach which finds increasing acceptance today, and, in the light of contemporary developments in biology, which gives decreasing attention to genes per se and more emphasis to interacting genes and their relations to environmental change. (For further details and discussion, see Waddington 1957, 1975.)

long-term evolutionary effects. Over time they are better suited to the new conditions. And it will be they who are best able to survive and leave offspring. In this way, ontogeny is linked to phylogeny, or long-term evolution. This approach to ontogeny, or lifetime development of organisms, is compatible with the organism-centred approach to phylogeny, or the long-term evolution of species. Both are different sides of the same coin. Lifetime development depends on genetic information accumulated over millions of years of evolution and long-term evolution depends on developmental changes in successive generations. Both also give special emphasis to interactions between organism and environment (Oyama 1985).

'God genes'

One of the most intriguing aspects of this new approach is the role of 'homeobox' genes. Recent research in genetics and development suggests that they are likely to be particularly significant as regards the link between development and evolution. A critical realist position emphasizes the key role of underlying structures and causal mechanisms. Homeobox genes are profoundly enduring structures and mechanisms, having existed for around one billion years and remaining conserved in all animals and plants (perhaps inevitably, they are referred to by some contemporary biologists as 'God genes'). They are in fact clusters of genes producing proteins which activate thousands of other genes in the organism in cascade-like manner. They lay down the basic components and ground plan for all animals: a head, back and thorax, for example, as well as eyes, brain-structure and appendages such as paws, fins or wings. Their relatively unchanging nature stems from their largely unchanging functions. Variations have nevertheless developed in relation to specific contexts. Some variations in appendages have allowed, for example, faster swimming, speedier running or better grasping. Some variations may even correspond to more extensive cognitive capacities, but this remains a far cry from saying that there are specific genes 'for intelligence' (see box 6.11).

In a similar way, it seems very likely that humans have (perhaps like other species) evolved with a strong sense of self-identity. It is one which young children develop as they mature and start relating to their environment (see box 6.12). Nevertheless, there is nothing here to suggest that humans have developed a specific kind of self (mutualistic, individualistic, narcissistic and so on). In line with the critical realist position discussed earlier, the form which this sense of self takes depends on the social context in which the human being develops.

The above forms of biology offer the possibility of a very productive liaison between the natural and social sciences. In particular, they allow recognition of

---

Box 6.11 'Master-control genes'

Homeobox genes provide the key to the modern understanding of evolution and development. Humans use their limbs for walking, holding knives and forks, etc. Other animals use their limbs for flying, swimming and so on. But they all have limbs. Similarly, they all have nervous systems, some obviously more sophisticated than others. They all have eyes, despite the variations in the *forms* of eyes. It comes as no surprise, therefore, to find that all higher organisms, from the fruitfly to humans, share a characteristic DNA segment. This is known as 'the homeobox' (see illus. 6.11). This cluster of genes has remained constant for about a billion years due to the fact that it has been serving basically the same underlying functions for which they originally evolved. (No wonder some scientists refer to them as 'God genes'.) One analogy in terms of design might be in the world of automobiles. Their underlying organization has not substantially changed because the purpose for which cars were originally designed has itself not changed.

Illustration 6.11 Homeobox genes

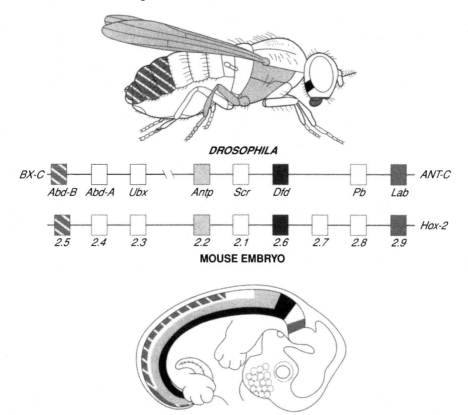

HOMEOBOX GENES control development in animals as different as *Drosophila melanogaster* (a fruit fly) and a mouse. These genes divide the embryo along its head-to-tail axis into bands with different developmental potentials. The location of a homeobox gene on a chromosome corresponds to where it is expressed in the body: proceeding from left to right, the genes control body areas closer to the anterior end of the animal. All homeobox genes seem to have a common evolutionary origin. In this diagram, related homeobox genes in *Drosophila* and the mouse and the body parts they control in each animal are shaded similarly. The mechanism that determines the head, trunk and tail may have arisen only once during evolution.

Source: De Robertis et al. 1990: 27

Box 6.12   Human development, evolution and the making of self

A sense of self and identity tends to emerge during the early development of the child and becomes an integral part of the human's mental structure. At the later stages of this early development process human beings increasingly make their own self-identities, again in the contexts of their environment. Research on autism in humans (where people have little awareness of themselves or of others) is showing up those parts of the brain necessary for the emergence of this sense of self (Goddard 1998; Frith and Happé 1999). But how these parts of the brain are activated depends on the society in which the individual develops. Hence the point of emphasizing the role of consumerism, the rise of new forms of employment and of 'the network society' in the formation of new kinds of self. In different kinds of society different kinds of self are likely to develop, emphasizing the 'plastic' nature of humans in adapting themselves to new circumstances.

the organism developing within particular contexts or types of society. Genetic reductionism is avoided. But we must now elaborate on precisely how this liaison should be put into effect. Development *in utero* and during the earliest stages of childhood turn out to be key meeting-points in the relations between lifetime development (and long-term evolution) and social relations.

Beyond biological reductionism: the significance of prenatal development

Recent research offers important explanations of how ill-health is passed on within families. It offers significant clues as to how an underclass of relatively unhealthy people is the process of creation and reproduction. Again, complex combinations of biological and social processes are involved, genes per se receiving relatively small explanatory weight.

'Weather forecasts'

Epidemiological work strongly suggests that a pregnant mother gives an unwitting genetically based 'weather forecast' to her unborn child, signalling via the uterus the kind of world into which her child is to be born (Barker 1998; Barker 2001; Eriksson et al. 2001). This is a well-recognized effect in non-human mammals but it has so far received little attention in studies on twins. Children from poor backgrounds, it now appears, are being biologically designed 'to make the best of a bad job' (Bateson and Martin 1999: 111). Their blood flow, metabolisms and production of hormones lead to altered bodily structures and functions. One effect is that their most essential organs, such as the brain, develop in a relatively normal way while organs less essential for immediate survival, such as the pancreas, are 'shortchanged'. In evolutionary terms they are thereby relatively well adapted to their environment. The survival of the child in such circumstances is ensured, at least in the short term. But as a result of their early treatment and their often shortchanged organs, they are more likely to suffer from a range of illnesses later on. These include diabetes and a range of other problems such as cardiovascular disease. Furthermore, the lives of these children are likely to be shorter than average (see box 6.13).

Most importantly, 'weather forecasts' are passed on from one generation to the next, the capacity of a woman to nourish her foetus being in part determined by her own intrauterine experience. Thus the effects of her mother's environment are transmitted to her *own* child. This strongly suggests a well-established biological mechanism which is contributing to the reproduction of an 'unfit' underclass over the long term – generations of people being not only born into poor circumstances but biologically 'designed' for such circumstances. They not only suffer ill-health and early death themselves but pass on these afflictions and fates to future generations. A kind of intergenerational 'cloning' is taking place, though not of the kind which now receives such prominence. Studies of marriage patterns show that mating takes place between people from similar social and educational backgrounds

---

Box 6.13 Diabetes: a global epidemic

The world is currently suffering from an epidemic of diabetes. An estimated 1.4 million people in the UK have this disease and around another 1 million remain undiagnosed. The illness is costing the British National Health Service around £5.2 billion per year. In the United States the numbers were 14 million in 1995, a figure expected to rise to 22 million in 2025. In the so-called developing countries the epidemic is expected to grow by 170 per cent over the same period. The greatest problem is in India, where the rise will be from 19 million to 57 million. (Institute of Science in Society, 2002)

(Lampard 1992; Prandy and Bottero 1998). This tendency must further widen the gap between the developmental endowments of the better and worse off.

Wrong bodies for modernity

Paradoxically, however, a child also suffers if he or she is born into conditions to which they are not well adapted. As long as an individual remains undernourished in postnatal life her or his glucose-insulin metabolism is adequate. But if, for example, a child whose mother has been starved is born into a world with high levels of sugar in food, this results in an increased predisposition to diabetes. People who have retained a traditional lifestyle in, for example, rural Africa or the highlands of Papua, New Guinea, experience low levels of diabetes or avoid this problem completely. Populations in Europe, North America and the western Pacific societies, by contrast, are much more affected. In the latter case, up to one-third of the population is afflicted by this problem. Similar outcomes have been found amongst populations that have undergone rapid migration. Ethiopian Jews who transferred to Israel during a famine in Ethiopia in the 1990s are a case in point. After only four years 9 per cent of those under the age of 30 had developed diabetes (Barker 1998). Something similar appears to affect people who are socially mobile. In a number of African societies, for example, the legal profession is recruited from people with relatively poor backgrounds and whose parents often suffer relatively short life-spans. A result is that many people in this profession suffer more health problems and die at a younger age than might be expected from their social status. In a sense they are in the 'wrong' body for someone of their social and economic standing.

Many people who are 'designed' for a poor environment are today experiencing versions of a 'Western' lifestyle with which their body cannot adequately cope. Fast foods, pre-prepared meals, fizzy drinks and low levels of exercise are amongst the characteristic features of modern life. And yet many people's bodies are not sufficiently robust to deal with this kind of treatment. The result is not just diabetes (see box 6.13), but also heart and circulatory diseases, which afflict people who have become considerably overweight, largely because of the sedentary, 'couch potato' lifestyle in which they engage. Many human bodies, in short, have not yet adapted to the modern ways of life to which they are being submitted.

The survival of the richest

Care must be taken not to adopt social stereotypes here, but it seems likely that it is the poorest people who are most likely to suffer from the results of poor food and low levels of exercise. Here, then, is another instance of the least 'fit' failing to deal with their environment, the result of which leads to relatively short and unhealthy lives. The better-off, and those able to eat better food and take exercise, on the other hand, are leading longer, healthier lives. Biology is involved in these people's lives, but there is an enormous difference between this kind of account and those of, say, Herbert Spencer and *The Bell Curve*.

Mother–infant conflict: the question of rights

The epidemiological studies conducted by Barker and his colleagues incorporate the idea that the environment itself is having direct major effects on human well-being. It insists on the social as well as the biological causes of illness and short lives. But it leaves some important social and political questions unanswered. One of these concerns the mother–child relationship. If it is accepted that the uterine 'environment' plus the wider social and environmental context can have either beneficial or deleterious effects, where does this leave the mother's rights? Is she no longer entitled to eat or drink what she wishes? In other words, the purely 'scientific' findings have important social and political implications. These will be taken up in chapter 7.

Further developing a non-reductionist perspective: 'intelligence'

Different schools of psychology interpret intellectual capacity in different ways, but few nowadays argue that intelligence is wholly innate. Many particularly emphasize the developing human being in her or his context.

Piaget and his followers understand intelligence as successful adaptation to the physical and social environment. They have studied in great detail the mental development of children from their earliest age (for a recent discussion, see Sylva 1997). It is a process of transition from a dependence on thought based on immediate experience to thought in which powers of abstraction are used to interpret the world and solve problems. These general changes in adolescent reasoning are accompanied by, and reflected in, the formation of personality, the construction of sexual identity and, more generally, the creation of self in relation to others. Such development, according to Piaget (1971), continued into the later stages of an individual's life. The individual emerges from the 'egocentrism' of childhood and comes to recognize the needs and levels of knowledge of others (Cox 1980). Such development constitutes the completed 'intelligent' individual.

Criticisms of Piaget

Piaget's work has been subject to criticism. His idea of human infants progressing towards some kind of final 'reasonable' state is somewhat mechanistic and now seems to overemphasize as 'natural' what Western civilization deems 'reason' to consist of. Nevertheless, Piaget's work is still highly regarded and has been much developed. In particular, it has been shown that general patterns of infant development actually differ according to the cultures in which they develop. Children in Western capitalist societies are quickest to grasp abstract ideas separated from their context (Buck-Morss 1982). Again, it is modern capitalist society which particularly promotes and develops a child's potential for abstract thought. Yet separating abstract from concrete ideas is potentially dangerous. Not only do people's intellectual competences remain inhibited, but environmental sustainability depends on connections between these kinds of understanding being regularly made.

Human development in context

There is now a further fast-growing literature showing that the social relations a child experiences in infancy, childhood and adolescence strongly affect how he or she develops in later life (see, for example, Karmiloff and Karmiloff-Smith 2002; Keating and Hertzman 1999; Keating and Miller 1999; Marmot and Wadsworth 1997; Montgomery et al. 1996; Montgomery et al. 1997). Emotional stability, educational performance, language acquisition, social mobility as well as cognitive capacities have all been demonstrated to be closely related to how a child has developed in the home, school and wider society. As Keating and Miller put it, following their survey of the literature, 'it is already clear that these findings are consistent with the notion that early experience becomes biologically embedded, especially during sensitive periods, and has pervasive and enduring effects on later development' (1999: 232). Such a perspective clearly again places a massive question-mark over arguments that such capacities or incapacities are genetically hard-wired into the human population. And once more it turns towards forms of explanation based on the causal powers and propensities of human beings as they develop in relation to their environment.

The above work on early childhood therefore largely supplants attempts to explain well-being and intelligence simply in terms of either 'genes' or 'environment'. The arguments in this new approach all take human development, and its implications for later well-being, as a common starting-point. The debates centre on precisely how the life-course affects later illness and life-expectancy. Are discrete events in early life responsible for problems in adulthood? Are such problems the product of cumulative social processes during the life-course? Or are they, as we might expect, a combination of both such processes? Discrete events in early life indeed combine with shocks during later life to affect overall levels of health (Power and Hertzman 1999). It seems clear that both such shocks are most likely to be experienced, however, by working-class people. It is they who are most subject to the classic risk factors generating later ill health. These include under-nutrition and other adverse circumstances affecting development, such as poor housing conditions, parental divorce and low levels of education during childhood. Note that the implications of this work for public policy are much more significant than that recognized by Herrnstein and Murray. For cognitive capacities and for health and well-being of all sorts, it is clear that educational or medical interventions at the very earliest stages of a child's life could well bring very important benefits.

Human development and intelligence: challenging *The Bell Curve*

Over a century ago, Darwin's cousin Francis Galton used identical twins to test the extent to which IQ is a product of heredity or environment. The assumption was that if the twins turned out to have similar levels of intelligence, this could be accounted for by the children sharing some inborn characteristics.

Today, identical twins are still very frequently used for this type of study, the idea being to find a pair who were separated at birth and brought up by two different adoptive families. The Spearman IQ test is somewhat different from the Piaget model, involving a range of assessments, including vocabulary and the mental manipulation of geometric forms. If their level of IQ remains similar despite their different upbringings, then an obvious conclusion is that the similarity is due to the fact that they have exactly the same genotype. If their IQ level is different, then the explanation is assumed to be environmental. On the face of it, recent studies seem to confirm the conclusion that genetic similarity is a powerful predictor of IQ level. Thus experiments by Bouchard et al. (1990) suggest that genes are responsible for between 60 and 70 per cent of variation in IQ.

Galton's work returns us to a perspective which is still alive and well today. If people are not succeeding in modern society, it is a result of their inherited characteristics. Similarly, the success of those who are succeeding is attributed to their inborn nature. This perspective informs *The Bell Curve*. However, more recent work has challenged such conclusions by questioning the use of twin studies for this kind of research (Daniels et al. 1997; Devlin et al. 1997).

Re-examining the role of genes

First, these authors re-examined the data from a number of studies of identical twins who had been reared apart. Furthermore, they explored data from two hundred studies of IQ correlations between different types of relative. They made the common-sense observation that twin studies necessarily emphasize the role that genes have to play. But as twins marry different people and pass their genes to the next generation, the twins' genes encounter a wholly different genetic context. Some of these genes' effects will change or even disappear. The genes from different parents will start combining with one another and create unpredictable results.

The above processes place a considerable question-mark over explanations of self-inflating 'cognitive elites' and 'underclasses' in the manner advanced by *The Bell Curve*. Genes are obviously inherited, but it is wrong to conclude, as did

Herrnstein and Murray, that IQ is therefore genetically inherited. Such a conclusion is unwarranted by the state of biological knowledge. Furthermore, there is evidence that people are quite capable of significantly increasing their IQ levels over their lifetimes. Finally, a review carried out by the American Psychological Association (Neisser et al. 1996) shows that employers are increasingly looking for people with a range of skills other than simple IQ. A premium is now being placed on, for example, interpersonal skills, 'personality' and what Goleman (1996) calls 'emotional intelligence'.

Why do twins have similar levels of intelligence?

A second challenge concerns the importance of the uterine 'environment': the earliest experiences and relationships of the developing child. Again, experiments with twins proved helpful. Dizygotic or fraternal twins are the result of the fertilization of different eggs by different sperm in the same mother. Their genetic 'similarity' is therefore the same as that of normal siblings born at different times. Nevertheless, fraternal twins still demonstrate a higher heritability of IQ than non-twin siblings who have been raised together.

These differences are well documented, and they are usually attributed to the fact that non-twin siblings are born at different times and are therefore raised under somewhat different conditions. But Daniels et al. (1997) show that the higher heritability of IQ amongst fraternal twins might not be a product of genes at all but a product of their shared intrauterine environment. Statistical analysis (using models which incorporated or did not incorporate the effect of uterine environment) provided the closest 'fit' to the data. Their conclusion is that only about one-third of the similarity in IQs can be linked to their genes. This is a far cry from the 60–80 per cent suggested by Herrnstein and Murray. This is an interesting example of how correlation might well not be the same as explanation.

So the genetically based conclusions of *The Bell Curve* are, to say the least, premature (see also Devlin et al. 1997). While genes per se may have a role to play, other factors are important in determining levels of intelligence. Specifically, the very earliest phase in a child's development is especially important. As Daniels et al. point out: 'Brain growth occurs during both the prenatal and perinatal period, with substantial growth occurring in utero and the majority of brain development completed by age one' (1997: 58).

Biology and society combining

But, while rejecting the purely genetic argument, the significant point is that biology and society are again *combining* to affect levels of intelligence. The kind of more complex model originally suggested by Waddington about half a century ago is more appropriate than the kind of genetic reductionism which often finds favour today. As Daniels et al. stress, much of the brain's growth takes place while the baby is still *in utero*. Excessive alcohol consumption, drug-use, cigarette-smoking and a poor diet amongst pregnant women are closely linked to the intellectual impairment of their children (Reinisch et al. 1995; Olds et al. 1994; Rush et al. 1981; Pagliaro and Pagliaro 1996). Daniels and his colleagues are not sociologists, but their discussion leads directly into areas where social scientists of many kinds have distinctive views.

Problems of drug-use and alcohol intake spread, like poor diets, across the social spectrum. But such practices are concentrated amongst the unemployed and those with few material resources. Furthermore, it has been shown that over 40 per cent of people with these problems are the children of one or more adults with the same problems, poor people having inadequate diets and engaging in excessive alcohol consumption, drug-use and cigarette consumption. Recent work on 'problem' drug-users suggests that the problem is indeed increasingly prevalent amongst the unemployed and those with few material resources (Das Gupta 1990).

Class, biology and intelligence

In short, we appear to be coming back to something resembling *The Bell Curve* thesis, but from a wholly different direction. Genes and their interactions are actually having a relatively small effect on intelligence and hence on social stratification. But social or class position can have significant effects on human biology, and on the development of generations of children and on their cognitive capacities. Note again that 'biology' has shifted away from mechanistic assumptions about genes 'for intelligence' and towards the causal powers of organisms, albeit genetically inherited causal powers. Whichever understanding of 'intelligence' is adopted, this seems like by far the best kind of explanation. But all these explanations emphasize the importance of family and community in affecting the human 'good life'.

Community and Human Development

The development of humans' physical and intellectual capacities is therefore best seen in context. There seems relatively little value in trying to understand why people are ill, or why some thrive or excel when others do not, simply in terms of their internal characteristics. Similarly, although development clearly has a genetic basis, an over-concentration on genes per se is not likely to produce useful insights.

All this entails placing a renewed emphasis on social setting, or using the term to refer to associating groups of people: 'community'. This message resonates well with the perspective developed by one of the founders of sociology, Emile Durkheim. It is also a perspective which is now finding increasing support in the sociology of health.

More than a hundred years ago Durkheim published his celebrated study of suicide. He argued that there are a number of different types of suicide. One is 'anomic'. Here, fluctuations of the economy cause instabilities and disruptions to social life, which generate great instabilities and changes to moral codes. Such disruptions are dangerous to individuals who have no sense of moral guidance and lose a grip on how to run their lives. Similarly, the complex division of labour in modern societies generates great instabilities for people in different work positions. Those in commerce and industry experience the greatest amount of change. Suddenly everything is possible. There is no longer any tradition holding them back, no sense of moral priorities which would help them make a choice as to how to run their lives. Meanwhile, other groups such as farmers do not experience such disruption. They remain contained within the existing moral order, oppressive as it may be, and were, at the time Durkheim was writing, much less likely to kill themselves.

This anomic kind of suicide is likely to decline, Durkheim believed. It is particularly associated with the transition from an old type of social order to new, industrialized, forms.

'Egoistic suicide': the significance of community

Egoistic suicide was, according to Durkheim, the form most associated with modernity. At the centre of his theory was the proposition that suicide rates are closely related to people's social context, and to levels of social integration. Those societies which are disintegrating are most likely to generate increased levels of suicide. The suicide rate in England, for example, was twice as high as that of Italy when Durkheim was writing. That of Denmark was four times as high as that of England. Suicide rates were lowest in Catholic countries and at their highest in Protestant ones.

These variations cannot be explained, Durkheim believed, solely in terms internal to the human psyche or inherited mental disorders. A sociological explanation had to be found. The most important differences between Protestantism and Catholicism, he believed, concerned the position of the individual. The individual is alone before God under Protestantism. In Catholicism, by contrast, the relation between the individual and God is mediated by the priesthood. This intervention brings with it an ordered set of beliefs and practices. The result is that Catholicism offers a more integrated form of community life. The individual feels her or himself to be part of a collectivity or community, even if this experience could be oppressive. These differences in the relation between the individual and the community are the main reasons, Durkheim believed, why there are different levels of suicide in different kinds of society.

Durkheim named the kind of suicide associated with disintegrated societies 'egoistic'. It could also be seen in other circumstances where the individual had been isolated from the community. An instance is unmarried people. How to explain the high suicide rates of the unmarried? Here again there was no protecting influence of the family. The individual was left unintegrated. Nowadays the relatively high levels of suicide amongst British farmers might be explained in this way. Not only have they suffered from a range of problems such as BSE and foot and mouth disease, but they also remain relatively unintegrated with the rest of society. Durkheim's proposition that 'suicide varies inversely with the degree of integration of the social groups of which the individual forms part' still seems to hold good (1952: 209).

Community and well-being: Durkheim updated

Durkheim's early work on the relations between psychic health and social support has been criticized. His distinctions between 'anomic' and 'egoistic' suicide are hard to maintain as completely separate categories. His reliance on statistics may underestimate the extent to which suicide is not admitted to or classified, particularly in Catholic societies. His reliance on correlation between local social structures and suicide leaves a lot to be desired in explanatory terms. He may have accounted for variations but, as he well knew, other disciplines such as biology and psychology would be needed to explain the final act of suicide.

Nevertheless, Durkheim's work has been highly influential. And it resonates well with contemporary work today on health and its relationship to local social relations. The links between social inequality and human well-being are a well-known feature of medical sociology. The association between absolute poverty and poor health is clear enough when we contrast the life expectancy of people in the so-called 'developing' countries and those such as our own. Average life expectancy in sub-Saharan Africa, for example, is 52 years. Contrast this with 75 years in the developed capitalist societies (World Bank 1993).

The new work, however, points to power relations and *relative* inequalities. In modern societies people's health and well-being is most likely to suffer in societies where inequalities of power take their most extreme forms. Life expectancy in countries with high levels of equality, such as Sweden, Norway and the Netherlands, for example, is higher than it is in Britain or the USA. According to this argument, then, the issue in the materially well-endowed societies is no longer the absolute living standards for different people, but where one is located in the social hierarchy (see box 6.14). Another way of putting this is that should 'community' be of a highly inegalitarian nature in different societies, then people's health is likely to suffer.

Durkheim gave rather little consideration to the actual mechanisms leading to people's psychic distress and possible suicide. Unlike the suggestion made by many of his critics, however, he was not averse to suggesting that psychological factors were almost certainly at work. Contemporary work allows us to pursue these further. Humans, like most other animals, have evolved powerful responses when confronted by a physical, mental or emotional threat. Their bodies automatically respond by preparing themselves to stay and resist or to capitulate or flee (the so-called 'fight or flight' syndrome). The biological processes are now becoming quite well understood. They include the release of sugar and fats into the bloodstream to provide fuel for quick energy, red blood cells flooding the bloodstream to carry more oxygen to the muscles of the limbs and brain, the heart beating faster, blood pressure rising and blood starting to clot in anticipation of injury (Patel 1996).

More recent work shows that continued exposure to stressful circumstances can severely affect the body's immune system. Normally, substances called antibodies protect us from foreign substances known as antigens. Furthermore, natural cells seek out and destroy cells that have acquired foreign characteristics such as infected or cancer cells. The central point, however, is that the resistance of people repeatedly exposed to stressful circumstances tends to be impaired (Seligman 1975).

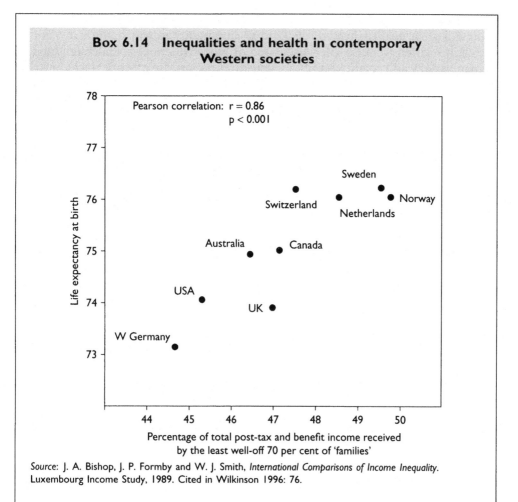

Box 6.14   Inequalities and health in contemporary Western societies

Pearson correlation: r = 0.86
p < 0.001

Source: J. A. Bishop, J. P. Formby and W. J. Smith, *International Comparisons of Income Inequality*. Luxembourg Income Study, 1989. Cited in Wilkinson 1996: 76.

In advanced capitalist societies, relative inequalities have a particular significance for people's health. This figure shows the relationship between the share of total personal income received by the least well-off 70 per cent of families and average life expectancy (in 1981). Life expectancy in countries such as Sweden and Norway, where the poorest 70 per cent of households receive a larger share of income than elsewhere, is higher than in countries like the former West Germany and the United States.

These studies therefore show that lack of power or control over your own life are key factors affecting ill-health in Western societies. Humans, like all other animals, are genetically programmed to adapt. But if such adaptation is intense or frequent it leads to 'wear and tear'. Eventually the structure and function of the organs of the body are damaged. The final effect may be serious illness of the body or the mind and even death. So, despite rising levels of affluence and longer life levels, modern society brings its own kinds of health problem. And this would appear to have a great deal to do with the kind of community in which you live. As suggested in relation to our earlier discussion of 'non-reductionist' understandings of human biology and cognitive abilities, general processes are at work (including that of people being genetically programmed as part of their evolutionary development to adapt to changing circumstances) but how this works out depends very much on the kind of society, or community, in which you live.

Human Transformation and the Risk Society

Some of the ways in which humanity is now transforming itself fit in well with the 'risk society' thesis. The new reproductive technologies are an example. Here are new ways in which modern science is attempting to transform nature. As a result, an array of 'manufactured' risks are possible. These include, for example, the distinct possibility of medical complications, multiple births and unknown long-term risks (see, for example, box 6.15). Here, then, are challenges to the whole idea of an inevitable 'progress' being made as a result of increased scientific intervention. As in the case of external nature, or 'the environment', scientific interventions are being conducted in 'open systems'. These are systems of interacting parts which do not change in constant and predictable ways. There is no simple 'cause-and-effect', whereby an intervention to a body or an ecological system has foreseeable outcomes. Risks stem, therefore, from interventions where the full implications cannot be fully known.

Developing the risk society hypothesis

But in other ways, the risk society thesis is not adequate to gain a purchase on how humanity is transforming itself and the risks that are being generated. As regards

---

Box 6.15 *In vitro fertilization and the risk society*

NEW INQUIRY TO CHECK HEALTH OF IVF BABIES

Britain is to launch a study into the potential health problems faced by the 68,000 children conceived as a result of fertility treatment since the first test-tube baby was born in 1978. Lord Winston said: 'Essentially, we have reason to believe that gene expression may change after different injuries and we've got some evidence to support that with frozen embryos. Basic functions such as growth, respiration and metabolism are regulated by genes, and if you change the way those genes are expressed – even temporarily – during times of rapid development, such as an embryo, you may well expect to see changes in the way the embryo develops'. (*Independent*, 22 October 2002)

Box 6.16   The uncertainties of *in vitro* fertilization

The Enlightenment ideals surrounding IVF are not necessarily realizable. On the one hand, science appears to be offering progress for the dynamic and self-seeking individual. It is a way of realizing the purpose for which she was born. On the other, it offers promises which are often not fulfilled. 'Hope' and 'opportunity' are offered but, as one of Franklin's interviewees says, the reality is somewhat different:

> When they said IVF was the only way I could have children, I came to the decision because, like you do, we just assumed that you have the operation and things are going to be fine. And when they said everything was fine (e.g. the tests) ... same with the first IVF treatment, great, the eggs were lovely, everything is fine, you know, we can't find anything wrong, and then you'd ring up two days later and they'd say sorry, it didn't work, and we'd say, well why, you know, if everything is fine? I think I'd accept it more if there was, if they'd said the egg count is not high, or the sperm count is not high. Then you would know, and you would know what they are treating. It's this not knowing all the time. (Franklin 1997: 151)

---

the new reproductive technologies, for example, risk society proponents underestimate the way in which they are being made into an industrialized labour process. The commodification and privatization of the birth process is only part of a more general development in which capital is finding further ways of realizing value in the manipulation of nature.

The risk society argument, particularly as it has been extended by Beck and others to include risk in the social rather than the environmental sphere, does not push the hypothesis far enough. This concerns the uncertainties generated by the new kinds of family being made with the aid of these technologies. These take two main forms. First, there are the uncertainties for those people actually engaging in this process (Franklin 1997). The new technologies are framed with powerful forms of language. Women are often construed as necessarily unfulfilled or incomplete if they do not have children. It is their 'natural' mission in life to have them. Their personal progress is to be achieved in this way, particularly since the new enabling science is now available. IVF is often promoted as not only 'natural' (giving nature a helping hand), but also as a relatively simple and straightforward sequence of events. In fact, as Franklin points out with the aid of her ethnographic work, each stage is problematic and a potential source of failure (see box 6.16).

These technologies can therefore lead to real uncertainty, distress and changes of plan. They are not necessarily the straightforward, progressive, 'natural' process which people are led to expect. As Franklin argues, the uncertainties stem not simply from having to make choices. Choice can in many ways be welcomed. But it has real downside risks, including insecurities as to whom you really belong and what it really means to be a person in modern society.

Critiquing the risk society hypothesis

In further respects the risk society idea is inadequate for understanding the nature of modern hazards. This is partly because it is centred on Western and advanced societies. The new reproductive technologies may be of pressing concern to some of the most wealthy people in those societies, but they are probably of much less interest to people in the so-called developing countries.

As discussed earlier, late-onset diabetes (known as Type 2) is set to rise especially fast in non-industrialized societies. There is a particular diabetes problem for children and adolescents. This is not the Type 1 form, associated infections or immune reactions which affect the ability of the pancreas to make insulin. It is the Type 2, supposedly adult, form. Among blacks in Charleston, South Carolina and Hispanics in Ventura, California, 45 per cent of new cases of diabetes in children are of Type 2. Among Japanese schoolchildren, Type 2 diabetes is seven times more common than Type 1, with incidence increasing thirty-fold in the last twenty years.

Some features of the risk society thesis may be to blame. It is possible, for example, that the rise of diabetes may be partly due to chemical pollution. But, as box 6.17 illustrates, these problems stem from people exchanging a life threatened by high death-rates resulting from infectious disease for a new over-fed and immobile way of life with which their metabolisms cannot yet cope. The risk society argument, in short, offers only a very partial understanding of the risks confronting the great mass of people at a global scale. The problems of human biology adapting to a new way of life are quite ancient, even if there is now every indication that they are becoming more intense. They cannot be understood within a thesis that argues that modern risk is a result of science and technology intervening too much

---

Box 6.17 Risk: the Pima Indians encounter modern ways of life

Welcome to the central Arizona desert, home of the Pima Indians and the birthplace of one of the strangest stories in medical research.

No one knows when exactly the Pima arrived – their stories say they came after a great flood survived only by Earth Medicine Man, Elder Brother *Se-eh-ha*, and Coyote. But in centuries past the Pima built themselves an unlikely paradise here along the banks of the Gila River, harvesting saguaro cactus fruit, hunting rabbits and lizards and irrigating crops of cotton, beans and squash through a system of canals. They called themselves the *Akimel O'odom* – River People.

In the late 1800s, all that started to change when Europeans settled upstream, diverting the water for their own use. Nowadays, the Pima live just outside of Phoenix, a city of 2.5 million people, frequently working in sedentary jobs. Many are obese, and the traditional diet is gone, replaced by a modern one rich in Twinkies, cheeseburgers and Coca-Cola. The Pima also suffer the highest prevalence of diabetes in the world. Fifty per cent of the over-thirties are affected, and whereas adult-onset diabetes usually strikes in late middle age, many Pima teenagers already have the disease. (Fox 1999)

in internal and external nature. The 300 million or so people now suffering from diabetes and related cardiovascular diseases do not yet have the luxury of entering the risk society. They are, if anything, looking for more scientific intervention, not less.

Summary

This chapter has been concerned with transformations to human nature. It first continued the discussion of *in vitro* fertilization and genetic engineering, this time with reference to human beings. The significance of these developments for human well-being is still not clear, but the suggestion has been that social science students would do well to address more holistic forms of biology and psychology which stress the role of the developing individual in her or his social context. This approach allows us to see that mental and physical health are closely related to people's social circumstances. Also clear are the implications of abstract knowledge being over-promoted in Western societies, with knowledge based on practical experience made marginal. This split is damaging to people since it does not fulfil their capacities for handling *both* types of information. It is especially damaging to those most dependent on practical, less theoretical types of knowledge. Furthermore, the split inhibits understanding of the complex social and ecological systems on which everyone depends. Moving towards socially just and ecologically sustainable societies means recognizing the two-way links between theoretical insights on the one hand and practical, 'everyday' understandings on the other. Both kinds of insight need one another.

FURTHER READING

New reproductive technologies

There is a developing literature on the ethical and moral implications of the new biotechnologies for human beings. Tom Shakespeare has been particularly influential in drawing attention to the possibility of using prenatal screening and genetic diagnosis as a new kind of eugenics – one in which parents are responsible for selecting those embryos that seem in some sense most 'fit'. This clearly has major implications for the oppression of disabled people. For discussion see, in particular:

T. Shakespeare, *Genetic Politics*. Cheltenham: New Clarion Press, 1999.

Habermas draws attention to the implications of biotechnology for identity, with the possibility of human self-evolution threatening humanity's self-understanding as autonomous, grown (as distinct from made) human beings. Biotechnology might also have severe implications for the balance of parent–child relations. Parents' choice of the infants' DNA could easily swing the balance of power against children and in favour of adults. See:

J. Habermas, *The Future of Human Nature*. Cambridge: Polity, 2003.

These are all very important issues. On the other hand, an over-emphasis on how human biology might or might not be manipulated can deflect attention away from how human biology and well-being are *already* being affected by social and environmental conditions.

There is a very fast-growing literature in this area. It includes:
> M. Strathern, *After Nature. English Kinship in the Late Twentieth Century*. Cambridge: Cambridge University Press, 1992.
> J. Edwards, S. Franklin, E. Hirsch, F. Price and M. Strathern, *Technologies of Procreation. Kinship in the Age of Assisted Conception*, 2nd edn. London: Routledge, 1993.

Much of the contemporary literature focuses on the experience of IVF. See, for example:
> G. Becker, *The Elusive Embryo. How Women and Men Experience the New Reproductive Technologies*. Berkeley: University of California Press, 2000.
> C. Cohen, 'Selling Bits and Pieces of Humans to Make Babies: The Gift of the Magi Revisited', *Journal of Medicine and Philosophy*, 24/3 (1999): 288–306.
> E. Kaplan and S. Squier (eds), *Playing Dolly: Technocultural Formations, Fantasies and Fictions of Assisted Reproduction*. Rutgers: Rutgers University Press, 1999.
> R. Mead, 'Eggs for Sale', *New Yorker* (5 August 1999): 56–65.
> H. Rogone and F. Twine (eds), *Ideologies and Technologies of Motherhood: Race, Class, Sexuality, Nationalism*. New York: Routledge, 2000.
> A. Turner and A. Coyle, 'What Does it Mean to be a Donor Offspring? The Identity Experiences of Adults Conceived by Donor Insemination and the Implications for Counselling and Therapy', *European Society of Human Reproduction and Embryology*, 15/9 (2000): 2041–51.
> N. Wolf, *Misconceptions: Truth, Lies and the Unexpected on the Journey to Motherhood*. London: Chatto and Windus, 2001.

A recent text which argues that the threat of commodification represented by the new reproductive technologies is overstated is:
> E. Jackson, *Regulating Reproduction: Law Technology and Autonomy*. Oxford: Hart, 2001.

While much of the above literature is about the 'consumption' of the new reproductive technologies (NRTs), there is rather little on the social organization of the system of reproduction – on, that is, the NRTs as an industrialized, profit-driven, production process. For exceptions, see:
> M. Gimenez, 'The Mode of Reproduction in Transition – A Marxist-Feminist Analysis of the Effects of Reproductive Technologies', *Gender and Society*, 5a/3 (1991): 334–50.
> R. Rowland, *Living Laboratories*. London: Lime Tree, 1992.

Critiques of reductionist biology and 'new' forms of biology

This is another large, and rapidly growing field, and one associated with emergent feminist approaches to the life sciences. A key book showing how biology and social theory can be productively combined is:
> S. Williams, L. Birke and G. Bordelow, *Debating Biology. Sociological Reflections on Health, Medicine and Society*. London: Routledge, 2003.

Other important texts include:
> E. Keller, *The Century of the Gene*. Cambridge, MA: Harvard University Press, 2000.
> L. Birke, *Feminism and the Biological Body*. Edinburgh: Edinburgh University Press, 1999.
> L. Birke, 'Bodies and Biology', in J. Price and M. Shildrick (eds), *Feminist Theory and the Body*. Edinburgh: Edinburgh University Press, 1999.

See also:
> T. Benton, 'Biology and Social Science: Why the Return of the Repressed Should be Given a (Cautious) Welcome', *Sociology*, 25/1 (1991): 1–30.
> V. Dusek, 'Sociobiology Sanitized: Evolutionary Psychology and Gene Selectionism', *Science as Culture*, 8/2 (1999): 129–69.

E. Steele, R. Lindley and R. Blanden, *Lamarck's Signature*. St Leonards: Allen and Unwin, 1998.

P. Dickens, 'Linking the Social and Natural Sciences. Is Capital Modifying Human Biology in its Own Image?' *Sociology*, 35/1 (2000): 93–110.

D. Barker (ed.), 'Type 2 Diabetes: The Thrifty Phenotype. *British Medical Bulletin*, 60 (2001).

Students interested in recent developments regarding homeobox genes and their key role in evolution and development might like to start with:

W. Gehring, *The Homeobox Story*. London: Yale University Press, 1998.

On homeobox or God genes, see:
<http:/copan.bios.unibas.ch/ch.homeo.html>

Health, intelligence and development

This is another large and understandably fast-growing field. Further references include:

M. Chorney, K. Chorney, N. Seese, M. Oliver, J. Daniels, P. McGuffin, L. Thompson, D. Detterman, C. Benvow, D. Lubinski, T. Eley and R. Plomin, 'A Quantitative Trail Locus Associated with Cognition Ability in Children', *Psychological Science*, 9/3 (1998): 159–66.

S. Fienberg, D. Resnick and K. Roeder (eds), *Intelligence, Genes and Success*. New York: Springer-Verlag, 1997.

H. Ghodse and D. Maxwell (eds), *Substance Abuse and Dependence*. London: Macmillan, 1989.

A. Hattersley and J. Tooke, 'The Foetal Insulin Hypothesis: An Alternative Explanation of the Association of Low Birthweight with Diabetes and Vascular Disease', *The Lancet*, 33 (1999): 1789–92.

L. Kohlberg, 'Stage and Sequence: The Cognitive Developmental Approach to Socialisation', in D. Goslin (ed.), *Handbook of Socialisation Theory and Research*. Chicago: Rand McNally, 1969.

R. Plomin, G. McClearn, D. Smith, S. Vignetti, M. Chorney, K. Chorney, C. Benditti, S. Kasarda, L. Thompson, D. Detterman, J. Daniels, M. Owen and P. McGriffin, 'DNA Markers Associated with High versus Low IQs: The Quantitative Tract Loci (QTL) Project', *Behaviour Genetics*, 24/2 (1994): 107–18.

7

Society, Nature and Citizenship

Overview

This book focused first on society's relations to the external environment and second on its relations to the 'internal nature' of people themselves. This chapter considers both internal and external nature, this time in relation to politics and the question of citizenship. Citizenship rights are the key way by which people become incorporated into a modern society. There are now a considerable number of arguments in favour of such rights being extended to non-human beings. This chapter, again using the themes of evolution, community, industry and risk, discusses the question of rights for humans and other species. It argues that the kinds of rights we now have and which are being proposed for non-humans are in many ways problematic. They are very much couched at the level of the individual, a result of the Enlightenment period in which they were developed. The problem with this kind of right is that it does little to counter or control class and other kinds of power. An alternative, more radical, view of rights is to develop them within their social and political and industrial contexts. Extending rights in this way will do much to protect human beings and other species. Environmental degradation and inequalities in people's well-being are a result of powerful social, economic and political forces. It may be that politics needs to develop beyond individuals choosing between the programmes of different political parties. (This can be seen as an extension of consumerism into the political realm.) It needs to develop in ways which enable people to secure a more thoroughgoing control over their lives and to assist other species in avoiding the excesses of commercialization and industrialization.

Box 7.1   The politics of the 'X generation'

American students are becoming decreasingly collective in their politics. In the 1960s and early '70s 45–50 per cent of college entrants rated 'keeping up-to-date with politics and helping clean up the environment' as very important personal objectives. About 40 per cent rated 'being very well off financially' as high in their priorities. By 1998 what Putnam (2000) calls the 'X generation' was entering college. 26 per cent were interested in politics and 19 per cent in the environment. Those rating affluence as high in their objectives had risen to 75 per cent.

Society, Politics and Rights

There are major questions as to what rights actually are and how they are supposed to improve relationships between society and nature. How can they assist humans to develop their own nature, bearing in mind that people develop in social and environmental contexts? How can they assist the environment, particularly as this applies to species caught up in industrialized food production or species under other kinds of threat? The system of rights we have now is certainly worth hanging on to, but it seems clear that it is not enough for the job in hand. What other kinds of rights are necessary? And are rights for animals to be the same as those for people? Furthermore, it seems clear that many people are decreasingly interested in the conventional political process. This particularly applies to younger people, precisely those whose outlooks have been made more personalized, individualized and narcissistic (see box 7.1). How can politics be made more interesting, something with which people might want to be involved?

The Evolution of Rights?

It is quite possible to be optimistic about the development of rights. One of the most influential optimists is the sociologist, T. H. Marshall (1964). His view is an evolutionary one in the sense developed in chapter 1. Applying an evolutionary model to the development of society, it incorporates strong notions of direction, progress and teleology (underlying purpose).

Rights as social evolution

Marshall argued that there are three elements to citizenship in the modern era, that is, the Enlightenment period from the eighteenth century onwards. These are:

- the civil element
- the political element
- the social element

The civil element

The civil element started to be established in the eighteenth century. At this stage, at least in the British, European and North American context, certain basic civil and legal rights were established. Note, as discussed in the Introduction, that these rights were very much organized around the liberty of the individual (see box 7.2). They offered full and equal justice before the law. Individuals from now on were no longer bound to the places in which they were born or the occupations they were born into. They had formal rights allowing personal independence, these being protected by the legal system. These rights, however, were only given to property-owners. It was therefore property-ownership which formed the basis of citizenship rights, property-owners being seen as people with a real and material stake in society. Note, however, that property-ownership was seen as entailing responsibilities. The person incorporated into the political community in this fashion was obliged to respect the possessions of other property-owners.

Box 7.2 Society as nature and the making of 'natural' rights

The notion of rights as developed in the eighteenth century derived from an idea of society as part of nature and people having rights as a natural being. On the one hand all social life and the state were seen as a product of free individual activity. A self-balancing, rationally ordered society was envisaged. Its predictability, certainty and potential irregularities could, it was imagined, be eventually gained. Newton's laws of physics were used as a model. On the other hand, humans were seen as possessed of a nature which must be expressed and which needed defending. The American Declaration of Rights, drafted in 1776, called for the protection of free speech, the security of the person, due process of law and the presumption of innocence in criminal proceedings.

As discussed in the text of this chapter, 'rights' as specified here are very atomistic and individualistic. 'Society' is envisaged in much the same way as it was envisaged by the philosophers of the Enlightenment. It is composed of a collection of individuals. For contemporary neoliberals, natural rights continue to be centrally important to protect the individual from the privations administered by society and particularly by states. They are a means of achieving a desirable *future* society, particularly by protecting individual autonomy. But those opposed to this form of individualized rights argue that since the eighteenth century until the present day such a conception has been used as a means of exerting class power. They argue that natural rights were actively used in the eighteenth century by rising commercial classes against arbitrary and absolutist power. (For further discussion see, for example, Blackburn 2001.)

Marshall's picture of rights-acquisition is a linear and directional one. He goes on to discuss the second phase in the evolution of citizenship, one that he assumes is emerging in all developing societies. From the nineteenth until the early twentieth century the rights to own property were greatly extended. They became universal, open to the whole population.

The political element

At this stage populations in Europe, the UK and the USA acquired the right, through electing representatives to parliament, to participate in the exercise of political power. Political citizenship was therefore the key means of incorporation into the community ('community' here being equated with the state). The idea was that members of the political, legal and moral community should be given new rights. This reflects the Enlightenment's scientific politics whereby people are able to engage in the decision-making processes that affect their lives. Specifically, this entailed being allowed to vote at the level of central or local government. Franchise was, in principle at least, now 'universal', as was the right of free speech, free association and freedom of movement. Note again, however, that certain obligations were involved: the new freedoms brought with them laws against libel and slander and a ban on acts of sedition or public disorder. So once more we find certain rules imposed on individuals, as well as certain freedoms.

The social element

Finally, in Marshall's directional and linear scheme, citizenship gained a social or economic component. The citizen gained 'a right to a modicum of economic welfare and security and the right to share to the full in the social heritage and to live the life of a civilized being according to the standards prevailing in the society' (1964: 72). The central institutions at this stage comprised the educational and welfare systems. Unemployment pay and sickness benefits were established. Industrial bargaining by unions and the right to join a union were fully established. Again, all these forms of citizenship were founded on the political rights already acquired. But note once more the obligations involved. These included the obligation to contribute to funds for the needs of strangers. In this way money could be provided for people who had been made unemployed, who had become ill or destitute. Until this third form of citizenship became established and administered through a state, the tacit common assumption had been that all these problems were a product of personal characteristics or individual difficulties.

Teleological development

Such has been the slow development of citizenship according to Marshall. Not only is it directional development but it is seen as progressive in the sense that it incorporates a sense of steady, almost inevitable, improvement to individuals' well-being. It also contains what we have earlier termed a 'teleological' element. That is, the model contains a strong notion that once the process of individual rights has been set in train, the outcome is almost inevitable. In line with Age of Enlightenment philosophy of the kind represented by John Locke, rights were first acquired by the property-owning middle classes, but in due course they began to spread to the working classes, particularly with the advent of the welfare state and publicly provided education. Such a process enables personal autonomy. It recognizes and encourages the development of the individual self and her or his ability to make rational choices as to how to consume goods and how to vote. Once started, the development of rights has a momentum of its own, basically because it is supportive of individual freedom.

Class relations

One of the most important aspects of Marshall's account (and one occasionally forgotten by later commentators) was that he saw the acquisition of all these rights as being in continuing tension with capitalism as a system of enduring class relations. More particularly, he was concerned with how emergent forms of rights were in fact mollifying or softening class struggle. According to Marshall, they certainly, therefore, did not abolish such struggle and it is unlikely that they would do so in the future. The best they could do was to alleviate matters, significantly improving people's autonomy and conditions while not removing the underlying relations creating social tensions. Rights, Marshall recognized, were a way in which society could be made to hang together, despite continuing class inequalities. This remains a fundamental weakness of contemporary politics, a point to which we will return.

Criticisms of the evolutionary view

Marshall's evolutionary account, one with an underlying sense of direction and progress and purpose, has been considerably criticized. It is obviously restricted mainly to the British case. It tends to treat the acquisition of rights as an almost automatically evolving process as distinct from a product of power relations. The development of social rights, for example, is now often seen as a product of a specific period around the Second World War, when levels of employment were high and the balance of class power shifted towards labour. An evolutionary view, on the other hand, implies an inevitable and linear process which has its own, unstoppable, dynamic (for further discussion see, for example, Turner 1993 and Janoski 1998).

The class basis on which social rights and collective forms of provision were based now appears to have weakened. In its place, a range of very varied rights is being demanded by diverse groups of people. These are articulated and put into practice by the new social movements, forms of politics to be discussed in the next chapter. In all, the collective demand for social rights has given way to very specific rights demanded by particular groups such as anti-racists and those supporting sexual minorities. There now seems to be no simple evolutionary pattern to the development of rights. Enlightenment-style commitment to 'progress' has given way to a diverse array of oppositional lifestyles. Many of these do not equate progress with purely material well-being and the steady acquisition of extra resources. Such a reversal of values, it must be admitted, often finds support and articulation from the more culturally oriented sections of the middle classes. Many of these, as discussed in chapter 4, find themselves leading comfortable, if not extravagant, ways of life.

Extending citizenship to more groups of people

Marshall's evolutionary model of citizenship therefore now looks very dated. Unsurprisingly, it failed to take into account elements of social diversity and the possibility of 'group rights', the allocation of special collections of people such as children, people of colour, aborigines, gay people and disabled people. Group rights in particular have been developed since Marshall's day. They go beyond purely individualistic rights and are a recognition of increasing social diversity, including the kinds of diversity associated with modern consumerism.

Group rights have been important both in recognizing and developing new forms of social identity and in developing the well-being of some subordinated groups (Isin and Wood 1999). On the other hand, the radical position as regards these kinds of right would still insist that, although 'diversity' and 'difference' are certainly advanced and recognized, these rights still do not seriously challenge established centres of economic and social power. They still do not seriously affect the social context which people need to control if they are to improve their lives.

Given the context in which he was working, Marshall gave women's rights only schematic and cursory attention, perhaps because women, at least in the British case, only acquired voting rights in 1928. Their full social rights are of course still now far from being realized and there are now important ongoing debates on what form the demands for female citizenship should take and whether the kinds of right outlined by Marshall are anything like sufficient as a form of emancipation (Isin and Wood 1999). Without wishing to decry the genuine advances achieved by women's rights, it is again still unclear as to how much genuine transfer of power these rights have achieved once applied to this (majority) group. They have not arrested, for example, increasing extremes in income and health. This is again because there is a systematic discrepancy between being allocated 'rights' and having the resources actually to realize them.

Environmental sustainability: extending citizenship to future people

Finally, the Marshall model gives little attention to the rights of *future* citizens. This has become of central importance to many concerned with the environment,

---

Box 7.3 Environmental justice

The concept of 'environmental justice' is largely a result of activism amongst community groups in the USA. Polluting factories and waste sites have often been placed in black neighbourhoods and people's reservations. Since its early days, however, the movement has been developed at a global and intergenerational scale. People in developing countries and future generations are likely to be badly affected by climate change caused by fossil fuel burning. And this is likely to have been caused in developed societies and by people in the present, and past, generations.

The environmental justice movement has found strong support in some government programmes. The United Kingdom government specifically links social and environmental justice:

> Everyone should share in the benefits of increased prosperity and a clean and safe environment. We have to improve access to services, tackle social exclusion, and reduce the harm to health caused by poverty, poor housing, unemployment and pollution. Our needs must not be met by treating others, including future generations and people elsewhere in the world, unfairly. (Economic and Social Research Council 2001)

---

including many governments concerned with what is sometimes called 'environmental justice' (see box 7.3). The environmental justice movement is now becoming widespread, even globalized. The demand is that everyone – including the poorest and most vulnerable – should, in the words of the United Nations Commission on Human Rights, 'have the right to a secure, healthy and ecologically sound environment'. Similarly, the Portuguese Constitution states that everyone should 'have the right to a healthy and ecologically balanced human environment and the duty to protect it' (cited in Economic and Social Research Council 2001).

These demands for environmental and social citizenship are difficult to argue against. On the other hand, the very fact that they give rise to relatively little controversy should give us some pause for consideration. They do not specify what a 'healthy and ecologically balanced human environment' actually is. Nor do they specify what kind of society they envisage providing environmental-cum-social justice for present or future 'citizens'. Dobson argues that 'policies for justice and sustainability will not always pull in the same direction' (1998: 242), but he argues that liberal, individualist theories of justice are compatible with most commonly understood versions of 'sustainability'. Benton, on the other hand, argues that the kinds of individualism implied by liberal and individualist theories of rights underestimate people's cultural as well as material needs; people need to relate to one another, to form social identities and satisfy their cultural requirements (1999c). He mentions, in particular, the struggles of indigenous peoples in Kashmir or the Amazonian region of South America. These popular struggles are in part about the protection of physical resources against 'modernization', the latter taking the form of, for example, the commercial exploitation of forests, ranching and the creation of hydro-electric schemes. But they are just as much about maintaining cultures and ways of life for future generations.

In sum, the demands made by the environmental justice movement are important, but they remain firmly set in the kinds of eighteenth-century citizenship norms explored earlier, in which one individual attempts to preserve her or his autonomy and property relative to another individual. People are social beings and it is not at all clear that the movement (one which seeks 'compensation' for individuals for harms done) can really provide the full justice which human beings deserve.

Extending rights to non-humans

The animal rights movement is also continuing the process of rights extension, seeming to further fulfil Marshall's evolutionary scheme. Here are other types of being for which their human representatives are demanding autonomy and freedom from harms. This time, however, the focus is no longer anthropocentric. Campaigners such as Tom Regan and Peter Singer challenge the human-centredness of conventional rights and, as part of this challenge, the assumption that humans can legitimately exercise power over or exploit other animals. Animals, such campaigners insist, can no longer be considered merely as 'resources'. The importance of animals, according to Regan, is that they (like humans) have a life and are therefore to be valued (see box 7.4). Note, however, that Regan's position still focuses on the individual animal. Indeed, he resisted citizenship at the ecosystem level because he believed it overrode the life chances of individual animals. Regan is still adopting the notion of the equality of citizenship which is assumed in Marshall's model and goes back at least as far as eighteenth-century political theory. He is still equating freedom with the kinds of freedom which humans have so far won. And he urges that 'the basic principle of equality that most of us recognize should be extended to all members of our own species' (1990: 163).

The same could be said of another well-known campaigner for animal rights, Peter Singer (see box 7.5). He directly compares animal liberation with earlier, human-centred, forms of liberation. His suggestion is that demands for animals are demands for removing 'the last remaining form of discrimination' (1990: 162). He, like Regan, asserts that making a sharp division between humans and animals

---

Box 7.4   Animals have value because they are subjects of a life

The really crucial, the basic similarity [between humans and animals] is simply this: we are each of us the experiencing subject of a life, a conscious creature having an individual welfare that has importance to us whatever our usefulness to others. We want and prefer things, believe and feel things, recall and expect things. And all these dimensions of our life, including our pleasure and pain, our enjoyment and suffering, our satisfaction and frustration, our continued existence or our untimely death – all make a difference to the quality of life as lived, as experienced, by us as individuals. As the same is true of those animals that concern us (the ones that are eaten and trapped, for example) they too must be viewed as the experiencing subjects of a life, with inherent value of their own. (Regan 1990: 185)

Box 7.5 Animals, like humans, are sentient beings

Surely every sentient being is capable of leading a life that is happier or less miserable than some alternative life, and hence has a claim to be taken into account. In this respect the distinction between humans and nonhumans is not a sharp division, but rather a continuum along which we move gradually, and with overlaps between the species, from simple capacities for enjoyment and satisfaction, or pain and suffering, to more complex ones. (Singer 1990: 165)

Box 7.6 Are some humans inferior in value to others?

Once we ask why it should be that all humans – including infants, mental defectives, psychopaths, Hitler, Stalin and the rest – have some kind of dignity or worth that no elephant, pig, or chimpanzee can ever achieve, we see that this question is as difficult to answer as our original request for some relevant fact that justifies the inequality of humans and other animals. (Singer 1990: 166)

---

fails to recognize the extent to which the two species share characteristics. Animals, like humans, can feel pain and are capable of having better or worse lives. Making clinical divisions between 'humans' on the one hand and 'animals' on the other is one means by which human domination over animals continues to be promoted and justified. Note that Singer even suggests that challenging humans' centrality could entail downgrading the claims of some humans relative to some animals. What we deem to be 'dignity' is the supposed 'dignity' of the human species as a whole. But do humans as a whole deserve such a label? (see box 7.6).

Comparisons between animals on the one hand and children and 'mental defectives' on the other must be a question of debate. Such defectives, along with most disabled people (who have also recently been compared unfavourably with animals by Singer) maintain specifically human capacities such as those for communicating complex ideas or remembering people and things from their early life. Such considerations do not seem central to Singer's thinking. Rather, the logic of his argument is to attempt to attribute to some animals which appear to have particularly well-developed capacities (and to be superior to many humans in this respect) rights equivalent to those of humans who are sufficiently sound in mind and body to have normal rights. The result, according to Singer, would be a 'community of equals', one in which apes and humans come together as 'equal citizens' (see box 7.7).

Giving rights to animals might therefore seem a further part of an ongoing success story, one in which all forms of life acquire rights and autonomy. There are, nevertheless, some obvious difficulties in attempting to recruit animals into

---

Box 7.7 Apes as members of a moral community of equals?

At present, only members of our own human species are recognized as members of the community of equals. And yet ethical argument combined with scientific evidence about the capacities of some animals is leading to considerable re-evaluation of whether it is right to distinguish animals from humans in this way. The Great Ape Project recognizes the close physical and psychological similarities between the apes and humans. Yet, it is argued, the apes are subjected to experiments that would be considered utterly abhorrent if conducted on humans. The following is an excerpt from the manifesto of the Great Ape Project, asserting a form of citizenship for the apes.

A DECLARATION ON GREAT APES

We demand the extension of the community of equals to include all great apes: human beings, chimpanzees, gorillas and orang-utans. 'The community of equals' is the moral community within which we accept certain basic moral principles or rights as governing our relations with each other and enforceable at law.

1 The right to life

The lives of members of the community of equals are to be protected. Members of the community of equals may not be killed except in very strictly defined circumstances, for example, self-defence.

2 The protection of individual liberty

Members of the community of equals are not to be arbitrarily deprived of their liberty; if they should be imprisoned without due legal process, they have the right to immediate release. The detention of those who have not been convicted of any crime, or of those who are not criminally liable, should be allowed only where it can be shown to be for their own good, or necessary to protect the public from a member of the community who would clearly be a danger to others if at liberty. In such cases, members of the community of equals must have the right to appeal, either direct or, if they lack the relevant capacity, through an advocate, to a judicial tribunal.

3 The prohibition of torture

The deliberate infliction of severe pain on a member of the community of equals, either wantonly or for an alleged benefit to others, is regarded as torture, and is wrong. (Cavaliri and Singer 1993)

---

the kind of individualistic idea of rights as outlined by Marshall and as developed by philosophers such as Regan and Singer. Animals, like indeed young children, disabled people and some 'mental defectives', clearly cannot exercise all the rights that they have won and been allocated. Animals cannot own property, vote or make serious demands on the welfare state. They cannot recognize moral principles and do not, as far as is known, have complex languages with which to communicate abstract ideas. They clearly depend on people (such as pet-owners, zoo-keepers and farmers) to act on their behalf. They cannot themselves enjoy individual fulfilment in 'the consumer society', these pleasures being limited to their owners. Many animals (including many 'wild' animals) have people permanently acting on their behalf who may or not protect them from the harms which can befall them, particularly as they are caught up in systems of power and industrialization.

In the end, the question is about the extent to which animals are caught up in human society and whether it is realistic to extend the whole panoply of 'rights' to them. Does it enable them to develop, or does it manipulate them in ways which leave them in pain, stressed and ill-developed? Debates about their inclusion as 'citizens' can easily become diversionary, as animals are caught up in, say, factory-farming or drug-testing regimes. This same lesson can easily be extended to human animals. The important issue is less that of 'citizenship' and more about the commercialized and industrialized systems in which they live. Do they provide the kinds of welfare needed to properly grow and develop?

Rights: the importance of context

This brings us to the heart of the 'rights' question, whether it is applied to humans or to animals. First, rights are couched in terms which only the kind of human society for which they were designed can start providing: voting, the ownership of property and so on. The types of citizenship to which Marshall refers and which remain dominant in contemporary society may well have some beneficial effects but they seem unlikely to pose any substantial threat to the existing social order. The Left in particular would suggest that they are only likely to lead to still more extensive forms of domination (Benton 1993). Furthermore, this political position argues that the kinds of right currently on offer are unlikely to deliver on their promises. Owning property, voting every four years and shopping more extensively are all, it is argued, unlikely to result in human emancipation.

But, second, and as many in the contemporary women's movement point out, there are severe problems here to do with the precise kinds of right which have evolved since the eighteenth century. They are, in other words, still largely founded on the kinds of right which are central to modern Western philosophy, rights which, apart from those offered by the welfare state, remain largely focused on the moral character and actions of *individuals*, human or otherwise. Again, they are typically concerned with the rights of individuals against the harms threatened or made by other individuals. An example from feminism, and one which has direct relevance to some of the work reported in the previous chapter, is given in box 7.8.

The argument against the individualistic kinds of rights handed down from the eighteenth-century Enlightenment period is, therefore, that they are couched in terms which do not recognize or challenge the real social and power relations which constitute a society. People, as discussed in considerable detail earlier, have the potential to develop in a number of different ways. But, as a critical realist perspective helps us realize, their actual well-being, their physical health, their

---

Box 7.8   Individual versus social and environmental rights: the case of mother–child conflict

Chapter 6 reported on research pointing to the effects on early childhood development of mothers' consumption patterns. Food, alcohol and drugs ingested by the mother can all have effects on the infant's early development and later life chances. This may seem relatively uncontroversial and is widely recognized as common sense by 'lay' people as well as by biologists and evolutionary scientists. It raises, however, some extraordinarily important and difficult issues about mothers' and children's rights. Is the implication that women are no longer to consume what they wish? Whose rights, those of the woman or those of the child, are to prevail? What about the position of low-income women who may be in no position to choose what kind of food they eat or, taking the environment to be more than just the womb, what kind of home or physical environment they live in? Clearly, the infant's 'environment' is broader than the mother's womb and what the mother chooses to consume.

These questions raise much wider issues, discussed by feminist theorists such as Firestone (1979). She argued that just as the working class should be enabled to rise up and seize the factories and machines on which they work, so women should be enabled to seize control of their own *reproductive* capacities. How would this come about? Firestone welcomed a future when the genital differences between the sexes were a purely cultural matter. She looked forward to an era when women are relieved of their reproductive capacities by artificial technologies of procreation. To the extent to which women are still giving birth, it would not be entirely down to them as individuals to ensure the well-being of children. It would be a collective and social enterprise. This implies that women's rights are social and collective. The environment affecting the child's development is produced by society and it is up to society to change that environment rather than to expect the individual woman to change her behaviour on behalf of her child.

---

identities and their cognitive capacities are all dependent on the particular social and environmental contexts in which they develop. The prized autonomy demanded by exponents of individual rights cannot be realized if the context in which they develop does not allow them to develop properly.

The same kinds of argument can be applied to non-human animals. On the one hand they have the genetically inherited potential to develop in a number of different ways. Most of the animals on which we depend for food have certain kinds of inbuilt ways of life. Like humans, most have elaborate forms of social life, involving communication, contact, social play and learning. Chickens, for example, normally socialize in flocks of up to one hundred members. Calves depend on their mothers at the earliest stages of their life for suckling. Yet, once we turn to how industry treats these and other kinds of being, we can see why an individualistic view of rights is often seen as cruel and inhumane.

Box 7.9 Industry and political citizenship

ANALYSIS: OIL AND THE BUSH CABINET

A majority of President Bush's new cabinet are millionaires and several are multimillion-aires. According to information from financial disclosure reports, released by the Office of Government Ethics, most cabinet appointees have amassed their fortunes in stock options.... It is not unusual for American politicians to be rich. For the last two decades more than half of all cabinet members have been millionaires.... What makes the new Bush administration different from previous wealthy cabinets is that so many of the officials have links to the same industry – oil. (BBC News: World: Americas, 29 January 2001)

BUSH ENERGY PLAN: POLICY OR PAYBACK?

A new power plant every week for 20 years, new nukes, drilling in the Arctic Wildlife Refuge – is this an energy policy, or a payback for President Bush's big campaign con-tributors? (BBC News: World: Americas, 18 May 2001)

Industry and Citizenship

The kind of criticism made of conventional democratic politics, as demonstrated in box 7.9, is not unusual. Equal citizenship does not produce the goods in terms of exerting real power. People do their duty by taking up their right to vote every few years but they are left feeling impotent. The key decisions (including those regarding the environment) are made by politicians who listen closely to, and are influenced by, corporate interests. Yet even this highly critical view of conventional democratic politics does not tell the full story. Supposing it was possible to have larger numbers of people participating in the political process and supposing that animals were given rights similar to those enjoyed by human beings, this would still leave the prime sources of power and inequality untouched. And, still more important, what would corporate interests do with their power?

The division of labour

An answer can be given by briefly examining how both people and animals are incorporated into industrial processes. The central feature of an advanced capitalist economy is the division of labour. Such a division has been a feature of virtually all human societies. The division of labour takes two forms, social and technical. The social division of labour refers to the division between organizations in society at large; between, for example, companies or between companies and households. The technical division of labour, which is the chief focus here, is the way in which capitalist industry is organized.

In modern societies such a division has been made especially complex. It is typically developed in a form which allows overarching control and coordination to be exerted. On the one hand, there are people such as managers who, on behalf of those investing capital, exercise a high level of control over the labour process. On the other are people whose work is increasingly mechanized and automated. The latter often find their skills and capacities ignored or unrecognized. Typically, they find their work mind-numbingly boring (Braverman 1974). And, as discussed earlier, there are major implications here for human well-being.

Animals and specialization

Very similar processes take place as animals are incorporated into the contemporary industrial labour process (Noske 1989). Animals of the same species are also often 'specialized' into the divisions of labour made by a capitalist labour process. Some cattle are raised for beef, for example, and others for milk. Some chickens are for humans to eat and some are for eggs.

Factory farming has a considerable impact on animals as social beings. Veal calves, for example, are only supposed to be fattened in confinement crates with little or no light. In this way they become the luxury-grade, milk-fed veal preferred by gourmets. They often lose association with their 'fellow' animals, because of restricted communication, contact, social play and social learning.

The impacts on their individual development can also be dramatic. Chickens kept in broiler houses or small cages are not allowed to develop in a normal way. Separated calves suffer from anaemia and neurotic behaviour as a result of being fed on high protein milk, and so on. Meanwhile, computerized mechanization means that they are increasingly separated from the 'stockman', the person who would previously have taken overall care of them and their development as individuals. Those concerned with animal welfare would argue strongly that animal well-being is suffering in ways similar to those experienced by humans.

This again leads to the conclusion that there may be little value in assigning rights to individual animals (or indeed to individual workers in the above-mentioned labour processes) if the context, in this case that of highly industrialized production regimes, is allowed to continue in its current form. This is the radical position against conventional 'rights'. Animal emancipation in this sense may well be a long time coming (see box 7.10).

Box 7.10   Rights in context: the case of factory farming

Factory farming includes most forms of animals which humans eat. It entails the tethering of pigs and cattle, and the long-distance transport of sheep and chickens packed close together (see illus. 7.10). The nature of factory farming strongly suggests that animal rights need to be formulated at the level of the industries as a whole rather than at the level of the individual animal.

Illustration 7.10 Notice advertising a National Rally to protest against factory farming

Note: the notice of a rally suggests that it is in the interests of humans (human physical well-being in particular) for factory farming to be stopped. The appeal is simultaneously anthropocentric and ecocentric.

Industry and human well-being: the transition to liberal economic policy

The changing relationships between industry and government are particularly significant for human and animal health. The particular kind of welfare state to which Marshall referred was very much a product of what we termed in the previous chapter the 'Fordist' era (Jessop 1994). It was introduced at a time when governments were centrally involved in balancing the relations between companies on the one hand and the labour force (as represented by the trade unions) on the other. National governments were then actively attempting to organize capitalist economies: manage wage-levels, influence levels of capital investment and use substantial government funds (especially the funds supporting people's welfare in the form of extensive health, housing and education programmes) to ensure that levels of economic activity (including levels of employment) were maintained when the private sector took a downturn.

Governments, in short, maintained a very active role in balancing the relations between capital and labour. With the development of post-Fordist industries and economies over the past thirty years, there have been corresponding changes to forms of state intervention. International competitive pressures and capital flows on a global scale and demands for a 'flexible' workforce (see figure 5.4, p. 160) all contributed to these changes. Especially important from our viewpoint have been the deregulation of the economy, combined with fewer concerns to reduce unemployment. What some call the 'workfare state' has been attempted, the idea being to make people work rather than pay them to be unemployed.

A two-tier system

A two-tier system of welfare has gradually been replacing the old form, one in which public sector provision is for those who cannot afford private sector fees. These are general tendencies, with significant variations between national governments, but the direction is one in which citizens' demands for state welfare have been subordinated to the needs of industries and companies operating in an increasingly internationalized setting.

One significance of this in terms of the Marshall model is that citizenship now appears to be evolving 'backwards'; ever-improving progress towards increased levels of welfare has been stopped in its tracks. High levels of health and education provision are provided for those able to afford them, while much lower levels are available via the public sector. At the same time, many national governments have been, to use Jessop's term, 'hollowed out'. On the one hand, supranational bodies such as the European Union are increasing in number and are to a large degree usurping the power of national states. On the other, local governments are tending to develop their own economic and social policies. These include attempts to provide infrastructure (in a way reminiscent of those attempted by central governments in the Fordist economic regime) to encourage companies to invest in their region. One of the more notable experiments in this regard was that attempted by the Greater London Council in the 1980s, one which challenged the market-oriented policies of central government and, as such, was closed down.

All this again suggests that Marshall's model of state intervention, and of forms of citizenship based on state-provided welfare, is by no means automatic. It may well go into reverse, though not (as also happened in the Greater London Council case) without resistance and struggle. The political 'community' represented by citizenship rights is unstable and may well, under pressure from powerful corporate interests, be subject to active degrading.

Industry and animal well-being

Meanwhile, what are the implications of these developments for the 'rights' of animals in the new, more liberalized form of state? Conditions appear to be getting significantly worse for animals in markets and systems of trade which are increasingly globalized. The BSE catastrophe was in large part the product of a deregulated food industry. The export of live animals for slaughter appears to be on the increase. The number of live animals exported from Britain rose from 440,000 to 700,000 between 1997 and 1998. The trade entails literally millions of animals being transported each year around Europe, often in appalling conditions. The particular kind of government 'community' designed to protect them (European Commission) is unable to stop the laws being (to use the EC's own words) 'systematically flouted' (see Compassion in World Farming 2002 for details).

Tests of new drugs on animals appear to have declined, at least in Britain. The figure has now levelled out at around 2.5 million a year. But experiments on genetically modified animals have actually increased from around 250,000 in 1995 to around 750,000 in 2001 (*Independent*, 25 July 2002). These are massive numbers. But they appear to be relatively unsuccessful in the attempt to breed animals with characteristics favourable for food production, while generating a number of problems for at least some of the animals concerned. Recall the fate of the Beltsville pigs (box 3.10).

One outcome of such developments is that the animal welfare lobby is driven increasingly to engage in direct action, since conventional politics fails to deal with the situation. In Benton and Redfearn's view, it is 'at least in part a response to growing frustration at failure to make headway by more orthodox means of exerting pressure' (1996).

Box 7.11 gives an example of how international flows of capital can be used to confront those protesting against the inhumane treatment of animals in laboratories. Huntingdon Life Sciences is close to where I work and I have been well aware of the protestors' repeated attempts to draw British investors' attention to conditions in the laboratory. At the same time, the company has been able to secure funding from a company in the USA. Meanwhile, the British government has been active in trying to attract alternative funding, arguing that this is a progressive form of science which will help to extend human life and keep jobs in Britain.

Box 7.11   Globalization and animal welfare

SALE OF HUNTINGDON LIFE SCIENCES GOES THROUGH

Huntingdon agreed to a takeover bid from LSR last October, and on Thursday said shareholders owning 89.5 per cent of the share capital had accepted the deal – enough to make the offer unconditional.

LSR was set up last year for the purpose of buying Huntingdon, which has been targeted by campaigners protesting against its use of animals in drug testing.

Huntingdon's market listing will now move to the New York Stock Exchange, and its London listing will be cancelled with effect from 24 January.

BANK TURNS BACK ON HUNTINGDON

On Wednesday it emerged that Huntingdon had lost one of its main backers, in a further sign that investors are becoming wary of being associated with the controversial firm.

Investment bank Stephens Groups, Huntingdon's biggest shareholder and one of its leading creditors, said it planned to sever all ties with the company by the end of the month.

All of Stephens' interests in HLS will be taken over by as yet unnamed new investors, the US-based bank said.

The move was a fresh blow to Huntingdon, which has struggled to attract investment since being targeted by campaigners.

Sources: <http://news.bbc.co.uk/hi/english/talking_point/newsid_1124014_stm>

Citizenship as Community

One way of summarizing the radical critique of classical citizenship is to say that it offers an 'alienated' or 'imagined' community (Marx 1975; Anderson 1993). Here we are back to the ideological sense of 'community' discussed in chapter 1. In this community they are all apparently equal. Everyone has a vote, a right to own property, a right not to be tortured, equality before the law and so on.

The problem is that this kind of political community largely ignores the rest of social, economic and political life. Humans are incorporated into it and yet they do not feel part of it. It ignores, for example, the social relations involved in a company, the exercise of power by the private sector over the state and so on. So what might be termed 'real community', in the sense of an equal recognition of people's powers and needs, remains a chimera. Animal rights protestors and those criticizing the kinds of right offered by conventional politics argue that other means of achieving social justice need to be developed.

Real communities of citizens?

'Community' is a recurrent idea in much environmental thought. The idea of a decentralized society is central here. Most obviously this means geographical decentralization. But it also often entails a separation from dominant forms of economic and political power. In this sense, a shift in place or locality is only part of the demand. Here we start to encounter other meanings of 'community': a place or locality, a set of social practices within locality and 'community' as a set of associations of a personal nature, one in which people commune with others and with their environment. Sharing the same space may or may not be important in achieving all these ends. More important is the question of economic, social and political power.

The deep greens

The phrase 'deep green' covers a number of different types of environmental politics. As represented by philosophers such as Arne Naess (1973, 1989), it allocates rights not just to human beings but also to ecosystems and the biosphere. Naess uses the principle of 'biocentric egalitarianism' to express this notion, arguing that all forms of life have 'the equal right to live and blossom' (see box 7.12). The emphasis here is therefore on life as a whole and the interdependence and reciprocity between all species and their environment. Its focus is above all 'ecocentric', though it focuses on the pleasure which humans can develop out of *being* ecocentric. Deep ecology recognizes the extent to which human beings are a product of their environment while at the same time they are transforming that environment. This leads to allocation of moral value to all life. As Naess puts it: 'the flourishing of human and non-human life on Earth has intrinsic value' (cited in Carter 2001: 20). At this point individualistic rights and responsibilities are being extended to fit the context. And, at the same time, the context of the environment is itself receiving its own right to life and development.

Box 7.12 Ecocentrism: the view from the deep ecology movement

The ecological field-worker acquires a deep-seated respect, or even veneration, for ways and forms of life. He reaches an understanding from within, a kind of understanding that others reserve for fellow men and for a narrow section of ways and forms of life. To the ecological field-worker, the equal right to live and blossom is an intuitively clear and obvious value axiom. Its restriction to humans is an anthropocentrism with detrimental effects upon the life quality of humans themselves. This quality depends in part upon the deep pleasure and satisfaction we receive from close partnership with other forms of life. The attempt to ignore our dependence and to establish a master-slave role has contributed to the alienation of man from himself. (Naess 1973: 95)

Interestingly, in light of the discussion in the previous chapters on human identity and developmental biology, deep ecology argues that this more holistic association of humanity with external nature will result in a transformed form of human consciousness. An 'ecological self' emerges, one which recognizes relations with and obligations to external nature. This would be contrary to the kinds of egoism and self-centredness which Naess, like many social theorists, sees as a characteristic feature of modern society.

Ecology and local community

A number of arguments and debates revolve around this kind of deep ecology programme. One again concerns 'community'. One implication of the deep ecology position is that *local* community, or the *local* ecosystem, is especially important. Does this mean that people's connection with their particular environment should be more significant than with the biosphere as a whole and to the forms of life with which we have no particular contact (Carter 2001)? Furthermore, what exact significance should be attached to humans as distinct from other species? In parts of his work, Naess seems still to be attributing a particular significance to the value of human beings as a species, which is in some way 'special', this despite the principle of 'biocentric egalitarianism' and the idea that all lives have an intrinsic value.

Furthermore, some versions of the deep ecology argument promote ecological systems as a whole, and if necessary at the expense of the living beings within them. This is the case with Leopold, whose 'land ethic' thesis holds that a thing is right when it tends to preserve the 'integrity, stability and beauty of the biotic community' (1949: 224–5). This leaves Regan, who we encountered earlier, arguing that the philosophy is tantamount to 'environmental fascism'. Preserving the larger good of the ecological community at the expense of individual lives within it has, Regan believes, distinctly sinister overtones.

The deep green programme also has some echoes in so-called 'bio-regionalism', as proposed by Sale (1984, 1985). The proposal is for humans to become 'dwellers in the land', to live as close to it as possible, to learn from it and to develop different types of politics in accordance with forms of regional nature and its rhythms. This last proposal is the most interesting and most controversial aspect of the programme, since Sale is quite frank in declaring that diversity in politics will include not only democracies, but 'aristocracies, oligarchies, principalities, margravates, duchies and palatinates as well' (cited in Dobson 1991: 81). In short, this is not only a diversity of politics but a diversity which includes forms of politics of which many environmentalists might not approve. External nature is setting the pace. Human politics comes second.

These arguments do much to counter the focus on individual citizens without context and on discussions of rights which focus on humans at the expense of other kinds of being. But they do not address the issues with which most sociologists are concerned. While taking a wider ecological view they have managed to abstract 'man's relationship with the environment' away from the social and power relations which constitute modern capitalist society. The clear hope is that by engaging with the environment differently, modern humanity will see the error of its ways and behave in more sustainable manners. The direct relations with the environment enjoyed by tribal peoples seems to be the model here. But is it possible to imagine all classes of people in modern capitalist society, or indeed all classes within a modern 'community', willingly going into reverse to recover this kind of relationship? Deep ecology is in danger of becoming a neo-Romantic utopia. Its somewhat mystic focus on 'organic' relations between people and nature is out of step with the ways in which the world works and the ways in which consciousness actually develops. Achieving the kinds of end to which the deep ecologists aspire would entail humans *working* differently on the environment in different ways, a point to which we return shortly.

Communitarianism: community as citizen?

Communitarianism is often presented as the radically opposite point of view from individualistic liberalism. It might at first sight seem to address some of the problems surrounding the development of the self and the maintenance of other species. But there are problems here too.

The primary emphasis is again on 'community', here sometimes expressed as 'society' or 'the nation'. The main focus is on making community or society actually work (see box 7.13). So the emphasis shifts away from the individual and equality couched at this very broad and abstract level. Instead, the good society is seen as being made through group activity and mutual support. Obligations under communitarianism tend to be towards some notion of a 'whole' society. The

---

Box 7.13 An environment for future generations: the communitarian thesis

Communitarianism is a movement which places considerable emphasis on 'community', on human association. This is seen as a way of restoring society, social cohesion and moral values, but without the heavy hand of the state, and without obsessive competitive individualism. Rights, as well as responsibilities, are central to this perspective. Amitai Etzioni, one of the main proponents of communitarianism, offers the following description:

> Although it is difficult to imagine rights without corollary responsibilities, we must recognize that we have some duties that lay moral claims on us from which we derive no immediate benefit or even long-term payoff. Our commitment to a shared future, especially our responsibility to the environment, is a case in point. We are to care for the environment not only or even mainly for our own sakes (although we may desire some assurance of potable water, breathable air, and protection from frying because the ozone layer is thinning out). We have a moral commitment to leave for future generations a liveable environment, even perhaps a better one than the one we inherited, certainly not one that has been further depleted. The same observations hold true for our responsibility to our moral, social and political environment. (1993: 11)

emphasis is on society envisaged as a kind of large organism. And it is to the whole of society that humans have obligations. Participation, mutualism and common identity tend to be the watchwords and we may well not expect anything back from having contributed to the community. Contribution is in itself sufficient reward. Communitarianism raises the whole issue of obligations as well as rights.

If society is not a mere bundle of unrelated individuals, as proposed during the Age of the Enlightenment, neither is it a kind of super-organism as proposed by communitarianism. The problem is that although communitarianism does indeed recognize some notion of society, it does so in a highly problematic way. It is a collection of interacting individuals and small groups. Industrial and economic power relations get little attention, as do their intimate connections to the institutions of state. The notion of a collective community becomes still more problematic once it starts being applied. Does 'the community' really mean the whole world? Or a nation-state? Or is it just a small part of the nation-state? In a loose kind of way communitarianism encompasses an idea of common humanity and the notion that the development of humanity takes place through human interaction both with other humans and with future generations of humans. But it remains human centred and, for many sociologists, it fails to take sufficient account of the nature of power in modern society.

Assuming that what we mean by 'community' is something that is locally based, the danger here is that of assuming (perhaps hoping for) a small-town politics and 'community', one mostly innocent of how advanced economies and forms of politics actually operate. Also largely missing is a concern with how society relates to external nature. As box 7.13 makes clear, communitarianism certainly takes a holistic view of society, one which includes a concern with the environment of future generations, as well as the families and governments of future generations. These are fine enough concerns, but communitarianism is not attempting to *link* a concern for social relations with a concern for external nature. This leaves a fundamental problem: that of human society being created precisely through its interaction with external nature. How it organizes itself to this end will deeply affect whether or not future generations are to inherit a 'liveable environment'.

We are so far left, then, with forms of citizenship which still do not seem to include what we have specified as a central objective: recognizing the intrinsic value of beings (human and non-human) but looking for settings which enable their capacities and skills to be realized. What are the ways forward, still recognizing that attribution of value to non-human beings must be a human-centred business?

Associational democracy and ecological citizenship

Associational democracy is a type of citizenship that has been born largely out of dissatisfaction with the kind of liberal politics that developed in the eighteenth century and with recent state socialism. Whereas both claimed to be democracies, they turned out in practice to be composed of large-scale, centralized hierarchies from which workers, consumers and non-experts were excluded. Associational democracy attempts to reduce the scale at which social affairs are organized, bringing decision-making down to the smaller scale or the level of the organization itself.

Associational forms of democracy begin to offer the far more extensive and more radical kind of citizenship which may be necessary to meet contemporary demands for a thoroughgoing form of animal rights. It does not offer rights and responsibilities to animals as such, but it does represent a form of politics which might enable the development of more humane relationships between humans and other animals. The key and central claim of associationalism is that 'individual liberty and human welfare are best served when as many affairs of society as possible are managed by voluntary and democratically self-governing associations' (Hirst 1994: 19). Entailed here, therefore, are forms of 'active citizenship' in which people are much more completely engaged in the organizations for which they work or the organizations which provide the services that citizens need. This would be an important way of restoring people's sense of a collective politics, one which incorporates a concern for the environment.

Associational democracy and diversity

Proponents of associative democracy insist on the diversity it offers. Radical feminist associations and self-sufficient ecological communities would join, for example, conservative religious groups as just different forms of self-organizing institutions. In this way, it is argued, democracy would be revivified, and people of whatever social or political persuasion would gain control and understanding over their own lives. It is difficult to argue against social diversity (analogous to ecological diversity) of this kind. Such forms of politics can enable groups of people to resist some of the main features of contemporary capitalism, particularly the tendency towards commodification and the growing polarization between the rich and the poor. They offer, in principle at least, the potential for some groups on the receiving end of a globalizing capitalism to take a degree of charge over their lives, while developing forms of society which are environmentally sustainable.

The dangers of associational democracy

On the other hand, there remain potential difficulties even with this type of more fundamental and deep-lying form of democracy. The forces of the market, and particularly of globally organized corporations, are unlikely, it may be argued, to be severely shaken by still small-scale groups organizing under the banner of associative democracy. For diversity, read fragmentation, divide-and-rule and, perhaps, self-organizing institutions which remain primarily self-serving, oblivious to animal cruelty and social justice (Hirst 1994). Indeed, as Martell (1994) has suggested in an argument which is both persuasive and uncomfortable, some kind of centrally or even cross-national agency is needed to ensure that local groups do in fact operate in a socially and environmentally benign way.

Nevertheless, it is noticeable that some of the organizations which are most actively challenging the socially and environmentally destructive effects of the global

---

Box 7.14 Community and cooperation: underlying tensions

The following, taken from a local pamphlet, describes some of the common features of cooperative organizations affecting the relations between work, the market, the environment and the development of individuals. Cooperatively organized food production is now becoming quite common in many societies. Note, for example, the 'Biocoop' organization in France and a wide range of organizations in developing societies which are combining to provide mutual assistance and advice and are in some instances able, as a result of collective organization, to acquire low-interest loans. But note the frequent reference to 'community'. What does this really mean in this context? How are inequalities of class, gender and race dealt with? Note also that the Fenland Community Enterprise Programme, UK, is financially supported by a wide range of local, regional, national and even international (European Union) government agencies. Does such support limit the coops' activities?

WHAT'S IT ALL ABOUT?

Community enterprises, social firms, social enterprises, coops, credit unions, not-for-profit businesses – confusing isn't it? Rather than attempting to define each type of organization, it may be more useful to identify their shared characteristics.

Key concepts

All such organizations contribute to the 'social economy', through their economic activity for social gain. Collective action for shared benefit by members (of the business and/or community) is key, as is skills development for all those involved.

Not-for-profit status

All enterprises are not-for-profit. This doesn't mean they can't make a profit, rather that any financial surplus is used for community benefit, not private gain. Indeed, profit-making is an important way in which these enterprises can achieve sustainability in the long term.

Scale of enterprise

Most enterprises tend to be small scale – by design of circumstances – servicing a local market.

Source: Fenland Community Enterprise Bulletin (Winter 1999/2000)

---

market and its institutions are indeed those organized in an associational way (see box 7.14). Their significance perhaps lies less in the real material threats to global forms of capitalism, which continue to treat nature as a mere commodity, and more in their assertion that there are indeed alternatives, even if problems of class and other forms of power remain to be confronted.

Associational democracy in action

Perhaps the most significant forms of associationalism, given the underlying strength of capitalist enterprises in generating both social hierarchy and environmental destruction, are those which have started at the workplace.

An example in the British case was the initiative by trade unions in Lucas Aerospace during the 1970s. Their version of 'self-government' took the form of developing skills and new ways of working which managed to be socially and environmentally acceptable. Following a programme of mass redundancies, the Shop Stewards' Combine Committee at Lucas drew up an audit of skills that would almost certainly be lost. The question asked of the workers is central to the concerns of this book. How could internal and external nature be simultaneously improved? How could human work be reorganized in ways which led to fulfilling and environmentally sustainable labour? In part, the answers included new kinds of product, including medical equipment, energy-efficient heat pumps and the development of alternative solar cell and fuel cell technologies. Even a lightweight coach which would run on both road and rail was proposed. But at the same time, the skills and potential of the industrial workers were to be actively used and exploited, thereby turning upside-down the usual industrial process of workers simply making what seemed to be economically profitable to shareholders and management. The promotion and use of human skills, new collaborative kinds of working together, combined with alternative environmentally friendly products, were therefore the result. Such democratized ways of working became the hallmark of the Greater London Council's interventions in the local economy in the 1980s. Significantly, the GLC was closed down by the Thatcher government pursuing neoliberal economic policy at the time, this particular kind of experiment in associative democracy being thereby brought to a premature end.

Associational democracy: the final analysis

Such experiments have been criticized even by commentators sympathetic to this type of leftwing politics. In particular, they can still be seen as somewhat narrow in scope. Industrial workers in each enterprise again focus on their own products and labour processes at the expense of remaining disconnected from other organizations; especially those engaging in the financing, distribution and consumption of their products (Rustin 1986). But such experiments have not even been allowed to thrive. The same can be said of earlier forms of industrial democracy. Organizations such as the reformed Lucas Aerospace or the old Greater London Council can in many respects be seen as the heirs of earlier kinds of decentralized economies which were based on non-capitalistic principles of cooperation and mutuality. They also allowed their workers to make alternative products, including products which benefit the environment.

They point to a kind of socialism, especially 'guild socialism' which was all but erased by experiments in state socialism and communism of the kind developed during the first half of the twentieth century. This entailed worker control over labour processes and technology and a notion that production could be for local consumers. It is a socialism to which many on the Left are once again looking. The GLC experiment did at least show how forms of small-scale democracy of this kind can be developed and made to work in a modern industrial society.

Towards an active citizenship

This chapter has discussed a number of different types of politics and forms of citizenship, starting with forms based on parliamentary and representative democracy and finishing with forms of democracy which seem to allow for greater fusion between consumption and production, greater control over means of production and a greater sense of people's involvement in the society which is affecting their lives (see box 7.15 for summary). These all rely on changing forms of human consciousness to enable the development of an environmentally sustainable society. On the other hand, the forms outlined towards the end of this chapter, some of which allow greater influence and control over institutions (and particularly institutions involved in the transformation of nature to make things) seem to offer a greater chance of developing environmentally sustainable and socially just kinds of society.

Box 7.15   Citizenship and forms of decentralized politics: a summary

Type of politics	Form of citizenship	Type of community
Liberal democracy	Individual/human	Imagined political
Communitarian	Group/human	Local practices
Land ethic	Ecosystems	Place/communion (including non-humans)
Deep ecology	All life forms	Place/communion (including non-humans)
Bioregionalism	All life forms (human politics secondary)	Place/communion/local practices
Anarchist	From human to all life forms	Social practices
Guild socialism	Worker control	Industry serving localities

This box compares different types of decentralized politics proposed in social and ecological philosophy. Note that overcoming the alienation of people from their own species is a recurrent theme. And overcoming the alienation of people from external nature is, with the exception of liberal democracy, another recurrent idea. 'Form of citizenship' refers to the type or level of entity whose life and autonomy are being protected and enhanced (human, non-human etc.). 'Type of community' refers to how community is defined.

Institutionalization and beyond

Such active engagement, rather than engagement solely through consumption and the fetishization of commodities, seems to offer the best chance of an altered human consciousness. And yet, extending the scope and importance of such environmental-cum-social organizations runs the real risk of their incorporation into the very political and social structures they are resisting. The history of successful organizations (including the history of a number of so-called non-governmental organizations) is the history of their being steadily 'institutionalized' (Carter 2001). This means that, as their growth and importance increases, their values and indeed their internal organization begin to mirror those of the well-established social and political systems which they were originally designed to resist. But such cooption can generate tensions. The likes of Friends of the Earth and Greenpeace need constantly to ensure that they are not sacrificing the values and priorities of their original supporters. Meanwhile, new, relatively untainted and unbureaucratized resistances endlessly come up from behind. These, sometimes known as new social movements, will be considered in the next chapter.

Citizenship and Risk

The politics of the risk society, according to the influential sociologist Ulrich Beck, is concerned with the avoidance of bads rather than with the distribution of goods. Health risks stemming from, for example, nuclear technology, the genetic modification of crops and global warming and the thinning of the ozone layer are operating at an increasingly global level. Furthermore, it is (according to Beck) difficult to pin down who exactly is responsible. It might be possible to pin the production of high levels of greenhouse gases down to a particular society, but such risks to human well-being are often not attributable to a particular source. This makes the suing of identifiable sources extremely difficult.

In this context, according to Beck, the politics of the risk society revolve around the avoidance of these bads, their prevention and (once they start taking effect) the difficulties these pose for the credibility and legitimacy of governments. All this, Beck believes, is quite distinct from conventional politics in which goods (income, jobs, social security) were allocated. These allocations still take place but they are, to use Beck's words, 'covered over' by conflicts over the distribution of 'bads'.

Beck's discussion offers important insights into some new tendencies, particularly as regards the globalization of at least some risks. But the discussion in this chapter suggests that Beck's idea of the politics of the risk society needs considerable development. In some central respects such politics may not be all that different from those of older modern society. Citizenship, based on individual and possibly group rights, still offers rather little protection against contemporary forms of 'manufactured risk'.

The politics of risk is much less new and much more mundane than Beck suggests. It is still primarily about people and other species with limited rights battling against corporate organizations with enormous economic power and considerable political influence. But this is not to say that there is nothing new taking place. Beck has established something important in his assertion that the sources of risks are difficult to track. But the reasons for this are worth exploring.

One of the most important general features of the new kinds of 'manufactured risk' is the risk's long-term impacts. They affect not only long-term health and development, but also possibly the well-being of later generations. This was, for example, the case in one of the most infamous early instances of industrial poisoning: the Minamata Bay incident, in which large numbers of people consumed spilt mercury as a result of an industrial accident. Victims, and relatives of victims, continued to be diagnosed for at least two decades afterwards.

Similarly, tens of thousands of US Vietnam War veterans and three generations of Vietnamese have continued to point to the defoliation spray, Agent Orange, as the source of large numbers of birth defects. In this case the risks appear to have extended through at least two later generations. Similar long-term risks were linked to the Chernobyl nuclear plant disaster in the USSR and to the Bhopal catastrophe in India. In the latter case some 20,000 people died immediately and today, two decades later, more than 120,000 people are still in need of urgent medical attention (see box 7.16). Similar stories might still be told about the BSE disaster in Britain.

Box 7.16   The politics of risk: the case of the Bhopal Union Carbide disaster

On the night of December 2–3, 1984, 40 tons of methyl isocyanate, hydrogen cyanide, mono-methyl amine and other lethal gases began spewing from Union Carbide Corporation's pesticide factory in Bhopal, India. Nobody outside the factory was warned because the safety siren was turned off. Not until the gas was upon them in their beds, searing their eyes, filling their mouths and lungs did the communities of Bhopal know of the danger.

Gasping for breath and near blind people stampeded into narrow alleys. In the mayhem children were torn from the hands of their mothers, never to see them again. Those who still could were screaming. Some were wracked with seizures and fell under trampling feet. Some stumbling in a sea of gas, their lungs on fire, were drowned in their own bodily fluids. It was a massacre. Dawn broke over residential streets littered with corpses. In just a few hours numberless innocents had died in fierce pain and unimaginable terror.

Over half a million people were exposed to the deadly cocktail. The gases burned the tissues of the eyes and lungs, crossed into the bloodstream and damaged almost every system in the body. Nobody knows how many died but in the next days more than 7,000 death shrouds were sold in Bhopal. With an estimated 10–15 people continuing to die each month the number of deaths to date is put at close to 20,000. And today (Autumn 2002) more than 120,000 people are still in need of urgent attention.

Some 43 per cent of the women from the severely affected communities who were pregnant at the time of the disaster aborted. Study of growth and development of children whose mothers were exposed to the gases during pregnancy revealed that the majority of children had delayed motor and language development. Studies have also presented evidence of chromosomal damage. (<http://www.bhopal.net/intro2.html>)

Manufactured risk and who to blame

The long-term unfolding of modern 'manufactured' risk is such that cause and effect become very unclear. Twenty to thirty years after a disaster people are still ill and dying from illnesses of many and diverse kinds. The connections between the original source of their problems and the problem itself can no longer be made. At the same time, companies transform themselves, merge with others, and evade long-term culpability. Meanwhile, governments are more often than not left picking up the bill; paying for resulting illnesses through public health systems. The financial implications of the risk have thereby been socialized, spread to all tax-paying citizens rather than focused on the original source of the problem. So individual citizens are not only relatively powerless to prevent or avoid corporate-induced risk, but they actually finish up paying for their own illnesses to be cared for.

All this is a further case for 'rights' to be made which are not only more social but which stretch to future generations. That is, they need to recognize the broader social context of risk and give people the chance to counteract such risk in a broader, less individualist way. However, the corporate *production* of risk also extends over people's lives and over several generations. How can 'citizenship' be still further extended to counter this emergent problem?

Summary

This chapter has been considering citizenship and its links to society and nature. Citizenship is the main way in which people still exercise power in their society. Citizenship rights have been increasingly extended to new groups of people and there is a growing emphasis on their extension to non-human species. This chapter has argued, however, that citizenship rights as presently constituted offer only limited autonomy and power. This is because they are couched in terms of the freedom of the individual when the reality is that human and non-human species are inevitably caught up in social relations and corporate institutions over which they have little control. Nevertheless, there are now emerging important new forms of citizenship and rights which allow control over the organizations affecting people's lives. They run the risk of further bureaucratization but they are also developing new forms of politics outside the kinds of citizenship offered by conventional forms of democracy. As articulated by new forms of political movement, they are pursuing new values, new relations between people and new relations between people and their environment. These alternatives are the subject of the next chapter.

FURTHER READING

Very useful guides to environmental politics are:
   N. Carter, *The Politics of the Environment*. Cambridge: Cambridge University Press, 2001.
   A. Dobson (ed.), *The Green Reader*. London: Deutsch, 1991.

With particular reference to some of the issues covered here, see:

E. Richardson and B. Turner, 'Review Article: Sexual, Intimate or Reproductive Citizenship?' *Citizenship Studies*, 5/3 (2001).

B. Turner, 'Risks, Rights and Regulation: An Overview', *Health, Risk & Society*, 3/1 (2001): 9–18.

A. Collier, *Being and Worth*. London: Routledge, 1999.

T. Hayward, *Political Theory and Ecological Values*. Cambridge: Polity, 1998.

K. Sale, *Dwellers in the Land: The Bioregional Vision*. San Francisco: Sierra Club Books, 1985.

R. Sylvan, 'A Critique of Deep Ecology', *Radical Philosophy*, 40–1 (1985): 1–21.

W. Kymlicka, *Multicultural Citizenship*. Oxford: Oxford University Press, 1995.

On forms of human association (including guild socialism and local money), see, in particular:

F. Hutchinson, M. Mellor and W. Olsen, *The Politics of Money. Towards Sustainability and Economic Democracy*. London: Pluto, 2002.

Debates continue on the left about the effectiveness of alternative forms of democracy. Monbiot, for example, argues for the continuing importance of electoral democracy, including such democracy at a national level. Wainwright, on the other hand, argues for popular engagement in public policy-making, organized mainly at the local level and making maximum use of practical knowledge. See:

G. Monbiot, *The Age of Consent. A Manifesto for a New World Order*. London: Flamingo, 2003.

H. Wainwright, *Reclaim the State. Experiments in Popular Democracy*. London: Verso, 2003.

British Social Attitudes offers useful periodic surveys of public responses to environmental questions. Especially relevant here is:

I. Christie and L. James, 'How Green are our Values?' 18th Report (2001): 131–57.

It shows, *inter alia*, that 'apathy towards environmental political protest has increased substantially among the young' (p. 149).

The journal, *Citizenship Studies*, is one of the best ways of keeping abreast with debates in this highly topical area.

On citizenship in the context of a 'nature' which is becoming thoroughly humanized, see:

C. Gray, *Cyborg Citizen*. London: Routledge, 2001.

There are several websites linking citizenship to environmental sustainability and community life. See, for example:

<http://www.cpn.org/index.html>

<http://www.ecocitymagazine.com/ref.htm>

The 1992 United Nations Declaration on Environment and Development gave special emphasis to actions at the local level. See, for example:

<http://www.un.org/esa/sustdev/agenda21.htm>

<http://www.sustainabledevelopment.org/blp/>

Further websites on local community as a basis for activating social-cum-environmental projects include that of the International Society for Third Sector Research:

<http://www.neweconomics.org>

Society, Nature and New Social Movements

Overview

If conventional parliamentary politics is now widely seen as problematic, what is the alternative? This chapter considers the 'new social movements'. These directly challenge the forms of 'scientific' politics inherited from the Enlightenment. They can be seen as a direct result of contemporary social and environmental change, including the risks resulting from environmental degradation. But they also create new values, cultures, forms of community as well as new kinds of human identity. There are continuing debates, however, over the 'newness' of these movements. Their resistance to the commodification of common space and public assets is shared by many in the 'old' movements. Furthermore, supporters of the old movements remain concerned that questions of social justice are being ignored. Finally, there are important debates as to how these movements do or do not relate to 'human nature'. For example, anarchist elements of the new social movements give special emphasis to education and to the linking of abstract ideas to knowledge based on everyday experience. This emphasis, it is argued, allows the full development of the human self. It also offers better prospects for understanding, and tackling, environmental degradation.

New Social Movements

Social movements that aim at overcoming the rift between people and nature are often described as 'new' social movements. This chapter aims to explore how these should be understood. What are their chief characteristics? Why are they coming into being? Are they all that new?

Table 8.1 Old and new social movements

	Old social movements	New social movements
Location	Polity	Civil society
Ideology and aims	Political integration	Autonomy
	Economic rights	New values/lifestyles
Organization of movement	Formal and hierarchical	Informal network and grass roots
Medium of change	Participation in political institutions	Direct action and cultural politics

Source: Martell (1994: 112)

What are new social movements?

What exactly are new social movements (NSMs)? They are usually said to include the green, women's, peace and civil rights movements and are contrasted with the older movements such as those associated with the workers' and trade union movements. Table 8.1 makes a broad contrast between 'old' and 'new' movements.

The old social movements are usually integrated into the formal political structure of the kind outlined at the beginning of the previous chapter. The workers' organizations have made and continue to make demands on government and indeed are often affiliated to a particular political party, such as the Labour Party. They therefore insist on being involved in the process of conventional politics and their demands are often of an economic kind, focusing on higher wages, for example. They are often organized in formal and hierarchical ways; the trade union leaders, for example, are at the head of large bureaucratic organizations, while the workers exercise influence on policy via their economic contributions and periodic ballots. The workers do not therefore have a 'hands-on' relationship with their workplaces, as might be the case in, say, a workers' cooperative.

The old movements are therefore content to engage with existing political institutions. The new movements have a quite different type of focus. They deliberately aim at *avoiding* conventional political power. They see their main battlegrounds in civil society – in, that is, the area of social life outside governments and state departments. They usually see themselves as developing new values and new ways of life outside those prescribed by conventional politics. They hope to organize themselves in ways which are unhierarchical and unbureaucratic. They are loose-knit, comparatively disorganized groupings and are concerned to build up participation at a grass-roots level.

Such, in broad terms, is a fairly conventional descriptive account of the NSMs and their difference from the old movements. But this leaves a number of jobs to be done. What has brought these movements into being? What, given that they are quite diverse, are their common features? Is the difference between 'old' and 'new' being exaggerated here? And how do both new and old types of movement link to the main themes of this study? We can begin to answer these questions by examining NSMs in terms of our themes of risk, community, industry and evolution.

Social Evolution and Risk

One obvious way of accounting for these new types of movement is simply to refer to the fact that the world has changed. Society has changed, as have its relations to nature.

New social movements and the metabolic rift

Thus the NSMs can in part be seen as a product of the 'metabolic rift' between society and nature. They can be seen as an emotional, Romantic reaction to those Enlightenment values which continue to allow humanity to exploit the environment as a mere object. Some environmental movements, particularly of the 'deep green' variety, seek relations with 'pure' nature, one in which people can develop their selves in a more fulfilling way by interacting with their environment and with other people more directly.

More materially, the new movements can be seen as a product of the real environmental risks which do now seem to be developing. The scientific 'facts' about, for example, the effects of global warming and the genetic modification of food are still not clear. But enough people feel they have sufficient knowledge of the risks involved to start developing alternative types of politics. The media, in combination with the advice of scientists and non-governmental organizations, have been responsible for drawing attention to these risks and for developing different forms of political engagement.

New social movements and social change

As regards social change, the new movements can be seen as a product of social evolution, as a product of a 'post-industrial' society (Touraine 1981, 1985). This perspective can be seen as Marxist in the sense that it draws attention to the changing forms of industry and employment and sees NSMs as a reflection of this change. Similarly, Eder (1993) points to the rise of what he calls 'the new middle class', who were amongst those discussed in chapter 4. 'The new middle class' in Eder's terms are those with high levels of cultural capital. They are amongst the leaders of the new kinds of values and environmental movements espoused by the NSMs. On the other hand, there is more to this perspective than this.

'The network society' was discussed earlier. It is a form of economy and social organization that gives particular prominence to the making and exchanging of knowledge. The media and the internet have a role to play, but this is not just a reference to the so-called 'dot.coms'. It refers to the ways in which all types of industry produce and exchange knowledge. This is an emergent and important way of realizing profitability, and is a distinct shift from societies which predominantly make and exchange things.

Connecting this argument to the NSMs, they can be seen as the political mirror of this social change. Like society itself, NSMs are increasingly about culture and ideas, as distinct from things. They are about making and exploring new ways of life in societies which are no longer organized around the manufacturing of physical objects.

Similarly, the NSMs can be seen as revolving around the making of new kinds of self or identity. This again runs parallel to some of the concerns in earlier chapters. Individualization, the making of apparently autonomous selves, is also a central feature of our society, one that results from consumerism and new types of employment structure. NSMs can also be seen as both reflecting these developments and challenging them. On the one hand, here are particular groups of middle-class people carving out new ways of life and new identities in a proactive way; not seeking anyone's permission and not hampered by traditions or precedents passed down through households. Still less are they hampered by the sense that they need to stay within the same firm all their lives.

On the other hand, many of the NSMs challenge the particular kinds of self outlined in chapters 4 and 5. While these movements may not express their priorities in psychoanalytic terms, their emphasis on social networks and active social engagement means they are attempting to overcome the particular kind of self-serving individualism of the narcissistic type. By the same token, they resist the rampant consumerism which lies behind this kind of psychic structure.

New society, new social movements

So the argument here is that NSMs reflect the kind of changing society in which we now live. Struggles which were once focused largely on the workplace have become displaced into other spheres of social life, particularly civil society. But these struggles are not simply a reflection of social and environmental change; they are challenging many of society's dominant Enlightenment values, priorities which are generating disaster at the environmental, social and personal levels.

Why a new form of politics?

But why should such concern lead to a 'new' form of politics? It is because the old form of scientific politics handed down from the Enlightenment is now seen as, at best, ineffectual and, at worst, too linked to the problems it is trying to resolve. Indeed, governments are a large part of the problem itself. Whereas the 'old' movements saw solutions and reconciliation via the medium of the state, many participants in the new movements see the state and its activities as a large part of the problem itself. Not only are governments remote, hierarchical and bureaucratic, but they also consistently align themselves with powerful vested interests. To make matters worse, they themselves engage in policies which promote environmental degradation and social injustice.

Paradoxically, however, the NSMs also often mourn the passing of this same hierarchical and bureaucratic state. Neoliberal policies in many societies mean that governments are now attempting to 'roll back' their activities, supporting the commodification of services (such as health, welfare and transport facilities) that were once allocated by bureaucratic means. But again, the promises offered in favour of such liberalization are not being wholly delivered. They do not benefit the environment, and they clearly benefit some groups of people much more than others. Either way, many supporters of NSMs appear to have had their fill of governments, either in their old or their 'rolled-back' forms. It is precisely for this reason that many of the NSMs are attracted to decentralized, relatively unhierarchical forms of government. Anarchism, a position to be explored later, falls into that category.

Revealing and Making Community

A linked dimension to the NSMs concerns the making of human association or 'community'. This is the particular emphasis developed by Alberto Melucci (1989). He argues that these movements should not be taken at face value. He is right to make this suggestion. On the other hand, there may be even more to the NSMs than he suggests.

Symbolism and submerged networks

According to Melucci, there are two important dimensions to the NSMs. First, their significance is mainly symbolic. That is, they are establishing new lifestyles and values. Second, they tend to be based on 'movement areas'. These are well-established networks already living out new, alternative ways of life. Collective action and political protest of the kind represented by the NSMs is realizing and developing the lifestyles already well developed within these networks:

> These take the form of networks composed of a multiplicity of groups that are dispersed, fragmented and submerged in everyday life, and which act as cultural laboratories. They require individual investments in the experimentation and practice of new cultural models, forms of relationships and alternative perceptions and meanings in the world. (Melucci 1989: 89)

If this understanding is accepted, it comes as no surprise that the NSMs are highly diverse in nature. This reflects the diversity of the networks from which they have sprung. But, for all their diversity, it is important to recognize that there may still be more material and economic processes underlying this diversity of social movement. These alternative cultural forms and attempts at remaking identity and community are all occurring in a particular kind of social and political context, an argument which has been made by a number of social movement theorists (Allen et al. 1992). Recognizing the social and political context leads to a possible extension of Melucci's work.

Putting submerged networks in context

In the material social world people are subject to massive and largely unknowable forces and relationships. This is emphasized by a number of contemporary social theorists, including Anthony Giddens (1990, 1991). One of the effects of globalization, as he points out, is to change the significance and meaning of everyday life. To an increasing extent, he argues, society is spread over space and time. This process of 'distanciation'

> increasingly tears space away from place by fostering relations between absent others, locationally distant from any given situation of face-to-face interaction. In conditions of modernity, locales are thoroughly penetrated and shaped in terms of social influences quite distant from them. What structures the locale is not simply that which is present on the scene; the 'visible form' of the locale conceals the distanciated relations which determine its nature. (Giddens 1990: 18–19)

Giddens is arguing here that social life which is mainly lived in local contexts and small-scale interaction is being 'disembedded', particularly under conditions of rapid globalization and the centralization of political power. In such a context, everyday life is being emptied of meaning. As discussed in box 1.8 (p. 43), it is shaped by processes and relationships well beyond most people's regular boundaries and knowledge. This leads, Giddens argues, to a condition of 'ontological insecurity' in which people are obliged to place their trust not in everyday experience and face-to-face interaction, but in markets and specialized forms of knowledge. This is a kind of anomie or alienation of the modern age, but one with a distinct spatial basis.

But at the same time, as Giddens points out, much of everyday life consists of 're-embedding', of people attempting to take their lives into their own hands and, in a proactive way, give themselves a new sense of meaning, identity and purpose. Seen in this light, NSMs as described by Melucci make even more sense. They are establishing a sense of identity in a globalizing society where social interaction is being emptied of significance. Those joining or supporting the NSMs are doing so in order to develop some understanding of, and possibly control over, their lives.

Re-embedding: an example

As an indication of the kinds of process to which Giddens is alluding, a statement from an individual contributing to the Mass Observation Archive, based at Sussex University, is reproduced in box 8.1 (for further details see Dickens 1992). From time to time the Archive asks correspondents to reply to 'directives' on specific topics. The particular directive used here elicited feelings about the most important developments of the 1980s. Many people chose environmental questions. And the account in box 8.1 of how one person became involved in a series of NSMs (including the Campaign for Nuclear Disarmament) gives one insight into what is happening. He was already part of a 'submerged network' of environmentalists. But becoming active was the direct result of his losing control over life and then 're-embedding' by joining the environmental movement.

Box 8.1 The making of an environmentalist

Why do people become environmentalists? The obvious answer is that they have a rising concern with the environment, with environmental degradation and the like. But another answer is more social and personal. They may also do so because they undergo a shift in values, perhaps as a result of a personal shock, often due to circumstances out of their control. In this context, environmental movements and politics offer not only new relations to the environment but new, less estranged relations between people. Those who join environmental movements do so for social as well as environmental reasons. The following individual had already been involved in a loose way with environmental politics. But his account shows how he became increasingly involved in the green movement:

Funnily enough 1980 to '90 were some of the most significant in my life. I had a nervous breakdown, sloughed off my conditioning and laid down new base rules which I believe at present to be correct.... For twenty odd years I had been bringing up a family earning my bread by running a mobile shop round the houses and working twenty-four hours a day, making as much money as I needed and ploughing the spare into the business.

One day the van broke down and I was sitting in a phone box waiting for the breakdown truck to come and tow me back to the garage for repair, when I thought what the hell am I waiting here for? All my profits this week will go to repairs and all I get out is another long week of work and work and I went home, stopped all my supplies and went down the DHSS and signed on for supplementary benefit...

I joined the Ecology Party and engaged in a lot of debate with my friends etc. and went to Worthy Farm Somerset to a Green Gathering. I had sold my van and bought a moped as being the cheapest form of transport than a bike and I thought I was too old to ride for long distances.

At Glastonbury I was involved with the Women for Life on Earth who were walking from Wales to Greenham to try and stop Cruise coming. For three days we sat in a marquee in a circle and debated whether it should be women only in order to get press interest. Although it was called Women for Life on Earth there were men involved as members and husbands of members. There we decided the men should leave the march...

Shortly after I read the theory of Gaia and everything became very clear to me that the earth had evolved me in ninety-six million years for the sole purpose of looking after her, in other words as her gardener and so in pure self-defence, since I could not survive without the world, I must make sure the world did [sic] survive. Since then I have stood as candidate for the European Parliament for the Green Party and am currently named in the [named region] Green Party.

If I make something happen every day then I am having an effect on the Chaos which is the world. I try and grow my own food and so have as little to do with the social system as possible except to change it. (Extracted from Mass Observation Archive, University of Sussex Library, Brighton, 23/2 (Autumn/Winter 1987); cited in Dickens 1992: 172–3)

Industry and the Red-Green Perspective

For many on the political Left, however, the kinds of analysis offered by Giddens and by other NSM theorists are missing the basic point. Why did the mobile shop owner turn to environmental politics? It was, in effect, because he had been made poor. Similarly, why is there environmental degradation? It is mainly due to capitalist industrialization.

According to this perspective, NSMs cannot afford simply to concentrate on remaking community within 'modernity'. What is this 'modernity' if it is not globalized capitalism? Similarly, questions of environmental sustainability and personal identity cannot be considered outside questions which have long been asked by critics of capitalism. These include questions of social justice as well as environmental degradation. Such is the 'Red-Green' position: one which argues that for all the focus of NSMs on new values, cultural diversity and the re-embedding of social life within 'modernity', the focus should remain on capitalist social relations and processes (Red-Green Study Group 1995; Benton 1999b).

The enclosure and privatization of common land and public resources has, for more than two centuries, been a prime feature of modern capitalism. And these, it is argued, lie behind much contemporary environmental degradation. Environmentalists must therefore look to the institution of private property and modern industrial economies if they are to fully understand environmental problems and their solution. Similarly, powerful classes and economic interests are now creating environmental degradation, and this must be confronted and changed. Again, as discussed in chapter 4, ecological problems are often ascribed to high levels of consumerism. And how does such consumerism come about? It is due to capitalist companies which, with the aid of extensive advertising, assure people that they need to surround themselves with more commodities if they are to be adequately fulfilled individuals. NSM-type environmentalists therefore need to be 'red' as well as 'green'.

The argument extends to many of the concerns which seem to be uniquely linked to NSMs. Here are three examples:

1   New social movements often emphasize the importance of 'building from below' or 'grass-roots' activity independent of the state. This is in line with the anarchist position often adopted by these movements. 'Red-Greens' now recognize the importance of 'building from below'. The idea of a state-imposed single, universal solution was clearly an enormous mistake. On the other hand, Red-Greens also insist on the importance of 'enabling from above', democratizing the state and other institutions such as transnational agencies in ways which support 'building from below'. Furthermore, state intervention (regarding, for example, the extension of citizenship or changes to the tax laws) may be necessary to overcome social inequality as well as environmental sustainability.

2   New social movements emphasize spontaneity and self-organization, again independent of state control. There is a lesson here for the Left. Unlike communists such as Marx and Engels (see chapter 2) Reds must now recognize

that there is no predetermined march of history towards a communist utopia. Again, the emphasis must be on diversity, self-management and the knowledge that societies may evolve in many, largely unpredictable ways.

3 New social movements give special emphasis to forms of social life outside paid work or the 'formal economy'. They therefore draw attention to the division of labour between the workplace on the one hand and the household or community on the other. Reds of the past have largely ignored these latter aspects of social life. This was another mistake, one which took caring and domestic work largely for granted. But Red-Greens also insist that the relationships between industry and household economies need better recognition. This entails not just organizing the formal sector in ways which allow home-workers to participate in the labour force, but also recognizing that what might seem like non-industrial concerns (for example, the raising of children) have close links with the industrial economy. 'Care', for example, includes care for children's health. And threats to health often stem from the formal economy.

Red-Greens therefore argue in favour of dialogue and coalition between NSMs and the 'old' type of social movement. NSMs cannot ignore capitalist production, democracy and social justice.

Water-melon politics?

However, these moves by representatives of the 'old' form of movement are sometimes met with scepticism and resistance by the new movements. They see the Reds as attempting to co-opt their independent politics into old and discredited forms of action. At worst, it is an attempt by a male, middle-class, middle-age minority to control new ways of thinking about the world. Furthermore, the Reds' emphasis on production and science is suspect. They are the source of the very problems which the new movements are trying to overcome. Those suspicious of the Red-Greens sometimes refer to their 'water-melon politics': green outside, red inside.

It is perhaps difficult to see how these arguments are going to be resolved. But there is also reason for optimism here. Many Red-Greens are already recognizing exploitation and struggle outside the workplace even if the coalitions between these struggles and those of, for example, black people and groups such as the 'New Agers' remain to be made (Red-Green Network 1995). The latter can be seen as the Romantics of our time, often idealizing 'nature' in a spiritual, quasi-religious way. This kind of Green is probably least likely to join the Reds.

Many of those engaging in NSMs have concerns which are very familiar to those in the supposedly 'old' and discredited leftwing politics. As box 8.2 indeed shows, many participants in NSMs are now clearly seeing across the supposed Red-Green divide to understand the social *and* environmental nature of the problem. Their critique of consumerism, for example, is one which goes back at least a century and a half to Marx, Engels and the early founders of the socialist and communist movement.

Box 8.2   May Day demonstration, Trafalgar Square, London 2001

Lola, a 24-year-old singer, explains why she was one of the thousands of protestors at this event:

> People are unhappy, seeing what big business has done to the planet. And there's this weird sort of mental exhaustion, as people strive after this dream and they're fed by big business: buy this, buy that, it scares me because you feel that everything's controlled by this massive faceless organization and that every government and politician is entwined in it. ('Why I Was There', *Guardian*, 2 May 2001)

Human Evolution and the Recovery of Human Nature

There are two recurring features of many of the new social movements. They are closely related. One is the resistance to hierarchy of all kinds. The other is the importance of knowledge and education. How are these concerns linked? Hierarchy, seen as social and political domination, is facilitated by the creation of specialized and abstract forms of knowledge. General knowledge, as discussed in chapter 1, has often been used to subjugate those whose understandings are of a more practical, local and everyday kind. Knowledge and education are amongst the prime concerns of the anarchist movement, one to which some NSMs subscribe.

Is hierarchy contrary to human nature?

As discussed in chapter 5, there is some debate between anarchists as to whether cooperation and mutualism is an inherent feature of humanity's evolved human nature. If Kropotkin (1985) is to be believed, the attempt by the new movements to make non-hierarchical organizations and associations is simply realizing what is fundamental to humans and other animals. It is the type of organization which fulfils their natural needs and predispositions. Such a position is in line with Freud's idea of an 'anaclytic' type of personality, one which recognizes the independence and needs of others. This is more healthy to the development of the individual than the narcissistic type of subjectivity developing in modern society.

If Bookchin (1997) is to be believed, on the other hand, hierarchy is very much a social product. It started with the domination of women and children by men and is perpetuated today with the domination of external nature by humanity. Bookchin's position suggests that mutualism should not be confused with sociality. This is a slippage which is often made in this type of discussion. Humans, many people would agree, are a social sort. They need to associate with one another and to communicate with them if they are to be fully developed individuals. Indeed, they have developed complex cultures, forms of communication and the capacity to express themselves in order to achieve just this sociality. But this is not to say that they are always and inevitably mutually supportive of one another. This latter smacks somewhat of idealism, a fault often associated with critics on the Left.

Ending the division of labour

One of the anarchists' main concerns is with the division of labour. The forms of associative democracy they propose entail collective ownership and control. The idea is not only to control what is made or produced but to create a new kind of integrated self. An enforced division of labour, one in which managers with specialist expertise have control of planning and technological innovation while workers are reduced to carrying out boring and repetitive work, would be abolished.

In the kind of decentralized society envisaged by Kropotkin (1985) people would therefore be neither intellectual nor manual workers. They would take part in planning and introducing new kinds of technological innovation while carrying out the sort of practical work necessary for the functioning of their organization. They would be able to link practical and more general forms of understanding, as a result of which human alienation would be overcome. The whole self would be used and linked; manual and intellectual capacities would be realized and combined.

Bookchin (1977) takes the argument still further. He was concerned not only with democratizing the division of labour in the sphere of paid work, but also with democratizing the social division of labour, within, that is, society as a whole. This fits in with his argument that the division of labour between men and women is more fundamental than that between classes. A priority is to release women from unpaid work in the home, a priority shared by many of the NSMs.

Modern education: 'a mass of rubbish'

Education and the manipulation of knowledge are central to the politics of anarchism, as indeed they are to many involved in NSMs (Woodcock 1977: Pt. 6). Kropotkin is one of the clearest anarchists on this. His rejection of the enforced division of labour was part of a wider project: that of rejecting the division between abstract and concrete forms of knowledge. The education of children starts off this essentially malign process. From school onwards general ideas are not properly linked to knowledge based on practical experience. 'Clever' individuals are those who can best handle abstract ideas.

Furthermore, 'brain' or 'mental' work of the kind emphasized in formal education consists of learning and reproducing these ideas in the form of parrot-like repetition of formulae. The result is that formal education is, in Kropotkin's words, 'a mass of rubbish' (see box 8.3). It is over-specialized and equates cleverness with the capability for handling abstract ideas out of their context. Meanwhile, those who do not have (or are trained not to have) such capacities for handling general ideas are directed to 'inferior' kinds of technical education. This is often the first stage in their relegation to tedious and unrewarding forms of labour. Abstract ideas, according to Kropotkin, should be impressed on the young mind in their concrete

---

**Box 8.3 Linking practical to abstract knowledge:
Kropotkin on the reorganization of knowledge**

Kropotkin firmly believed that school education, especially scientific education, is 'a waste of time' and 'a mass of rubbish'. The laws of nature should be understood, he believed, through practical experience rather than through rote-learning and parrot-like repetition. Even the tools and instruments children use in science should be constructed by the children themselves:

> The waste of time in physics is simply revolting. While young people very easily understand the principles of chemistry and its formulae, as soon as they themselves make the first experiments with a few glasses and tubes, they mostly find the greatest difficulties in grasping the mechanical introduction into physics, partly because they do not know geometry, and especially because they are merely shown costly machines instead of being induced to make themselves plain apparatus for illustrating the phenomena they study. ... In reality, all apparatus used to illustrate the fundamental laws of physics ought to be made by the children themselves. (1995: 177)

Kropotkin was writing a century ago. Is school education, particularly scientific education, 'a waste of time' or 'a mass of rubbish'? And do Kropotkin's proposals for linking abstract and concrete forms of knowledge still make sense today?

---

forms. This could be achieved by, for example, solving problems 'in the playing-ground with a few sticks and string'. But the actual result of modern industry is that these connections remain unmade. Human beings' full capacities again remain under-developed.

Knowledge and new social movements

The implications for understanding the relations between society and nature are self-evident. Enlightenment thinking has long given a special premium to the development and understanding of abstract ideas. Furthermore, it is right to have done so. Modern science remains central to understanding humanity's relations with nature. The problem is that abstract ideas have been projected as immune to development and testing with reference to the knowledge derived from everyday experience and observation. Such knowledge is not simply a case of understanding how, for example, the laws of nature relate to practical experience of them 'on the ground'. They can also be used to create new theoretical ideas which can be tested by experiments.

Perhaps in the end the knowledge question may turn out to be the most important contribution of the new social movements. It is certainly a central component of the environmental movement. Some members of NSMs remain deeply suspicious of science and of the whole Enlightenment project which promoted scientific enquiry. But this is regression and a counsel of despair. The idea of scientific knowledge must be accepted, but science must constantly justify itself, with reference to what people are experiencing. The other side to this same coin is that people whose understanding is not scientific can actually contribute to the development of scientific knowledge. This entails opening up to different kinds of contextual and local knowledge and memories (Irwin 2001). Such understandings are not usually considered 'scientific', but they are important because they can demonstrate how more abstract understandings work out not in laboratories but in 'open systems'. Scientific and lay knowledge are not inherently in conflict. NSMs show that they can be combined. One result is a new kind of enlightened self.

Summary

New social movements are very diverse in nature. This can be seen by examining those in the 'anti-globalization' movement, first established in the mid-1990s. Under this umbrella are, for example, anarchists, pro-Lenin communists, anti-war campaigners, anti-racists and those demanding state intervention to counter further ecological degradation. This seems to many like a recipe for instability, incoherence and impotence. At the same time, as this chapter has indicated, there are a number of common themes connecting many of these movements. These include the creation of participatory forms of politics, the exploration of alternative values and lifestyles, the development of new kinds of education and the support of new, less narcissistic forms of identity. Furthermore, many of the new movements' concerns, such as the commodification of public property, are shared with the older movements. They address those sources of economic and political power responsible for degrading both internal and external nature.

It is now frequently suggested that attempts be made to channel and coordinate these various forms of politics at a global scale. This, it is argued, would give them greater strength against those institutions and classes which wield economic and political power. But this strategy too brings potential dangers. It could easily be a first stage towards the cooption and containment of the new movements within centrally run bureaucracies. Such a move would directly undermine what many of the NSMs are attempting to achieve. Diversity can be considered a source of weakness, but it can also be celebrated as a source of strength.

FURTHER READING

The literature on the new social movements is now very considerable. A useful introduction is:

A. Scott, *Ideology and the New Social Movements*. London: Routledge, 1990.

See also:

J. Allen, P. Braham and P. Lewis, *Political and Economic Forms of Modernity*. Cambridge: Polity Press, 1992.

L. Martell, *Ecology and Society*. Cambridge: Polity Press, 1994.

R. Inglehart, 'Values, Ideology and Cognitive Mobilization in New Social Movements', in R. Dalton and M. Kuechler (eds), *Challenging the Political Order*. Cambridge: Polity Press, 1990.

Those who challenge the rigid division between 'old' and 'new' movements include:
  L. Ray, *Rethinking Critical Theory: Emancipation in the Age of Global Social Movements*. London: Sage, 1993.
  R. Brulle, *Agency, Democracy and Nature. The US Environmental Movement from a Critical Theory Perspective*. London: MIT Press, 2000.

The latter text is a new departure, using the work of Jürgen Habermas to assess whether American environmental movements are facilitating the opening up of a new 'public sphere' in which rationality and open communication of public opinions prevail. Brulle concludes that this goal is being partially met, though the range and diversity of environmental movements in the US remains very diverse. Klaus Eder was a student of Habermas. He argues that rationality within environmental politics must resist Enlightenment-style assumptions that the environment is merely there to be exploited. Aesthetic considerations and questions of moral responsibility also need incorporating. See:
  K. Eder, *The Social Construction of Nature*. London: Sage, 1996.

A text which links closely to Giddens and 'disembedding' is:
  A. Franklin, *Nature and Social Theory*. London: Sage, 2002.

Franklin argues, *inter alia*, that environmentalism should be seen in the context of social convulsions of modern life. 'Nature', in this context, is construed and engaged in as it represents harmony, balance and peace. Further criticism of new social movements literature is that they are insufficiently placed in historical perspective. See Brulle 2000, op. cit. But note that some authors have attempted to make this link. See, for example:
  R. Dunlap and A. Mertig (eds), *The US Environmental Movement, 1970–1990*. London: Taylor and Francis, 1992.

A helpful overview of the field is:
  C. Rootes (ed.), *Environmental Movements*. London: Cass, 1999.

The contemporary anti-globalization movement seems likely to give a new boost to the literature in this area. As a first indication of this development, see, for example:
  S. George, G. Monbiot, L. German, T. Hayter, A. Callinicos and K. Moody (eds), *Anti-Capitalism. A Guide to the Movement*. London: Bookmarks, 2001.
  M. Klein, *No Logo*. London: Flamingo, 2000.

See also the website of the World Social Forum:
  <www.worldsocialforum.com>

See also the website of La Via Campesina, an international movement coordinating peasant organizations of small- and middle-scale producers, agricultural workers and indigenous communities from Asia, Africa, America and Europe:
  <http://ns.rds.org.hn/via/quienes_erg.htm>

A very useful introduction to Kropotkin is:
  P. Kropotkin, *The Conquest of Bread and Other Writings*, ed. M. Schatz. Cambridge: Cambridge University Press, 1995.

Bookchin's publications are several. One of the most relevant here is:
  M. Bookchin, *The Ecology of Freedom*. Palo Alto, CA: Cheshire Books, 1992.

For a recent very useful survey which pays particular attention to Bookchin, see:
  R. Eckersley, *Environmentalism and Political Theory. Toward an Ecocentric Approach*. London: UCL Press, 1992.

As regards anarchism today, a valuable study is:
  D. Pepper, *Communes and the Green Vision*. London: Merlin Press, 1991.

Modern anarchism in relation to today's anti-capitalist movement is covered in:

M. Albert, 'Anarchists', in S. George, G. Monbiot, L. German, T. Hayter, A. Callinicos and K. Moody (eds), *Anti-Capitalism. A Guide to the Movement*. London: Bookmarks, 2001.

One of the heroes of the anti-capitalist movement is José Bové, a French farmer who identifies himself as a 'peasant farmer' and founding member of the Confederation Paysanne. He appears to have anarchist leanings, the highlights of his colourful career so far including the destruction of three tons of Novartis transgenic corn and the dismantling of his local branch of McDonalds. See:

J. Bové and F. Dufour, *The World is Not for Sale*. London: Verso, 2000.

See also:

C. Heller, 'From Scientific Risk to Paysan Savoir Faire: Peasant Expertise in the French and Global Debate over GM Crops', *Science as Culture*, 11/1 (2002): 13–37. Paradoxically, this particular form of anarchy is deeply dependent on EC farm subsidies.

The new social movements make very active use of the internet. Some of the most prominent representative organizations in the social/environmental field include:

Community Recycling Network   <www.crn.org.uk>
Earth First   <www.eco-action.org/ef/index.html>
Food First   <www.foodfirst.org>
Friends of the Earth   <www.foei.org>
Genetic Resources Action International   <www.grain.org>
Green-Socialist Network   <http://member.lycos.co.uk/leonora/gsn.html>
Green Party   <www.greenparty.org.uk>
Greenpeace International   <www.greenpeace.org>
Peoples Food Sovereignty Network   <www.peoplesfoodsovereignty.org>
Our World is Not for Sale   <www.ourworldisnotforsale.org>
Reclaim the Streets   <www.reclaimthestreets.org.uk>

Appendix

Interacting with the Environment, Transforming Ourselves: Suggestions for Further Research

As people interact with nature they finish up transforming their own natures. This is an old theme in the social and political sciences, one which students may wish to follow up.

Jean-Jacques Rousseau (1712–78) argued, for example, that in a 'pre-political' state of nature people were independent, self-sufficient individuals. They were easily capable of acquiring and looking after the resources they needed for survival, yet also able to exercise compassion. (This included, Rousseau believed, compassion towards other species as well as towards other humans.) But the development of agriculture and the extension of private property made these individuals increasingly dependent on one another and hence, in Rousseau's eyes, *un*free. Furthermore, those with advanced physical or mental strengths started to exploit those with fewer abilities. At this stage in human development 'political society' emerged; community laws were needed as 'the most honest men learned to count it as one of their duties to slay their kind' (1994: 70). Rousseau believed that the emergence of private property was largely responsible for alienating people from one another and increasing human antagonism. It also estranged people from their environment.

Rousseau strongly influenced Georg Hegel (1770–1831), who developed no less than a theory of world history, in which concepts competed for dominance, leading to the increasing development of a world mind. People are thereby progressively emancipated through the development of increasingly scientific and rational understandings both of themselves and of the external world. Hegel's picture is broadly in line with Enlightenment thinking. He argued, however, that the development of a *collective* form of knowledge was more significant than the development of *individual* rationality. Remarkably, he also argued that the development of agriculture and industry meant that people no longer had a direct engagement with nature. In this way they were made into mere passive consumers of products, their knowledge no longer being derived from first-hand experience (see Plant 1973, 1977a,b).

Marx based his understanding on Hegel. As discussed in chapter 2, however, he argued that world history consisted of the struggle between social classes, rather than ideas. People make social relations in working on their environments to produce the things they need such as food and houses. But humanity makes not only new social relations but also new biological and mental structures. Modern capitalist society, incorporating the institution of private property, systematically separates or alienates people from the rest of the natural world and undermines people's capacities. In this respect Marx was following Rousseau. Hegel believed that the possession of private property was an important means by which people could relate to and understand external nature.

Other early social scientists developed similar perspectives. Auguste Comte (1798–1857), for example, is sometimes seen as the founder of sociology. He also built up an entire theory of social change based on how people understand both their environment and themselves. As briefly discussed in box I.4 (p. 13), Comte saw the earliest era of modern society, 'the theological stage', as based on religious understandings both of nature and of humanity's place in nature. During the next 'metaphysical' stage, people began to see themselves as natural, rather than supernatural, entities. Astrology was used to understand the movements of the planets, for example, and society was seen as not so much God-given but as stemming from human nature itself. Finally, in the 'scientific' stage, the thinking of such giants as Newton came to dominate humanity's understanding of their environment and of themselves. Furthermore, the new science of 'sociology' would enable people to build a better society, one based on a scientific understanding of human nature as well as their environment.

In the modern era this theme has been relatively neglected, mainly because of social science's changing priorities. 'Humanity's interaction with nature' has been largely interpreted as 'humanity's *interpretation* of nature'. There has been little emphasis on how people's physical and psychic natures are transformed. The work of Adorno and Horkheimer is, however, worth exploring (see Introduction, 'Further reading'). They argue that Enlightenment science has been made a means by which human nature and the environment are dominated. In the process, a new kind of human identity has been created: a highly rational self, relating to the environment as a mere object to be manipulated. An over-quantified and scientifically defined 'nature' therefore leaves people's capacities underdeveloped; individuals feel powerless, their creative and imaginative capacities neglected.

All these perspectives can be criticized. Comte's faith in modern scientific method as a means of understanding human society now seems, for example, misleading and over-optimistic. The Frankfurt School, in contrast, tends to be over-pessimistic about the gains made by the Enlightenment. (It also has relatively little to say about the effects of humanity's domination over *external* nature.) Nevertheless, these older ways of linking society and nature are worth revisiting. An example of how historical research can be conducted within the general framework outlined here is given in box A.1.

Box A.1   Interacting with nature, transforming humanity: the case of ship navigation, Enlightenment science and the making of the British Empire

In the late seventeenth century ships were having enormous problems orienting themselves. It was the problem of establishing longitude – one's exact position east and west – while in the middle of the sea and out of sight of land. In March 1675 Charles II appointed John Flamsteed, a 28-year-old clergyman and mathematician, as his first Astronomer Royal to try to crack this problem. Flamsteed was instructed by the king to 'apply himself with the most exact care and diligence to the rectifying of the tables of the motions of the heavens, and the places of the fixed stars, so as to find out the so much-desired longitude of places for the perfecting the art of navigation' (<www.nmm.ac.uk>).

The problem was partly solved using observations made at Greenwich Royal Observatory, designed by the distinguished architect, Sir Christopher Wren. By the early eighteenth century sailors were able to orient themselves by reference to the moon and the stars, though by this time they also had access to the 'sea clock', whereby longitude is established by comparing the time on a ship with that at the home port. (The 'sea clock' concept was outlined by Newton in 1714 but was not finally established as a working idea until some 60 years later.)

The important point here is that the observations made at the Observatory proved crucial in the development of Isaac Newton's own theories. He wrote to John Flamsteed, providing information about the likely changes in the moon's position. But Newton also sought information about the actual observed movements of the planets. Using this information allowed him to develop his lunar theory, showing how variations in the moon related to the gravitational effects of 'massive bodies' such as the earth, the moon and the planets. Partly to deflect criticism that he had pilfered Flamsteed's star maps, Newton acknowledged the assistance he had been given by the young Astronomer Royal: 'All the world knows that I make no observations myself and therefore I must of necessity acknowledge their author: and if I do not make a handsome acknowledgement, they will reckon me an ungrateful clown' (cited in Forbes 1975: 67).

The development of Enlightenment astronomy in turn assisted a new round of interactions between society and nature. Accurate navigation allowed British fleets to supply and extend a vast trade and military empire based on the global exploitation of people and natural resources. This was symbolized by the Greenwich Meridian being made the reference point for time-zones throughout the whole world in 1884. Note, however, that the key symbolic importance of the Greenwich Observatory attracted the attention of several political activists. A French anarchist attempted to blow up the Observatory in 1894, the first case in Britain of 'international terrorism'. Similarly, in 1913 two policemen claimed to have overheard a group of suffragettes plotting to destroy the Observatory at the heart of the British Empire. This threat did not come to anything, but it was sufficient to alarm the then Astronomer Royal, Sir William Christie.

Source: Royal Greenwich Observatory Archives, University of Cambridge Library. File RGO 7/58.

Glossary of Terms

Actor-Network Theory (ANT) Emphasizes context and relationships between people, organizations, ideas and learning. Argues that no distinction can be made between a pure 'nature' and a non-natural 'society'.

Age of Reason/Enlightenment A period of remarkable development and innovation in philosophical thought, starting in the seventeenth century. It was characterized by a belief that people could understand and control the universe by means of rational thought and empirical work.

Agri-industrial complex A term used to refer to the fusion of farming with other industries (seed and chemicals production, plant and animal breeding and scientific research establishments) into a major, connected, industrial enterprise.

Alienation Used mainly in historical materialism to describe the separation by capitalism of people from the product of their labour, from their own creative capacities, from other people. Less well known in Marx's work is the idea of alienation from **external nature** which Marx envisaged as integral to humanity's spiritual, as well as material, well-being.

Altruism The phenomenon of people doing what is in the interests of others and not in their self-interest. Sometimes contrasted with egoism.

Anaclytic/anaclysis In Freudian psychology the child turning to those objects of love (e.g. the mother) who assist in its helplessness and gratify its self-preserving needs. As the child matures, this love is transferred to a range of others who protect, feed and so on. See also **narcissism**.

Anomie A social condition in which social norms governing social interaction have broken down. Associated with Emile Durkheim's sociology, especially with his analysis of suicide.

Anthropocentric Most people are anthropocentric insofar as they affirm the intrinsic value (that is, the value in their own right) of human beings. See also **ecocentrism**.

Associationalism/associative democracy Proposals to strengthen associations such as unions, works councils, neighbourhood associations, as an alternative to the kinds of liberal democracy emergent since the nineteenth century. These are seen as no longer able to cope with modern conditions and are steadily losing popular support.

Biological reductionism   A critique of biology arguing that biological understandings of human beings cannot, on their own, provide adequate understanding of social practices, social relations and social change. A similar critique can be made of certain branches of sociology. 'Sociological reductionism' takes little account of biology, ecological systems and the organic bases of social life. See also **sociobiology**.

Biotechnology   Transplant of genes from one strain or species to another. Can entail transfers between wholly different species; from, for example, fish to tomatoes, bacteria to humans, and vice versa.

Closed systems   A term used in **critical realism** to describe a situation in which the operation of a causal mechanism can be examined independently of external influences. See also **open systems**.

Commodification   The making of a facility previously collectively or state-owned into a commodity to be bought and sold. Human labour can also be commodified.

Commodity fetishism   A concept derived from Marx referring to the worship of commodities in themselves and the neglect of the social relations and **labour processes** involved in their making.

Communitarianism   A call for reinvigorated social and political institutions which would resist both rampant **liberalism** and overpowerful governance to reassert a strong sense of community.

Consumption/consumer society   Consumption refers to the purchase of all kinds of commodities: goods, holiday, leisure, etc. Consumer society entails a claim that modern societies are increasingly organized around consumption and this has major implications for people's identities and politics.

Critical realism   Realism, unlike positivism, recognizes relations and processes which are independent of our beliefs about the world. Structures and processes therefore underlie what can be observed, though they may well not be observable themselves. Critical realism maintains a critique both of our understanding of these structures and processes and of the social processes under examination. Critical realism is often contrasted with constructionism or constructivism. The strongest version of this argument is that what may seem to be independent real objects are actually social or cultural constructs.

Diseases of affluence   Illnesses such as diabetes and heart problems stemming from people leading relatively traditional ways of life (in, for example, subsistence farming) encountering modern, Western lifestyles.

Ecofeminism   A position which argues that women are closer to nature. Some ecofeminists argue that this connection is one of a spiritual nature, a connection to be celebrated. Materialist ecofeminists argue, however, that the closeness to nature is due to the division of labour and patriarchal exploitation.

Egocentric/ism   Term borrowed from Freudian psychology. Children are seen as developing through a series of stages: oral (sucking, feeding and so on), anal and phallic. Adults are capable of regressing to this egocentric, self-centred type of disposition and behaviour. See also **anaclytic, narcissism**.

Ecological modernization   The belief amongst academics and policy-makers that contemporary societies have the capability of dealing with environmental crises.

El Niño   A warm water current which recurrently changes direction. It has climatic effects throughout the Pacific region. Whether the extremes of drought and flood generated by El Niño are becoming more exaggerated and whether human interventions are responsible are still matters of scientific discussion.

Empiricism   A term used to describe those forms of scientific enquiry which give a particular place to experience in the acquisition and development of knowledge.

Enlightenment See **Age of Reason**.

Environmental Justice Movement A global movement to resist the dumping of toxic, radioactive and hazardous substances on, for example, communities of indigenous peoples, Hispanics and African-Americans.

Epidemiology The study of the incidence and distribution of diseases and illnesses in human beings.

Evolutionary psychology A form of psychology which attempts to explain human behaviour via an understanding of humanity's **phylogeny**, or evolutionary history.

External and internal nature External nature is usually referred to as 'the environment'. Internal nature is the biology (and chemical processes, etc.) of human beings and their development. External and internal nature draw attention to the fact that human beings are themselves part of nature.

Feudalism A social structure that predominated in tenth–twelfth-century Europe and in many other regions such as Egypt and China. Consisting of, *inter alia*, lord–peasant relationships, the subordination of the individual to group interests in feudal society is of particular interest to sociology.

Frankfurt School of Sociology An influential group of sociologists working at the Institute of Social Research, Frankfurt, from the 1920s to the 1930s. Amongst their interests was the fusion of Freudian and Marxist theory and a critique of the rationality celebrated by **Enlightenment** thought.

Functionalism A position which has roots in the application of evolutionary and biological ideas to the understanding of society. In much the same way as parts of a body (for example, the heart) 'functions' to keep the body alive, so too do certain institutions (for example, the family or religion) 'function' to keep society operating as a whole.

Gaia hypothesis Named after Gaia, the Greek name for Mother Earth, this postulates that the chemical and physical conditions of the earth, its atmosphere and oceans is a product of life itself. This contrasts with the view that life adapted to planetary conditions.

Genetic reductionism See **reductionism**.

Historical materialism A position first outlined by Marx which asserts that social change, forms of culture and politics are primarily determined by material and economic relations and processes. See **materialism and idealism**.

Inductive method/induction An argument or assumption that regular associations in the past will continue into the future.

Just-in-case/just-in-time Refers to modern industrial enterprises no longer holding large stocks. Instead, stocks are delivered 'just-in-time' as and when they are needed. These changes allow greater flexibility of production and savings in warehousing costs. See also **Post-Fordism**.

Labour process The process of production in which labour power (the capacity to work) is applied to raw materials from nature and to machinery to make commodities.

Liberalism and neoliberalism Liberalism was a position developed during the **Enlightenment** to assert the liberty of the individual relative to the coercive power of government. Neoliberalism continues to assert the continuing importance of the minimal state in achieving maximum individual autonomy.

Materialism and idealism Materialism is a position in which the true nature of the world is taken to be wholly physical or material. Idealism takes true reality to consist of ideas, consciousness or culture. Materialists argue that ideas stem from material relations and processes. Idealists argue that the material world offers a set of misleading appearances.

Metabolism/metabolic rift   Metabolism refers to the conversion of living matter into energy, the latter being central to the reproduction of organisms and society. Metabolic rift refers to the overloading and exhausting of ecological systems.

Mode of production   A concept of particular importance to Marxist theory. It refers to the relationships between the forces of production (tools and technologies) and the relations of production (typically, the relations between the owners and non-owners of the forces of production). The concept enables distinctions to be made between, for example, feudal and capitalist modes of production.

Modern movement   In architecture, the application of scientific rationality to the construction and design of buildings. The machine (buildings built by machines, buildings as 'machines for living in', a 'machine aesthetic') had key significance for the architectural modern movement. See also **postmodernism**.

Narcissism   A term used in Freudian psychology to refer to self-love, more particularly an image of the self. People take themselves, their own bodies, as their 'love objects', this being seen as a reversion to infantile behaviour when the developing infant is aware only of her/himself. Narcissism is often contrasted with **anaclysis**.

Nationalization   Bringing a commodity (land, for example) into public ownership.

Open systems   A term used in **critical realism** to refer to circumstances in which causal mechanisms interact with one another. This circumstance is the norm. See also **closed systems**.

Phylogeny   The evolutionary history of a species of animal or plant. See also **evolutionary psychology**.

Positivism   A doctrine in the philosophy of science which argues that science can only be developed with the aid of observable, experienced entities. As developed by Comte, Durkheim and others, it entailed the proposition that social science could be developed using the methods of science. See also **critical realism**.

Post-Fordism   A term (used often by **historical materialists**) to describe a relatively new phase in capital accumulation. Production is increasingly organized in a flexible way around changing, and varied, forms of consumption. Workforces are themselves made 'flexible' and governments are having to adjust to this emergent type of production.

Postmodernism   Developments in architecture, painting and culture generally which include, *inter alia*, the assembly of diverse styles from different contexts and a rejection of traditional boundaries between 'high' and 'low' cultures. They therefore reject the claims of the **modern movement** that culture, including architectural forms, can be interpreted in a single way or in the way intended by the artist/architect.

Psychic structure   The organization of the human mind. Usually considered to be rooted in survival and reproduction and with implications for personal identity or 'subjectivity'.

Rationalization   In sociology, a term usually associated with Max Weber to refer to the tendency in modern society for every aspect of human activity to be subject to calculation, measurement and control. According to Weber, these processes leave the monitored individual in an 'iron cage', stripped of moral values and spirituality.

Reductionism   An explanation is said to be reductionist when it attempts to account for a diverse range of phenomena in terms of a single determining factor. Thus genetic reductionism attempts explanation in terms of genes alone. Sociological reductionism attempts to explain the diversity of social behaviour with reference only to social processes and without reference to the physical and biological processes that affect human society.

Reflexivity/reflexive modernity As used by Beck in *Risk Society* (1992), this refers to a new stage in social development in which scientific knowledge is used to overcome the results of earlier forms of technological intervention. As applied to human beings, it refers to people becoming separated from traditional ties and forms of knowledge. To an increasing extent they are 'writing their own biographies'.

Risk society The argument, advanced particularly by Ulrich Beck, that contemporary society is characterized by a wide range of risks. Some of these are environmental, the application of science generating a range of unforeseen outcomes. Some of these risks are social, contemporary life becoming more 'risky' as tradition offers few guides for personal life and people increasingly 'write their own biographies'.

Romanticism A reaction to rationalism, re-emphasizing the irrational, the sublime, the supernatural and the aesthetic dimension of human experience.

Situationists A modern, radical French philosophy which argued that much of social life is turned into mere 'spectacle'. One result is the decline of spontaneity.

Sociobiology A form of biology which argues that the behaviour of humans and other animals can be largely explained by their 'selfish genes' attempting to reproduce themselves into future generations. Sociobiology was developed partly to explain 'the problem of altruism'. Organisms, including humans, assist others so that assistance will be later reciprocated.

Sociological reductionism See reductionism.

Subjectivity The quality of resting upon subjective facts or mental representations. Interpreting objects in the light of one's own subjective or mental state.

Teleology The notion that there is some kind of purpose or end towards which societies or evolutionary processes are working.

Third sector Organizations, such as local exchange trading systems and voluntary organizations, which are neither capitalist nor government-run.

Utopia A word describing an ideal community free of conflict and based on a clear set of values which allows human needs to be satisfied.

References

Allen, J., Braham, P. and Lewis, P. (1992) *Political and Economic Forms of Modernity*. Cambridge: Polity Press.

Anderson, B. (1993) *Imagined Communities*. London: Verso.

Ardrey, R. (1961) *African Genesis: A Personal Investigation into the Animal Origins and Nature of Man*. New York: Atheneum.

Avery, D. (1993) *Biodiversity: Saving Species with Biotechnology*. Hudson Institute Executive Briefing. Available from Hudson Institute, Herman Kahn Center, P.O. Box 26–919, Indianapolis, Indiana 46226, USA.

Avery, D. (1998) 'Feeding the World with Biotech Crops', *The World and I*, special edn of *Natural Science at the Edge* (May): 154–61.

Baldi, P. (2001) *The Shattered Self. The End of Natural Evolution*. Cambridge, MA: MIT Press.

Barker, D. (1998) *Mothers, Babies and Health in Later Life*. London: Churchill Livingstone.

Barker, D. (2001) *Type 2 Diabetes: The Thrifty Phenotype*. Special issue of *British Medical Bulletin*. Oxford: Oxford University Press.

Bateson, P. and Martin, P. (1999) *Design For a Life: How Behaviour Develops*. London: Cape.

Baudrillard, J. (1998) *The Consumer Society. Myths and Structures*. London: Sage.

Baumann, Z. (1989) *Modernity and the Holocaust*. Ithaca, NY: Cornell University Press.

Beck, U. (1982) *Risk Society*. London: Sage.

Beck, U. (2000) *The Brave New World of Work*. Cambridge: Polity.

Beck, U. and Beck-Gernsheim, E. (2002) *Individualization. Institutionalized Individualism and its Social and Political Consequences*. London: Sage.

Bell, C. and Newby, H. (1976) 'Community, Communion, Class and Community Action: The Social Sources of the New Urban Politics', in D. Herbert and R. Johnston, *Social Areas in Cities*. Vol. II: *Spatial Perspectives on Problems and Policies*. London: Wiley.

Benton, T. (1993) *Natural Relations. Ecology, Animal Rights and Social Justice*. London: Verso.

Benton, T. (ed.) (1996) *The Greening of Marxism*. New York: Guilford Press.

Benton, T. (1999a) 'Evolutionary Psychology and Social Science. A New Paradigm or Just the Same Old Reductionism?' *Advances in Human Ecology*, 8: 65–98.

Benton, T. (1999b) 'Radical Politics – Neither Left nor Right?' in M. O'Brien, S. Penna and C. Hay, *Theorising Modernity. Reflexivity, Environment and Identity in Giddens' Social Theory*. London: Longman.

Benton, T. (1999c) 'Sustainable Development and Accumulation of Capital: Reconciling the Irreconcilable?' in A. Dobson (ed.), *Fairness and Futurity. Essays on Environmental Sustainability and Social Justice*. Oxford: Oxford University Press.

Benton, T. and Redfearn, S. (1996) 'The Politics of Animal Rights. Where is the Left?' *New Left Review*, 215: 43–58.

Bhaskar, R. (1993) *Dialectic: the Pulse of Freedom*. London: Verso.

Blackburn, S. (2001) *Being Good. A Short Introduction to Ethics*. Oxford: Oxford University Press.

Bookchin, M. (1982) *The Ecology of Freedom*. Palo Alto, CA: Cheshire Books.

Bookchin, M. (1997) *The Murray Bookchin Reader*, ed. J. Biehl. London: Cassell.

Bouchard, T., Lykken, D., McGue, M., Segal, N. and Tellegen, A. (1990) 'Sources of Psychological Differences: The Minnesota Study of Twins Reared Apart', *Science*, 250: 346–53.

Bourdieu, P. (1984) *Distinction. A Social Critique of the Judgement of Taste*. London: Routledge.

Braverman, H. (1984) *Labor and Monopoly Capital. The Degradation of Work in the Twentieth Century*. New York: Monthly Press.

Brown, L. (2001) *State of the World (2001)*. London: Earthscan.

Buck-Morss, S. (1982) 'Socio-economic Bias in Piaget's Theory and its Implications for Cross-cultural Studies', in S. Modgil and C. Modgil (eds), *Jean Piaget: Consensus and Controversy*. London: Holt, Rinehart and Winston.

Burkett, P. (1999) *Marx and Nature. A Red Green Perspective*. New York: St Martin's Press.

Carter, N. (2001) *The Politics of the Environment*. Cambridge: Cambridge University Press.

Castells, M. (1996) *The Rise of the Network Society*. Oxford: Blackwell.

Castells, M. (2001) *The Internet Galaxy. Reflections on the Internet Business and Society*. Oxford: Oxford University Press.

Cavaliri, P. and Singer, P. (1993) *The Great Ape Project*. London: Fourth Estate.

Chagnon, N. (1992) *The Last Days of Eden*. New York: Harcourt Brace Jovanovich.

Clarke, A. and Linzey, A. (1990) *Political Theory and Animal Rights*. London: Pluto.

Compassion in World Farming (2002) *Live Exports. A Cruel and Archaic Trade that must be Ended*. Petersfield: CIWF.

Couper-Johnston, R. (2000) *El Niño. The Weather Phenomenon That Changed the World*. London: Hodder and Stoughton.

Cox, M. (1980) *Are Young Children Egocentric?* London: Batsford.

Craib, I. (1989) *Psychoanalysis and Social Theory. The Limits of Sociology*. Hemel Hempstead: Harvester.

Crompton, R. (1996) *Class and Stratification*. Cambridge: Polity.

Cronon, W. (1991) *Nature's Metropolis. Chicago and the Great West*. New York: Norton.

Crouch, D. and Ward, C. (1988) *The Allotment. Its Landscape and Culture*. London: Faber and Faber.

Cunningham, S. (1996) *Philosophy and the Darwinian Legacy*. Rochester, NY: University of Rochester Press.

Cypher, J. and Higgs, E. (1997) 'Colonizing the Imagination: Disney's Wilderness Lodge', *Capitalism, Nature, Socialism*, 8/4: 107–30.

Daniels, M., Devlin, B. and Roeder, K. (1997) 'Of Genes and IQ', in B. Devlin, S. Fienberg, D. Resnick and K. Roeder (eds), *Intelligence, Genes and Success: Scientists Respond to The Bell Curve*. New York: Copernicus.

Darby, H. (1956) *The Draining of the Fens*, 2nd edn. Cambridge: Cambridge University Press.

Darby, H. (1976) 'The Age of the Improver: 1600–1800', in idem (ed.), *The New Historical Geography of England after 1600*. Cambridge: Cambridge University Press.

Darwin, C. (1901) *The Descent of Man*. London: John Murray.

Das Gupta, S. (1990) 'Extent and Pattern of Drug Abuse and Dependence', in H. Ghose and D. Maxwell (eds), *Substance Abuse and Dependence*. London: Macmillan.

Davis, M. (2001) *Late Victorian Holocausts. El Niño Famines and the Making of the Third World*. London: Verso.

Davis, M. (2002) *Dead Cities: A Natural History*. New York: The New Press.

Davis, S. (1997) *Spectacular Nature. Corporate Culture and the Sea World Experience*. Berkeley: University of California.

Dawkins, R. (1976) *The Selfish Gene*. Oxford: Oxford University Press.

Dean, K. (2000) 'Capitalism, Psychic Immiseration and Decentred Subjectivity', *Journal for the Psychoanalysis of Culture and Society*, 5/1 (spring).

Dean, K. (2003) *Capitalism and Citizenship: The Impossible Partnership*. London: Routledge.

Dent, N. (1988) *Rousseau*. Oxford: Blackwell.

De Robertis, E., Oliver, G. and Wright, C. (1990) 'Homeobox Genes and the Vertebrate Body Plan', *Scientific American*, 231/1 (July): 26–32.

Devlin, B., Daniels, M. and Roeder, K. (1997) 'The Heritability of IQ', *Nature*, 388 (31 July): 468–71.

Dickens, P. (1988) *One Nation? Social Change and the Politics of Locality*. London: Pluto.

Dickens, P. (1992) *Society and Nature. Towards a Green Social Theory*. Hemel Hempstead: Harvester.

Dickens, P. (2000) *Social Darwinism. Linking Evolutionary Thought and Social Theory*. Buckingham: Open University Press.

Dickens, P. and Parry, J. (1998) 'Ecological Competence in a Modern Age: A Role for the New Information Technologies', in A. Bolder (ed.), *Work and Education Handbook 98. Ecological Competences*. Cologne: B&A Publications.

Dobson, A. (ed.) (1991) *The Green Reader*. London: Deutsch.

Dobson, A. (1998) *Justice and the Environment*. Oxford: Oxford University Press.

Drayton, R. (2000) *Nature's Government. Science, Imperial Britain and the 'Improvement' of the World*. New Haven: Yale University Press.

Durkheim, E. (1952) *Suicide*. London: Routledge.

Durkheim, E. (1954) *The Elementary Forms of Religious Life*. London: Allen and Unwin.

Durkheim, E. (1964) *The Division of Labour in Society*. New York: Free Press (originally published 1893).

Eckersley, R. (1992) *Environmentalism and Political Theory. Toward an Ecocentric Approach*. London: UCL Press.

Economic and Social Research Council (2001) *Environmental Justice. Rights and Means to a Healthy Environment for All*. Special Briefing No. 7. Brighton: University of Sussex.

Eder, K. (1993) *The New Politics of Class. Social Movements and Cultural Dynamics in Advanced Societies*. London: Sage.

Elias, N. (1978) *The Civilising Process*. Vol. 1: *The History of Manners*. Oxford: Blackwell.

Elias, N. (1982) *The Civilising Process*. Vol. 2: *State Formation and Civilisation*. Oxford: Blackwell.

Elsworth, S. (1990) *A Dictionary of the Environment*. London: Paladin.

Engels, F. (1969a) 'The Part Played by Labour in the Transition from Ape to Man', in *Dialectics of Nature*. Moscow: Progress.

Engels, F. (1969b) *The Housing Question*. Moscow: Progress.

Erdal, D. and Whiten, A. (1996) 'Egalitarianism and Machiavellian Intelligence in Human Evolution', in P. Mellars and K. Gibson (eds), *Modelling the Early Human Mind*. McDonald Institute Monographs. Cambridge: McDonald Institute for Archaeological Research.

Eriksson, J., Forsén, T., Juomilehto, J. and Barker, D. (2001) 'Early Growth and Coronary Heart Disease in Later Life: Longitudinal Study', *British Medical Journal*, 322 (21 April): 949–53.

Etzioni, A. (1993) *The Spirit of Community. The Reinvention of American Society*. New York: Touchstone.

Featherstone, M. and Hepworth, M. (1991) 'The Midlifestyle of "George and Lynne": Notes on a Popular Strip', in M. Featherstone, M. Hepworth and B. Turner (eds), *The Body. Social Process and Cultural Theory*. London: Sage.

Firestone, S. (1979) *The Dialectic of Sex. The Case for Feminist Revolution*. London: The Women's Press.

Fischer-Kowalski, M. (1997) 'Society's Metabolism: On the Childhood and Adolescence of a Rising Conceptual Star', in M. Redclift and G. Woodgate (eds), *The International Handbook of Environmental Sociology*. Cheltenham: Elgar.

Fishman, R. (1982) *Urban Utopias in the Twentieth Century*. Cambridge, MA: MIT Press.

Foster, J. (2000) *Marx's Ecology. Materialism and Nature*. New York: Monthly Review Press.

Foster, J. (2002) *Ecology Against Capitalism*. New York: Monthly Review Press.

Foucault, M. (1977) *Discipline and Punish: the Birth of the Prison*. Harmondsworth: Penguin.

Fox Keller, E. (2000) *A Feeling for the Organism*. New York: Freeman.

Fox, D. (1999) 'The Famished Road', *New Scientist* (13 November): 38–43.

Franklin, S. (1997) *Embodied Progress. A Cultural Account of Assisted Conception*. London: Routledge.

Freeman, C. and Louca, F. (2001) *As Time Goes By. From the Industrial Revolution to the Information Revolution*. Oxford: Oxford University Press.

Frith, U. and Happe, F. (1999) 'Theory of Mind and Self-Consciousness. What is it Like to be Autistic?' *Mind and Language*, 14/1: 1–22.

Fukuyama, F. (2002) *Our Posthuman Future: Consequences of the Biotechnology Revolution*. New York: Farrar, Strauss and Giroux.

George, S., Monbiot, G., German, L., Hayter, T., Callinicos, A. and Moody, K. (2001) *Anti-Capitalism. A Guide to the Movement*. London: Bookmarks.

Giddens, A. (1990) *The Consequences of Modernity*. Cambridge: Polity.

Giddens, A. (1991) *Modernity and Self-Identity: Self and Society in the Modern Age*. Cambridge: Polity.

Gimenez, M. (1991) 'The Mode of Reproduction in Transition – A Marxist-Feminist Analysis of the Effects of Reproductive Technologies', *Gender and Society*, 5a/3: 334–50.

Goddard, A. (1998) 'Sense of Self Sets Humans Apart', *Times Higher Education Supplement* (11 September).

Goleman, D. (1996) *Emotional Intelligence*. London: Bloomsbury.

Goodman, D. and Redclift, M. (1991) *Refashioning Nature. Food, Ecology and Culture*. London: Routledge.

Goodman, D., Sorj, B. and Wilkinson, J. (1987) *From Farming to Biotechnology*. Oxford: Blackwell.

Gordon, S. (1991) *The History and Philosophy of Social Science*. London: Routledge.

Gorz, A. (1994) *Capitalism, Socialism, Ecology*. London: Verso.

Goudie, A. (2000) *The Human Impact on the Natural Environment*. Oxford: Blackwell.

Gould, S. (1980) *Ever Since Darwin*. Harmondsworth: Pelican.

Gray, J. (2002) 'Ulrika is a Sign that we've Got it All', *New Statesman* (28 Oct).

Hall, S. and Jefferson, T. (eds) (1976) *Resistance Through Rituals. Youth Subcultures in Post-War Britain*. London: Hutchinson.

Haraway, D. (1991) 'Situated Knowledges: The Science Question in Feminism and the Privilege of Partial Perspective', in idem, *Simians, Cyborgs and Women: The Reinvention of Nature*. London: Free Association Books.

Haraway, D. (1991) *Simians, Cyborgs and Women: The Reinvention of Nature*. London: Free Association Books.

Hardin, G. (1968) 'The Tragedy of the Commons', *Science*, 162: 1243–8.

Harner, H. (1977) 'The Ecological Basis for Aztec Sacrifice', *American Ethnologist*, 4: 117–35.

Harvey, D. (2000) *Spaces of Hope*. Edinburgh: Edinburgh University Press.

Hawkins, M. (1997) *Social Darwinism in European and American Thought: Nature as Model and Nature as Threat*. Cambridge: Cambridge University Press.

Herrnstein, R. and Murray, C. (1994) *The Bell Curve*. New York: Free Press.

Hirst, P. (1994) 'Can Secondary Associations Enhance Democratic Governance?' in J. Cohen and J. Rogers (eds), *Associations and Democracy*. London: Verso.

Ho, M.-W. (1999) *Genetic Engineering. Dream or Nightmare?* Bath: Gateway Books (rev. edn).

Hofstadter, R. (1959) *Social Darwinism in American Thought*. New York: Braziller.

Hughes, J. (1999a) 'The Classic Maya Collapse', *Capitalism, Nature, Socialism*, 10/1.

Hughes, J. (1999b) 'Conservation in the Inca Empire', *Capitalism, Nature, Socialism*, 10/4.

Hughes, J. (2000) *Ecology and Historical Materialism*. Cambridge: Cambridge University Press.

Inglehart, R. (1997) *Modernization and Postmodernization: Cultural, Economic and Political Change in 43 Societies*. Princeton: Princeton University Press.

Irwin, A. (2001) *Sociology and the Environment. A Critical Introduction to Society, Nature and Knowledge*. Cambridge: Polity.

Isin, E. and Wood, P. (1999) *Citizenship and Identity*. London: Sage.

Jablonski, D. (1997) 'The Origin of Animal Body Plans', *American Scientist* (March–April). <http://www.amsci/articles/9/articles/Erwin-1.html>

Janoski, T. (1998) *Citizenship and Civil Society*. Cambridge: Cambridge University Press.

Jessop, B. (1994) 'Post-Fordism and the State', in A. Amin (ed.), *Post-Fordism. A Reader*. Oxford: Blackwell.

Karmiloff, K. and Karmiloff-Smith, A. (2002) *Pathways to Language: From Fetus to Adolescent*. Columbia, MA: Harvard University Press.

Keating, D. and Hertzman, C. (1999) *Developmental Health and the Wealth of Nations*. New York: Guilford.

Keating, D. and Miller, F. (1999) 'Individual Pathways in Competence and Coping', in D. Keating and C. Hertzman, *Developmental Health and the Wealth of Nations*. New York: Guilford.

Klein, M. (2000) *No Logo*. London: Flamingo.

Kloppenburg, J. (1988) *First the Seed. The Political Economy of Plant Biotechnology*. Cambridge: Cambridge University Press.

Kloppenburg, J. (1991) 'Social Theory and the De/Reconstruction of Agricultural Science: A New Agenda for Rural Sociology', *Rural Society*, 56: 519–48.

Knauft, B. (1991) 'Violence and Sociality in Human Evolution', *Current Anthropology*, 32: 391–428.

Kropotkin, P. (1985) *Fields, Factories and Workshops Tomorrow* (with introduction and commentary by C. Ward). London: Freedom Press (first published 1899).

Kropotkin, P. (1987) *Mutual Aid: a Factor of Evolution*. London: Freedom Press (first published 1902).

Kropotkin, P. (1995) *The Conquest of Bread and Other Writings*, ed. M. Schatz. Cambridge: Cambridge University Press.

Lampard, R. (1992) 'An Empirical Study of Marriage and Social Stratification'. Unpublished DPhil dissertation, University of Oxford.

Lasch, C. (1979) *The Culture of Narcissism. American Life in an Age of Diminishing Expectations*. New York: Norton.

Latour, B. (1987) *Science in Action*. Cambridge, MA: Harvard University Press.

Latour, B. (1988) *The Pasteurization of France*. Cambridge, MA: Harvard University Press.

Latour, B. (1993) *We Have Never Been Modern*. Hemel Hempstead: Harvester.

Latour, B. and Woolgar, S. (1979) *Laboratory Life*. Princeton: Princeton University Press.

Leopold, A. (1949) 'A Land Ethic', repr. in A. Dobson (ed.), *The Green Reader*. London: Deutsch, 1991.

Lindley, K. (1982) *Fenland Riots and the English Revolution*. London: Heinemann.

Luhmann, N. (1989) *Ecological Communication*. Cambridge: Polity.

MacKenzie, D. and Wajcman, J. (eds) (1999) *The Social Shaping of Technology*, 2nd edn. Milton Keynes: Open University Press.

Marmot, M. and Wadsworth, M. (eds) (1997) 'Fetal and Early Childhood Environment: Long-term Health Implications', *British Medical Bulletin*, 53/1 (January).

Marshall, T. (1964) *Class, Citizenship and Social Development*. Chicago: University of Chicago Press.

Marteau, T. and Richards, M. (1996) *The Troubled Helix*. Cambridge: Cambridge University Press.

Martell, L. (1994) *Ecology and Society. An Introduction*. Cambridge: Polity.

Maruyama, S. (1991) 'Seikatsu: Japanese Housewives Organize', in C. Plant and J. Plant, *Green Business. Hope or Hoax?* Bideford: Green Books.

Marx, K. (1970) *Capital*. Vol. 1. London: Lawrence and Wishart.

Marx, K. (1975) *Early Writings*, ed. L. Colletti. Harmondsworth: Penguin.

Marx, K. (1976) *Capital*. Vol. 1. Harmondsworth: Penguin.

Maryanski, A. (1992) 'The Last Ancestor: An Ecological Network Model on the Origins of Human Sociality', *Advances in Human Ecology*, 1: 1–32.

Maryanski, A. and Turner, J. (1992) *The Social Cage: Human Nature and the Evolution of Society*. Stanford, CA: Stanford University Press.

Maynard Smith, J. (1998) *Shaping Life: Genes, Embryos and Evolution*. London: Weidenfeld and Nicolson.

Meadows, D., Meadows, D. and Behrens, W. (1983) *The Limits to Growth: A Report for the Club of Rome's Project on the Predicament of Mankind*. London: Pan.

Melucci, A. (1989) *Nomads of the Present*. London: Hutchinson Radius.

Merchant, C. (1990) *The Death of Nature*. New York: Harper and Row.

Mies, M. and Shiva, V. (1993) *Ecofeminism*. London: Zed Books.

Miller, D. (1995) 'Consumption as the Vanguard of History', in *Acknowledging Consumption*. London: Routledge.

Mol, A. (1994) *The Refinement of Production. Ecological Modernization: Theory and the Chemical Industry*. The Hague: CIP-Data Koninklijke Biblioteek.

Montgomery, S., Bartley, M. and Wilkinson, R. (1997) 'Family Conflict and Slow Growth', *Archives of the Diseases of Childhood*, 77: 326–30.

Montgomery, S., Bartley, M., Cook, D. and Wadsworth, M. (1996) 'Health and Social Precursors of Unemployment in Young Men in Great Britain', *Journal of Epidemiology and Community Health*, 50: 415–22.

Murphy, R. (1994) *Rationality and Nature. A Sociological Inquiry into a Changing Relationship*. Boulder, CO: Westview.

Murphy, R. (2000) *Sociology and Nature. Social Action in Context*. Boulder, CO: Westview.

Murphy, R. and Steward, J. (1955) 'Tappers and Trappers: Parallel Process in Acculturation', *Economic Development and Cultural Change*, 4: 335–55.

Murray, R. (2002) *Zero Waste*. London: Greenpeace.

Naess, A. (1973) 'The Shallow and the Deep, Long-Range Ecology Movement. A Summary', *Inquiry*, 16: 95–9.

Naess, A. (1989) *Ecology, Community and Lifestyle*. Cambridge: Cambridge University Press.

Neisser, U., Boodoo, G., Bouchard, T., Boykin, A., Brody, N., Ceci, S., Halpern, D., Loehlin, J., Perloff, R., Sternberg, R. and Urbina, S. (1996) 'Intelligence Knowns and Unknowns', *American Psychologist*, 51: 77–101.

Nisbet, R. (1966) *The Sociological Tradition*. London: Heinemann.

Noske, B. (1989) *Humans and Other Animals. Beyond the Boundaries of Anthropology*. London: Pluto.

O'Connor, J. (1988) 'The Second Contradiction of Capitalism: Causes and Consequences'. Santa Cruz, *Capitalism, Nature, Socialism*, Pamphlet 1.

O'Connor, J. (1998) *Natural Causes*. Part 1: *History and Nature*. New York: Guilford Press.

Olds, D., Henderson, C. and Tatelbaum, R. (1994) 'Intellectual Impairment in Children of Women who Smoke Cigarettes in Pregnancy', *Pediatrics*, 93: 221–7.

Oyama, S. (1985) *The Ontogeny of Information*. Cambridge: Cambridge University Press.

Pagliaro, A. and Pagliaro, L. (1996) *Substance Use among Children and Adolescents*. New York: Wiley.

Parker, J. (2001) 'Towards an Ecofeminist Ethics: A Critical Realist and Social Movements Approach'. DPhil thesis, University of Sussex, Brighton, UK.

Patel, C. (1996) *The Complete Guide to Stress Management*. London: Vermillion.

Piaget, J. (1971) *Biology and Knowledge. An Essay on the Relations between Organic Regulations and Cognitive Processes*. Edinburgh: Edinburgh University Press.

Pinker, S. (1997) *How the Mind Works*. Harmondsworth: Allen Lane/Penguin Press.

Plant, C. and Plant, J. (1991) *Green Business. Hope or Hoax?* Bideford: Green Books.

Plant, R. (1973) *Hegel*. London: Allen and Unwin.

Plant, R. (1977a) 'Hegel and Political Economy I', *New Left Review*, 103 (May–June): 79–92.

Plant, R. (1977b) 'Hegel and Political Economy II', *New Left Review*, 104 (July–August): 101–13.

Plomin, R. (1999) 'Genetics and General Cognitive Ability', *Nature*, 402 (supplement): C25–9.

Porter, D. (2000) *Enlightenment. Britain and the Creation of the Modern World.* Harmondsworth: Penguin.

Porter, D. (2001) *The Enlightenment.* Basingstoke: Palgrave.

Power, C. and Hertzman, C. (1999) 'Health, Well-Being and Coping Skills', in D. Keating and C. Hertzman, *Developmental Health and the Wealth of Nations.* New York: Guilford.

Prandy, K. and Bottero, W. (1998) 'The Use of Marriage Data to Measure the Social Order in Nineteenth-Century Britain', *Sociological Research Online*, 3/1.

Pretty, J. (2002) *Agri-Culture. Reconnecting People, Land and Nature.* London: Earthscan.

Putnam, R. (2000) *Bowling Alone. The Collapse and Revival of American Community.* New York: Simon & Schuster.

Redclift, M. (1987) *Development and the Environmental Crisis. Red or Green Alternatives?* London: Methuen.

Redclift, M. (1996) *Wasted. Counting the Costs of Global Consumption.* London: Earthscan.

Red-Green Study Group (1995) *What on Earth is to be Done? A Red-Green Dialogue.* Manchester: Red-Green Study Group (c/o Pat Devine, 2 Hamilton Road, Whitefield, Manchester M45 6QW).

Regan, T. (1990) 'The Struggle for Animal Rights', in P. Clarke and A. Linzey, *Political Theory and Animal Rights.* London: Pluto.

Reinisch, J., Saunders, S., Mortensen, E., Robin, D. and Robin, D. (1995) '*In Utero* Exposure to Phenobarbitol and Intelligence Deficits in Adult Men', *Journal of the American Medical Association*, 274: 1518–25.

Rennie, J. (1994) 'Grading the Gene Tests', *Scientific American*, 270: 66–74.

Richards, M. (n.d.) Private communication from Professor Martin Richards, Faculty of Social and Political Sciences, University of Cambridge.

Rousseau, J.-J. (1979) *Emile.* New York: Basic Books.

Rousseau, J.-J. (1994) *Discourse on Inequality.* Oxford: Oxford University Press (first published 1775).

Rush, D., Stein, Z., Sussex, M. and Brody, N. (1981) 'Diet in Pregnancy', in D. Rush, Z. Stein and M. Sussex (eds), *Diet in Pregnancy.* New York: Liss.

Rustin, M. (1985) 'Lessons of the London Industrial Strategy', *New Left Review*, 155: 75–84.

Sahlins, M. (1972) *The Use and Abuse of Biology.* London: Tavistock.

Sahlins, M. (1974) *Stone Age Economics.* London: Tavistock.

Sale, K. (1984) 'Bioregionalism. A New Way to Treat the Land', *The Ecologist*, 14: 167–73.

Sale, K. (1985) *Dwellers in the Land. The Bioregional Vision.* San Francisco: Sierra Club Books.

Saunders, P. (1995) *Capitalism. A Social Audit.* Buckingham: Open University Press.

Savage, M., Barlow, J., Dickens, P. and Fielding, A. (1992) *Property, Bureaucracy and Culture. Middle-Class Formation in Contemporary Britain.* London: Routledge.

Sayer, A. (1995) *Radical Political Economy.* Oxford: Blackwell.

Schandl, H. and Schulz, N. (2000) 'Using Material Flow Accounting to Operationalize the Concept of Society's Metabolism. A Preliminary MFA for the United Kingdom for the Period of 1937–1997'. ISER Working Paper No. 2000–3. University of Essex, UK.

Schettler, T., Solomon, G., Valenti, M. and Huddle, A. (1999) *Generations at Risk. Reproductive Health and the Environment*. Cambridge, MA: MIT Press.

Schmidt, A. (1971) *The Concept of Nature in Marx*. London: New Left Books.

Seligman, M. (1975) *Helplessness*. San Francisco: Freeman.

Sennett, R. (1974) *The Fall of Public Man*. Cambridge: Cambridge University Press.

Sharp, G. (2001) 'Ecology and the Labour Process: Towards a Prefigurative Sociology on the Labour–Nature Relation'. DPhil Thesis, University of Sussex, Brighton, UK.

Silver, L. (1998) *Remaking Eden. Cloning and Beyond in a Brave New World*. London: Weidenfeld and Nicholson.

Singer, P. (1990) 'All Animals are Equal', in P. Clarke and A. Linzey, *Political Theory and Animal Rights*. London: Pluto.

Smiles, S. (1862) *Lives of the Engineers*, Vol. 1. London: David and Charles Reprints.

Smith, M. and Kollock, P. (1999) *Communities in Cyberspace*. London: Routledge.

Sonnenfeld, D. (2000) 'Contradictions of Ecological Modernisation: Pulp and Paper Manufacturing in South-east Asia', in A. Mol and D. Sonnenfeld, *Ecological Modernisation Around the World. Perspectives and Critical Debates*. London: Cass.

Spaargaren, G. and Mol, A. (1992) 'Sociology, Environment, and Modernity: Ecological Modernization as a Theory of Social Change', *Society and Natural Resources*, 4 (Oct–Dec): 323–44.

Spallone, P. (1989) *Beyond Conception: The New Politics of Reproduction*. Basingstoke: Macmillan.

Spence, M. (2001) 'Environmental Crisis in Prehistory: Hunter-Gatherers and Mass Extinctions', *Capitalism, Nature, Socialism*, 12/3.

Spencer, H. (1898) *Principles of Biology*, 2 vols. New York: Appleton.

Steele, D., Lindley, R. and Blanden, R. (1998) *Lamarck's Signature. How Retrogenes are Changing Darwin's Natural Selection Paradigm*. London: Allen & Unwin.

Sylva, K. (1997) 'Critical Periods in Childhood Learning', *British Medical Journal*, 53/1: 185–97.

Tansey, G. and Worsley, T. (1995) *The Food System. A Guide*. London: Earthscan.

Thompson, E. (1991) *Customs in Common*. London: Merlin.

Todd, M. (1972) *Everyday Life of the Barbarians. Goths, Franks and Vandals*. London: Batsford.

Tönnies, F. (1955) *Community and Association*. London: Routledge (originally published 1887).

Touraine, A. (1981) *The Voice and the Eye*. Cambridge: Cambridge University Press.

Touraine, A. (1985) 'An Introduction to the Study of Social Movements', *Social Research*, 52: 749–88.

Turner, B. (1993) 'Outline of the Theory of Human Rights', in B. Turner (ed.), *Citizenship and Social Theory*. London: Sage.

Urry, J. (1990) *The Tourist Gaze*. London: Sage.

Urry, J. (2000) *Sociology beyond Societies. Mobilities for the Twenty-first Century*. London: Routledge.

Waddington, C. (1957) *The Strategy of the Genes*. London: Allen & Unwin.

Waddington, C. (1975) *The Evolution of an Evolutionist*. Edinburgh: Edinburgh University Press.

Weisz, H., Fischer-Kowalski, M., Grunbuhel, C., Haberl, H., Krausmann, F. and Winiwarter, V. (2001) 'Global Environmental Change and Historical Transitions', *Innovation*, 14/2: 117–42.

Wheale, P. and McNally, R. (1988) *Genetic Engineering. Catastrophe or Utopia?* Hemel Hempstead: Harvester.

Wheale, P. and McNally, R. (1990) *The Biorevolution. Cornucopia or Pandora's Box?* London: Pluto.

Wilkinson, R. (1996) *Unhealthy Societies: The Afflictions of Inequality.* London: Routledge.

Williams, R. (1973) *The Country and the City.* London: Chatto.

Williams, S. (1999) 'Is Anybody There? Critical Realism, Chronic Illness and the Disability Debate', *Sociology of Health and Illness*, 21/6: 797–819.

Wills, C. (1989) *The Wisdom of the Genes: New Pathways in Evolution.* New York: Basic Books.

Wills, C. (1993) *The Runaway Brain.* London: Flamingo.

Wolf, E. (1982) *Europe and the People Without History.* Berkeley, CA: University of California Press.

Wolman, A. (1965) 'The Metabolism of Cities', *Scientific American*, 213/3: 178–93.

Woodcock, G. (1977) *The Anarchist Reader.* London: Fontana.

World Bank (1993) *World Development Report 1993: Investing in Health.* Oxford: Oxford University Press.

Wrangham, R. and Peterson, D. (1997) *Demonic Males: Apes and the Origins of Human Violence.* London: Bloomsbury.

Yoxen, E. (1983) *The Gene Business. Who Should Control Biotechnology?* London: Pan.

Ziman, J. (2000) *Technological Innovation as an Evolutionary Process.* Cambridge: Cambridge University Press.

Index

Lightning Source UK Ltd.
Milton Keynes UK
UKOW04f2043261016
286227UK00016B/333/P